THE TRIALS OF RICHARD GOLDSTONE

THE TRIALS OF RICHARD GOLDSTONE

DANIEL TERRIS

RUTGERS UNIVERSITY PRESS

New Brunswick, Camden, and Newark, New Jersey, and London

Library of Congress Cataloging-in-Publication Data

Names: Terris, Daniel, author.
Title: The trials of Richard Goldstone / Daniel Terris.
Description: New Brunswick : Rutgers University Press, 2018. | Includes
    bibliographical references and index.
Identifiers: LCCN 2018012694 | ISBN 9780813599960 (cloth)
Subjects: LCSH: Goldstone, Richard. | Judges—South Africa—Biography. |
    Prosecution (International law)—Biography.
Classification: LCC KTL110.G65 T47 2018 | DDC 347.68/03334 [B]—dc23
LC record available at https://lccn.loc.gov/2018012694

A British Cataloging-in-Publication record for this book is available from the
British Library.

www.rutgersuniversitypress.org

Manufactured in the United States of America

In memory of my father, David
and for my grandson, Ralph David
"...from generation to generation..."

CONTENTS

ABBREVIATIONS

ABA	American Bar Association
ACABQ	Advisory Committee on Administrative and Budgetary Questions
ANC	African National Congress
ARAC	Africa Risk Analysis Consultants
CHR	Commission on Human Rights (U.N.)
HRC	Human Rights Council (U.N.)
ICC	International Criminal Court
ICTR	International Criminal Tribunal for Rwanda
ICTY	International Criminal Tribunal for the Former Yugoslavia
IDF	Israel Defense Forces
IFOR	Implementation Force (NATO)
IFP	Inkatha Freedom Party
JNA	Jugoslovenska Narodna Armija (Yugoslav People's Army)
KLA	Kosovo Liberation Army
MAG	Military Advocate General
NGO	nongovernmental organization
NICRO	National Institute for Crime Prevention and the Rehabilitation of Offenders
NUSAS	National Union of South African Students
OFP	Oil for Food Program
OHCHR	Office of the United Nations High Commissioner for Human Rights
ORT	Organization for Rehabilitation and Training
OTP	Office of the Prosecutor
PLO	Palestinian Liberation Organization
SAJBD	South African Jewish Board of Deputies
SRC	Student Representative Council
TRC	Truth and Reconciliation Commission
UDF	United Democratic Front
U.N.	United Nations

THE TRIALS OF RICHARD GOLDSTONE

PROLOGUE
Icon and Pariah

I N THE BALLROOM of the Grand Hotel Amrâth Kurhaus, champagne glasses clinked and chandeliers sparkled. It was May 25, 2009, and the occasion had brought together the leading lights of the international community in The Hague, the capital of the Netherlands. Judges from the world's most influential global courts mingled with ambassadors from thirty-two nations, alongside scholars, activists, and journalists. They had assembled in this lavish room to celebrate a cause and the man who embodied it. That man was Justice Richard Goldstone, and on this evening, the MacArthur Foundation was conferring upon him its prestigious Award for International Justice.

Images of war and brutality flashed on the screen above the podium. A block of bombed-out apartment buildings. A fiery explosion. Rifle fire and a man slumping to the ground. Women in headscarves bearing portraits of loved ones. "Human suffering cries out for justice," intoned a voiceover. "The worst crimes must not go unpunished." The camera cut to a white man in his sixties with a wide round face, spectacles, and a neatly knotted necktie. "When I think back on the war criminals that I was involved with," Richard Goldstone shared in his clipped South African accent, "I think that what they all really have in common is that on the face of it they were all ordinary human beings like you and me. Anybody is capable of doing terrible things, given the circumstances."[1]

Jonathan Fanton, the president of the MacArthur Foundation, took the podium to hail the evening's honoree as a man of courage, a pathbreaker, the leading of figure of a singular global development. Few had done more than Richard Goldstone to bring the world's worst regimes and individuals to justice: as a widely respected judge, as a leading figure in the transition to democracy of his native South Africa, as a lawyer in The Hague prosecuting the perpetrators of war crimes in the Balkans and Rwanda. He held honorary degrees from a dozen prestigious universities. The city of The Hague had named him as its first "peace philosopher." In presenting the MacArthur Award, Fanton touted the judge's "moral authority and legal credibility" and proclaimed that "his unquestioned competence and integrity won the faith of the world." In his tribute, Fanton channeled Goldstone's hope, an aspiration shared by the hundreds of distinguished men and women who had gathered to celebrate his work: "No longer will dictators or oppressive governments be able to violate the fundamental rights of citizens with impunity. We are moving into a new and different world. . . . The twenty-first century will witness the growth of an international criminal justice system and victims of war crimes will no longer be ignored."

The audience stood and gave a prolonged and refined ovation that managed to combine enthusiasm and dignity, and as the man of the hour himself arrived at the podium and surveyed the applauding crowd, a broad grin spread across his face. These were Goldstone's people, and this was his moment. Just two decades earlier, international criminal justice had scarcely existed. Now it was an established fact, and he was happy to savor the occasion. His work had brought him face to face with some of the ugliest truths of human behavior, yet he had managed to preserve throughout a sense of uplift and possibility. "For any human endeavor to succeed, there have to be optimists running it," he told the assembly in the ballroom. "If human beings were pessimists, we'd all be in caves."

Four months later, in September 2009, Richard Goldstone faced a very different sort of public recognition. Speaking before the United Nations

(U.N.) Human Rights Council (HRC) in a meeting hall in Geneva, Switzerland, a Canadian lawyer named Anne Bayefsky read a prepared statement that accused him of authoring a vehicle of hate and of repeating an ancient blood libel. Scarcely looking up from her text, Bayefsky refused to address the astonished judge by his title or even as Mr. Goldstone. "Richard," she inquired brazenly, "how does it feel to have used your Jewishness to jeopardize the safety and security of the people of Israel and to find yourself in the company of human rights abusers everywhere?"[2]

In the fall of 2009, Richard Goldstone had chaired a U.N. mission that suggested that the state of Israel was guilty of war crimes during the 2008–2009 conflict in Gaza. In the wake of that report, its principal author was reviled as an "evil, evil man," a "quisling," a perpetrator of modern-day "blood libel," a "racist hyena," a traitor akin to a Nazi collaborator. He was accused of selling out his principles, of unforgivable naïveté, of hypocrisy, of turning his back on his own people and even his family. His fiercest critics included anonymous bloggers, distinguished scholars, and even Shimon Peres, the venerable president of the state of Israel, who disparaged him as "a small, small man." With an explosion of critiques in newspapers, on television, and across the echo chamber of social media, few individuals had ever absorbed such a barrage of invective from their own people as Richard Goldstone.

In the waning decades of the twentieth century and the early decades of the twenty-first, nationalist leaders around the globe advanced their agendas through ugly rhetoric, intimidation, and violence. The idealistic spirit of global cooperation, nurtured in the wake of World War II, was giving way to naked expressions of self-interest. Emboldened leaders whipped their followers into frenzies of hatred, and then refused responsibility for the consequences.

The field of international criminal justice was born, in part, as an antidote to these dangerous developments. Richard Goldstone believed that individuals—especially political and military leaders—should be held accountable for violence and violations of human rights committed against men, women, and children on their watch. He also believed that accountability should be universal, not restricted to weaker nations or isolated regimes. International justice could punish those who committed atrocities, create a historical record so that crimes could not be covered up, and deter future leaders from abusing their power.

The ideals of international justice were inspiring, but the practical realities often offered a cautionary tale. New courts did indeed punish some of the world's worst perpetrators, but unscrupulous actors on the world stage also found ways to manipulate the laws of human rights and the laws of war for their own purposes. Justice sometimes contributed to peace, but at other times the crude mechanisms of the law undermined the foundations of reconciliation. Leaders delivered high-flown rhetoric about law and justice, and then behind the scenes did everything possible to short-circuit them. Politics often perverted international law just as politics often intruded into the legal realm, even in the world's most advanced democracies.

Despite these shortcomings, international criminal justice became a fixture. People continued to argue about how it should be achieved, and powerful nations kept their distance from some of its most important institutions. Yet what was unthinkable a century ago became a commonplace. By the early years of the twenty-first century, it was a truism that if political and military leaders wantonly sacrificed the lives of innocents in the course of war or repression, they should be punished in the name of humanity.

Richard Goldstone became the most important exemplar of the rise of international criminal justice. His courage, determination, political skills, and intelligence represented the contributions of one extraordinary individual to a new set of moral and legal ideals. At the same time, his sacrifices—and sometimes his errors of judgment—exemplified the most daunting obstacles to establishing fairness and accountability on a global scale. Along the way, Goldstone also fell victim to one of the dispiriting trends of the contemporary era, the triumph of hyperpartisanship and personal recrimination over reasoned debate. Richard Goldstone diverted the stream of history, but history also swept him along in its treacherous currents.

1 ▸ DIVISIONS

IN THE SOUTH AFRICAN autumn of 1944, six-year-old Richard Goldstone loved to play in the study of his grandfather, Albert Jacobson. As he ordered his toy soldiers, he watched his grandfather rearrange flags across the map of Europe in response to news of the war being fought there. Boy and grandfather listened loyally to the radio, and late in the evening, when the broadcast shut down for the night, the pair stood up when the radio played "God Save the King."[1]

The boy learned that on the little island in the upper left of the map was a place called England, where his grandfather had been born. From there Albert first ventured to South Africa by ship in 1892 as a boy of sixteen. By the turn of the twentieth century, Albert Jacobson was settled for good in the country as a buyer for the Imperial Tobacco Company.[2]

Richard's grandfather told him that he had a special future: he would grow up to be a lawyer. The boy did not question his grandfather's decision. He sensed that the old man was conferring an honor, and that it was his duty to accept it. His grandfather challenged the boy with tasks, encouraging him to read aloud and hone his ability to make the keys fly on a clackety old typewriter.

Why the law? His grandfather was not a lawyer himself, and there were no lawyers in the family. Did the old man have a deep-seated commitment to the ideal of justice? Did he see the law as a bulwark against the politics of separation and contempt that were gaining strength in his adopted country? Was it simply that law was a respectable profession, secure in status and income? Or did the old man see some specific quality in his grandson that made him sure that the boy would flourish in the halls of justice? Richard Goldstone never fully knew why his grandfather chose the law for him, but he grew up with a rare kind of certainty about his future. "I was fortunate in a way," he remembered later, "because I never didn't know what I was going to do."

By the time Richard Goldstone came along, his grandfather's principal occupation was owning and running the Prince's Court apartment complex in the town of Benoni, some thirty miles from the city of Johannesburg. Originally a mining town, Benoni was in the postwar years a respectable commercial center, notable for its large population of English speakers, in a country where most White citizens spoke Afrikaans, and for its sizable Jewish population.* In his earlier years, Albert Jacobson had been a salesman, a merchant, a labor leader, and a player in local politics, once making an unsuccessful run for Parliament on the United Party ticket. Now Albert managed the complex of some thirty units, whose residents were mostly young professionals scraping by in South Africa's middle class.

Richard was born on October 26, 1938, a few miles away in the town of Boksburg, but his family soon moved to Benoni. His father, Ben Goldstone, worked in sales for one of South Africa's largest retailers. His grandmother, Fanny Levy Jacobson, helped her husband Albert manage the apartment complex. Fanny hired and oversaw the Black workers who kept the complex clean and in good repair. Albert and Fanny had arranged with a Zulu chief from Natal to provide a steady supply of labor for the Prince's Court. Black workers came and lived for months or years at a time in segregated hostels on the outskirts of Benoni, sending wages home to their families and community. Most South African Whites spoke with their Black workers in English or Afrikaans, but Richard's grandmother and his mother, Kitty Goldstone, learned enough isiZulu to communicate well with the chief and their employees.

---

* When speaking of pre-1994 South Africa, this book uses the custom of capitalizing the names of racial groups, except within direct quotations.

Richard grew up hearing his family members issuing orders and praise and reprimands in an African language. Fanny and Kitty left no doubt who was in charge at the Prince's Court, but Kitty also did her best to instill in her son an ethic of care and compassion for the individual men and women who served the family. "I grew up in a home where there was respect for Black people, which perhaps wasn't so common at that time," Richard remembered later.[3]

The underlying reality, however, was that this footing was not equal at all, because Albert Jacobson, Kitty Goldstone, and Richard Goldstone were White South Africans, beneficiaries of a warped social structure. For more than two centuries, Whites had slowly contained and constricted the lives of Blacks through violence and intimidation. For the last twenty-five years, during the 1920s, 1930s, and 1940s, they had increasingly done so through law and bureaucracy, creating new regulations about where Blacks could live, what work they could do, whom they could marry, and what property they could own. While the direction of this trajectory had been clear, its course had been uneven. Under the ruling United Party, extensive debate roiled the White community about how to balance social control with a modicum of fairness for Blacks and others of non-European descent. South Africa's courts, shaped by a deep-seated tradition of respect for the law, created occasional roadblocks.[4]

In April 1948, when Richard was nine, South Africa held national elections. On the wall where he had charted the course of the war in Europe, Albert Jacobson now posted election returns by district. The National Party won an unexpected victory and South Africa's first exclusively Afrikaner government came into power. The news was shocking. The National Party had run on a platform of "apartheid," a word coined only a decade earlier to describe an imagined separate development of the races, consolidating White power and resources, and promising non-Whites a future at the margins of the country. Would the Nationalists really dare to implement the far-reaching implications of segregation? For Richard, a different question weighed on him: Would he and his schoolmates be forced to give up English, compelled to speak in class the guttural Afrikaans that he heard in the market and on the radio? This thought thoroughly terrified him.

Like all South Africans, then, Richard Goldstone lived in a world of many divisions. The boy was healthy but not particularly athletic, his body slightly pudgy, his brown hair neatly trimmed across the top of a forehead that even on a ten-year-old looked improbably broad and forceful. Race necessarily colored his interactions with those around him, but as a boy Richard did not think of the boundaries between people as fixed or certain. The isiZulu he heard in his household told him that, with the right tools, there were flexible ways to mitigate the harshness of division.

In South Africa in the 1940s, Richard's skin color marked him within the social structure of his country. But in other ways, he was set apart, not as a White person, but as a Jew.

Jews had come to the Cape and gradually to other parts of South Africa by the dozens and the hundreds from England and elsewhere in the first half of the nineteenth century, as they did as in small numbers to every corner of the British Empire. But beginning in 1880, a wave of Jews began to arrive from a tiny section of the northwest corner of the Pale of Settlement, especially from the communities of Kovno and its environs in Lithuania.[5] Son followed father, family followed family, escaping repressive laws and violent pogroms that endangered the Jewish community in the late years of the nineteenth century. The diaspora from Lithuania to South Africa remained remarkably cohesive and homogenous, sharing hometown connections and traditions. Over the next thirty years, 40,000 "Litvaks," as they were known, overwhelmed the 4,000 or so Jews who had arrived with the British.[6]

They clustered in the suburbs of Johannesburg and Cape Town, although they eventually formed tight-knit communities in most of South Africa's major cities. The country's Jews were upwardly mobile, especially in the world of merchandise and retail, but large pockets of poverty persisted. Their religious observance was solidly Orthodox and rational, by tradition unreceptive to both the reformist and mystical currents that had swept through other corners of the Jewish world.

In traveling 5,000 miles to the south, Lithuanian Jews made a nearly instant transition from victim to beneficiary of a culture of injustice. Their European origin established them as Whites, and in some quarters other White South Africans welcomed them as another bulwark in the establishment of European civilization at the tip of the continent.[7] In the delicate dance of the South African White community, the new immigrants attached themselves to the English language and to some extent to English traditions. They made little effort to hold on to the Yiddish language or to pass it along to their children.[8]

Being White and speaking English did not, however, make the Jews of South Africa secure; nor did they feel secure. By the time Richard Goldstone was born in 1938, 100,000 Jews constituted only the tiniest sliver of South Africa's 4,000,000 people. Jewish ears stayed closely attuned to murmurs of anti-Semitism that sometimes broke openly into the nation's political dialogue and its policy. In 1930, Parliament passed a law with a new quota system restricting entry into the country for immigrants. The law did not mention Jews by name, but it was obvious to all that Jews were its principal target. Throughout the 1930s, as National Socialism came to power and gained strength in Germany, anti-Semitic voices in South Africa were emboldened. Small numbers of Jews fled to South Africa from the Nazi regime, igniting both calls to restrict this new influx and not-so-subtle public reminders that the Jews were mere "guests" in this Christian country.

South African Jews argued with one another about how best to respond to their combination of privilege and insecurity. Yet almost all of them united around the goal of establishing a Jewish state in the land of Palestine. Their first national Jewish institution, the South African Zionist Organization, had been founded even before the turn of the twentieth century. Through the 1920s and 1930s, South African Jews remained zealous and active in the Zionist cause, second only to the Jewish community of the United States in their fundraising for the project of nation-building in the Middle East. Zionist youth organizations absorbed the energies of the young. For these Jews at the outer edge of the diaspora, Zionism was both a cause and a source of meaning.

Richard's parents, Ben and Kitty Goldstone, represented different strands within the Jewish community. On Richard's father's side, the line back to Lithuania was direct and unaltered. His paternal grandparents, Davis and Sarah Goldstone, had arrived in South Africa as part of the great wave. They settled in Boksburg, some thirty miles from Johannesburg, kept a kosher home, and joined an Orthodox shul. Ben and Kitty also lived for a time in Boksburg and then in Benoni, some ten miles from Boksburg.

Kitty's parents, Albert and Fanny Jacobson, were originally of Sephardic origin, but their families had lived in England for generations. While Jewish identity was strong in the Jacobson family, Albert's religious observance had mostly fallen away by the time that he made the long trip south after a painful break with his wealthy parents. The spirit of Judaism in Albert's household was relaxed. His wife Fanny might have preferred more traditional Jewish practice, but Albert took a more private approach to his faith. On Yom Kippur, the old man avoided synagogue, choosing instead to mark the day with fasting and solitary reflection in his own study. Annual traditions in the Jacobson house included both a Passover Seder and a Christmas lunch.

In raising their daughter Kitty, Albert and Fanny had emphasized the greatness of Western culture, and she achieved diplomas that qualified her to teach elocution, ballet, and the piano. She developed the special spark of culture, leadership, and organization that made her an excellent teacher of young children and later a leader in Jewish communal life.

Ben Goldstone lacked Kitty's vivacity, and he also lacked his own parents' dedication to Jewish observance. Ben had a successful career in business and played an active role in the South African Chamber of Commerce. Kindhearted and beloved, Ben tended to yield to his wife in household matters and child-rearing, so between Richard's parents, his mother was the greater influence on his upbringing.

In 1948, the year the National Party took over the South African government, the Jewish community celebrated as the state of Israel declared its independence. The jubilation transcended any outpouring that Richard had seen before. Being Jewish was no longer something private and separate and personal; it was, for the first time, a public act, a mark of pride, a source of meaningful action. The new state allowed a boy on the southern edge of the globe a way to see himself as a player on the world stage.

That same year, the Goldstones moved from Benoni to an apartment in the Johannesburg suburb of Parktown. Ben Goldstone had a new position as the CEO of a large group of department stores. Richard Goldstone gained a new school, a new social network, and a new, larger city to explore.

In Johannesburg the Goldstones entered a Jewish world much larger, more diverse, and more contentious than the small community they left behind in Benoni. Time, growth, and history had eaten away at the relative homogeneity of Jewish Johannesburg. There were now Reform synagogues as a complement to the Orthodox shuls. Class divides were more evident, as some Jewish families had climbed into the upper reaches of White South Africa. Tensions over South African politics were making themselves felt in Jewish circles. Kitty Goldstone, an ardent Zionist, found a broader canvas for her Jewish commitments in Johannesburg. She had been involved with the women's Zionist organization in Benoni, but in Johannesburg this work became her principal occupation outside her home.

Convenience and style brought the Goldstone family into the orbit of Temple Israel, a Reform congregation established in the 1930s by Rabbi Moses Cyrus Weiler. As Richard approached thirteen, the Jewish age of manhood, he fully expected that Rabbi Weiler would preside over his bar mitzvah ceremony in the synagogue's modern building down the street from his home. A family crisis intervened. Richard and his parents lived not far from his paternal grandparents, whose strict observance of tradition was at odds with the Reform insurgency. Davis Goldstone insisted that he would never set foot in a Reform synagogue, and for a time the crisis threatened to upend the joy of the occasion. Rabbi Weiler prevailed on the family to accede to the grandfather's wishes and celebrate Richard's event in an Orthodox setting.

Three weeks before the bar mitzvah service, Davis Goldstone was stricken by a heart attack and died. His death cast a shadow over his grandson's celebration, but in the Goldstone family there was also an undercurrent of relief. Had they proceeded with plans for Temple Israel, what would his family have thought? Under the current circumstance, no one could say that Davis Goldstone had been driven to his death by his family's heartless apostasy.

Richard's bar mitzvah launched the teenager into his first and only period of intensive Jewish observance. He rose early each morning and donned the *tefillin*, the black boxes with their leather straps binding the forehead and arm of the young man in his prayer. He attended weekly services at the Orthodox synagogue, and he insisted that his mother keep a kosher kitchen.

Richard declined to wear a yarmulke on the streets or at school, and he made no other exterior show of his commitment. He prayed and took Hebrew lessons, but he undertook no extensive program of Jewish study and showed little curiosity about the mysterious ways of God. Instead, he seemed to take comfort in ritual, in the steadiness of practice and order, a commitment with obligations only to himself. By the time Richard turned seventeen, he had "lost the light" of Jewish observance.

Albert Jacobson died in Benoni in December 1953. The days at Albert's feet in his study were long past, but the grandfather's dreams for his grandson were still intact. The boy, now in Jewish terms a young man, still had his sights set on the law.

King Edward VII, a government school, sat precariously on the border between two sides of the Johannesburg Jewish community. It had been educating boys of the Johannesburg suburbs on its ridgetop campus since 1911, projecting the solidity and care of the upper crust, but falling just below the highest rank. King Edward VII was now Richard Goldstone's school, a curious combination of hidebound conservatism in the British style and underlying ferment.

Arriving at King Edward VII as a pampered only grandson and only child, Richard hoped to find there a broad canvas on which to display his talents.[9] The school, however, turned out to be a terrible match. Its institutional culture, shaped by its ties to the British educational system, valued brawn over brains. Military exercises were held weekly and were compulsory. Nothing mattered as much as success on the athletic field, especially in sports of muscle and blood like rugby. For a boy whose physical talents were modest, the "Old Edwardian" spirit proved endlessly frustrating. Despite his lofty ambitions, the teenaged Richard Goldstone suffered the indignity of mediocrity. He hated the place.

With his interest in the law, it was natural that Richard should seek distinction on the debate team. On one occasion he argued for the affirmative on the question, "History serves no essential purpose in the school curriculum," and in his final year the school yearbook reported that in the "Masters vs. Boys" debate Richard and his partner "did not find it too difficult to persuade an audience that was 80 per cent schoolboys that 'Education is Interrupted by Schooling.'"[10] Even in an area of strength Richard could not quite find a secure place. As president of the debate club, he proposed that the members spar over the question of whether access to abortion should be made easier for women in South Africa. The school administration quickly quashed that topic. Although Richard was not punished, he understood clearly that it would not be in his best interests to test the limits of propriety in the future.

"I don't know that Richard ever had a childhood in the conventional sense," one friend remembered. "In his early teens he had a pretty shrewd idea about who he wanted to be. I think that he had great ambitions not to be another drone like most of the rest of us. He pursued his objectives. Richard always would identify a person who he thought could be useful in advance of his aims or his career. And those he would cultivate. So he was not 'one of the boys.'"[11]

In the years between Richard Goldstone's move to Johannesburg in 1948 and his graduation from King Edward VII in December 1956, apartheid in

South Africa took tangible shape. Parliament, with its National Party majority, passed the Prohibition of Mixed Marriages Act in 1949. The Group Areas
Act followed in 1950, allowing the government to codify and enforce the
restriction of residential options for Blacks, Coloureds, and other non-
Europeans. Other pillars of apartheid followed: the Bantu Authorities Act,
the Prevention of Illegal Squatting Act, the Native Building Workers' Act, the
Reservation of Separate Amenities Act.[12] The National Party consolidated
its power in national elections in 1953, a contest where Richard, emulating
his grandfather, kept careful charts following the returns on the walls of his
bedroom in his Johannesburg apartment.[13]

These years also saw the incipient form of organized resistance. In 1952,
the Defiance campaign, though it was short-lived and did not achieve its
goals, used peaceful demonstrations and boycotts and showed the economic
and political power that Blacks could muster in a country that depended upon
their labor. The African National Congress (ANC) swirled with debates, as
new young activists like Nelson Mandela and Oliver Tambo voiced their rest-
lessness with the courteous politics of the past. The Communists and other
parties more revolutionary in their rhetoric than the ANC were gaining
adherents in the townships. The leftists even attracted a few followers among
Richard's fellow White students at King Edward VII.

By 1956, when Richard Goldstone graduated and joined the ranks of Old
Edwardians, larger political questions were still secondary for him. The young
man had bided his time in secondary school, eager to free himself from the
confines of a competitive culture. Or rather, he was eager to enter an arena
where the competition was more suited to his particular skills and talents.

The young man crossed the lawn and headed toward the columned portico
across the center of the imposing building in the campus quadrangle of the
University of the Witwatersrand. The drive in his new car from his home in
the Johannesburg suburb of Houghton to the university was only a few minutes, but already he felt a world away. He passed the looming columns and
followed the flow of other slightly dazed young people toward lunch in the
campus cafeteria.

As Richard Goldstone took his place in line, he felt the thrill of the unfamiliar. Another young man fell in behind him. He wore a short-sleeved shirt
and tie, and his skin was a deep chocolate brown. Richard captured the
moment in his head, almost as though he was being photographed from

above. Here they were, two students, one Black, one White, in the same lunch line, in the same university. For the first time in his life, at the age of nineteen, he was side by side with a Black person in a moment with every appearance of perfect equality. The two young men struck up a conversation. The Black student showed Richard the passbook that he was required to carry if he left his neighborhood, without which he would be subject to arrest. The image of that passbook stuck in Richard Goldstone's mind for many years, an early tangible introduction to the human and legal costs of the brutal system that had gripped his country.[14]

This encounter across the racial divide was possible in apartheid South Africa in 1957 because the University of the Witwatersrand, known familiarly as "Wits," was one of two so-called open universities in the country. Most South African universities were segregated by race. At Wits and at the University of Cape Town, however, both Blacks and other non-Whites could legally enroll alongside White students, if they met the admissions standards. The numbers were small. At Wits there were fewer than 100 Black South Africans out of nearly 6,000 students, but they were present.[15] Richard felt the exhilaration of doing something important just by standing in line.

Richard was not yet fully liberated himself. He was still living at home, sleeping in his own bedroom, making the commute to campus in an automobile that his parents had given him for his high school graduation, but now the characteristics that he had developed under his grandfather's tutelage began to count for something. The orderly march of the pins on the World War II maps, the lengthy games of chess, the systematic immersion in Arthur Mee's *Children's Encyclopedia*—Albert Jacobson had instilled in Richard a love of order, a deep satisfaction in collecting, analyzing, and mastering knowledge.

Richard recognized that the discipline that served him so well in his academic studies had a practical application as well. At university, a young man did not have to succeed as an athlete or deliver a booming speech in order to acquire power. Richard's talents for organization, his relentless discipline, and his extraordinary capacity for work all served him well as he vigorously pursued a new route toward the recognition he had long craved. It was called politics.

Like so much else in the Transvaal, the University of the Witwatersrand owed its origins to the gold mines that had driven the region's economy for half a century. The mines needed engineers and managers, so the South African School of Mines was founded in the town of Kimberley before the end of the nineteenth century, moving its operation into the center of Johannesburg in 1904. In 1922, it was incorporated as a full-fledged university, developing colleges of arts, medicine, law, engineering, and business. By the postwar period, the University of the Witwatersrand and the University of Cape Town were rivals at the pinnacle of South African higher education, catering principally to the country's English-speaking business and professional classes, or at least to those who could not afford to send their children abroad to Oxford and Cambridge.[16]

Despite its national aspirations, Wits was still essentially a Johannesburg institution. The vast majority of its students came from the city, its suburbs, and neighboring areas of the Transvaal, commuting daily from home to campus. Jews made up nearly a quarter of the Wits student body, nearly twice their proportion in the overall population of Johannesburg.[17] King Edward VII was virtually a feeder school.

On matters of race, the university mirrored the contorted logic and policies of the country as a whole. Its identity as an "open university" did not have its origins in a commitment to social and political equality. To the contrary, the "open" character of the university was built on a solid foundation of racism.

South African leaders had for half a century been building a society in which the segregation of the races was a leading principle. Yet Whites still had a stake in the overall well-being of Black communities. After all, White prosperity in the mines and comfort in the home depended on Black labor. Some of South Africa's leading White thinkers argued that if non-White communities were to develop and thrive separately from Whites in South Africa, they would require their own professional leadership. Most crucially, Black communities needed Black physicians to minimize the spread of disease and keep workers healthy. It was also important to train Blacks and other non-Whites in other professions, such as law and teaching, in order to preserve the social and civic order. This argument fueled the policy of admission to Wits and the University of Cape Town for a small but perceptible number of non-Whites among their student bodies. The universities were "open" not to enshrine equality, but to fortify the structure of inequality.

Not everyone among the Wits faculty and administration embraced enthusiastically the education of non-Whites. Once undertaken, however, it worked its way from policy to principle. With the training of doctors as the highest priority, the greatest concentration of Blacks and Coloureds at Wits was in the medical school.[18]

The admissions policies of Wits and the University of Cape Town were obvious and visible targets for the new National Party government, bent on eliminating race-mixing. The vice chancellor, Humphrey Raikes, resented government interference. He opposed the National Party's efforts to eliminate open admissions, even though he was in fact quite open about his belief in White supremacy. Raikes saw education of a small segment of Black leaders as an essential bulwark against the dangerous tendency to what he called "Native degeneracy." So he steered what he proudly thought of as a middle course: a policy of "academic non-separation and social separation."[19] In the classroom, according to this policy, Black and Coloured students would be side by side with their White classmates. They would study together, but Whites and non-Whites would conduct their extracurricular and social activities apart.

Apartheid was anathema to the majority of English-speaking White students who made up the majority of the Wits population, but there were deep divisions about whether to resist it with principled opposition or with outrage. The official Wits student government organization, the Student Representative Council (SRC), became the locus of intense battles between liberals and radicals.

Shortly before Richard arrived on campus, Wits had a change of leadership. Humphrey Raikes retired, to be followed as vice chancellor by W. G. Sutton, a civil engineer also committed to social separation but with few of the administrative and political skills of his predecessor. Sutton viewed politics with distaste, and did his best to withdraw from the fray. Student activists filled the vacuum in leadership with their own priorities.

In South African political terms, Richard Goldstone was marked early on as a liberal. Fairness, decency, respect: these were the commitments that came most naturally to him.[20] To the liberals' political right were acknowledged proponents of the still-recent South African policy of apartheid. Many students from this side of the spectrum were Afrikaners who hailed from Pretoria and other parts of the Transvaal outside of the Johannesburg metropolis. At the left wing of the spectrum the radicals joined together in advocating for a confrontational approach to challenging apartheid, both inside and outside the university. By and large the non-White students avoided overt participation in student politics. The ANC, though emerging as a serious political force in the nation during the 1950s, had minimal visible presence at Wits.

During Richard's first year at the university, students and the Wits faculty and administration alike resisted a new bill introduced in Parliament that year, the Separate University Education Act, which threatened to roll back the open university model and firmly entrench the establishment of entirely separate White and non-White institutions of higher education. The SRC organized a mass protest in May 1957, late in Richard's first term. Goldstone found himself swept up by the soaring rhetoric of one of the speakers, an Indian Wits law student named Ismail Mahomed who was also one of the leaders of the SRC.

Inspired by the protests and unintimidated by older students, Richard Goldstone made the unusual choice of standing for election to the SRC at the end of his first full year as a student. In late 1957 he won election to the only political office he would ever hold.

With his entrance into university politics, Goldstone became a familiar and visible figure on campus. Of medium height and a slim build, he was notable for the briskness of his pace and the briskness of his manner. His dark hair was already receding slightly around the edges, so that his forehead, now even more prominent, gave him the advantage of looking somewhat older than his twenty years. The young student leader hated the insidious way that the apartheid mind-set came to pervert basic principles, especially within university life. He zeroed in on the hypocritical notion of the "open" university. Allowing Blacks and Whites to sit side by side in the classroom and then refusing to let them dance or play together was absurd. The administration's policy positively offended him for its blatant and tormented form of compromise. In response, Goldstone became a master tactician within the Wits student movement, urging a reasoned and logical response to the university's policies.

Respected by many for his thoroughness and his skills, appreciated for his contributions to the anti-apartheid spirit, Richard Goldstone could be seen as cool, self-serving, a bit remote from the passions of the moment. Yet these aspects of his reputation did not interfere with Goldstone's rise in Wits campus politics. He was elected a member of the SRC at the end of his first year, vice president at the end of his second year, and president at the end of his final undergraduate year.

In 1958, during his second term on the SRC, he began, unknowingly, a life-long trajectory by chairing his first commission, an examination of the whole question of social segregation on campus. His report urged the administration to open the university further by establishing minimum quotas for Black and Coloured students in its various schools and by ending artificial barriers to segregation on campus.[21] Later in the year, he authored a second report, this time with SRC president John Shingler, that focused exclusively on the question of university admissions. Here his argument penetrated deeper. The open university, he said, could not be defended only on the basis of university autonomy. Autonomy was useless if not based on underlying values. In another circumstance, he warned, the principle of autonomy might be used to *support* segregation in the face of demands by a more liberal government. The student leaders did not abandon the principle of academic freedom, but they modified it. Goldstone's report called for university autonomy on admissions decisions as long as race, religion, and sex were not factors in the selection process.[22] In the end, however, the university simply brushed aside these reports, maintaining social segregation as an entrenched policy.

In one instance, Richard arguably overplayed his hand while in a position of power. When the student newspaper, itself an arm of the SRC, began to criticize the student council for being too conservative and too unwilling to challenge directly the administration, Richard, then the SRC president, swung into action. Freedom of expression was all very well as an abstract principle, but it made no sense to the young man that the student government's own media arm should have the right to mount a public challenge to its leadership. Goldstone dismissed the editor from his post. "I have no problem with freedom of expression," he told his SRC colleagues, "but this is *our* newspaper. We appoint the editor, and if we don't like the editor, we get rid of the editor." Leftist students responded with a petition for a student-wide vote of no confidence. The mass meeting was held at the Wits swimming pool, the only space large enough to accommodate the huge turnout. Richard and the SRC leadership survived the vote, but not before the proposer of the motion was tossed into the pool by a group of rowdy students from the engineering faculty. Goldstone was within his formal rights as SRC president, but his actions suggested that he gave little thought about how the ideal of an independent press might flourish on the Wits campus. In later years, he would show more acuity in thinking about how to balance competing rights.[23]

On the national level, the picture was becoming even bleaker. The 1957 Separate University Education Act failed, but it was only a postponement. In 1959, Goldstone's final year as an undergraduate student, Parliament passed a successor statute, the Extension of University Education Act, a broad measure whose name was designed to disguise its real intent: a chilling restriction on the open universities. In the future, Wits and the University of Cape Town would be permitted to admit Black and Coloured students only by special ministerial dispensation. In practice, this meant that Wits and UCT remained technically integrated into the 1960s, but the already small numbers of non-White students dropped to fewer than a dozen.

One day in early 1959, at the beginning of Richard's third and final year as an undergraduate, the president of the SRC, John Shingler, brought titillating news. There was a spy in their midst.

This news was not altogether shocking. After all, it was common knowledge that the South African Police and others within the state's security apparatus kept a close watch on student activism all over the country. It had been national news in 1957 when a spy for the authorities was exposed at Rhodes University in the Eastern Cape. Ever since his first year at university Goldstone had been aware of the presence of the police: the bulky figures hovering toward the rear at public meetings and protests, the shadowy men who followed him in slow-moving Volkswagens as he walked Johannesburg streets.[24] "Some of them you could see from a mile away," he recalled later. "They made no bones about it. They wanted you to know that you were being followed."[25]

Goldstone had heard from Black classmates stories about the brutality of the South African police, but shielded by his own sense of privilege he could not see overweight men in overcoats as a serious threat. "We sort of enjoyed it. We joked about it. We knew that our phones were being tapped and talked all sorts of rubbish on telephones and said that we were looking forward to this meeting when there wasn't one, hoping to inconvenience them by sending them on a wild goose chase."[26] The police presence had always struck the young leaders as clumsy and oafish.

This spy, John Shingler said, was altogether different. Not old. Not bulky. Not Afrikaner. Not even a man.

Her name was Priscilla Lefson. She had just completed her BA studies at Wits, and she was working part time as a model. Richard knew her, of course.

She was a familiar in their circles, a good friend of the woman whom Shingler was dating at the moment. Indeed, Shingler's girlfriend had broken the news, telling Shingler that for months Lefson had been paid to deliver information on their activities to the police.

Goldstone and Shingler were gripped with excitement. Here was a chance to turn the methods of apartheid regime on its head. The situation demanded an inquiry. Goldstone and Shingler approached Ernie Wentzel, a former president of the National Union of South African Students (NUSAS), a mixed-race organization that represented the anti-apartheid universities. Wentzel had already built a successful practice at the Johannesburg bar. Together the three men concocted a plan to smoke the spy out.

On a warm January evening, Priscilla Lefson arrived at Ernie Wentzel's flat in the Johannesburg suburb of Berea dressed for a party. Wentzel's wife greeted her at the door, showed her into the living room, and retired to the bedroom. Ms. Lefson found that the party consisted of Ernie Wentzel, John Shingler, and Richard Goldstone. There was no music. There was only the invisible reel-to-reel tape recorder that Richard had hidden behind a large potted plant.[27]

The three men confronted their surprised detainee with the information that they had acquired. After several minutes of badgering her to confess to their charges of espionage, the questioners ramped up the pressure, admitting that they were going to "get a little bit brutal because we have been brutally treated." They let the young woman know that the facts about her activities would be a "right royal story for the Press which we shall not hesitate to use," and they made it clear that her name would be front and center in leaks to the media.

The threat of publicity bore fruit. The inquisitors extracted a confession, although Lefson maintained her spunk and sense of humor in the face of their onslaught. For the last two years, she admitted, she had been giving reports of the activities of the SRC to one Sergeant Kruger of the South African Security Police. She brought him detailed accounts of meetings, conferences, and conversations. She was instructed to keep a special eye out for "people who were making trouble," though she insisted that she had not, in the end, singled out any particular individual for special attention. This was not about money for her, she told the men. This was about keeping some kind of check on Communists and others who might foment unrest or even violence. Her questioners had no doubt that she had been paid for her services, but they could not persuade her to admit to this detail on their surreptitious tape.

The next day, with a documented confession in hand, Goldstone and Shingler dramatically played excerpts from the recording at an emergency meeting of the SRC. Their fellow students endorsed and ratified their leaders' action, decried the government's intrusion into academic freedom, and authorized the public dissemination of this shocking news. The students delivered a copy of the transcript of the tape to the *Sunday Times*, the most widely read English newspaper in the country. On Sunday, February 15, 1959, all of South Africa woke up to Richard Goldstone's photograph on the front page of the newspaper and a full account of the activities of the woman identified in the story only as the "Blonde Spy."

The Blonde Spy scandal dominated the South African news cycle for the better part of a week. The English press lambasted the heavy-handed tactics of the police. Priscilla Lefson was imagined as a femme fatale, using her wiles to charm secrets out of inexperienced young men in the student movement. Goldstone and Shingler were lauded for their courage in making the issue public. In Parliament, the outspoken anti-apartheid legislator Helen Suzman demanded an explanation. The commissioner of police denied any involvement. He threatened that anyone who raised the issue would get "a kick in the pants."[28]

Speaking to reporters, Richard kept a straight face and talked seriously about civil liberties and government interference. But he could not suppress the shiver of pleasure each time he saw his photograph in the papers. More than 1,000 students demonstrated to support free expression and denounce spying. On the Wits campus Richard was a hero, and he accepted the accolades with every appearance of humility.

As the story unfolded, the South African police turned the tables and started their own investigation of the accusers and the SRC. The commissioner of police charged that in his opinion Wentzel, Shingler, and Goldstone had used "Gestapo tactics" against the young woman, and the minister of justice repeated the phrase in Parliament. The police demanded that the original reel-to-reel tape of the confession be turned over. The young men dodged the request, claiming that the original had been misplaced.

In fact, Richard had made a trip to Cape Town and left the tape with anti-apartheid friends. When he flew back home, agents met him on the tarmac and whisked him roughly into a back room at the Johannesburg airport. A pair of policemen loomed over him, barking questions for an unsettling half hour. Eventually they abruptly turned Richard loose, but not before he got a taste of what it felt like to be exposed and alone in his native country.

Feeling the pressure, Goldstone and his fellow conspirators decided to turn the tape over to the authorities, after they made sure that a few politically embarrassing remarks by Wentzel, a leading member of the Liberal Party, had been spliced out.

The incident had some salutary results. English editorials decried the incident as an example of the overreach of the security establishment. "To the ordinary man," one newspaper editorialized, "there is something repugnant in the idea of people who belong to the same fraternity or group spying and reporting on the words and actions of their associations and friends often expressed in unguarded moments or twisted out of context. . . . It is a picture not very flattering to South Africa."[29] Opposition to segregation of the universities stiffened, and it seemed for a short time as though the passage of the Extension of University Education Act would be imperiled. As the account of Lefson's role became generally accepted as fact, the commissioner of police was forced to resign. A cartoon in one of the local newspapers depicted him on the receiving end of the blow to the rear end that he had promised to deliver to others.

Four weeks after the original revelation, however, the tables began to turn. Priscilla Lefson went public, and the *Sunday Times* published the Blonde Spy's story. She presented herself as a patriot, with no more of a role than keeping an eye out for Communists and others who might intend harm to the state. She was no paid spy, she averred. As her photograph revealed, she wasn't even a blonde.

By this time, too, the actions of her accusers came under more intensive scrutiny. At the time the pushback came from the pro-government press, eager to portray Lefson as a principled guardian of national values protecting the apartheid regime from scurrilous opponents. Even in the English-language press, the young men's "melodramatic behaviour over the tapes also served to damage their own public standing," according to one historian.[30] By the standards of fair procedure and human rights that Goldstone later stood for, the inquisitors' methods were, after all, somewhat excessive. If Goldstone and Shingler were so concerned about civil liberties and underhanded tactics, then what about their own actions in making a secret tape recording and then hastily making it public? Three men had lured a vulnerable young woman under false pretenses to an apartment, and then ganged up to interrogate her for two hours, threatening her with public exposure if she did not make a full confession. Goldstone was willing, as a young man pursuing his cause with a touch of self-righteous fervor, to stretch the boundaries of due process and fairness.

These considerations did not faze Goldstone, either at the time or in recalling the incident years later. He and Shingler had done what needed to be done to a woman whose actions were "contemptible and dishonest," in the service of informing the public about the desperate and nasty lengths to which the government was willing to go. He had support from the broader public. "If the students revolt against being spied upon, they are simply doing what any other citizen would do in similar circumstances," opined the *Sunday Times*.[31] Goldstone's excesses were understandable in the context of a country in the grip of a racist and increasingly authoritarian regime.

The young man savored the moment as the Blonde Spy scandal made the transition from the news pages into the annals of South African popular culture. A few months after the story broke, a new musical was hustled into production on the Johannesburg stage. It was called "I Spy." One lyric memorialized the Priscilla Lefson figure as a "special duty cutie." He attended the premiere with not-so-secret pride, though the fictionalized cast of characters contained no part called Richard Goldstone.

In addition to his work on the SRC, Richard became an active member of the executive committee of NUSAS. Through his work with NUSAS he came into more frequent contact with Blacks inside and outside of Wits. He accepted an occasional invitation to visit a fellow student in his home in one of the townships. There the physical circumstances made a mark on him: the shacks without electricity and running water in neighborhoods where city services were remote or nonexistent. For the first time he saw close-up the gulf between White and Black,

Through his activities as a student leader, he met some of the leading figures of the anti-apartheid movement. Bishop Ambrose Reeves of the Anglican Church hosted multiracial gatherings in his Johannesburg home, where the atmosphere was freer than student meetings on campus. In the Reeves home Richard heard Black and Coloured people speaking up with an articulate candor that he seldom heard in SRC meetings, where the White majority tended to dominate the discussions.[32]

Moving further afield, he left South Africa on his own for the first time. As a representative of NUSAS he traveled to an international faculty/student conference in Nigeria.[33] He was anxious about the trip, conscious that as a

White South African even fellow activists might treat him as a pariah. But he found his reception warm and embracing, and he socialized comfortably with Black students from every part of Africa and the wider world. He took off on his own to see more of the country, feeling conspicuous and self-conscious in his white skin, and apprehensive that those he met would judge him harshly as a White man from the home of apartheid.

Traveling in remote parts of Ghana after the conference, he seldom volunteered that he hailed from South Africa, but only once did he feel it necessary to tell an outright lie about his origins. He acquired a nasty skin infection on a rural sojourn and found himself in a tiny clinic, treated by a Black doctor. The physician was making small talk as he picked up an oversized syringe to treat Richard with antibiotics, and he asked his White patient where he was from. Cognizant of his surroundings, with a skeptical eye on the needle, the young man answered without hesitation, "I'm from Australia."[34]

A year later he accompanied other South African student leaders on an annual trip to England. On the way home, he stopped on his own for two weeks in Israel, where he walked for hours in Jerusalem and experienced firsthand the nation that was for so long a dream in the eyes of his fellow South African Jews. He witnessed also the uneasy relationship between Jews and Arabs in the new country, and he reflected on what it meant in comparison to the troubled state of race relations in his own country. He had lived for most of his life with an abstract image of Israel and its central place in the life of the Jewish people. Faced with the gritty, chaotic reality, he could not quite feel comfortable in this alien place, with its Mediterranean messiness and its mélange of languages foreign to him. But Israel also offered him a lifeline, a sense of identification beyond the beautiful but deeply flawed nation of his birth. He did not have to live his life trapped and branded as a White South African. In recent history, being Jewish had meant confinement and death for millions. For Richard Goldstone in the late 1950s, the Jewishness with which he identified in the new land of Israel was a means of transcending the confines of his identity under the apartheid regime.

2 ▸ THE STRIVER

Sixty-nine people were dead in a place called Sharpeville. The township lay thirty-seven miles from the University of the Witwatersrand campus in Johannesburg. On March 21, 1960, the police opened fire on a demonstration, and the news of the Sharpeville massacre radiated quickly around the country and around the globe. It was now clear to the world what had been clear for many years to South African activists: this government was prepared to use violence as a tool to repress dissent. It was a galvanizing moment for South Africa. The government tightened its grip by declaring a state of emergency. The ANC began to debate in earnest whether tactics of nonviolence were enough to topple such a determined regime.

The news from Sharpeville reached Richard Goldstone at a leading Johannesburg restaurant where, as president of the SRC, he had been invited by a Johannesburg businessman who was also a Wits alum interested in supporting the work of the SRC. The news from Sharpeville appalled the young lawyer-to-be. It confirmed the worst that he had heard from his Black classmates, and it threatened to open a new phase in South Africa's climate of repression. But as hard as Sharpeville hit him, his time for activism was now limited. Working on the SRC by day, he was now a full-time law student in the evenings.[1] South Africa's massive problems were competing for Goldstone's attention with his personal priorities. He was becoming a master of compartmentalization.

The law school at Wits, the most prominent in the nation, was known for its ability to turn out both servants of the apartheid state and the South African government's most strident critics. It was a place of extraordinary intensity. Of the forty students who entered with Richard Goldstone, fewer than half graduated three years later.[2]

While converting his copious class notes from scrawls to neatly catalogued typescripts, Goldstone discovered deep intellectual pleasure in the study of the mysteries and intricacies of South Africa's legal system.[3] South African law was based on the Roman-Dutch tradition, brought from continental Europe by the Dutch colonists in the seventeenth and eighteenth centuries. That tradition gave great weight to the law as written, and especially the law as an expression of the will of the executive and the legislature. Roman-Dutch law tended to bolster the authority of government rather than to serve as a check on its power. The arrival of the British in nineteenth-century South Africa added a rich new layer. With its origins in checking the power of the king at the time of the Magna Carta, the British tradition of common law provided a crucial counterweight to the authoritarian framework that the Dutch had left behind.

In Richard Goldstone's South Africa, attachment to the principle of the rule of law ran deep. Supporters of the government in power counted on the primacy of laws passed by Parliament as a bulwark of the legal order. South Africa was, as one observer put it, "at once a country of extreme injustice and elaborate legality."[4]

Both the Roman-Dutch and the British traditions were the tools of propertied men of European descent. Law's benefits flowed principally to Whites. Under White rule, law served as a brutal tool of exclusion, oppression, and violence, especially since the ascent of the National Party in 1948. Yet opponents of the regime could also look to the law as a potent tool for challenging the blatantly unjust structure of South African society. Even those who bore the brunt of South African injustice tended to see it that way. The two young leaders of the ANC, Nelson Mandela and Oliver Tambo, had been trained as lawyers. As working attorneys, they performed a vital service for Black clients, and they also came to understand the structure of South African law from the inside.

In the early 1960s, however, using the law to challenge authority was not uppermost in Richard Goldstone's considerations. He was mastering the complexities of contracts, torts, and other tools of the law of commerce. No classes dedicated to human rights or civil liberties graced the Wits law school curriculum.

On a chilly morning in June 1961, Richard Goldstone stood under the giant columns of the Wits administration building, comparing notes on torts with a law school classmate, when two students spilled out of the building into the winter sunshine. One was a cousin of a friend of Richard's companion. The other young woman confessed laughingly that she had just emerged from a psychology lab, where all the rats in her experiment were running the wrong way. Richard's attention had been wandering, but the charming irreverence of the speaker caught his attention. She was attractive, Jewish, curious, and with a bit of spunk. Her name was Noleen Behrman. The next day, acting on the suggestion of his companion, he asked her out. Years later, Richard Goldstone liked to laugh that on that day in 1961 *he* was the only rat who did *not* get away.

Studying at Wits had been a second choice for Noleen Behrman. Growing up in the Johannesburg suburbs, her dream was to study speech and drama in one of the seaside cities, Cape Town or Durban. However, her father had died suddenly at the age of forty-one, just two years before she was to enter university. Not wanting to leave her mother behind, Noleen gave up her plan to leave town, settling instead for pursuing a degree in social work at Wits, the local university.[5]

Somehow Richard found extra hours in the day for his new girlfriend. Music was their initial bond. The couple attended evening concerts, and spent hours together at the Goldstone family home with music in the background while Richard studied. He chose the music. She flipped the disc when the needle slid to the center.[6] By the end of 1961, as Richard completed his second year of law school, the young lovers had an understanding. As soon as Richard completed his degree, they would embark on their life together.

In December 1962, Richard Goldstone and Noleen Behrman were married under a *chuppah*, a symbolic Jewish wedding tent, on the same altar in the same Johannesburg synagogue where he had become a bar mitzvah just over a decade earlier. The ceremony came right on the heels of his law school graduation, where he was honored by the Society of Advocates as the most outstanding law student of the year. The wedding photographs, interweaving two extended Jewish families, could have been taken in Europe, America, or any corner of the Jewish world. But this young couple were stepping into their future in the warped and vulnerable nation of South Africa in the 1960s.

Although Jews were disproportionately represented in the active struggle against apartheid, Jewish lawyers' relationships to the South African state took many forms in the 1960s. Richard Goldstone crossed paths with most of his Jewish contemporaries during that decade.

Arthur Chaskalson was at the defense table when Nelson Mandela was arraigned on charges of conspiracy, alongside a dozen other activists who had been trapped and arrested at an ANC safe house in the Johannesburg suburb of Rivonia. A young Cape Town lawyer named Albie Sachs found himself drawn so strongly to the cause of the ANC that he joined the banned organization and went into exile to serve it. Joe Slovo entered directly into the armed struggle from inside South Africa. Percy Yutar, on the other hand, made his mark in the same Old Synagogue courtroom as Arthur Chaskalson in 1963, but from the other side. Yutar faced Nelson Mandela and the Rivonia defendants as their accuser, serving as the lead prosecutor for the South African state and arguing for the death penalty in the trial that sent Mandela to prison for twenty-seven years.[7]

Many Jewish lawyers found a different way out, leaving South Africa for a more comfortable living and a less fraught climate abroad. Between 1960 and 1994, tens of thousands of Jews emigrated from their South Africa homeland, many of them seasoned professionals in medicine, law, and other fields. Emigration was more difficult for lawyers than for doctors, since legal skills, rooted in the South African system, were less portable than the more universal expertise of the physician. Retooling was the cost of escaping the moral complexities of their home country.

As for Richard Goldstone, he simply applied himself to the profession of the law, advancing as fast as he could. He followed the Rivonia trials from a distance, knowing well the part that other Jews like Chaskalson and Yutar were playing there. He was far from the courtroom when Mandela, at the close of his trial, declared that he was prepared to die, if necessary, for "the idea of a democratic and free society in which all persons live together in harmony with equal opportunities." Goldstone had decided he would devote himself to law and family and community, while taking every opportunity within his own circle to defend values of fairness. Rather than an activist, he thought of himself as an "interested observer," one who was "increasingly frustrated and full of despair at the enforcement of laws designed to impose apartheid in greater and greater measure."[8]

Within a year of completing law school, Goldstone secured a place in Innes Chambers, the stately downtown quarters of the Johannesburg bar. This in itself was no small achievement, for it meant that he had broken into the ranks of the advocates, the higher rank of the South African legal profession. Advocates argued cases in court. They received their cases from attorneys, lawyers of a lower rank, who actually did the work of consulting with clients and much of the preparation work on the legal and substantive issues. Starting out as an advocate was no guarantee of success, since advocates depended on their relationships with the attorneys for drumming up business. It was, as one lawyer friend put it, a "leap of faith" on the young man's part.[9] To become an advocate required not only the appropriate law degree and success in the bar exam, but a kind of invitation process akin to joining an old and established club, which is indeed what at times Innes Chambers most resembled.

Goldstone began acquiring commercial cases, the main field of opportunity for a young lawyer on the rise, at a swift and steady rate. A tireless worker, he became an accepted, if not wholly beloved, figure in Innes Chambers, where fellow advocates saw him as competent but also, according to one friend and colleague, envied his rapid accomplishments.[10] He became known for his rapid but thorough preparation, and for his compact and logical courtroom style. As an orator, he would never hold an audience spellbound with high-flown rhetoric and courtroom theatrics. Instead, he acquired an extraordinary ability to synthetize complex material succinctly, to delve right to the heart of a matter and construct arguments that appeared unassailable. He loved working in Innes Chambers: the camaraderie of the bar, the library he built in his "lovely chambers," the adrenaline rush of performing in court. His unflappable exterior, however, disguised inner tension. "I was always nervous before a big case," he recalled. "I enjoyed preparation and cross-examination. It was like playing chess in many ways."[11]

The Johannesburg bar was by reputation the most liberal in South Africa, and Goldstone felt at home among the group of mostly English-speaking advocates, most of whom earned a comfortable living as White South Africans while at the same time privately deploring the National Party regime. Innes Chambers itself was an all-White fraternity when Goldstone arrived. As a young advocate, he played a part in breaking that color barrier. In 1964, Ismail Mahomed, classified as Indian within the South African racial system, was considered for Goldstone's group within the bar. Mahomed, seven years his senior, had impressed the younger man as a brilliant orator during their brief overlap at Wits, so Goldstone could speak to Mahomed's strengths from personal experience. He politicked among his older colleagues, arguing not for the symbolic value of Mahomed's admission, but for the talents that he would bring to Innes Chambers. Privately he treated Mahomed's successful candidacy as his own small contribution to the battle against apartheid.

The Goldstones moved further north as Richard's income grew and as they could afford a larger place in a more upscale community. They also needed the room for their expanding family. Glenda was born in 1965. A second daughter, Nicole, followed three years later. Yet work always came first, even within the home. After a long day in downtown Johannesburg, the young lawyer's evenings after dinner were mostly devoted to preparation for the next day's appearances, often using Noleen as a sounding board as he wrestled with complex problems.[12]

Goldstone's work was consuming, but he also developed a taste for the good life. As he rose on the professional ladder, he found the time, despite his punishing professional schedule, to indulge this taste. Already a tennis player, he took up golf as well. His talent in both sports was no better than moderate, but he played with an understated manner and an insouciance that belied a fiercely competitive spirit. Richard also developed a passion for fine wines, and he and Noleen began to visit the hidden corners of South Africa's developing vineyards during annual vacations in Cape Town.

During Goldstone's early years at the bar, he became involved for the first time in Jewish organizations, echoing his mother Kitty's commitment to the Jewish Women's Benevolent Society. The Six Day War in 1967 galvanized the global Jewish community, stimulating both concern about Israel's isolation within the Middle East and enormous pride in its swift and thorough military victory over the surrounding Arab nations.[13] One of Goldstone's first substantial engagements was with the South African Jewish Board of Deputies (SAJBD), the principal umbrella organization for the national Jewish community. Dominated by leading professionals and businessmen, the

SAJBD was bedeviled by the question of how the Jewish community should respond to apartheid.

For years, the SAJBD had clung to the argument that as an umbrella organization it should stay out of politics. Its membership, the argument went, encompassed a broad spectrum of political convictions. Since the board could not speak in one voice on behalf of the entire membership, it should not speak at all. The subtext was clear. In speaking up on behalf of Blacks and other excluded minorities, the Jewish community had little to gain and much to lose if it incurred the wrath of political leaders and other powerful figures in the Afrikaner community. Better to wear the cloak of neutrality than be exposed to retaliation for gestures that would not, in the end, achieve much of anything.[14]

As tensions mounted and the apartheid regime consolidated its power and expanded its policies, however, this argument sounded increasingly hollow, especially when confronted with the prophetic and activist spirit of the Jewish tradition. Goldstone joined the SAJBD's public relations committee and pressed for statements that would call the government to account, based both on Jewish principles of justice and an appeal to Christian South Africans, whose biblical tradition shared Old Testament values. These efforts were to little avail. The majority of the members of the public relations committee, and of the board as a whole, diluted drafts of statements until they turned to unsatisfying pablum. Goldstone believed that the SAJBD's excuse of serving Jews of all political persuasions was a "cop-out," but he rated himself as only "20 percent successful" in having an impact on the organization's public posture.[15]

Uneasy that his service to the Jewish community consisted only of rearguard battles, the young lawyer jumped when he was offered another opportunity: to take a leadership role within the worldwide organization known as ORT, the Organization for Rehabilitation and Training. Founded in Russia in 1880, ORT provided technical training in practical fields to young Jews and non-Jews alike in many corners of the world.[16] Technical training was a field entirely unfamiliar to Goldstone, whose personal proficiency barely extended to changing a light bulb. But for this reason, he welcomed both the challenge to learn something new and the chance to contribute to more practical results than empty public statements.

ORT proved amenable to the talents of the young lawyer, who rose as quickly in its ranks as he did in the bar. In the mid-1960s, when Goldstone became involved, ORT South Africa was purely a fundraising organization, supporting the global organization's training programs in Israel and Eastern Europe, as well as within significant swaths of the Arab world. A leadership role provided Goldstone with reasons to embark on eye-opening trips overseas. As early as 1967, he traveled to Iran, where ORT had successful operations. In the 1970s he was overwhelmed by the experience of watching new immigrants to Israel from the Soviet Union kiss the tarmac on arrival at Lod Airport. Within his own country, however, he could make no field visits, because World ORT had never established programs in South Africa itself. The international board did consider instituting programs in South Africa in the 1970s, but Goldstone reluctantly had to advise against it. ORT activities would be seen, he argued, as legitimizing the apartheid regime. The reputation of the organization worldwide would be tarnished. The leadership of World ORT agreed.

Goldstone was nevertheless invited to join World ORT's international board, and he would much later serve seven years as its president.[17] He took pride in witnessing World ORT's concrete results: technical schools built, skills acquired, lives transformed piece by piece, in tangible ways.

The intersections between South African and world events shaped Richard Goldstone's direction and commitments during his rise in professional life.

In 1966, Senator Robert F. Kennedy visited South Africa. His first stop was Johannesburg, where he visited Innes Chambers and made a deep impression on Richard Goldstone, then just twenty-seven years old. Goldstone admired Kennedy's candid account of progress made in civil rights in the United States, and the distance that America still had to travel to achieve equality for the "Negro." He took to heart RFK's famous "ripple of hope" metaphor for the power of individual men and women to change the course of history.

Kennedy's visit spurred the young lawyer to more readings in the law and culture of the United States. When he had his chance to visit the country for the first time on business for one of his commercial cases, he jumped at it. Goldstone extended his American visit as long as possible, riding buses through the Northeast to see Washington, D.C., New York, and Boston. Without being blind to the continuing inequalities within the United States, he admired the creativity that American civil rights lawyers had shown in *Brown v. Board of Education* and other landmark cases. It was the beginning of the young man's lifelong love affair with American culture and ideals.

Although Israel's victory in the Six Day War in 1967 thrilled the South African Jewish community, Israel became increasingly isolated over the next decade as Palestinian nationalism took hold and turned into a global cause. The humiliation of the Arab armies and the occupation of the Gaza Strip and the West Bank launched a narrative that painted Israel as a proto-colonial power, with the Palestinians as its oppressed victims. The Palestinians made common cause with other like-minded movements around the world, including with the opponents of South African apartheid. An isolated Israel, with few friends on the African continent, built strong economic and military ties with the South African government. This connection between two pariah nations created fissures in the global Jewish community, torn between its commitment to Israel and its support for ideals of freedom and justice.[18]

Richard Goldstone understood that a fragile Israeli state had few options, but he grew increasingly concerned about the consequences of persisting in the occupation of the West Bank and Gaza. He feared that Israel was making choices that could undermine its stability for many years to come.[19]

Closer to home, the temperature of the political climate in South Africa rose during the 1970s. Riots during 1976 in Soweto, the massive township southwest of Johannesburg, marked another turning point in the South African struggle, the most explosive moment since the Sharpeville massacre. A younger generation of Black South Africans, who had never known anything but the National Party's apartheid regime, pressed for the isolation of their country. They asserted that any form of cooperation with South African society constituted support for its apartheid policies. This argument fueled the global movement for economic and political sanctions against South Africa, and it also began to put White South African liberals, who benefited from apartheid even if they opposed it politically, on the defensive. Richard Goldstone, who in the late 1970s was in the prime of his successful years as a commercial lawyer, felt the sting of this argument.

Across the Atlantic, U.S. president Jimmy Carter made human rights a centerpiece of his foreign policy. The discourse of human rights, thought by many before then as a vocabulary of aspiration, came into its own as a practical tool for changing the behavior of governments and even individuals. Concerns about the rights of Jews in the Soviet Union echoed concerns with the rights of South African Blacks in the worldwide Jewish community. The politics of human rights increasingly put the struggle against apartheid into a global context.[20]

Human rights ideas and language had been part of the student movement at Wits when Richard Goldstone attended, but they had little direct connection to the work of a commercial lawyer. As the concepts gained credibility around the world, however, Goldstone found himself encountering human rights advocates on his travels for business and Jewish communal work. He was not yet a close student of the field, but it was working its way into his consciousness. In the late 1970s, two anti-apartheid lawyers, John Dugard (within South Africa) and Albie Sachs (living in exile) published books on human rights and the South African legal order.[21] Dugard in particular offered a line of thinking that offered legal opponents of apartheid a range of choices from the common law and human rights discourse with which to challenge the established order on its own terms. In 1979, the first international conference on human rights in South Africa took place in Cape Town, featuring a stirring address by Judge Michael Corbett. Corbett, in language astonishing for a sitting judge of the Supreme Court, told the conference frankly that in South Africa "one cannot avoid the conclusion that in many areas the freedom of the individual and his basic human rights are severely curtailed. . . . Among the questions we, as South Africans, will have to ask ourselves are whether such curtailment actually promotes the common weal."[22] While not a direct participant in these conversations, Goldstone was a close student of these developments, which would have a profound influence on his thinking and actions in later years.

Two years after the Soweto uprising, in 1978, the judge president of the Transvaal Division of the Supreme Court of South Africa offered Goldstone an appointment as an acting judge for a few weeks to fill a temporary vacancy. Goldstone accepted the post and spent the spring of 1978 in temporary quarters in the sprawling courthouse across the street from Innes Chambers. In some ways a stint as judge was a welcome respite. From the start, Goldstone recalled, "I loved the bench . . . the research, the quiet. Compared to a very busy practice at the bar it was really very relaxing."[23] As a judge, Goldstone could keep regular hours, control the pace of the proceedings, and take the time that he needed to reflect on the issues before him. As much as he enjoyed the parry and thrust of argument and oratory as an advocate, he discovered that he had a taste for listening too. Then, too, there was the plea-sure of being the decider.

Goldstone served his six weeks in 1978, and he was pleased to accept another temporary appointment in 1979, but he thought little about the impli-cations. Acting judge appointments provided a break from the work of an advocate, but these were fill-in positions with no special status and no exten-sive commitments. Whatever his ambitions, he expected to be a practicing lawyer for at least another decade or more. Especially in the political climate of contemporary South Africa, he did not expect that a lawyer still remem-bered for his anti-apartheid work as a student activist would be chosen as a permanent judge.

He was wrong. In 1980, Richard Goldstone received a phone call at his home from the minister of justice. He was offered an appointment as a per-manent member of the Transvaal Supreme Court bench.

The news was as exhilarating as it was unexpected. It was a step toward the culmination of a lifelong dream, yet it also set off a chain of anxiety. If he were to accept permanent appointment, his life would be transformed. Gone would be the professional camaraderie of Innes Chambers, the diverse and interesting give-and-take of representation of clients from around the coun-try and around the world. He would be entering instead a world of compara-tive isolation. Also gone: the large and comfortable income that he had finally attained through his work in commercial law. As a judge, he would be a public servant. His salary would be significantly less than half of his cur-rent income.

The Goldstones had no extensive resources on which to draw. They would have to cut back expenses, take fewer vacations. They would be a long way from poverty, but they would forego, quite possibly forever, the prospect of wealth and financial security. Yet at the age of forty-one, Goldstone had the chance to make his mark on the nation, and there was no telling whether the opportunity would ever come again. He and Noleen decided together that they would simply have to make the best of the financial sacrifice.

Finances were not, however, the only difficult consideration. A moral issue was at stake as well, one impossible to gloss over. As an acting judge, he had been able plausibly to maintain his independence from the government, since his service was temporary. To become a permanent judge in South Africa in 1980, however, was to become a servant of the apartheid state, bound to apply its laws, barred by matters of ethics and decorum from the active politics of dissent. The moral dilemmas of a private citizen in South Africa were challenging enough. Could an individual maintain his integrity while serving as a guardian of justice under the apartheid regime? Goldstone could not say yes to the minister before wrestling with this question.[24]

In 1980 the Supreme Court of the Republic of South Africa consisted of eighty-seven judges, divided into seven provincial districts. Richard Goldstone was asked to serve as a judge of the Transvaal province, one of twenty-nine judges based in Pretoria and Johannesburg.[25] Those judges sat alone as the highest trial court in civil and criminal cases, and two or three judge benches heard appeals on civil and criminal cases from the lower courts, where the presiding judicial officers were called magistrates. Most of those on the "Supreme Court" bench, including the post on which Goldstone had been asked to serve, were more akin to judges of a Federal Court of Appeal within the U.S. system. Their decisions were not necessarily final. There was one further level of review: ten members of the Supreme Court sat on the Appellate Division of the Supreme Court, the highest judicial authority in the country, based in the central city of Bloemfontein.

All South African Supreme Court judges in 1980 were White. All but one were men. Diversity on the South African bench in 1980 meant that two-thirds of the judges were native speakers of Afrikaans and the other one-third were native speakers of English. Richard Goldstone was not the first Jew to be named to the South African bench, but compared to their representation in the bar, the number of Jewish judges was disproportionately small.

Although the law as an abstraction was venerated in South Africa, the power of judges was also circumscribed. Parliament, the legislature, was the supreme legal authority in the land. South Africa's 1961 constitution specifically excluded power of judicial review; that is, judges were not permitted to rule on whether or not Parliament's laws were constitutional.[26] So, for example, the laws governing the separation of people by skin color, the laws of apartheid, could not be overturned by judges on the basis of a constitution or any other legal instrument. The South African legal system permitted no option for judges to apply the concept of universal human rights or to refer to a higher moral authority in rendering their decisions. The Appellate Division had been crystal clear on this point: "Parliament may make any encroachment it chooses upon the life, liberty or property or any individual subject in its sway, and . . . it is the function of courts of law to enforce its will."[27]

Within these constraints, however, judges did have considerable power and flexibility. They might not be able to overturn laws, but they could rule on their implementation. They could decide whether government agencies and organizations were complying with the letter and spirit of the law in their regulations and actions. Judges were seldom able to alter the big picture with large, sweeping strokes. But they had latitude to effect change by focusing on specific cases and details.

So while the courts could not overturn apartheid, judges had been able over the years to slow down its advance at key junctures. In the 1950s, the Appellate Division used a technicality to strike down laws regarding separate but equal recreation facilities for Whites and Blacks. In the same era courts prevented the government for many years from striking Coloured people from the voting rolls in the Cape province.[28] In both of these instances Parliament eventually passed stronger, judge-proof legislation, but the cat-and-mouse game between the courts and the legislature offered some slight means of protection for those who bore the brunt of injustice in the country. The veneration of the rule of law also offered a sliver of hope to those who preferred that legal processes, rather than violence, might serve as the country's path to democracy.

Since 1948, the National Party had at times tried to pack the bench with judges friendly to the apartheid project, but the behavior of individuals, once appointed, was not always predictable. Moreover, by the 1970s, the government was beginning to appoint known liberals to the bench, as a way of demonstrating to a critical world that South Africa was indeed a nation with a respect for the independence of the judiciary. The risk to the government of appointing liberals to the bench appeared, on the face of it, to be low. How much harm could judges really do when Parliament could always rewrite the laws? The selection of Richard Goldstone appeared consistent with this trend.

None of this made Goldstone's decision easy. Harsher laws with fewer loopholes had made it harder to use the courts to resist apartheid. One observer called for those on the bench already to resign "as a statement of judicial despair and outrage, . . . an assertion of the judge's absolute fidelity to justice, a protest against the abuse of law."[29]

When Richard Goldstone consulted with Arthur Chaskalson, his friend told him that he personally could never accept a judicial appointment in an undemocratic South Africa. Despite his personal qualms, Chaskalson actually encouraged Goldstone to accept the appointment. It is a matter of self-interest,

Chaskalson told his friend. We need people on the bench who will give us a fair hearing. Chaskalson pointed to the example of John Didcott, a liberal who had become a judge in Natal five years earlier. Didcott had found a way to make a series of courageous rulings against the government. "The judge who invokes the presumption in favour of individual liberty in interpreting the security laws is not 'lying', but applying a rule of positive law," John Dugard wrote. "So, too, a judge who allows himself to be guided by the common-law principle in favour of equality in interpreting a discriminatory statute does not lie, but acts in accordance with the best traditions of the law."[30]

With Noleen already behind him, the conversation with Chaskalson sealed his determination. In August 1980, he took the oath of office and became a permanent member of the judiciary of the Republic of South Africa.[31]

3 ▸ CRACKS IN THE WALL

DURING THE 1980S, the apartheid regime in South Africa both approached its breaking point and tightened its grip. Within the country, an emboldened younger generation of Black activists and the increasingly effective political and military tactics of the banned resistance organizations undermined the authoritarian power of the regime. External pressure, in the form of political and economic sanctions, made South Africa more than ever into a pariah state. The government responded with crackdowns, culminating in a five-year state of emergency beginning in 1986. During the same period, however, more far-sighted members of the ruling elite recognized that the end of minority rule was inevitable, and they opened secret talks with the still-imprisoned Nelson Mandela and other leaders of the resistance parties.

Richard Goldstone made an impact on the incipient transition to democracy in two distinct ways. First, he almost single-handedly destroyed one of the pillars of the apartheid structure, a law called the Group Areas Act. He did so in a way consistent with his preference for incremental change, rather than by taking on the entire system head-on. Second, he used the office of judge to bring small but crucial reforms to the institutions of South African law enforcement: the prisons, and the courts themselves. In doing so, he challenged norms of separation between Blacks and Whites, and he demonstrated to members of the resistance that they had allies within the legal system. His practical and symbolic actions helped make the case that the law itself, rather than violence, could be a powerful tool for bringing dramatic transformation to the country.

When he came onto the permanent bench in 1980 at the age of forty-one, Richard Goldstone was at least a generation younger than most of his colleagues. Nevertheless, Judge Goldstone settled into his work quickly and comfortably, moving his large and growing library into the spacious quarters in the courthouse, right across the street from his old office in Innes Chambers. The judge president made things easy for him by assigning him mostly the same kinds of commercial cases that he had argued as an advocate, but a Supreme Court judge inevitably fielded a wide range of cases. In his first month on the bench, a criminal case involving the South African security apparatus proved the first test of his thinking and his confidence in his new position.

On the evening of January 27, 1979, two members of the Gambling and Vice Squad of the South African Police were on the trail of a crime. On the strength of a tip, they were keeping watch on the apartment of a young White woman in South Africa's capital city, Pretoria. Early in the evening, the woman left her apartment in the company of a man whose skin was suspiciously dark. In the eyes of the vice squad officers, the man appeared to be a member of the Indian racial group. Since he was in the company of a woman who appeared to be a member of the White racial group, the officers felt that they had strong reason to believe that they were on the track of a violation of the Immorality Act of 1950. This act prohibited sexual relations between South Africans of different racial groups under the official government classifications. Offenders were subject to a maximum penalty of seven years in prison.

The woman and the dark-skinned man returned to the apartment in the wee hours of the morning, along with another man. At 4:00 A.M. the five policemen broke down the door of the apartment. They raced immediately to the bedroom, where their flashbulb captured the young woman, alone and partially clothed, staring with alarm into their camera. In the living room the officers found two young men, fully clothed, sprawled across the sofas. The man whom they had supposed to be Indian managed to find his identity papers, which showed that he was in fact a member of the White racial group.

In that Pretoria apartment, there had been no interracial sex. Indeed, it appeared that there had been no sex at all. The policemen's investigation collapsed on the spot.

The outraged woman filed a case against the police for illegally invading her apartment. The five vice squad officers were charged in Pretoria court with performing an unlawful search, a criminal offence under the South African code. A magistrate found the five men guilty and sentenced them each to a nominal fine of 100 rands or a prison sentence of six months. The officers appealed their conviction. On August 18, 1980, their case, *S v. Boshoff and Others*, was heard in the courtroom of Judge Richard Goldstone.[1]

His first case involving the conduct of security forces did not rouse the newly appointed judge to excessive zeal when he delivered his judgment. Indeed, he bent over backward to give the police the benefit of the doubt. Goldstone accepted without comment the officers' claim that their faulty observations about the young man's skin color constituted probable cause of a crime. He likewise accepted their argument that this probable cause justified their forced entry into a young woman's apartment. The judge conceded that 4:00 A.M. would not ordinarily be considered a reasonable hour at which to conduct a search. Nevertheless, given that the supposed offense was often a nighttime activity, he believed that the timing of the police action may well have been reasonable. He made no comment at all about the Immorality Act and the assault on human dignity that resulted from a legal proscription of interracial sexual activity.

Instead, the judge seized on the young woman's uncertainty about exactly which officers conducted the thorough search of her belongings. The five policemen did not contest the fact that they were all present in the apartment, but they sowed doubt about exactly which of them undertook which parts of the task. Judge Goldstone indicated that he would have preferred that the police had knocked and announced themselves before entering the apartment, rather than precipitously breaking down the door. In the end, however, he concluded that there was not sufficient proof that any specific policeman conducted an unreasonable search. He set aside the conviction and the sentences of all five officers.

It was a rather timid start to Richard Goldstone's judicial career. He showed reluctance to question the actions and intentions of the police. He was quiescent about the Immorality Act and the spurious on-the-spot judgments about racial identity that officers of the law had to make in order to enforce it. Offered the chance to comment on the case years later, he merely observed that the officers "were incorrectly found guilty in reliance by the State on that provision and that was really the end of the matter."[2] If anyone in the Ministry of Justice was following the case, it was likely seen as a favorable omen about Goldstone's "reliability" for the government position. In that respect, the case turned out to be misleading.

In 1981, Goldstone heard another case that bore more directly on the laws of apartheid. With a full year of experience under his belt and working with another judge, he seemed willing to go out farther on a limb. For the first time, he concurred in a decision that gave his liberal principles a chance to constrain the impact of the laws of separation.

The 1981 case, *S. v. Sekwati*, involved a fifty-seven-year-old Black man who was living illegally in a certain neighborhood of Johannesburg.[3] His residency there was in violation of the Urban Areas Act of 1945, which permitted Blacks to live in that area only if they were legally working on a full-time or almost full-time basis. Mr. Sekwati could not prove that he was employed, but he refused to vacate his residence when ordered to do so by a commissioner who was empowered to enforce the segregation of Johannesburg housing. Because Mr. Sekwati refused to cooperate with the law, the commissioner sentenced him to a year's imprisonment on a work farm.

Acting Justice Slomowitz sat with Richard Goldstone on the *Sekwati* case when it came before the Transvaal court on appeal. Slomowitz signed their joint judgment, which was more distinctly skeptical about the motives and the methods of the authorities than Goldstone had been in *Boshoff*. Slomowitz did not directly challenge the segregationist intent of the Urban Areas Act, but he was clearly distressed that Mr. Sekwati did not receive anything like due process from the commissioner. With scarcely a thought or a question, a man had been deprived of his liberty. The commissioner, said Slomowitz, should have investigated much more thoroughly Mr. Sekwati's circumstances, including his health, his finances, and his available options, before sending him off to a term of confinement for a violation that was not, after all, of a criminal nature. The judge said that it was perfectly proper under the law to order Mr. Sekwati to leave the area, but the opinion ordered the man to be released from his term on the work farm.

Goldstone concurred in this decision. Slomowitz demonstrated how the law could be challenged indirectly by scrutinizing procedures, rather than going head-on after underlying principles. The *Sekwati* decision relied heavily on the idea that in enforcing the law, the government had to examine the particular circumstances of the individual involved, and to ascertain whether that person had any reasonable options. Goldstone was moving toward a "natural rights" approach to the law that would help to liberate him from the "plain fact" tradition in South Africa.[4] As it turned out, he would borrow and enlarge the *Sekwati* argument the next year, in a case that shook the foundation of the apartheid system and brought him to nationwide prominence.

Mrs. Gladys Govender resided with her children and grandchildren at 37 Hanover Street in the Mayfair area of Johannesburg. Mayfair was designated as a residential area for the White racial group under the Group Areas Act. This law was first enacted by Parliament in 1950 to codify residential segregation in South Africa. With its restrictions on land ownership by non-Whites and its containment of non-White populations in ever-smaller and less desirable areas, the Group Areas Act remained in 1982 one of the cornerstones of the apartheid system. Mrs. Govender was a member of the Indian racial group and was legally prohibited under the 1966 revision of the Group Areas Act from living on Hanover Street. In March 1982 she was brought before a magistrate, who found her choice of domicile to be in violation of the law. He duly sentenced her to a fine of fifty rands or fifteen days in prison, suspended if she was not convicted of a similar offense in the next three years. Following the custom in these types of cases, the magistrate also ordered Mrs. Govender and her family evicted from their home.

The problem, however, was that Mrs. Govender and her family had nowhere to go. Her lawyer told the magistrate that there were simply no alternative housing options for Indians in Johannesburg. The Govender family had been on a waiting list already for seven years, and another decade might go by before they found a new home. The magistrate agreed to suspend the eviction for nine months, until December 31, 1982. But Mrs. Govender appealed the decision, saying that she should be able to stay in her house for as long as it took to find a suitable alternative.[5]

S. v. Govender came before Judges Richard Goldstone and Louis Le Grange on the morning of November 30, 1982. There was no particular reason for the plaintiff to have any strong hope of success. After all, thousands of non-Whites had been prosecuted under the Group Areas Act. Conviction and eviction had followed with regularity. The prerogative of Parliament seemed to give little room for judges to maneuver.

After hearing the arguments from the lawyers for the government and for Mrs. Govender, Judges Goldstone and Le Grange adjourned the court for lunch and to discuss the case. Goldstone took the lead in their discussion. The two judges agreed that there was nothing that they could do about Mrs. Govender's conviction, her fine, or her suspended sentence. After all, the Group Areas Act was unambiguous about which people could live in which places. The judges' personal opinions about the appropriateness of the law were immaterial. The magistrate's decision to evict the Govender family from their Hanover Street home was another matter, however.

The Group Areas Act, Goldstone pointed out to his colleague, had been revised on more than one occasion. The original 1950 version stated that if a person was convicted for living in the wrong neighborhood, then that person *shall* also be evicted from his or her home. When Parliament updated the act in 1966, however, the new version said merely that the judge *may* order an eviction if a person is found guilty. Over a glass of wine with Judge Le Grange, Goldstone suggested that the change from "shall evict" to "may evict" was highly significant.

His reasoning followed this line of argument:

South African judges were supposed to follow closely and respect deeply the intentions of Parliament.

If Parliament had changed the law to allow judges to exercise more discretion, then it must have had a good and deliberate reason for making this change.

If evictions were no longer to be automatic, it was reasonable to assume that Parliament wanted judges to consider evictions on a case-by-case basis.

If Parliament had wanted judges to consider evictions on a case-by-case basis, then this meant that a judge was not only allowed but was obligated to take a close look at individual people's circumstances before tossing them out of their homes.

It strained credibility to entertain the idea that the South African Parliament in 1966 made this small change in the language of the Group Areas Act in order to protect the rights of Blacks and other non-White people living in White areas. But justifying a judgment in terms of the black of Parliament's text was an unimpeachable approach in South Africa. Goldstone's argument turned a blind eye to the strict intent of the legislators, perhaps, but it was eminently persuasive.

It was obvious from the record that the magistrate did not in fact fully take into account Mrs. Govender's circumstances before ordering her eviction. Indeed, the magistrate seemed to have ordered the eviction as an automatic corollary to the sentence, with the stay of the order as an afterthought.

As far as Richard Goldstone was concerned, this was not good enough. In writing the judgment for himself and Le Grange, Goldstone cited many factors that might persuade a judge to hesitate before ordering an eviction: the character of the neighborhood, or the attitude of the neighbors, or whether the tenant owed money to the landlord. Goldstone's list went further. A judge might want to take into consideration the personal hardship that an eviction might cause, or whether it was likely that the evicted person would be able to find somewhere else to live. Presumably the number of dependent family members could be another consideration. The magistrate, Judge Goldstone pronounced, had not sufficiently explored any of these circumstances.

So Judges Goldstone and Le Grange ordered that Mrs. Govender and her extended family could stay at home, an Indian family right in the middle of Mayfair, in a Johannesburg neighborhood legally designated as White. Her conviction remained intact: she would still have to pay a fine. But she was spared the further consequence of losing her home.

On the face of it, this should have been a pyrrhic victory for Mrs. Govender. If she remained on Hanover Street, the government could theoretically return, charge her again with a violation of the Group Areas Act, and fine her or send her to prison for this repeat offense. After all, the judges' decision did not directly attack the basis of the law.

In practice, however, the eviction, although treated in the law as a secondary matter, was the real punishment. Eviction fulfilled the law's underlying purpose, which the *Govender* decision challenged. If someone convicted under the Group Areas Act could pay a fine but still remain in her house, she would, in the end, still be integrating the neighborhood. Non-Whites would be living side by side with Whites. In the absence of other housing options, Judge Goldstone's order effectively gave Mrs. Govender the right to stay put indefinitely.

The *Govender* decision sent shockwaves through the South African legal community. The Ministry of Justice mysteriously failed formally to publish the decision until 1986, almost four years later. In the meantime, unofficial copies of the judgment made their way through the circles of activist lawyers representing the disempowered groups within South African society. The implications of the decision were clear. If the government wanted to pursue policies of segregation under the Group Areas Act, it would now have to do so on a case-by-case basis, rather than wholesale. In point of fact there were few housing options for *anyone* other than Whites in Johannesburg, so slowing down the eviction process was a serious wrench in the works of the apartheid machinery. In the wake of the *Govender* decision, prosecutions under the Group Areas Act virtually ground to a halt. As a result, mixed-race neighborhoods gained a precarious foothold in South Africa's cities.

Lawyers working on Black housing rights quickly picked up the thread and applied Goldstone's reasoning and judgment to a string of cases that challenged the nation's housing laws.[6] "For the practitioners, it gave a ray of hope," recalled Justice Moloto, a leader in the Black Lawyers Association at the time. "We could defend our clients a little more successfully than before, because the interpretation before was very restrictive."[7] Kate O'Regan, who was then defending non-White clients in the Cape province, noted the nationwide impact of this Transvaal case, calling it "sensitive to human rights concerns, imaginative and legally sustainable. . . . It was a really landmark judgment."[8] The *Govender* case was no frontal assault on the apartheid regime, but it was the most dramatic instance of the weakening of apartheid through the conventional tools of the law. It created a crack in the wall that weakened the structure.

The *Govender* decision catapulted Richard Goldstone once again to nationwide fame, for the first time since the Blonde Spy scandal a quarter century earlier. The decision also brought him into close contact with an important constituency, the country's Black lawyers. In recent years, the small Black professional class had expanded. There were now more Black attorneys, and there were Black advocates in Innes Chambers, nearly two decades after Ismail Mahomed broke the color line there.

The Goldstones had had for many years some Black acquaintances and they had hosted Black people as guests in their home. The attitude of respect for all that Kitty Goldstone had fostered when Richard was growing up was reflected in the household that he and Noleen established, and in the values that they tried to instill in their daughters. "From early on, if he was sitting in a room and someone made a racist comment, he didn't have any tolerance," his younger daughter Nicole remembered.[9] Before Goldstone became a judge, however, the family's connection with the Black community was general and occasional.

In 1980, shortly after Goldstone arrived on the bench, his colleague, Judge Herbert (Nick) Nicholas, with whom he sat on the *Boshoff* case, invited him to become involved with an organization called the National Institute for Crime Prevention and the Rehabilitation of Offenders, known as NICRO. The organization had been founded early in the twentieth century to help former prisoners reintegrate into society. NICRO provided a range of training, education, and support services to those returning home after sentences for both ordinary and political crimes. NICRO's leadership had always been drawn principally from among White professionals from Johannesburg, with liberal judges playing a leading role.

Goldstone immediately found the work of NICRO compelling and essential. As a judge, his job involved punishment, but he strongly favored second chances. Despite the demands of his work on the bench, he found himself quickly involved in NICRO's leadership, rising within two years to the position of the president of the organization.

The judge developed a strong bond with a NICRO staff member named Isaac Meletse, a Black man in his fifties who had grown up in the multiracial community of Sophiatown, before it was flattened in 1955 as one of the consequences of the Group Areas Act. As a boy, Isaac had come under the influence of a famous anti-apartheid minister named Trevor Huddleston. Huddleston's tutelage led to Meletse's lifelong commitment to working on behalf of the marginalized, and a lifelong commitment to the Anglican church as a lay minister. As a young man, he played soccer professionally before working in academic administration and as a furniture salesman, until the Soweto uprising of 1976 inspired him to work more closely in the community and led him to NICRO.[10]

Meletse and Goldstone, the lay preacher and the judge, developed first a strong working relationship, then a close personal friendship. Goldstone found Meletse's dedication to the individual offenders in NICRO's programs inspiring. Meletse appreciated that the judge brought to his board leadership a deep respect for the opinions of those like Meletse himself who were working closely in the community. Over its seventy-year history, NICRO's offices had all been headed by White staff. Furthermore, the organization's offices were all in White areas outside the Black townships where most of its clients lived. Goldstone, sensing Meletse's leadership potential, set out to change both of these defects.[11]

In 1982, around the time of the *Govender* ruling, a bus full of White judges traveled from downtown Johannesburg into the heart of Soweto. The visit was Richard Goldstone's way of generating momentum for a drive to establish a NICRO branch in the Black community, with Isaac Meletse as its director. Over the next four years, Goldstone participated directly in delicate negotiations with Soweto residents to purchase property and build a facility that would best serve the community's needs. The new site, opened in 1986, included classrooms, hands-on workshops, and a shopping center where returning convicts learned to manage small-scale retail stores. Goldstone connected his NICRO work directly to the courtroom; he sentenced one man convicted of a shooting in Soweto to five years of service with the organization. It was the first instance of community service sentencing in a South African court.[12]

The friendship between Goldstone and Meletse affected Nicole Goldstone, now a teenager. Nicky became enthralled by the political struggle against apartheid; she began to sport "Free Mandela" T-shirts and to attend occasional parties in Soweto. At school her friends called her "Judgy," perhaps because of her father's position, perhaps because of her own tendency to make bold pronouncements. At one point, Nicky announced her intention to find a way to join the ANC. She attributed her activism to her father's influence. "I was brought up that politics is who you are in South Africa. You can't just live here. You've got to be somehow a part of fixing society."[13] But her father the judge could go only so far. Richard applauded her sentiments, but he discouraged her from joining an organization that was still illegal in South Africa. This would be bad for both of them. Nicky reluctantly bowed to his wishes.

Goldstone's engagement with NICRO led him to think deeply and actively about the role of prisons in the South African justice system. Later in the 1980s, he focused his attention not only on former offenders, but also on those men and women who were still serving their time.

In June 1986, P. W. Botha, who now occupied the newly created position of state president of the Republic of South Africa, declared a state of emergency. Botha justified new regulations as an essential tool against what he called the terrorist threat. Under the emergency, the police had the power to detain prisoners without cause and for extended periods. The regulations even contained what was informally called an "ouster clause," language that explicitly barred the courts from intervening to protect the rights of citizens. In 1986 alone, as many as 10,000 South Africans were held without charges filed against them.[14]

During the year before the state of emergency went into effect, Judge President Wes Boshoff asked Richard Goldstone if he would be willing to undertake a special assignment. There had been complaints about the proper administration of prisons and police cells. Would Judge Goldstone be willing to set aside his other duties for some months in order to make official visits to the Transvaal's penal and police facilities? Goldstone hesitated, worrying that Black lawyers and prisoners themselves might view this as an attempt to cover up misdeeds. He would be making his reports privately to the judge president and also confidentially to the International Committee of the Red Cross, rather than to the public. He did not like the idea that the judiciary might be perceived as helping to implement a system of detention without trial.

He decided, on advice of his lawyer friend George Bizos, to ask the prisoners themselves. One day in 1985, he walked from his chambers to the notorious police station in John Vorster Square in Johannesburg to visit Zwelakhe Sisulu, the son of famed ANC leaders Walter and Albertina Sisulu. The younger Sisulu, the editor of a weekly newspaper, had been held without charges and in solitary confinement for weeks. The cell was damp and had no running water; the prisoner was under twenty-four-hour video surveillance; and the authorities had provided him no reading material, not even the required Bible.[15] In a spartan room usually used by the prison's attending physician, Goldstone listened carefully to Sisulu's litany, and then told him that he wished to ask his advice.

The detainee looked up in surprise, then broke into a deep laugh. "It's rich," Sisulu said, "for a Supreme Court judge to ask a prisoner for his counsel." Goldstone assured the young man that he genuinely wanted to know whether Black inmates would welcome his visits and his inquiries about the conditions they faced. The prisoner offered his endorsement without hesitation, even if the reports were not to be made public. "Remember we never had any access to a person of similar value," Sisulu said later. "The only people you heard in detention and in authority were the security police or at the very least court officials. And so when he asked me that question I was very clear that we wanted him to do what he was supposed to do because it would have been to our benefit. And indeed it was to our benefit because an hour or two after my first meeting with him we actually had running water."[16] Later that day, Goldstone informed the judge president that he would undertake the assignment.[17]

Over the next three years, Goldstone made hundreds of visits to prisons and police cells in every corner of the province. These visits settled into a pattern. He arrived at the facility without prior warning and asked that the detainees, generally Black and Coloured activists, be assembled in the dining hall or the chapel. He asked whether they wished to meet with him alone, or whether the prison authorities should be invited to sit in. Almost invariably the prisoners voted for the authorities to stay and hear their thoughts. He asked whether they wished to speak in Afrikaans or in English. The cry was always for English, to the dismay of the Afrikaans-speaking wardens. Then he heard the detainees' concerns, first collectively, then in a series of one-on-one conversations for the details.

Goldstone was deeply moved by the resilience and the humanity of the thousands of non-White detainees whom he met. He encountered righteous anger, but not the self-pitying, misanthropic tone of bitterness. The prisoners might with justice have lashed out at him as a representative of the system that had consigned them to these cells, but they did not. "If anything made me optimistic about the future of our country," Goldstone recalled later, "it was the attitude of the detainees I visited, their friendship, their positive reaction. Their welcome to a white judge was a very emotional experience for me."[18] The detainees hungered, more than anything, for a connection to the outside world, especially through reading materials. To address this eminently reasonable request, Goldstone had to tilt against the prison authorities, for whom deprivation and censorship were principal tools of punishment. With the help of his friends and colleagues around the world, he began to deliver stacks of magazines (the only actual book allowed was the Bible). He also persuaded the minister of police to ease the procedures for family visitations. The visits clearly cheered many detainees. Years later, a former prisoner named Mathatha Tsedu remembered his encounter with the judge "deep in the rural outback of South Africa when in terms of my own resources as a person to keep myself together I was probably reaching the lowest ebb. He provided for me something that lifted me and gave me hope."[19]

Goldstone was also pleasantly surprised by the professionalism and fairness of the administration of many of the prisons. The wardens, he found, were mostly career civil servants who took pride in their work, and he believed that most tried to provide conditions that treated prisoners with at least a modicum of respect. During the period that he conducted the visits, he knew of no unnatural deaths of prisoners in the Transvaal, and he saw little evidence of widespread violence and abuse within the prison system.

The judge knew that in visiting the prisons he was seeing only part of the picture. Many of the horror stories emerged from holding cells in the basements of police stations, where security forces extracted information from detainees, far from the eye of public scrutiny. These holding cells were beyond the reach of a traveling judge.[20] Goldstone did, however, encounter abuses in the prisons as well. Stories of physical violence against prisoners were rare, but he was sensitive to violations of their dignity. When one warden required prisoners to kneel when the visiting judge arrived, Goldstone asked the men to stand, and he later quietly saw to it that the warden was reassigned.[21]

He also used the occasion to challenge the mistakes of the legal system itself. In one instance, where a group of men had been detained because they had complained about being exploited by a factory for which they worked, Goldstone's threat to have the Legal Resources Centre intervene on their behalf led to their speedy release.[22] On another occasion, he met eight Black prisoners who, in addition to their term of confinement, had been sentenced to corporal punishment, a prescribed number of strokes from a whip. They had been convicted of armed robbery, rape, and murder, all before the same magistrate, who justified the additional corporal punishment because the crimes were serious in nature. Goldstone took advantage of a clause in the Criminal Procedure Act that allowed a judge to review formally any lower-court sentence that might not be in accordance with justice.[23]

Reviewing the convictions and the sentencing, Goldstone was outraged by the casual racism of the magistrate. He castigated the lower-court judge for making demeaning comments about Black-on-Black violence, and for ignoring mitigating evidence. He found the practice of whipping brutal and abhorrent, as well as counterproductive. Those whose dignity is assaulted, he said, will inevitably "harbor a strong feeling of injustice and nurture an understandable grudge against society." In four of the cases he found that the magistrate's sentence lay outside the acceptable standards for corporal punishment, and he set aside the strokes. But whipping as a punishment had a long tradition within the South African criminal code. As recently as the 1960s it was still a mandatory punishment for many categories of crime. Goldstone found that in two cases (involving four defendants), the magistrate applied the standards correctly, and he could not overturn the sentence on appeal. In these two instances, he could not see his way to transcend his legal authority on behalf of his personal moral principles.[24]

As the state of emergency lengthened, men and women held without charge spent longer times in prison, and the anger rose among those whom Goldstone visited. Disillusionment set in, as prisoners languishing for weeks and months felt that they had been forgotten. Some even begged to be interrogated, hoping at least to move their situation forward. The visits became deeply troubling to the judge. Even as the momentum in the battle for the country was shifting toward the ANC and its supporters, he worried that the nation might be moving toward an era of explosive violence. From the bench, he looked for ways to push back against government overreach.

Circumscribed though his options were by South African law and custom, Richard Goldstone used his position to bring respect and inclusiveness to the court system itself. In 1987, he broke a color barrier by inviting a Black attorney to sit with him on a criminal case. The case, for which Goldstone had to travel to Tzaneen in the Limpopo region, involved a Black man accused of shooting a White policeman. The rules called for the presiding judge to appoint two "assessors," essentially ad hoc judges who would hear the case with him. Goldstone felt that the matter "cried out" for a Black assessor, but qualified Blacks were reluctant to serve, feeling that their appearance on the bench would symbolically legitimize the apartheid regime. Eventually, Miriam Thloka, who was teaching at a local university, agreed to sit with him. "It's a small world," she said when the judge asked her why she was willing. "You visited my brother yesterday in prison yesterday, and you brought him a scrabble set." Besides, she continued, she and her family were prominent members of the United Democratic Movement, the legal political resistance organization, and no one in the community could question her credibility.

The appearance of a Black woman on the bench caused an uproar in Tzaneen. The local court officials closed the women's restroom and compelled employees to walk a half mile to city hall rather than integrate their facilities. Local restaurants refused to seat the judge and his two assessors for lunch. On the first day of the trial, people were pushing their way to peer into the courtroom, some shocked at, some proud of Thloka's presence.[25]

In a 1987 case, Goldstone struck a blow for the treatment of Blacks as defendants and witnesses within the court. The case involved the conviction of a Black man, one Mr. Gwebu, for auto theft, but the appeal focused on the "inexcusable" conduct of the magistrate who had presided at the original trial and his "rude, bullying and unfair treatment" of the defendant. Goldstone deplored the practice of many magistrates who refused to use proper names when addressing Black defendants and witnesses. Instead, many magistrates addressed Black defendants in their courtrooms as the "accused" (*"beskuldigde"* in Afrikaans), and Blacks who were testifying as "witness" (*"getuie"*). "This depersonalising of people is disrespectful and degrading," read Goldstone's judgment. "It is no cause for difficulty for people to be called by their proper names. I can find no reason for the appellant, in this case, when addressed directly by the magistrate, not being called 'Mr. Gwebu.'"[26] The opinion put magistrates across the country on notice that their treatment of Blacks in their courtrooms could serve as a basis for overturning their decisions.

Inside the Transvaal Supreme Court chambers in Johannesburg, Goldstone broke another barrier. Through a professor at Yale Law School, he learned of a student, Vernon Grigg III, who wanted to clerk in South Africa as a part of his training. The catch was that Grigg was Black. Not only had there never been a Black judge in South Africa; there had never been a Black law clerk.

Goldstone took the precaution of discussing the move with the head of the Johannesburg Black Lawyers' Association, Justice Moloto. What would their reaction be to Vernon Grigg's presence in the judges' chambers? Would they cheer this as a step toward equality? Or would they shun the student for participating as a functionary within the formal apparatus of the apartheid regime? The Black lawyers debated this vigorously among themselves. In the end they gave their blessing: every barrier broken now was a step toward a fuller expression of freedom.[27]

Vernon Grigg's first day in the Transvaal courthouse was "utterly terrifying," but Goldstone's unwavering support helped him through it. Other court officials, all of them White, did not bother to hide their disdain for the Black newcomer. The judges themselves, however, were scrupulously polite, and the barrier was ultimately broken without incident. Within months, two other judges on the Transvaal bench had followed Goldstone's lead and brought on Black law clerks.[28]

The strength of Richard Goldstone's convictions fueled courageous and forthright rulings, but he could not avoid the agonizing moral choices that serving on the bench in South Africa imposed. The balance between his oath to the South African constitution and his commitment to broader principles of justice forced him into awkward trade-offs.

The death penalty itself posed one such conundrum. As Goldstone knew very well, South African law not only permitted capital punishment, it also prescribed many situations in which judges were compelled to apply it. Goldstone instinctively recoiled from the death penalty on moral grounds, but his opposition fell short of a stand on principle. "I never liked the death penalty, but I wasn't a sort of conscientious objector," he remembered. "I wouldn't have gone on the bench if I had been, because I knew that I might have a duty to impose it."[29] As a trial judge, he confirmed the death sentence twice. Both times came in cases when armed robberies escalated into gratuitous murders. The law, Goldstone believed, required the death penalty in these instances, and he found no extenuating circumstances that might lead him to mitigate the punishment.[30]

The issue became even more prominent when he was promoted to the Appellate Division of the Supreme Court, the nation's highest judicial body, in 1990. Death penalty sentences automatically came before an Appellate Division panel. The panels were allowed to overturn the death sentence only if they concluded that the lower court had misapplied the law. This gave the higher-court judges very little discretion. As a member of the Appellate Division, Goldstone served on dozens of such panels, and he voted with his colleagues to confirm death sentences on a number of occasions.[31] However, given that South Africa suspended the execution of prisoners in February 1990, none of those whose death sentences Goldstone voted to uphold were actually executed.

In one of the few cases available where Goldstone actually authored an Appellate Division decision on a capital punishment case, he did not sound altogether hesitant. Confirming a death sentence in the case of one particularly gruesome murder, Goldstone used language that suggested that he believed that the death penalty could indeed act as a deterrent to future crime. "Hired killers," he wrote, "must be made aware that, save in possibly exceptional circumstances, the courts will impose the ultimate sentence upon them. Furthermore, society is unlikely to regard even a life sentence as adequate retribution. For these reasons, in my opinion, the only proper sentence is the death sentence."[32] Goldstone was clearly no absolutist.

In the aftermath of questions decades later about his record on the death sentence, some of South Africa's most prominent lawyers emphasized that Goldstone showed tremendous restraint on this issue from the bench. "He passed far fewer death sentences then many other judges would have done," remembered Albie Sachs, his colleague on the Constitutional Court.[33] Gilbert Marcus, who spent much of the 1980s representing Black defendants in South African courts, put it more bluntly: "You would pray that you got Goldstone if you got a death penalty case."[34]

Richard Goldstone himself did not accept the idea that his conscience and his duties as a judge came into conflict. "I never felt uncomfortable about having accepted the position as a judge," he recalled almost thirty-five years after his initial appointment. "I was never put into a position where I had to apply law that was morally unacceptable to me." This reflection suggested that while Goldstone may have disliked the death penalty and felt that in some instances it had been wrongly applied, its persistence as an option for punishment was not a moral issue for him. It also pointed to the tremendous compartmentalization that being a liberal judge in South Africa required. Judge Goldstone *did* have to rule with regard to some laws that he considered morally unacceptable. Yet because he often worked assiduously to soften those laws' impact—as he did in the *Govender* case—he could conclude years later that he had never, in fact, actually had to apply any law that violated his conscience. Indeed, he believed that finding a way to maneuver within an unjust system was itself a kind of judicial responsibility. "I would suggest that the role and conduct of judges should be dictated very much by the political reality obtaining in his or her society," he said in 1997. "There is nothing to be gained by Quixotic acts."[35]

Twenty years later, Goldstone's record as a judge in South Africa became a source of controversy when critics of his Gaza report castigated him for alleged hypocrisy over his role as a so-called hanging judge.[36] How could he stand in judgment of Israel, critics argued, when he himself had willingly served under apartheid, sentenced dozens of Black prisoners to death, and upheld the laws of an oppressive regime? It was easy to construct a narrative of moral depravity from Goldstone's decision to join the bench and the cautious style he exercised in challenging its injustices. It was also easy for Goldstone and his friends to construct a narrative of heroic opposition: the liberal judge who undermined the apartheid regime from within. Neither story in its purest form held up. Richard Goldstone agreed to serve as a judge in his native country because he believed that the law—perverted though it was—could nevertheless serve the cause of justice. The record showed that he did indeed serve the cause of justice, albeit with human short-comings that history could not erase.

By 1990, Richard Goldstone, at the age of fifty-one, occupied the highest post for a South African lawyer: he had been appointed to South Africa's highest judicial body, the Appellate Division of the Supreme Court. He was lionized within important circles in both White and Black South Africa for his cre-ative rulings, and at least one of his judgments, in *S v. Govender*, had served as one of the landmark blows against apartheid.

He also had developed strong international connections, with a global rep-utation as a South African judge of strong liberal leanings. He was particularly well known in legal circles in the United States. He spent a leave at Harvard University comparing South Africa to other repressive societies; he was a guest at the prestigious Aspen Institute; and he met with leading lights from the legal community at conferences around the globe.

Like some other prominent White South African liberals, Goldstone did not support international sanctions against his country, on the grounds that such measures inevitably harmed the most vulnerable members of society.[37] "Many people who call for [sanctions], for the most part, are driven by emo-tion," he said in 1988, "without a thought for the hardship and deprivation already resulting from unemployment." He admired the position of British prime minister Margaret Thatcher, appreciating the "balance that enables her to appreciate that one can oppose sanctions and racial discrimination simul-taneously. There is no contradiction at all."[38]

The Appellate Division met in the city of Bloemfontein, in the Orange Free State, in the center of the country. With Glenda and Nicky now adults living on their own, Richard and Noleen no longer felt so tied to their Johan-nesburg home. The Goldstones decided to move their permanent residence to an apartment in Cape Town, in the Sea Point district looking over the Atlantic. Richard commuted regularly to Bloemfontein, as well as to Johan-nesburg and Pretoria on other business.

Toward the end of 1988, Goldstone spoke at the graduation at King Edward VII School. He told the young men that when he had graduated from the school thirty-two years earlier, many people, White and Black, disaffected with the climate in South Africa, were leaving the country. They believed that nothing could be done to bring meaningful change to a nation where injustice was built into the structure of everyday life. Little did those people appreciate, the commencement speaker continued, what an important contribution they could have made to transforming South Africa into a better place. He cited the many meaningful improvements that had been made since the 1950s. South Africa still has a long way to go, he argued, but it could not have come this far without the participation of those who stayed inside the country and worked slowly and tirelessly for a better form of justice. He counted himself among those reformers.

"I have no regrets," Richard Goldstone told the graduates, "at having decided to remain in this country." He knew that the young people before him had many options, and might also be tempted to leave South Africa and establish themselves in countries with a better moral track record. But he encouraged them to make the same decision that he had made, to stay at home and address the challenge of moving South Africa toward genuine democracy. "We owe it to each other," he urged the graduates, "to stay and rise to that challenge and not run from it. . . . We can all build those bridges so essential to a harmonious future. Those bridges and those points of contact can yet be crucial in the final resolution of the problem as to the kind of South Africa in which we will live in the twenty-first century."[39]

4 ▸ DEMONSTRATIONS

By 1990, APARTHEID was on its last legs, but how it would end was very much in question. In a climate of free-floating anger and fear, there was every reason to anticipate a tide of blood. At first the worst seemed destined to come to pass. Violence spiraled out of control in the province of KwaZulu-Natal, and in Richard Goldstone's own Transvaal. Pressed into service by F. W. de Klerk and Nelson Mandela, Goldstone brought into this maelstrom his experience as a judge, some newfound skills as an investigator, and his unflappable temperament. He also discovered and nurtured a side of his personality that had lain dormant since his days at the University of the Witwatersrand—a taste and a talent for the world of politics. "Mr. Justice Goldstone has become a household name with the best of the politicos, his position synonymous with judicial integrity in the face of political adversity," one reporter noted at the end of 1992.[1] As it turned out, he needed every ounce of that skill—and his talent for public relations—to keep enough peace to allow the South African "miracle" to take hold.

On September 20, 1989, F. W. de Klerk became state president of South Africa, succeeding P. W. Botha, who had been impaired by a severe stroke earlier in the year and had stepped down in the summer. Observers expected no dramatic change in policy by de Klerk, a colorless National Party stalwart. In December 1989, however, de Klerk agreed to a one-on-one meeting with the still-imprisoned Nelson Mandela.[2] Clandestine talks between the government and Mandela and other leaders of the ANC had been in progress for three years, but a one-on-one meeting between the state president and the ANC leader-in-waiting represented a major step forward.

Then, on February 2, 1990, in his first formal speech to Parliament, de Klerk jolted the country and the whole world. He announced the unbanning of the anti-apartheid political organizations: the ANC, the Pan African Congress, and the South African Communist Party. He promised the release of large numbers of political prisoners. He lifted many of the restrictions of P. W. Botha's state of emergency. And he told the world that, twenty-seven years after the Rivonia trial, Nelson Mandela would within days be a free man.[3]

A Supreme Court judge would not go out for a drink to celebrate publicly a heartening political development, but Richard Goldstone welcomed the news privately with friends and family. He watched on television when, on February 11, Nelson Mandela appeared on the steps of Cape Town City Hall (just two miles from the Goldstones' beachfront apartment) and declared, "Our march to freedom is irreversible. We must not allow fear to stand in our way. Universal suffrage on a common voters' role in a united democratic and non-racial South Africa is the only way to peace and racial harmony."[4]

Goldstone also witnessed the turmoil on the day of Mandela's release. The authorities misjudged the size and volatility of the crowds that waited to greet Mandela, and when the ANC leader was delayed and arrived hours late, angry chaos ensued in and around Cape Town. New circumstances were giving more room for the expression of pent-up anger among South Africa's Black communities. Conservative elements among South Africa's Whites were also publicly threatening to resist the National Party's new direction from the opposite political vantage point. South Africa would be sitting on more than one powder keg in the coming months and years.

At this heady moment, Richard Goldstone accepted a small but delicate role that thrust him into the middle of this emotional cauldron. Four days before de Klerk's speech, on January 30, 1990, a Black man named Clayton Sizwe Sithole was found hanged in the shower room in John Vorster Square, the notorious Johannesburg police station where Goldstone had visited Zwelakhe Sisulu. Sithole had been arrested some weeks earlier to stand trial for his activities as a member of the still-illegal Umkhonto we Sizwe, the military wing of the ANC. The police reported that Sithole had taken his own life—end of story. Sithole's family was unconvinced. For years Blacks had been dying in South African prisons, deaths that were often explained as accidents or suicides. There was every reason to think, as far as they were concerned, that Sithole had met his death at the hands of the police themselves, and that the authorities were engaged in a cover-up.

Under many other circumstances, the authorities simply ignored Black people's outcries. This case, however, posed a political challenge. Clayton Sithole was the boyfriend of Zindzi Mandela, the daughter of Nelson and Winnie Mandela. His death in a prison cell was more than a family matter. At a time when the Mandelas' role in the future of South Africa was a topic of open speculation, Sithole's death threatened unrest.

The minister of justice, Kobie Coetsee, wanted to take no chances. A formal and enigmatic man, Coetsee had managed to survive as a loyal National Party minister for almost a decade while at the same time quietly promoting reform. He both shored up the government's legal strategy behind its state of emergency and participated in the secret talks with the ANC. Coetsee did not want Clayton Sizwe Sithole turned into a martyr. So he decided to appoint a senior judge to get to the bottom of the story. There were no Black judges to whom he could turn, so he chose a man whose rulings had sometimes challenged the government, but who was known for his steadiness of judgment and his even-handed temperament. On January 31, 1990, the day after Clayton Sithole's death, Kobie Coetsee called Richard Goldstone.

Goldstone accepted with alacrity. His experience visiting South African prisons made the terrain familiar. After years of sitting on trials that by their very nature lagged behind the pace of history, he relished the opportunity to participate in real-time events.

Immediately he made an unusual choice, one that heralded his style in this new role and showed his instincts for the symbolism of investigation. Rather than hearing the evidence in the Supreme Court building, Goldstone moved his investigation's base of operations into an unused room in Johannesburg City Hall.[5] The judge understood instinctively that this locale offered a more neutral venue than courtrooms, where Blacks had felt themselves on so many occasions victimized by the legal proceedings of the state.

Goldstone listened to oral testimony in city hall over the course of five long days. He gave considerable attention to the medical evidence, which, as far as he was concerned, made it "clear beyond any question" that Sithole hanged himself.[6] The autopsy showed no signs of beatings or other forms of coercion. While it was natural for Sithole's family to question whether the forensic specialists who testified were truly independent, Goldstone could find no reason to doubt their conclusion that this was a suicide.

The conclusion carried additional weight because the judge uncovered a reason why Sithole might have wanted to take his own life. Over the course of a five-hour interrogation Sithole had given evidence about his own part in recent violence in the Transvaal townships. He confessed to his involvement in several murders, including the notorious killing of a man named Thole Dlamini in 1988.[7] This murder was itself part of an even larger story, a series of criminal activities organized and perpetrated by members of the so-called Mandela United Football Club, which was led by Winnie Madikizela-Mandela. Sithole had apparently killed Dlamini to keep him from informing to the police on the activities of the organization.

A delicate situation had now turned explosive. While rumors had previously circulated about Winnie Mandela's activities, these new revelations from a man now dead were unsubstantiated, and her status as a hero of the resistance movement was still intact. A public release of Sithole's allegations threatened to stir up even more unrest over the young man's death.

Goldstone proposed a resolution. He called the lawyers for Sithole's family and for the government into the city hall office and laid out the scenario. He would announce publicly that he was ruling Sithole's death a suicide, and that he had the medical evidence available to back up this conclusion. The judge indicated that one of the reasons for the prisoner's suicide was likely his remorse at having implicated people very close to him in criminal conduct. But Goldstone refused to make public any specific allegations regarding an organized criminal network overseen by his girlfriend's famous mother. After all, Goldstone told the lawyers and the public, the allegations against Winnie Mandela were not proven; she was not a party to the proceedings, and he would not play a role in trying her in the press.[8]

The report worked out well for both sides. The government felt itself absolved of a murder of a prisoner, and the Black leadership's dirty laundry for the time being escaped exposure. Both sides pronounced themselves satisfied. It would be several more years before the full extent of Winnie Mandela's criminal activities would become public knowledge in South Africa, and by then the country had already crossed its great divide.

On Monday, March 26, 1990, in townships throughout an area known as the Vaal Triangle, tens of thousands of Black people gathered for protest marches. Sixty kilometers south of Johannesburg, close to the river border where the Transvaal met the Orange Free State, the Vaal Triangle was a center of South Africa's heavy industry, and also the infamous site of the Sharpeville massacre and other tragedies in the country's troubled history. A region populated principally by speakers of Sesotho, its demographics began to change in the 1970s and 1980s, with the establishment of large residential hostels that housed men who came from outside the region for the jobs in the Triangle's iron and steel factories. Many of the migrant workers were Zulus from the southeastern region of Natal, and competition over jobs, resources, and politics began to erupt in the 1980s. The South African government, fond of a divide-and-conquer strategy, exploited ethnic rivalries in the Vaal Triangle. By the time the state of emergency was declared in 1986, violence had engulfed the region.

The marches were organized by the United Democratic Front (UDF), but authorities, citing local laws about advance permission, had turned down their request.[9] The marchers' demands were extensive and generic: better housing, better schools, better work opportunities; and the organizers refused to give up in the face of the denial of a permit.

On the morning of March 26, 50,000 Black demonstrators converged on Moshoeshoe Street in the township of Sebokeng and were marching in the direction of the police station. Hemmed in by the shanties and stalls on either side, the demonstrators moved up the road toward a line of forty-seven policemen at the gates of the Sondela Brewery. Arriving at a barricade of armed men and vehicles, the demonstrators at the front tried to halt, but those in the rear continued to press forward. The policemen could see raised kieries, and men with their arms extended, as though hurling objects into the air. The front wave of marchers was within thirty meters of the police line.

And then there was gunfire. First a single report, and then within seconds a volley of shots. The marchers at the front turned and fled in every direction. The harsh clatter echoed off the walls of the brewery. There were people fallen and bleeding and crying on Moshoeshoe Street. Five of them were dead.

There had been thousands of deaths in Black townships in recent years, but the tragedy at Sebokeng in March 1990 was the first major disaster since

F. W. de Klerk announced the road map to the new South Africa. The shootings occurred just five days before de Klerk and the leadership of the ANC were scheduled to have their first formal negotiation since Nelson Mandela's release. Those meetings were abruptly canceled. The violence threatened to derail the peace train before it had even left the station.

Another inquiry was required. Minister of Justice Kobie Coetsee turned once again to Richard Goldstone. The quick and successful resolution of the Sithole inquiry made him the obvious candidate. The judge knew immediately that this task would be much more daunting than the earlier investigation. For this assignment, Goldstone needed more than a room in city hall. He needed an investigative team.

Here Richard Goldstone got lucky. Through the Sebokeng inquiry he acquired not only a competent investigator for a single incident, but a man who would follow him for years and become a lifelong friend.

The man whom Kobie Coetsee loaned to Goldstone to head the investigative team was Johan du Toit, known as "JJ," a deputy attorney general. Du Toit hailed from Bloemfontein, right in the middle of the Orange Free State, the heart of the conservative Afrikaner community. JJ's English was tinged heavily with traces of the old Dutch, and his roots in Afrikaner culture and in the Dutch Reformed Church were deep. He had worked for his entire career within the Ministry of Justice, under the overall authority of the National Party government. By his background and his résumé, it was reasonable to wonder whether this man could be trusted to be independent, or whether he was really assigned to protect the interests of the government and the police.

Richard Goldstone set a tone of disinterested professionalism, and he was happy to find that du Toit insisted that a commitment to the truth was his only priority. Besides, there was in some ways a distinct advantage to having an Afrikaner as his lead investigator. The majority of the policemen, and nearly all of the officers involved in the incident, were themselves Afrikaners. Speaking both English and Afrikaans equally fluently and coming to the investigation as a kind of "insider," du Toit brought some natural advantages when it came to questioning the motives and the actions of the South African Police.[10]

Together the judge and the investigator retraced the march's route along the streets of Sebokeng to see exactly where the events took place. Du Toit presided over a painstaking set of interviews with all of the policemen who were present, as well as with dozens of marchers and other witnesses. The contradictory stories threatened to swamp the investigation. The police claimed that they were under assault by stones and weapons. Black witnesses insisted that the crowd was orderly, and that the firing was unprovoked. Goldstone was worried that he would have little to report beyond this conflicting set of accounts.

Then an anonymous package arrived at the investigation headquarters. It contained a videotape, shot right at the gates of the brewery at the very time of the incident. It did not show the gunfire, but it did show which police officers were present. This new evidence inspired Goldstone to try a novel tactic. The judge ordered every police officer present at the brewery gates to return to the scene on a day in early May, six weeks after the shooting. He had du Toit line up the officers in the exact positions where they were on the fatal day. The investigator then quizzed the policemen closely, both on the street and in interviews immediately afterwards. Du Toit asked them not only about their own actions, but about the actions of the men immediately to their right and their left.

The reenactment opened up the full story. There had been no plan to repel the marchers with violence. In fact, there was no plan at all. The police line was cobbled together from several unrelated police units, with different command structures, and no coordination between them. The commanding officers were sitting in a parked vehicle on the side and at the rear, out of sight of their officers, out of earshot, and in no position to exercise any authority. When a White civilian in short pants and a short-sleeved shirt armed with a pistol showed up and wanted to take his place in facing down the Black crowd, he was allowed to take his place right on the front lines. In short, the police preparation was a textbook case in law enforcement incompetence.

The reenactment also enabled Goldstone and du Toit to identify the first shooter, one Constable van Rhyn. Van Rhyn first denied his role. Under more intense questioning he then conceded that he had fired a tear gas canister by accident, a claim that was completely implausible, given the sequence of steps necessary to launch the device. The other policemen on the line, jittery already and without any leadership from their commanders, panicked and fired a variety of weapons, including guns with lethal ammunition. When the crowd started to run, they simply kept firing. Of the 161 people hit by gunfire at Sondela Brewery gate, eighty-four were shot from behind.

In June 1990, Richard Goldstone sat down and typed out a seventy-four-page report on the Sebokeng incident, writing "every word" himself. In style and method, the report echoed the judge's canny combination of meticulous detail and carefully contained outrage. He devoted nearly five pages at the start to the driest possible technical detail about the ammunition carried by the various men on the police line. Yet as he came to describing the human actors, his prose became more pointed. He noted that Constable van Rhyn, who fired the tear gas canister that started the shooting, "was not an impressive witness." Goldstone refused "to accept his rather lame excuse" for not initially reporting that he had fired his weapon. "In the present case," he concluded, "the use of force was quite immoderate and disproportionate to any lawful object sought to be attained."[11] Goldstone did not let the UDF organizers entirely off the hook, however. He cited their lack of organization and communication with the authorities, calling their actions "negligent if not irresponsible." But the weight of his judgment was clear: the police at Sebokeng were leaderless and indifferent. Goldstone recommended that those who fired the lethal shots be prosecuted, especially those who showed, as he called it, a "callous attitude" and "an attitude of unconcern for the lethal nature of their ammunition and for the consequences of its use."[12]

Despite this tough language about the men on the front lines, the judge pulled his punches when it came to the commanders who sat out the tragedy on the sidelines. He lambasted one Sergeant van Huysteen for admitting "quite brazenly" that it didn't matter that his men had loaded lethal ammunition in their weapons, and he criticized Captain du Plooy for doing "nothing by word or deed to reassure his men that the situation was being kept in hand and under proper control."[13] Yet despite saying that du Plooy "erred in a number of respects," Goldstone concluded that, because the commanders had given no orders to shoot, he could not recommend prosecuting them. Those who fired the shots themselves were directly responsible, not the officers whose poor decisions and discipline put their men in a dangerous situation. A few years later, when it came to assigning blame for ethnic cleansing in the Balkans and genocide in Rwanda, Goldstone would become a proponent of the legal doctrine of "command responsibility," the idea that military officers may bear responsibility for large-scale misdeeds by those they command, even in the absence of direct orders.[14] But in his first inquiry into a massacre, Goldstone placed the blame principally on those who pulled the triggers.[15]

Finally, in offering "general comments," Goldstone looked ahead, presciently looking at the Sebokeng tragedy in the context of the ongoing process of achieving democracy. "If this type of demonstration is to become a regular feature of political expression in South Africa," he concluded, "the sooner that it is subject to known and sensible rules the better."[16]

The Sebokeng report was the most specific and concrete formal account to date of the shoddy and callous operations of members of the South African Police.[17] It was "the first real finding against the government," according to George Bizos, who represented the protesters in the hearings.[18] The *Saturday Star* congratulated Goldstone for avoiding "judicial pussyfooting" and opined that the report "firmly established the independence and impartiality of the country's judiciary at home and abroad."[19] Even though the report stressed negligence rather than intention as the cause of the violence, it confirmed in a public and visible way what many South Africans already knew from experience: in many instances the South African Police were more likely to cause violence than to prevent it.

Richard Goldstone did not escape unscathed. In the wake of the report's release, hate mail and anonymous late-night telephone calls came to the Goldstones' apartment in Johannesburg. Even a judge does not like to make enemies within a security establishment seething with anger, anxiety, and unpredictability. On the street and in the office, Goldstone knew that he would have to keep his eyes open, but he and Noleen refused to change their lifestyle. Living under the threat of violence, after all, was a daily condition of life for the vast majority of South Africans in the early 1990s.

While the day-to-day negotiations between the South African government and the Black parties still stumbled over issues of trust, several agreements in 1990 and 1991 created discernible momentum toward a political solution to South Africa's long struggle. Looming over the political discussions, however, was the long shadow of continuing, indeed accelerating, violence that was gripping the country. Between 1984 and 1989, more than 3,500 people had died in political clashes.[20] In the months after de Klerk's February 1990 speech, new outbreaks of conflict threatened to dwarf those numbers.

A focal point of the violence in the early 1990s was conflict of renewed intensity between supporters of the ANC and the newly formed Inkatha Freedom Party (IFP). This party's roots extended back to the 1920s, when it was founded by Solomon, the king of the Zulu nation, to promote Zulu culture and secure Zulu power. Its original base was in the province of Natal. After losing momentum as an organization in the early years of apartheid, the IFP got a shot in the arm in 1975 when a local Zulu chief, Mangosuthu Buthelezi, became its leader. Buthelezi had been an active member of the ANC, but he drifted away from his ANC colleagues in the late 1970s and early 1980s, establishing his own idiosyncratic stance as an opponent of apartheid who nevertheless accepted the leadership of KwaZulu, one of the "homelands" that the apartheid government had established in order to segregate the country by tribal region. Straddling the line between cooperation with the South African authorities and seeking to undermine them, Buthelezi had a fiercely loyal following among his Zulu base but was seen as a polarizing figure by opponents in the ANC and beyond. In 1990, with the march toward democracy under way, Buthelezi wanted to transform his organization from a social and cultural movement into a political force that could play a major part in the new South Africa. He established the IFP to achieve that end.[21]

This development put Buthelezi and the IFP on a direct collision course with the ANC, and the political contest played a part in fomenting violent conflict. Violence had become commonplace in Natal, where IFP and ANC supporters vied for control of townships and regions, as well as in areas of the Transvaal like the Vaal Triangle. The conflict drew on many sources. Many White observers liked to blame the violence on traditional rivalries between the country's African tribal groups. While conflict between Zulus and Xhosas and other African peoples did indeed have deep historical roots, those tensions meant less than more pressing contemporary problems.

All Black South African communities in the 1980s and 1990s faced serious and ongoing economic distress, partly as a result of apartheid, partly as a result of the poor overall shape of the South African economy. So it was no surprise that tensions between the parties were erupting at key points over local economic issues: between rural and urban taxi drivers, for example, fighting for business and pride in the suburbs of many of the country's cities. Housing was another flashpoint. With available housing opportunities in short supply, tensions flared as groups of men moved from one place to another in search of better economic opportunities.

It was also clear that the South African government itself was playing a decisive role in the acceleration of conflict in Black communities. The government wanted a Black force within the country that could be controlled and could provide a check on the rise of the ANC, which the National Party rightly saw as its most powerful and serious rival. The IFP, with its own reasons to challenge the ANC, became a regular (if publicly undeclared) ally of the government.

In the late 1980s, stories about the government's part in catalyzing violence began to come to light. In November 1989, a policeman named Dirk Coetsee went public with an account of his role in a unit of the South African Police based in Vlakplaas, a farming area just a few miles west of Sebokeng in the southern Transvaal. Coetsee gave details about his own involvement in helping to arm and train IFP supporters at Vlakplaas and in other locations. Shortly thereafter, the anti-government *Daily Mail* newspaper broke a story about secret government funding for the IFP, a tale of corruption that earned the moniker "Inkathagate." The South African government alternated between denying the allegations altogether and blaming them on rogue elements in the police and security forces.

Wherever the blame lay, violence was becoming an inescapable phenomenon in the Black townships, and ordinary people were paying the highest price. The March 1990 massacre that Richard Goldstone investigated at Sebokeng, where five people lost their lives, was soon eclipsed by other incidents in 1990 and 1991 that left hundreds more dead.[22] There was a very real chance that these local conflicts could erupt into all-out civil war, and that the promise of South African democracy could devolve into a bloodletting that would derail any chance of forming a new nation.

All the parties that were committed to the negotiating process had an incentive to create some mechanism to try to understand and defuse the violence. In September 1991, those parties signed a detailed National Peace Accord, which formally created an independent commission to investigate the violence and propose solutions for containing it.[23] It was a slender reed, but on it rested the hopes for a peaceful transition for South Africa.

This time, when Kobie Coetsee called to offer him the chance to chair another commission, Richard Goldstone was more hesitant. The two men met in Coetsee's Cape Town apartment, just a few blocks from the Goldstones' seaside residence. The two men refrained from going on a first-name basis; they preferred to call each other "Minister" and "Judge." They shared nevertheless a preference for a practical, undogmatic approach to the legal profession and to the world of politics beyond.

The National Peace Accord had stipulated that the commission should be chaired by a judge or senior lawyer with at least ten years of experience to "ensure that the Commission has suitable, independent and objective leadership, fully versed in the law and fearlessly given to grant all parties an equal opportunity to state their views and give their facts." The accord further indicated that when it came to appointing the chair and the other members of the commission, "consensus will be the key word." In other words, the chair of the commission would have to be acceptable not only to F. W. de Klerk, but also to Nelson Mandela. George Bizos, who had represented the ANC in the investigation of the Sebokeng massacre, suggested to Mandela that Goldstone would be the ideal candidate to lead this new round of inquiries.[24] So the judge knew from the beginning that he would begin with the support of both the government and its principal opposition.

Goldstone also had practical matters to consider. For one thing, as Kobie Coetsee told him frankly, chairing the commission might threaten the judge's job security and leave him "politically tainted." Furthermore, would it be possible to conduct such a far-flung inquiry and still retain enough independence and authority to serve on the country's highest court? If he accepted this crucial assignment, Goldstone might well have to give up his position on the bench.

Coetsee sympathized with Goldstone's personal dilemmas, but he graciously deflected the judge's hesitations about accepting the role.[25] The minister sweetened the pot by dangling the prospect that should he have to resign as a judge, a prestigious ambassadorship might follow. The minister needed the judge to accept. If Goldstone turned the post down, the parties might be arguing about alternative candidates for months to come.

The opportunity to play an important part at a crucial moment in South African history was too much for a man of Goldstone's talents, ambition, and sense of public service to resist. He offered Coetsee three conditions. First, he wanted an office in Cape Town, so that he could spend time in his new home. Second, he asked that JJ du Toit, who had performed such exemplary work at Sebokeng, be seconded to the commission as its lead investigator. Finally, Goldstone wished to continue his work as a judge, even while chairing the commission. He told Coetsee that under these terms, he would be happy if his paycheck would come only from his judicial salary. As the chair of the commission he would work formally as a volunteer and preserve his independence as an active judge.

Kobie Coetsee was by this time at the seat of government in Pretoria, so Goldstone flew there to discuss his terms. The minister agreed, and then brought the judge to see President de Klerk to seal the arrangement. "I'm absolutely confident that this violence is going to disappear and you won't have much to do," de Klerk assured the judge. "How wrong he turned out to be," Goldstone recalled drily later.[26]

Goldstone's appointment won plaudits in the South African press. "He will make a bloody good chairman," an anonymous "liberal judge" told the *Sunday Times*. "We don't need someone who will go overboard." Another unnamed judge offered the backhanded praise that Goldstone was "definitely not wishy-washy" but that "he won't stick his neck out too far."[27]

One of Goldstone's first acts was to request a meeting with Nelson Mandela. His earlier investigations had established his credibility with F. W. de Klerk, but he had had no such personal contact with the ANC. After all, until the previous year nearly all of its leadership had been either in exile or in prison. So one morning in the fall of 1991, Goldstone ventured to the home of ANC leader Walter Sisulu in Soweto.[28] Through his work with NICRO Goldstone had visited the unofficial capital of Black South Africa many times before, but this meeting had a special charge. All of the top leadership had gathered in the Sisulus' living room: Nelson Mandela, Walter Sisulu, Oliver Tambo, and Cyril Ramaphosa of the ANC, as well as Chris Hani, the magnetic leader of the South Africa Communist Party. It was the first time that Goldstone had met any of them, with the exception of Ramaphosa, whom he had gotten to know during the 1980s when Goldstone's ORT work brought him into contact with the then secretary-general of National Union of Mineworkers. Goldstone did not know what to expect. Would a White judge be greeted with skepticism, or even hostility, despite the fact that Mandela had tacitly approved his appointment?

He received a warm personal welcome in Walter Sisulu's living room. Nelson Mandela himself set the tone by pronouncing his confidence in Goldstone's appointment. A leisurely and amicable conversation spilled through lunch and into the afternoon. The ANC leadership were pleased that the commission had been formed, but they were open in their skepticism about whether it could operate truly independently of the government. They did not question Judge Goldstone's personal integrity, but each of them had a lot of experience watching the South African government overtly and covertly exercising its will.

Goldstone took the opportunity to make a practical proposal. In recent weeks, the South African government had been pressuring the ANC to disclose the extent and whereabouts of its weaponry within South Africa. The party had formally renounced violence the previous year, but in the summer of 1991, public accounts revealed that some ANC operatives had undertaken a backup plan to hide arms around the country in case the talks broke down and the leadership felt that the armed struggle needed to be revived. Goldstone's suggestion responded to the government's public call for transparency. Perhaps, he offered, the ANC could agree to disclose information about its arms supplies if the government simultaneously agreed to provide a public accounting of its own weaponry.

Mandela listened thoughtfully, and then asked Goldstone what the government's attitude to this proposal was. "Mr. Mandela, I have no idea about the government's position," Goldstone responded. "I'm putting it to the ANC first."

Mandela appeared pleased by this response. "It is not often that the Black side is consulted first," he smiled.

Several days later, the ANC leadership agreed unconditionally to a reciprocal disclosure of information about their arms. The judge followed up with President de Klerk, but the government had no interest in providing any more information than was absolutely necessary about its stockpiles. Nevertheless, the discussion had proved useful in establishing the chairman's credibility with the ANC. It would not be the last time that he would consult with the "Black side" first.

The Goldstone Commission, formally known as the Commission of Inquiry regarding the Prevention of Public Violence and Intimidation (hereafter "the Commission"), held its first meeting on October 26, 1991, the occasion of its chairman's fifty-third birthday.[29] The parties had named four members, two Black, two White, in addition to Goldstone. The Black lawyers were Lillian Baqwa, an attorney from Natal, and an advocate from Pretoria, Msakasi Solomon Sithole, who was known as Solly. Neil Rossouw, named vice-chair, had served most recently as attorney general in the Cape. Gert Steyn was completing a career as a regional court judge.[30]

Goldstone understood that the Commission would face fierce external pressures regarding its findings. Beginning in September 1990, Nelson Mandela and other Black leaders began to talk publicly about a shadowy organization that lay beyond the first two "forces" of the South African government, the army and the police. It was hard to pin down exactly what the "third force" *was*, but the ANC and other Black leaders said that they could identify its impact. The third force, they said, was committing and provoking violence within Black communities around the country, creating divisions, cutting down strong leaders, planting evidence of misdeeds that would undermine public trust in the Black political parties. Black leaders expected the Commission to point to the ultimate source of the violence.

The Commission's first interim reports, published in early 1992, were models of balance and caution. Reports on the areas of Thokoza in the Transvaal and Mooi River in Natal blamed both the ANC and the IFP for violence, and also pointed to the neglect of the security forces in permitting clashes to continue unabated. In the charged atmosphere of the time balance meant that the Commission's first reports satisfied no one. "This 50-50 thing I found at times rather distressing," recalled Albie Sachs, who at the time was an ANC activist recently returned from exile. "Quite often the reporting was missing out on deep structural institutional causes of violence that were part of the program."[31] The chairman took a practical approach. "What was crucial for the success of the commission was that all the major parties would remain cooperative," Goldstone recalled. The Commission's "huge compulsion to be seen to be independent" was essential to its credibility.[32]

Goldstone himself remained skeptical during the first months of 1992 about the idea of a "third force" to destabilize the Black parties. "My own feeling, and it's nothing more than that," he told an interviewer in January 1992, "is that there isn't a third force. I think there are third *forces*. I would be surprised if there weren't right wing policemen involved in undercover violence operations."[33] In an interim report on violence in Mooi River in Natal, Goldstone detailed the failings of the security forces in failing to prevent the loss of life. Yet he ended the fact-finding section report with a strong lecture aimed at the ANC and the IFP, refusing to allow them to deflect blame by pointing fingers at the government. "The Committee in no way suggests that the security forces are to blame for the violence at Mooi River," Goldstone stated bluntly. "The blame for that falls squarely on those who were participants in attack and counter-attack, irrespective of which party they support."

For Richard Goldstone, there was a crucial difference between the responsibility of individual policemen for contributing to a climate of violence, on the one hand, and the existence of a mysterious, government-approved organization on the other. He accepted with alacrity the notion of individual malfeasance. He genuinely was not convinced, however, that the evidence pointed to the idea of a sanctioned conspiracy. Given the personal bond that he had built with Kobie Coetsee, Goldstone may have found it difficult to believe that the minister of justice or his colleagues had really overseen a nefarious network designed to shore up apartheid in its dying days.

When Richard Goldstone sat down in April 1992 to write a six-month report on the work of the Commission, his frustrations of the previous months spilled over into the text, under the veneer of formal language in numbered and subnumbered paragraphs.[34] Rather than subsiding, the pace of blood-shed was accelerating. Despite the lack of evidence on a "third force," the report clearly placed the blame for the current violence on the legacy of apartheid. Goldstone cited as contributing factors "a police force and army which, for many decades, have been the instruments of oppression by successive White governments."

Having completed this analysis, Goldstone delved into what he cared most about: the specific steps that he and the other members of the Commission proposed to reduce the opportunities for violence. One suggestion was to deploy police to work in tandem with local dispute resolution committees, thereby trying to establish a spirit of cooperation between the security forces and local civic actors. Noting that "hostels are common to most of the worst areas of violence," Goldstone also recommended the simple measures of pro-viding adequate security fencing and prohibiting the flow of arms in and out of the temporary housing. Finally, the Commission recommended that the carrying of any dangerous weapons in public should be outlawed, including the so-called traditional weapons favored by the Zulu members of the IFP.

Richard Goldstone delivered this second interim report of the Commis-sion to President F. W. de Klerk on April 29, 1992. De Klerk's government sat on the report for a month, then released a misleading summary to the public that asserted that the Commission blamed the violence on the Black parties. Nelson Mandela was furious at reading the government's summary, though he later read the report in full and apologized to the chairman in a statement to the media. The incident made a large impression on Goldstone, and immeasurably increased his respect for the character of Nelson Mandela. "In my experience," he concluded, "few leaders would have acted in that fashion. To apologize was one thing, to call a press conference to correct the record was another."[35]

On the night of June 17, 1992, Simon Moloi and his wife Elizabeth were asleep in their corrugated shack in a squatters' settlement in Joe Slovo Park, on the outskirts of the township of Boipatong. The township sat in the Vaal Triangle, just a few miles south of Sebokeng, a community of tiny, neat bungalows, with hundreds of people living in temporary housing in the open spaces at the margins. Boipatong was known as an ANC stronghold, but tensions had been building between the people of the township and the residents of a large hostel called KwaMadala, across the train tracks from the town center on the property of the Iron and Steel Corporation, known as Iscor. The KwaMadala residents were Zulus, brought from outside the region to work in the factory, and the hostel had become a stronghold for the IFP.

Increasing tension had followed the breakdown of the latest round of peace talks in May, when the ANC had returned to a strategy of mass mobilization. Just a day earlier, on June 16, South Africans had marked the sixteenth anniversary of the uprising in Soweto, with the vast majority of Blacks staying home from work. Tens of thousands had gathered peacefully to hear Nelson Mandela and Desmond Tutu. In other places, demonstrations had turned to confrontation. By the South African Police count, thirty-four people died on June 16 across the country, and accusations were flying in every direction about who was responsible.

Shortly before 10:00 P.M. on the night of June 17, Simon and Elizabeth Moloi awoke to the sounds of shouts, gunfire, and the screams of a woman. The couple ran outside their shack, where they saw through the darkness two Black men attacking a woman and her child with axes. In the panic and chaos and in a hail of gunfire, Simon and Elizabeth were separated. Simon managed to find a hole in the barbed wire fence at the end of the settlement and run to the safety of a nearby swamp, where he spent the night, well within earshot of the continuing mayhem. When he crept back into Joe Slovo Park the next morning, Simon found Elizabeth wrapped in a blanket by the fence, her body riddled with cuts and the marks of the two bullets that killed her. A few yards away lay the knife-cut corpses of the pair whom Simon had seen under attack, nine-month-old Aaron Mathope and his mother Rebecca.

Events had transpired quickly and under the cover of darkness, but Simon later claimed to remember some telling details. He said that he had been able to see "four or five" armored police transports and a yellow police bus, and that he had been able to see dozens of Black men, presumably Zulus, emerging from those vehicles. He also said that as he was fleeing he had heard two White men, dressed in camouflage, shouting in Zulu, "Let us kill the dogs."[36]

By daybreak on June 18, the narrative of the Boipatong massacre was beginning to take shape. More than 200 Zulu residents of the KwaMadala hostel, armed with spears and knives but also with powerful and sophisticated rifles, had gone on a rampage, leaving a bloody trail in their wake. More than forty bodies lay on the streets and yards of the township. It was the largest death toll for an incident in a single township since the transition period had begun with F. W. de Klerk's 1990 speech.

Representatives of ANC, building on these accounts, made it clear that they believed that the South African Police had played a central role in insti-gating the violence. Cyril Ramaphosa, the chief negotiator in the talks with the government, put it bluntly: "We charge de Klerk and his Government with complicity in the slaughter that has taken place in this area."[37]

For Nelson Mandela, Boipatong represented a tipping point. Although he had eventually accepted Richard Goldstone's assurance that his Commission had not yet accumulated hard evidence about a "third force," Mandela firmly believed that agents of the government were deeply involved in fomenting violence in Black communities. Boipatong seemed like the clearest—and most tragic—indication of "third force" activity.

The scale of the killings and the depth of the ANC's outrage thrust Boipa-tong into the headlines, both within South Africa and around the world. Archbishop Desmond Tutu, Nelson Mandela, and even President F. W. de Klerk rushed to the township, though de Klerk's visit was cut short after pro-testors surrounded his motorcade.[38]

The next day, the ANC, which had called de Klerk's visit to Boipatong a "cynical public relations exercise," announced that it was suspending nego-tiations with the government. "I can no longer explain to our people why we continue to talk to a government which is murdering our people," Nelson Mandela told a rally. He went on to say of the police, "I am convinced that we are no longer dealing with human beings, but with animals."[39]

On the night of the Boipatong massacre, the chairman of South Africa's most important commission on violence was spending ten "fascinating" days in France as the guest of its government. The optics were not ideal. Goldstone was meeting with French police officials to learn about crowd control at demonstrations, but at the very moment when the worst crisis of violence was unfolding in a Black township, the Goldstones' sojourn was not entirely absorbed in conversations with police commanders. In plan-ning for the trip, Richard had jokingly hinted to the French ambassador that he was particularly interested in policing in the wine regions. So the chairman's itinerary had duly included a "memorable" weekend as guests in the mansion of the famous champagne maker Moët et Chandon.[40]

It was obvious, however, that Boipatong demanded a response from the Commission. The day after the massacre, Richard spoke with Kobie Coetsee, who relayed what he said was de Klerk's request that, in investigating Boipatong, the Commission should include a distinguished international jurist on the panel. Goldstone readily agreed, and decided to ask Proful Bhagwati, a former chief justice from India whom he had met in Johannesburg some months earlier. While in London on the next leg of his overseas journey, he added a second foreign observer, P. J. Waddington, the director of criminal studies at the University of Reading, to focus specifically on the actions of the police.

By the time that Richard Goldstone returned to South Africa on July 2, the sense of crisis that Boipatong had catalyzed was gripping the country. Negotiations were stalemated, recriminations were flying, and confidence in the future was at a perilous low. For two days, he and Bhagwati heard from legal representatives of the government, the ANC, and the IFP about how to proceed with their Boipatong inquiry. What was most clear was that nothing was clear, everything was disputed. Goldstone knew there was no way for the Commission to avoid a full-fledged investigation of Boipatong, but he also despaired, because the complexity and sensitivity of this single incident threatened to overwhelm his small staff. Truth-seeking could bring light into dark corners, but it could also become a morass from which the Commission might never emerge.

These frustrations came to the surface when Goldstone spoke to the press on July 6, 1992. The Commission, he pronounced, was "distressed" that so many of its recommendations—like the simple matter of better security around the hostels—had been ignored. The country was "turning a deaf ear to Goldstone," headlined the *Star*.[41] The tone of the chairman's remarks seemed to confirm that he was tired of what one overseas newspaper had called his "Cassandra" role, "always listened to, never heeded."[42]

Yet he also came forward with his toughest language to date about the Black parties. Reiterating that no one had presented the Commission with any clear and convincing evidence of systematic "third force" involvement in the country's violence, Goldstone made it clear that he was losing patience with the public airing of those charges. "In the absence of such evidence [of 'third force' complicity in violence]," he said, "the Commission considers that allegations to the effect that Government and Security Force leaders are themselves directly responsible for the commission of violence are unwise, unfair, and dangerous. They are dangerous particularly because they are likely to exacerbate the climate of violence and frustrate and retard attempts to curb violence."[43] While Goldstone did not mention the ANC by name, it was the ANC that had been airing such charges with particular regularity and intensity since Boipatong. It was the first time that the chairman had expressed so direct and biting critique of Nelson Mandela and his circle.

In the meantime, P. J. Waddington completed a report in three weeks that found that in Boipatong the police were woefully unprepared but not directly complicit in the violence that unfolded on the night of June 17.[44] Richard Goldstone made the Waddington report public almost immediately. He was pleased that the Waddington report undermined what he considered the "fiction" that the South African Police had a history of ruthless efficiency. "I have no doubt that this whole idea of an efficient police force is incorrect both in relation to the actual methods used, but also in relation to manpower," he told one interlocutor shortly after the report's release. "I think it's a tremendously over-stretched police force and one is seeing more and more admission of that." He thought this exaggeration of police capability all the more dangerous "because it's particularly unfair on de Klerk."[45]

The main committee of inquiry on Boipatong finally began on August 4, 1992. As Goldstone had feared, the level of detail, the conflicting stories, and the exhausting cross-examinations by the lawyers for the various parties created a confusing maze of information. Dozens of witnesses bravely came forward to testify about the events of June 17, and many more submitted affidavits. Outside experts, brought in to help verify the eyewitness testimony, buried the Commission in an avalanche of data. One expert report, delivered in forty-three closely-typed pages, was devoted entirely to an analysis, complete with oscillation graphs, of the moonlight, starlight, and streetlamps in Boipatong between the hours of 10:00 P.M. and midnight on June 17.

Boipatong was a low point for the transition process for South Africa, and it also proved a low point for the work of the Commission. In the aftermath of the massacre, violence spiraled even further, and controversy nearly derailed the negotiation process. By September 1992, three months after the tragedy at Boipatong, the Commission had issued no authoritative account of the incident. Indeed, the report would remain incomplete throughout the lifespan of the Commission, which failed to unravel the most infamous incident of violence during its tenure. With limited resources, the Commission was unable to keep up with the fast pace of events and was threatened with irrelevance.

One problem was that the chairman had simply overextended himself. Despite his ferocious capacity for work, the demands of the moment were considerable. After all, in addition to chairing the Commission, Goldstone was still sitting on cases as a judge of the Supreme Court of Appeal. "It was very difficult for us to get his attention," JJ du Toit remembered, "because he was involved in cases in Bloemfontein. He still wanted to be involved with the law."[46]

Despite these public setbacks, Richard Goldstone had quietly created a solid foundation for the success of the Commission's work. He had criticized the government, but he had also taken pains not to weaken F. W. de Klerk, whom he believed to be the best option to lead the National Party toward accepting true democracy in South Africa. "The interesting thing about Richard Goldstone is how calm he was during all this stuff," remembered Princeton Lyman, then the U.S. ambassador to South Africa. "You could imagine someone turning this into a political matter, like a district attorney. . . . He exposed all these things, but I never heard him do a diatribe about how evil all these people were."[47]

In July 1992, when he might well have succumbed to despair, Goldstone retained a spirit of optimism. Above all, he believed that the process toward democracy had to keep moving forward, even amidst bloodshed and imperfections in the process. "I don't believe that in the process of moving to a really democratic, non-racial government we can afford to hold it up until there's some halcyon situation in which there can be a proper free and fair election," he told one interviewer at the time.[48] In the coming months, the Commission began to play its part in the transition in a more visible, dramatic, and successful way.

5 ▸ THE THIRD FORCE

IN JULY 1992, at the same moment as the Boipatong aftermath was spiraling downward, important developments were already quietly turning things around for the Goldstone Commission. The chairman's preference for forward-looking processes that would focus on violence prevention, more than the assignment of blame, began to pay off. Furthermore, in the months that followed, his political skills would finally expand the resources and capacity of the Commission, opening the door to more thorough investigations than were possible in its early months. With more resources, more discipline, and some good luck, Richard Goldstone would finally bring the shadowy "third force" into the light of day and play a central role in the run-up to South Africa's first democratic elections, which would be scheduled for April 1994.

Goldstone's own early investigation of the deaths after a political march in Sebokeng in 1990 had helped him understand the tinderbox nature of mass demonstrations in South Africa's transition period. Tragically, the Sebokeng violence had been repeated many times over at marches over the previous two years, with hundreds more deaths and thousands of injuries. It was not just Black demonstrators who were at risk. Violence at political rallies was taking a toll on the South African Police as well. Over 100 policemen died in 1990 and 1991 combined, and the pace was accelerating. In the first half of 1992 alone, 125 policemen were killed in action.[1] The government, as well as the political parties, had a stake in reducing tensions and conflict on the streets of the country's townships.

In April 1992, Goldstone took the initiative to address this issue by forming a special panel of the Commission with a novel composition and a novel mandate. Under the authority of the subcommittee on the "Regulation of Gatherings," which he chaired, he established an international panel of experts that would be tasked with producing recommendations for the Commission. South Africa could benefit, Goldstone reasoned, from the experience of other countries that had dealt—often much more successfully—with crowd control at political rallies. To lead the group, Goldstone tapped a Harvard Law School professor named Philip Heymann, whom he had met only recently at a conference in Durban. It was the first time that any inquiry nominally under the auspices of the South African government had used foreign experts to advise on a major policy change. By July, the panel made a long list of recommendations for the regulation of political gatherings in South Africa. Four ideas stood out.

First, the panel recommended that police should not have sole responsibility for logistics and crowd control at mass rallies. Second, the police should be well trained and have access to a broad range of nonlethal methods of crowd control, with lethal force used only in extreme circumstances. Third, all parties should commit to advance planning and more flexibility. Finally, and most controversially, all demonstrating parties should commit to a policy that marchers were not allowed to carry weapons of any kind.[2]

Goldstone knew that the recommendations of this panel—and of his Commission more generally—were only as powerful as their acceptance by the full range of parties, including the government. He also knew that airing the recommendations in public would make it more difficult for the parties to block meaningful change. So in July 1992, just after his public statement criticizing both the government and the ANC, he convened three days of hearings in Cape Town on the regulation of public gatherings. Heymann and his team presented the findings of their report, and representatives of all the parties had a chance to weigh in. As Goldstone expected, the public forum made it difficult to oppose the panel's commonsense suggestions. By the end of the week in Cape Town, it was clear that there was a general consensus behind the development of draft legislation for Parliament that, if passed, would enact the Heymann panel's principal recommendations.

There were two problems, however, with waiting for legislation to solve these problems. The first was time. With demonstrations organized in some part of the country on a nearly daily basis, the continuing threat of violence was enormous. South Africa simply could not afford to wait for months of parliamentary debate to address this issue. The second problem was legitimacy. Goldstone understood that new regulations could only be effective if they were formally embraced by all the parties, rather than imposed by fiat by a legislature in which Blacks had no representation.

On July 9, at the end of the Cape Town hearings, Goldstone called together the attending representatives of the government, the ANC, and the IFP, and he put them all on the spot. Why wait for Parliament? he proposed. Let's hammer out an agreement that you can all live with right now. Philip Heymann admired the chairman's self-assurance and boldness. "I had this feeling of the parties having no leverage," he remembered, "no place to put their feet down. The country was in turmoil, moving to a new stage, and he was just creating a new law of demonstrations on the spot."[3] JJ du Toit was less surprised. The Richard Goldstone he knew was a man whose manner said, "'If you don't agree with my recommendation, that's your right, but you're not going to ignore me.'"[4]

Under the pressure of the chairman and the public spotlight, the parties agreed immediately to adopt the recommendations of the committee. The document called for a detailed but flexible planning process where the organizers, the government, and the police would commit to work hand in hand.

Yet the document's most important and revolutionary statement was its first clause, drafted by Goldstone himself: "Members of the public have the right to demonstrate peacefully in public, in order to convey their views effectively and the South African Police have the duty to protect this right." The formal articulation of a right to public protest—signed and endorsed by the South African government—represented a sea change in the political landscape. In the absence of a constitution and with apartheid still in many ways the law of the land, the language of rights was still a foreign tongue in the South African legal context. Richard Goldstone had found a way to bring the right of political expression—and with it a reliance on the concept of human rights more generally—to the center of the country's attention.

Furthermore, this clause had a practical consequence. Over the years, the South African government had established a complex set of laws and practices designed to make almost any public demonstration technically illegal. There was always a pretext to shut down a demonstration: crowds on the sidewalks, or people marching through a red light.[5] The "right to demonstrate," combined with a mutually agreeable planning process, effectively undermined those laws.

A few days later, Kobie Coetsee called and dispensed with the usual pleasantries that he and the chairman had generally enjoyed. The minister of justice was startled at what he was reading, and he was shocked that Goldstone was already preparing to go public with the agreement. Most startling to Coetsee—and to F. W. de Klerk—was the idea that the Commission was telling the people of South Africa that they did not need to obey the law. Goldstone conceded that this was indeed one way to look at it.

The minister did not want to provoke a head-on collision, especially because over time the chairman had previously gone out of his way not to undermine the de Klerk government. Coetsee told Goldstone that he was reluctant to dictate to a judge, but he pressed the point about how the Commission might handle the public release.

"President de Klerk is very unhappy," Coetsee continued. "He asked whether you would in making it public say that the agreement doesn't suggest that the law need not be obeyed."

"Minister," Goldstone replied, "I can't say that because that's what the agreement DOES say."

"I'm surprised to hear a judge suggesting that people shouldn't obey the law," Coetsee countered.

"This is an unusual situation," Goldstone said. "The law was made by White South Africans and the Black majority had nothing to do with it." When Coetsee paused, Goldstone pressed his advantage. "Minister, this is a subject that we should debate over a lunch and not on the telephone."

"You're quite right," Coetsee finally conceded. "You must do what you have to do."[6]

On July 16, 1992, as promised, Goldstone released the agreement publicly, praising the parties for the spirit of cooperation that they brought to the task. Later that day, Kobie Coetsee placed another call to Richard Goldstone. "I owe you an apology," the minister said. "You were right and we were wrong." It turned out that the ANC had planned for that very day a march of 90,000 people in Pretoria, and the government had been exceedingly anxious about how it would turn out. But in the wake of the agreement, the ANC leaders had instantly shown their willingness to work with the Pretoria City Council and the South African Police in negotiating a route and procedures that would minimize the possibility of disturbance. Goldstone could not resist a bit of self-congratulation. "I pointed out to Coetsee," he recalled later, "that when people are made part of a process and are fully consulted, they generally adhere to the terms that they agree upon. That is really what democratic government is all about."[7]

In August 1992, Richard Goldstone took advantage of the public spotlight to offer a bold proposal. He called for an amnesty for those who agreed to testify before the Commission about matters relating to the promotion of violence. With a promised amnesty, Goldstone believed, individuals would be more likely to come forward and provide the Commission with specific and credible evidence regarding all perpetrators of violence.[8] Goldstone had, however, misjudged the moment. The South African government upped the ante by making a public call for an unconditional amnesty that would go far beyond the Commission and exonerate hundreds of its own officials from prosecution.[9] The ANC, after the government's response, rejected both amnesty proposals, saying that it was impossible to promise forgiveness in advance, that the nature of the crimes would have to be revealed.[10]

For the moment, then, Goldstone's August 1992 suggestion went nowhere. Three years later, however, amnesty would return as a major feature of South Africa's Truth and Reconciliation Commission (TRC). Goldstone's 1992 proposal anticipated the development that many observers would credit as the defining and innovative feature of the TRC process.

In the same statement when he called for the amnesty, Goldstone also reiterated his public pressure for more resources and support for the Commission. This time, he had the backing of a report from the secretary-general of the U.N. In September 1992, President de Klerk approved funding for the formation of five new investigation teams. The teams would include lawyers and policemen reporting directly to the Commission, in the person of JJ du Toit. These additions transformed the Commission from an underfunded body with a skeleton staff to a robust organization with twenty-six investigators based in five cities.[11]

The creation of the investigation units was a watershed moment for the Commission. None of the important revelations that followed later in 1992 and right through the 1994 election would have been possible without them. Some observers had been complaining that the Commission was essentially toothless. It was becoming clear that Richard Goldstone had a knack for creating teeth.

The increasing stature of the Commission paid off almost immediately. In September 1992, it issued a swift report following a march that had turned violent in Bisho, the capital of one of South Africa's self-governing "homelands." Where Boipatong had sent the negotiations into a tailspin, Bisho had the opposite effect. The bloodshed seemed to catalyze the parties, with its stark reminder that negotiations were the only route to ending the cycle of violence. At the end of September, as the Commission was delivering its crisp, clear report on Bisho, Nelson Mandela and F. W. de Klerk were signing a new "Record of Understanding" that got the talks back on track. Among the key items in the document: the agreement on the fencing of hostels that had been a key recommendation of the Commission.[12]

Creating the investigation units was no simple task. Inevitably the bulk of qualified investigators to join these teams would have to be drawn from the South African security apparatus itself—from the very forces whose actions the Commission might be scrutinizing. Goldstone believed strongly, however, that there were many men of integrity within those forces who would be willing to put the discovery of the truth before their loyalties to the government. Still, he wanted his investigators to be vetted well, so he took the unusual step of publicizing the names of those whom he intended to appoint before any formal offer was made. This gave South Africans—particularly in the Black community—the chance to identify any officers known to be hostile or derelict in their duties.

During this time, the chairman also extended and refined his team approach to leadership. His style was to consult frequently with all of those who were part of the Commission, but he made no pretense that he was delegating the ultimate authority. He was consultative, but decisive. "He would always bring us together and say what he thinks, and ask for views, and then we would argue it," JJ du Toit remembered. But his team could not dither. "He was already drafting what to say. He's a fast mover, that guy. If you're going to stop him, you have to have very good arguments to stop him in his tracks."[13] With the investigation teams in place, the Commission finally had the opportunity to make a dramatic move.

On October 30, 1992, a liberal Afrikaans-language newspaper called *Vrye Weekblad* published a two-page spread under the sensational headline "New

Evidence of a 'Third Force' in Massacre Ordered by the SAP."[14] A former soldier from Mozambique named Joao Cuna had come forward to say that in
July 1991 he had participated in a drive-by shooting in the province of Natal
in an operation directed by the South African Police. Cuna said that he had
been recruited, given an AK-47 rifle, and that he had been ordered to shoot
men known to be ANC members in a house and at a taxi stand in the city of
Pietermaritzburg. The next day, Cuna alleged, he was taken to Johannesburg
and paid 4,000 rand for his part in the operation. The editor of *Vrye Weekblad*,
in an accompanying editorial, said that Cuna's sworn affidavit settled once
and for all that a "third force" was poisoning the South African landscape.

It was not the first time that a South African newspaper had uncovered
"third force" activity.[15] *Vrye Weekblad*'s allegations, however, were significant
at this moment because President F. W. de Klerk had worked mightily to convey the impression that illicit operations by the South African security
forces were a thing of the past. Cuna's charges suggested that operations were
continuing on de Klerk's watch, and during the time frame in which the Commission had jurisdiction.

The South African Police immediately began their own investigation of
Cuna's charges, but Goldstone knew that the whole point of an independent
commission was to take on situations where the police could not be trusted
to investigate themselves. Interviews with Cuna and dogged legwork following a trail of credit card receipts led the Commission to a shadowy organization called Africa Risk Analysis Consultants (ARAC).

At this point, Goldstone decided to act under the unusual authority that
had been granted under the National Peace Accord, which allowed the Commission "to inspect any premises and demand and seize any document on
or kept on such premises."[16] The Commission needed no judicial or governmental approval. It had, formally at least, virtually unlimited powers of search
and seizure. Ironically, Goldstone was fighting a tyrannical system with a
search and seizure power outside a normal framework of checks and balances.
"I was doing many things on the Commission that in a democracy would have
been unthinkable and unconstitutional. The fact that we could conduct a raid
on government offices without a court order. . . . We were taking advantage
of the undemocratic nature of the regime."[17]

On November 11, 1992, a team of investigators and policemen reporting
to the Commission swooped down on the headquarters of ARAC, located
in a colorless mall on the outskirts of Pretoria. Goldstone had ordered the

team to be selective: they were only to seize materials directly related to the evidence that Joao Cuna had provided. He did not want to be accused of exceeding his authority by undertaking an extensive "fishing expedition." The five files that the investigators removed proved explosive enough.

The files revealed that ARAC was in fact a front for a unit called the Directorate of Covert Collection (DCC), a military intelligence arm of the South African Defence Force. During 1991, the DCC had employed a man named Ferdi Barnard, a former drug squad sergeant who had participated in dirty tricks operations throughout the 1980s and had twice been convicted of murder. The documents showed that Barnard had been charged with infiltrating the military wing of the ANC and identifying ANC members who were involved in criminal activity. If no criminal activity could be found, then Barnard would compromise them by associating them with illegal activities involving prostitutes, homosexuals, bar owners, and drug dealers. The DCC went so far as to operate a brothel whose express purpose was to entrap ANC representatives. These activities went forward under the racist code name "Operation Baboon."

The documentation was clear and specific. Senior officials in the South African Defence Force, during the presidency of F. W. de Klerk, had approved and supported the employment of one of the notorious evildoers of the apartheid era.

The situation presented Richard Goldstone with a conundrum. Under the law that formed the Commission, the results of all inquiries were to be reported first to the state president. The chairman, however, did not wish to turn over the ARAC files to the Ministry of Justice, given the real prospect that the government would then delay their release and sanitize the information. So Goldstone donned his metaphorical robes and issued a kind of judicial ruling in his own favor. He decided that "inquiries" referred only to formal reports and proceedings by the Commission. Materials gathered by search-and-seizure, he determined, were therefore not "inquiries" and did not have to be turned over. It was a clever interpretation, and perhaps even a subversion of the original law—an echo of the strategy that he had sometimes used as a judge. But this conclusion served Goldstone's sense of justice, in the wake of revelations that the chairman found "morally unacceptable."

Instead of producing a private report for F. W. de Klerk, Goldstone decided to go public. On November 16, 1992, he issued a thirteen-page statement, and he held what was only his second press conference since the formation of the Commission. He began by reminding the public of de Klerk's promises to clean up the security forces, and he thanked the president for respecting the Commission's independence. He revealed the details of Ferdi Barnard's employment and his blackmail activities (though he was careful not to mention the incendiary name of the operation). He also gave the government some cover by stating that "the Commission believes that no decent member of the Security Forces would support or approve of such conduct by any branch of those Forces."[18]

The revelations made headlines across the country and around the world.[19] The "dirty tricks" of Ferdi Barnard were frankly on a small scale in comparison to the direct acts of violence committed by the apartheid regime over the years, but the "smoking gun" nature of the documents made the story irresistible. Liberal papers in South Africa cheered the Commission's work and excoriated the government, although some external commentators complained that Goldstone was, through his caution, protecting de Klerk's regime. After all, Joao Cuna's original story of contracted murder had been reported in the press, and observers wondered why it did not figure in the Commission's revelations. "Judge Goldstone is a brilliant Appeal Court judge, but he is something of a legal pedant," complained the British newspaper the *Guardian*, arguing that the chairman should have gone public with the more serious charges of a "much broader and more violent campaign of murder."[20]

Caught unawares by Goldstone's public announcement, F. W. de Klerk seethed. He despised "the sensational manner in which Goldstone had publicized preliminary and untested findings," and he deplored the chairman's "precipitate and sensational statements to the media."[21] When the two men met the next day, de Klerk "made no effort to hide his resentment" of Goldstone's actions. Yet he also decided to act quickly—and to try to take matters out of the Commission's hands. Just two days after Goldstone's press conference, the state president appointed the head of the South African Air Force, General Pierre Steyn, to conduct the government's own investigation of the Commission's allegations.

The ANC, for its part, decided not to overplay its hand. Although the initial reaction of the ANC's representatives was to call for the resignation of this "totally discredited government," cooler heads quickly prevailed. Negotiations had been back on track since September, and Nelson Mandela recognized that allowing these new revelations to fatally weaken de Klerk as a negotiating partner was not in the ANC's interest. Rather than calling for the president's head, Mandela called de Klerk's appointment of General Steyn "a good, encouraging step." Indeed, Mandela used the scandal to make a public offer to the National Party, a proposal that offered the White minority a formal power-sharing arrangement in a democratic South Africa. The *New York Times* called these "conciliatory gestures" "an important shift in strategy" for the ANC.[22]

In mid-December, General Steyn presented a private interim report to F. W. de Klerk indicating that the revelations about the DCC were only the tip of the iceberg. Steyn said that there was reason to believe that higher-ups within the South African Defence Force had been involved in train massacres in the Transvaal, with supplying poison to assassins, with stockpiling arms in various African countries, and with training paramilitary forces in game reserves.[23] De Klerk claimed later that he and his senior advisers "listened, dumbfounded" to this information.[24]

On December 19, 1992, de Klerk announced that he was firing or placing on leave twenty-three members of the Defence Force, including some of the country's most senior military officers.[25] The Commission's raid in Pretoria had unleashed a powerful wave. More than a year in advance of the scheduled election, accountability was coming to South Africa, and the leaders of the security establishment were on notice.

The sensational revelations of November and the dismissals in December made it clear that Richard Goldstone himself had become a pivotal player in South Africa's transition. For the first time, a government-appointed Commission had made specific findings against the security forces, leading to concrete action. The findings had strengthened the case that de Klerk's National Party could not be trusted by itself to lead South Africa to democracy. By bringing his findings directly to the public, Goldstone had also burnished his own standing and reputation.

He was the "Man of the Year" according to one South African newspaper, and the "Newsmaker of the Year" according to a radio station. The *New York Times* called him "a cross between King Solomon and the Ghostbusters."[26] The *Sowetan* featured a cartoon with a billboard showing a balding, large-eared White man blasting upward as the line on a graph labeled "Optimism in South Africa's Future Chart." Looking at the billboard, an observer remarks to her companion, "(Gold)stone Is Going Up!"[27]

The Jewish community, both in South Africa and abroad, proudly claimed Richard Goldstone as one of their own. In January 1993, he was the guest of honor at a gala dinner in Cape Town hosted by the South African Jewish Board of Deputies. "We gather tonight to pay tribute to him as a famous South African Jew," said the SAJBD's national chairman, Mervyn Smith. "This community is deeply proud that one of its sons should be one of the peace makers in our troubled country. None of us is yet blasé enough not to feel a swell of pride when the name Goldstone appears nightly on our television screens or daily in our newspapers." The SAJBD presented Goldstone with a *shofar*, a ram's horn "symbolic of his commitment to the call in Leviticus for 'Liberty throughout the land for all the inhabitants thereof.'"[28]

Richard Goldstone loved the limelight, and he was getting better at courting it. His close friends discerned a growth in his ability to thrive in a public role. One friend remembered that before the 1990s, Richard was a "very dry speaker" whom one observer had termed "the great borer." Yet with the practice of exposure he had grown comfortable on television and in the glare of the public eye. He was speaking frequently as a guest of honor across the country, a task that he considered a natural responsibility of the Commission chairman. He clearly enjoyed the accolades, but also encountered his own thin skin. "I have discovered how much I hate being criticized," he confessed wryly to a group of journalists in Durban. "Unfair criticism is not so bad. What I really dislike is criticism which is justified—fortunately there has not been too much that I place in that category."[29]

"Mr. Justice Goldstone has become a household name with the best of the politicos, his position synonymous with judicial integrity in the face of political adversity," one newspaper opined at the end of 1992. "But *everybody* will remember him for his astonishing role this year. . . . From being a Supreme Court judge with a bent for human rights, Mr. Justice Goldstone has forged for himself a reputation for himself a reputation this year as South Africa's moral guardian."[30] These were heady times for the "moral guardian," but they were dangerous times as well. In finally directly taking on the security establishment, Richard Goldstone was cultivating some powerful enemies who were still determined to impede their country's march to democracy.

By the beginning of 1993, South Africa was looking with anticipation and trepidation to national elections, which had at last been set for April 1994. An established date was a triumph for the negotiation process, but it also increased the stakes. South Africa's transition was now inevitable, so the battle for political power intensified. Nevertheless, the continued deaths in the townships led some observers to wonder whether South Africa was really ready to move forward.

"Anybody who thinks this is going to be a beautiful smooth transition to wonderful democratic rule has got a hell of a shock in store for them," Richard Goldstone said in a private interview in January 1993. "It a question of trying to reduce the number of lives that are lost and not to prevent it." It was a sobering concession by the chairman of the Commission of Inquiry regarding the Prevention of Public Violence and Intimidation, but he fervently believed that the alternative would be even worse. "We've got to have this election," he continued. "Otherwise the country is simply going to dissolve in the most unbelievable violence. . . . If the election is called off because of violence we're never going to have an election. If you give in to blackmail—particularly violent blackmail—then you can never recover from it."[31]

During 1993, the chairman turned his attention to the quiet part that he could play in the political process in the run-up to the elections. At the heart of his efforts were the relationships that he developed and cultivated with the key figures who were transforming the country.

The chairman of the Commission had a formal obligation to the state president, but his face-to-face meetings with de Klerk were relatively infrequent. De Klerk claimed that he "had a healthy respect" for the judge's "fairness and thoroughness." But he also deeply disliked Goldstone's insistence on going directly to the public with his findings. "As the chairman of a judicial commission of inquiry," de Klerk complained later, "he was supposed to submit his reports to the state president after all the evidence had been properly tested and weighed—and not make precipitate and sensational statements to the media."[32] De Klerk was playing fast and loose with the facts, since the only time that Goldstone went directly to the press was in the case of the ARAC raid in November 1992.

Richard Goldstone wrestled with the question of what part the state president was actually playing in the violence that continued to wrack the country under his leadership. At each revelation and long after he left office de Klerk presented himself as an outraged leader whose integrity had been betrayed by corrupt subordinates. "In my relationship with security forces, I sometimes felt like a man who had been given two fully grown watchdogs—say, a Rottweiler and a bull terrier. Their previous owner had doted on them. He had given then [sic] the tastiest morsels from his table and had allowed them to run free and chase cats all over the neighbourhood. I had put a stop to all that. As a result, they did not particularly like me. . . . I could guide them, but I knew that if I pulled too hard, I might choke them—or they might slip their collars and cause pandemonium in the neighbourhood."[33]

For his part, Richard Goldstone went out of his way not to implicate de Klerk directly, and it appears that he generally accepted the state president's self-portrait. Two decades later, Goldstone still claimed that he could not be definitive about de Klerk's responsibility for the actions of his security forces, but he admitted that his instinct was always to give the state president the benefit of the doubt. "It's highly unlikely that he knew," Goldstone reflected. "His conduct was inconsistent with a man who was covering up."[34] As with Kobie Coetsee, Richard Goldstone always maintained a certain understanding for the ways in which leaders had to operate within the constraints of their political circumstances.

At first, Goldstone had virtually no personal connection with Nelson Mandela. But as the transition period went on, he developed a close bond with the ANC leader that bolstered the Commission and helped create a role for the judge in South Africa's later history. After their initial conversation at the Sisulu house in Soweto in 1991, he had little direct contact with Mandela for some months. Goldstone's telephone conversation with Mandela after the ANC's angry denunciation in the press began to build a relationship. Not long after that, Goldstone informed de Klerk that he planned to meet regularly with Mandela to brief him on the Commission's work, just as he was keeping de Klerk himself informed.

"Absolutely not," de Klerk fumed. "I'm in government and he's not in government."

"Mr. President," Goldstone replied. "One of these days he will be in government. I need to meet with him, and I don't want to do it behind your back."[35]

Beginning in the second half of 1992, Richard Goldstone paid regular Sunday evening visits to Nelson Mandela's home in Houghton, the same Johannesburg suburb where Goldstone himself had lived as a teenager. The two men would watch the 8:00 P.M. national news together, and then chat for an hour or two, starting with the work of the Commission but expanding the conversation into the broader South African scene. Many times Mandela was exhausted, finally letting his fatigue show at the end of a week of a punishing schedule. But Goldstone felt that the "Old Man" also was lonely and "craved social interaction" in the quiet and comfortable confines of his home. On one occasion, the men met in Mandela's upstairs bedroom, the ANC leader in his pajamas and dressing gown. Mandela passed along advance news of soon-to-be-public political developments in order to give the chairman the chance to prepare for the impact on his Commission. In one case, with regard to a particularly sensitive matter, Mandela wrote the gist of it on paper, from justified concern about government eavesdropping. Goldstone sometimes passed along sensitive information of his own, at one point alerting Mandela that he had picked up credible rumors that a leading ANC figure had acted as an informant for the government.[36]

The two men became friends in a way that Goldstone never did with either Coetsee or de Klerk. As shrewd navigators of the political landscape, both men also used their friendship to promote their agendas. They were savvy veterans, a pair of seasoned lawyers for whom the pleasures of friendship and the relentless quest for political capital were naturally and comfortably intertwined.

The personal bond between them was genuine, and it spilled over into Richard Goldstone's family life. Goldstone's daughter Nicky had admired Mandela since she was a teenager. Her father had successfully persuaded her to not to put herself at risk by involving herself in protest politics, but Nicky's finely tuned social conscience permeated her personality. By 1993, she had been living for several years in Israel. She had become an ardent Zionist and a passionate advocate for the ideals of Israel. Yet as South Africa approached a transition to democracy, and as her father was playing a leading role, Nicky felt a paroxysm of guilt about not being present to play a part in this historic moment in the country of her birth. She felt keenly the moral burden of having benefited as a White child under apartheid, and now the new challenge of feeling inadequate in the face of her father's courageous and visible contributions to the cause of justice. In the middle of 1993, she wrote out her cri de coeur in the form of a letter to Nelson Mandela himself, which her father made sure that the ANC leader received.

Mandela's response, dated August 4, 1993, was sent to Nicky in Jerusalem on two single-spaced typed pages on ANC letterhead. The veteran activist sympathized with the young White woman's plight on a personal level. There is no reason, he told Nicky, for "you to feel the guilt of your elders or to take responsibility" for the legacy of apartheid. At the same time, Mandela reiterated his position that he wanted Whites to remain in the country. "I have appealed to White South Africans not to leave," he wrote, "simply because we need their expertise and knowledge to help build a new South Arica out of the ashes of apartheid. It is one way that White South Africans can reconcile their past with a new present and future, to show that they wish to make amends." Yet he refused to judge his friend's daughter personally: "If you are to remain in South Africa, feeling unhappy and not being able to give your all, as we will have to do if we are to achieve our dreams, then you must find a niche for yourself where you will be happy, whole and be able to contribute your best."[37]

The letter resonated deeply with both father and daughter. Mandela's message blended a stern commitment to principle with enormous generosity of spirit, a combination of traits that he shared with Richard Goldstone. Describing himself and the White judge as fellow soldiers in the war against apartheid, Mandela captured in a few words a conviction that the fight for social justice requires many people of many temperaments and in many different roles.

On April 10, 1993, Richard Goldstone traveled to New York City to brief the U.N. on the progress of the Commission and the prospects for containing the violence in South Africa. The U.S. visit put him for the first time front and center on the international stage alongside major players in global politics. He met with senior ambassadors at the U.N., representatives of the World Bank, and key figures from the U.S. State Department and both houses of Congress.

The fortnight that Goldstone was away from South Africa was among the most dangerous periods in the transition. The murder of Communist Party leader Chris Hani just before the chairman's departure had spawned angry outbreaks in every part of the country. Only a dramatic appeal for calm by Nelson Mandela had kept South Africa from exploding. The South African Police discovered that Hani's killer had been recruited by Clive Derby-Lewis, an Afrikaner politician who had been one of the founders of the Conservative Party, a group that found the National Party too soft on apartheid. When the police opened up Derby-Lewis's computer, they found a hit list of prominent anti-apartheid figures in South Africa. Nelson Mandela was the top name on the list, and Chris Hani's was number three. Richard Goldstone appeared as number five.

Friends and colleagues had been warning Goldstone that he needed to take more precautions about his family's personal safety. After all, the Commission's work was probing the activities of some of the most murderous groups in the country. Until this point, Richard and Noleen had been cavalier, unwilling to accept the intrusions on their lives that more precautions would entail. The Hani assassination, however, made it clear that famous figures were vulnerable. As the election date neared, the temptation to disrupt the process by targeting well-known individuals would only be greater.

Reluctantly the Goldstones accepted round-the-clock security, which continued through the rest of the life of the Commission. Richard chafed against some of the conditions. He particularly disliked not being able to leave his Cape Town apartment for a spontaneous walk on the beach. Yet he also enjoyed the warmth and professionalism of the policemen assigned to him. He could have wallowed in resentment over the restrictions. Instead, he chose to redefine his security detail as an extension of his social circle.

Then, in the crucial weeks running up to the election, Richard Goldstone faced his sternest test as chairman. A series of stunning revelations thrust his Commission back into the national spotlight and threatened to upend the chairman's life and derail everything that he had been working for over the previous two and a half years.

On February 10, 1994, a representative of a Pretoria nongovernmental organization (NGO) informed Goldstone that an unnamed South African policeman was willing to come forward with information about "third force" activities. The catch: he would speak only directly to Richard Goldstone himself.

Three days later, on the evening of February 13, Goldstone waited with trepidation in a darkened corner of the swimming pool area at the Sandton Sun Hotel just outside Johannesburg. Three burly White men crossed the courtyard and took their places in the poolside plastic chairs. Two of them introduced themselves as police officers, majors in the "Department of Efficiency Services." The majors informed Goldstone that their companion, who sat slightly slouched in his chair, was prepared to speak to the chairman only on the condition that his name and identity should never be revealed. Goldstone said that he agreed, as long as the officer gave him, as chairman, his full name and rank. The men decided to refer to the informant outside their conversation simply as "Q."[38]

On that evening and in subsequent interviews Q described how the notorious paramilitary unit of the South African Police at Vlakplaas, thought to be disbanded five years earlier, was still maintaining an active operation. At this farmstead near Pretoria, a secret unit of policemen was manufacturing guns, supplying them to the IFP, and sometimes planning and executing murders themselves. At the center of the operation was Eugene de Kock, a former policeman with a long résumé as an apartheid government hit man. He had performed simple executions, he had pummeled a man to death with a spade, and he had killed one political activist by sending him a set of Sony Walkman headphones that exploded when he turned them on.[39] De Kock's reputation for violence and terror had earned him the sobriquet "Prime Evil." Q maintained that de Kock, who had been thought to be sidelined after public revelations about Vlakplaas in 1990, was still active, and collecting millions of rand from the government and from the illegal sale of arms.

Q's story was only one man's word. JJ du Toit began to conduct interviews with Q's Vlakplaas colleagues, but they professed to know nothing. Q met with the chairman again, now reporting that he and five other Vlakplaas operatives had that very day been ordered to move heaven and earth to find any information with which to blackmail Richard Goldstone himself. Two of them focused on the chairman's tax records; another pair had been assigned to find out whether he was having any extramarital affairs.[40]

Goldstone now turned to JJ du Toit and his team of investigators to find any promising leads. Q had mentioned a safe deposit box in de Kock's name in the ABSA Bank in Pretoria where damaging information might be held. In the box the investigators found a handgun registered to de Kock, and a set of undeveloped photographic negatives. When they developed the photos, the investigators were puzzled. All they saw, apart from family photographs was an image of a group of men gathered around a car in the middle of the veldt laughing and apparently enjoying a barbeque. Du Toit felt a twinge of disappointment. What were the photos of a social occasion doing in a safe deposit box?

In his next interviews with one of the Vlakplaas policemen, du Toit dramatically produced the photographs, placing them on the table in front of the witness and staring him down intently. The young policeman squirmed in his seat, and then his story spilled out. The barbeque was a party, a spontaneous celebration on the way home after a successful mission to "take out" certain targets. Q's story no longer stood alone. The Commission had corroboration.[41]

Using the policemen's leads, the Commission's investigators fanned out across the Transvaal, uncovering documents and conducting further interviews that revealed an extensive network of active attempts to undermine the

ANC and the peace process itself. Above all, Vlakplaas had turned into an active arms bazaar, selling weapons principally but not exclusively to the IFP, with the aim both of weakening the ANC but also of promoting violence more generally. These were not just the unapproved actions of low-level thugs. The evidence pointed to the active involvement and leadership of three senior members of the police: Generals Johan le Roux, Basie Smit, and Krappies Engelbrecht.

One week after the poolside meeting with Q, on February 20, Goldstone met with F. W. de Klerk and Kobie Coetsee at the president's official residence in Cape Town.[42] Goldstone found the state president "visibly shocked" by what he learned. The two leaders promised the full cooperation of the government, including funds for witness protection and the investigative support of South Africa's intelligence services. In early March, Goldstone sat down with Nelson Mandela and outlined the findings to him.

By the middle of March 1994, time was of the essence. Over the previous month, the Commission had uncovered the most convincing evidence to date of widespread and continuing criminal activity in the security forces. The November 1992 findings had been sensational and damning, but de Klerk could argue that he had contained the damage by removing from active service some of the individual officers responsible. The investigation that began with Q pointed to pervasive and systematic activities approved by generals, uncovered with just six weeks to go before the South African election.

The chairman ordered his investigators to confront Eugene de Kock and the three generals with the information that had been accumulated. On March 16, all four men vigorously denied involvement, and refused to cooperate further. The chairman decided that it was time to go public. He would have liked more time to investigate, but he felt that he had no choice. "If those intent on further destabilization succeed in aborting the election," he explained, "an investigation afterwards would be a futile exercise."[43] His staff did not fully agree. Some of the investigators worried the evidence against the perpetrators was still not solid, that going public would undermine their ability to continue their work. The chairman felt that the political ramifications overrode a law enforcement strategy.[44]

In hindsight, some later critics would complain that Goldstone, as a judge, should not have stooped to airing unproved allegations in the court of public opinion, especially because the reputations of three senior officers were involved. The alternative, however, was to bury the story until after the election. Goldstone had promised that he would come forward if credible "third force" evidence surfaced. Breaking this promise would have had costs both for his own integrity and for the health of the country.

On March 18, 1994, Goldstone presented an interim report simultaneously to de Klerk and Nelson Mandela with the full information about what he called a "horrible network of criminal activity." He exhorted the government and all relevant authorities "to take all possible steps" to neutralize those who "may or might be likely to cause or encourage criminal acts of violence and intimidation between the present time and the election."[45] This time the state president had no choice but to release the report immediately to the public. Although Goldstone went out of his way to insist that "it would be unfair and dangerous to tar the whole Police Force with the brush of Vlakplaas," the public identification of three generals with the "horrible network" undermined the credibility of the National Party at a key moment in the election cycle.

With their backs against the wall and nothing further to lose, the targets of Goldstone's investigation now tried to strike back. A volley of insinuations reached the witnesses who had come forward. Their direct testimony, after all, posed the gravest danger to the Vlakplaas operatives, who could not only lose their jobs but could be held criminally responsible. It also proved impossible to keep the informants' identities a secret. Within days of the press conference, "Q" was revealed as Kobus "Chappies" Klopper, a member of de Kock's unit C10. With the help of the British and Danish governments, the Commission spirited the key witnesses out of South Africa, bringing them to the comparative safety of Europe, where the Commission could question them further.

The threats did not stop with the witnesses. Richard Goldstone received a call from an anonymous caller who seemed to know everything about his movements, and who warned ominously that both he and Noleen were in danger of being killed. The Goldstones were rattled. They had a full-fledged security detail, but was it enough? After all, Richard had now directly implicated the men behind the most dangerous arm of the apartheid regime, men with vast experience in murder and intimidation.

The Goldstones moved quickly. On the advice of the head of National Intelligence they decided to bring forward by twenty-four hours a visit that had been planned to London and Copenhagen where Goldstone wished to interview the witnesses who were receiving protection in England and Denmark. They hastily packed two bags and sent a remaining suitcase and some personal items to the house of their friends, Errol and Ruth Friedmann, in a Johannesburg suburb. Richard called Errol, asking his longtime friend to look after his mother in case that anything happened to him.[46] While Richard and Noleen flew on an overnight flight to London, the Friedmanns' house was burgled, and the Goldstones' possessions rifled. British authorities met the Goldstones at Heathrow and escorted them first to a military installation by the coast, and then to a safe house in the country. Richard found the whole exercise hasty and alarming, but in the end it also had its compensations: the farmer who owned the "safe house" turned out to have "a splendid collection of Bordeaux wine."[47] He and Noleen returned to South Africa with trepidation ten days later, grateful to the other members of the Commission, and to JJ du Toit, who had remained in the country and on the front lines.

The Commission's March 1994 interim report effectively ended the debate about whether or not a "third force" was operating in post-1990 South Africa. The chairman made a half-hearted attempt in the report to protect the government by insisting that no "other" third force activities besides the ones detailed in this document were known to the Commission. But "a horrible network of criminal activity" involving senior officers of the police was a "third force" by most South Africans' common understanding of the term. F. W. de Klerk and Kobie Coetsee continued to insist that they knew nothing about this, and Richard Goldstone professed to believe them. If such an extensive operation was operating without the state president's knowledge, that itself was damning enough.

Richard Goldstone's March 1994 revelations only told part of the story. They revealed some of the details regarding de Kock's unit at Vlakplaas, but a wealth of other information uncovered by the investigation remained out of the public eye. The investigation of Vlakplaas had revealed an array of misdeeds extending back into the 1980s. These included the documentation of "hit squads," the blackmail of a prominent Black clergyman, the shredding of documents after the 1991 Inkathagate scandal, and details of "Operation Romulus," a disinformation campaign designed to destabilize the ANC. Early in April 1994, Goldstone brought these revelations to President de Klerk, saying that he was ready to issue another, more extensive report on these "third force" activities. De Klerk made it clear to the chairman he had no desire to see further sensational press reports that would only threaten the prospect of a peaceful election.

Goldstone put the same question to Nelson Mandela, and the ANC leader agreed. No good purpose would be served in releasing further information in this time frame. Goldstone reluctantly agreed to quash the report. "In light of that political judgment by the two men who were really guiding the events in South Africa at that time," he said later, "I felt there was no option but to comply."[48]

Like millions of other South Africans of all colors and backgrounds, Richard and Noleen Goldstone waited in a long and joyous line on April 27, 1994, to cast their ballots in South Africa's first truly democratic election. The election proceeded in a national climate of remarkable calm. That night, Richard celebrated with white wine from South Africa's own Western Cape.

The Commission could take some credit for many of the positive developments that allowed the election to proceed with relative ease. Few violent incidents had marred the political demonstrations of the final weeks, governed by the regulations that the Commission had developed. Furthermore, after months of threatening to boycott the election, Chief Buthelezi had in mid-April announced that the IFP would participate after all. Pressure on the IFP from its international supporters had increased since the Commission's March report had shown the continuing extent of cooperation between the party and the South African government. While Buthelezi had many motivations for participating, the fact-finding work of the Commission had played its part in bringing the last political holdout into the democratic fold.

In addition to its specific findings, the Commission had played a crucial symbolic role as well. It gave life to the idea that formal legal processes— even under an undemocratic government—could serve the cause of the truth. By bringing together Black lawyers and Afrikaner policemen under the leadership of an English-speaking Jew, the Commission also provided a very public example of cooperation across the divides of South African society.

Now Nelson Mandela was in line to become South Africa's president, and the Commission could wrap up its work. For the next six months, its various committees of inquiry published their reports and worked on making the archives of the Commission a permanent resource for the nation. These final reports focused principally on a detailed examination of the underlying causes of violence in the country, along with policy recommendations for the future. The Commission would live on as a newly formed Human Rights

Institute, with a mandate to focus on rights and violence prevention under the new democratic polity.[49]

The transition of South Africa from apartheid to democracy was the twentieth century's most spectacular success for human rights in the developing world. Richard Goldstone's contribution to that dramatic process was not only critical for South Africa's history. It also reframed the possibilities for law and justice in conflict-ridden and postconflict societies around the globe.

The Commission's most glaring success and its most glaring failure were one and the same: the simultaneous persistence and containment of political violence in South Africa. In the four-year run-up to that election, 15,000 South Africans lost their lives, at a rate that by most counts actually accelerated in the months leading up to April 1994. The Commission proved powerless to stem this tide of blood. Yet the election itself was a spectacular triumph. Millions voted, the National Party handed the reins of government to the ANC, and the predicted civil war never materialized. Richard Goldstone's leadership of the investigations that exposed the "third force" and of the processes that limited the potential for violence in demonstrations deserves a large share of the credit for the success of the South Africa transition.

It would have been easy for the ANC and other opponents of the apartheid regime to turn their backs on the law as an instrument for justice. After all, the law had been perverted in so many ways in South Africa that it would have been natural for those who suffered from its barbs to remain skeptical of its usefulness. Yet South Africa's transition was built on a commitment to a robust constitution that would allow the country to start afresh, but also to incorporate some crucial elements of its traditional legal system. Richard Goldstone and the Commission played a central role as well in fortifying faith in law's possibilities at the dawn of the transformation.[50]

6 ▸ IN THE FOOTSTEPS OF ROBERT JACKSON

IN JUNE 1994, Richard and Noleen Goldstone embarked on a long-delayed vacation to the Tuscan hills in Italy. Although the Goldstone Commission would not file its final reports until October, the chairman's delicate work was essentially complete, and his own future was uncertain. What role would there be in the new South Africa for a white judge who had worked to serve both the law under an apartheid regime and principles of universal human rights?

As it turned out, a new and dramatic development was about to take Richard Goldstone's life and work in unexpected directions, thousands of miles from his native country. For the next two years, he would play the leading role in building two other brand-new courts and would bring to life an abstraction known as "international criminal justice."

Two years earlier, in June 1992, while Richard Goldstone and his commission in South Africa were sorting through the aftermath of the massacre at Boipatong, a twenty-seven-year-old man named Ibro Osmanović was sweltering on the concrete floor of a military hangar near the banks of the Sušica River in eastern Bosnia-Herzegovina. More than 500 other men and a handful of women were crowded into less than 500 square meters. Some daylight made its way through the windows high above, but the panes were sealed shut, so little air flowed through the hangar to relieve the stifling summer heat. A lucky few had brought their own bedding, but most slept directly on the concrete. Food arrived once a day, at 11:00 A.M.; the allowances were more fit for a child than for grown men. Armed guards blocked the doorways, their barking orders punctuating the low murmur of talk and fear.[1]

Just a few weeks earlier, Ibro had been living in his hometown of Vlasenica, just a few miles away. Vlasenica was a town of 7,500, its population a mixture of Muslims and Serbs, with Muslims in the slight majority and holding many of the prominent positions in local and civic leadership. Ibro was Muslim, but he had grown up with Serbs as neighbors, friends, and co-workers. They spoke the same language, haunted the same coffee shops. Ibro had a good job with one of the large companies involved in aluminum, forestry, and other industries in this resource-rich section of Yugoslavia.

In April 1992, Ibro's hometown was turned upside down. Bosnia-Herzegovina had recently declared its independence from the Federal Republic of Yugoslavia, and two weeks later, troops from Yugoslavia's national army, the Jugoslovenska Narodna Armija (JNA), appeared on the outskirts of town. Artillery shells fell into the center of Vlasenica, terrorizing the population. Then local Serb men—people with whom Ibro worked and sometimes drank—appeared on the streets of the town in white armbands, operating as local militia. Armed men went door-to-door to Muslim homes, demanding that any weapons in the house be turned over "for security reasons." Bosnian Serbs took over the administration of the town, and some of the Muslim leaders disappeared. Within days, Vlasenica was transformed into a municipality run by Bosnian Serbs, and its Muslim residents faced a double bind. On the one hand, their movements were restricted, and they were required to apply for passes to move to specific locations in or out of the province. On the other hand, many were being forced to leave their homes. In some cases they escaped to other Muslim areas of Bosnia. Others, like Ibro Osmanović, ended up in the local prison.

Over and over again Ibro swore to his captors that he owned no weapons, that he was not part of any "armed resistance," and that, in fact, there was no armed resistance at all among the Muslims of Vlasenica. But his protestations fell on deaf ears. On June 18, 1992, Ibro was moved out of Vlasenica and taken one kilometer out of town to a place called Sušica camp. Originally a warehouse and later a military installation, Sušica was now festooned with barbed wire and high-intensity spotlights.

When Ibro arrived, he saw a tall, hatless Serb in military camouflage, sporting a pistol and a knife in his belt, with a rifle slung over his shoulder and a baton he was juggling between his hands. Ibro recognized the man. His name was Dragan Nikolić, known informally around Vlasenica as "Jenki." Ibro did not know Jenki well, but he knew that he had worked in the aluminum industry, and he had seen him around in the town coffee shops. He had known that Nikolić was a bit rough, but what he saw and heard now shocked him. Jenki announced himself as the commander of the prisoners' new home, emphasizing the point by swinging his baton in the air. Then, in a swift motion, he swung his rifle from his shoulder and fired several rounds over the heads of the detainees, the bullets clanging off the metal shed behind them. "In this place," Dragan Nikolić told the cowering men, "I am God, the stick, and the law."

Sušica housed Muslims from all over the Vlasenica district. Conditions during the day were bad enough. The guards took Ibro and other men outside the camp and forced them to work in cleaning out and sometimes destroying homes of Muslim families. Even worse, the prisoners were forced to dispose of bullet-ridden corpses in some of the smaller villages. But the real horror was at nighttime. The bare, airless hangar became a house of fear, as guards roughly pulled prisoners from the floor, interrogating them on the spot or bringing them outside the hangar to a patch of ground by an electricity pole close enough to the doorway that screams of pain could be heard by those inside. When the guards pulled one of the women out of doors at night, she returned in silence.

Dragan Nikolić, true to his promise, was a prominent player in these nighttime visits. One night, Ibro watched in horror as the camp commander unsheathed the bayonet of his rifle, forced open the mouth of another inmate named Fikret "Cice" Arnaut, and thrust the knifepoint deep into his throat. Another night, Jenki oversaw the beating and eventual death of a man in his sixties named Durmo Handzić.

Compared to Arnaut and Handzić, Ibro was fortunate. He escaped the outdoor beatings, though Jenki forced him on one occasion to sit in standing water for more than forty hours. But Ibro survived his experience at

Sušica, and later in the summer he was transferred to another camp, in a place called Batković, where he was confined for another year before he was finally released. Nevertheless, Ibro remembered with blazing intensity the face of Dragan Nikolić, "the God, the stick, and the law."

In the summer of 1995, three years after his term in Sušica, Ibro told his story in a modern, high-tech courtroom in The Hague, the capital of the Netherlands, where lawyers questioned him closely about the actions of the camp commander. But Jenki was not present at the hearing. In fact, no one in the courtroom knew exactly where he was. Instead, the purpose of the proceeding was to establish the basis for an international arrest warrant for Mr. Dragan Nikolić, on charges of war crimes and crimes against humanity. Among the charges were the torture of Cice Arnaut and the murder of Durmo Handzić. The hearing was based on a formal indictment of Dragan Nikolić, which had been confirmed by Judge Elizabeth Odio Benito on November 4, 1994. The signature on the indictment, above the title of "prosecutor," was that of Richard J. Goldstone.[2]

Half a year before he signed that indictment, Richard Goldstone had never heard of Dragan Nikolić, and the events in the former Yugoslavia were no more than a flicker across his consciousness as he read the world news during the period of the South African election.[3] He was more preoccupied with the establishment of the new court that would approve and then interpret his country's permanent constitution, the first in South Africa's long and bloody history.

The Constitutional Court would consist of eleven judges, and President Mandela was required by the interim constitution to select four members of the initial bench from among the dozens of judges currently serving at the Supreme Court level across the country. Richard Goldstone was not ashamed to admit to friends and family that he coveted one of those slots. He had already had some discreet conversations about this with George Bizos, the legendary anti-apartheid lawyer who was close to Mandela and with whom Richard had first crossed paths during his days as a student leader at Wits. Bizos had broached the subject with Goldstone as the two men rode together to the new president's inauguration in May.[4]

Yet on July 5, 1994, when the Goldstones returned from holiday, a surprising fax was waiting in the judge's office. Dated four days earlier, on July 1, it came on letterhead bearing the mark of the U.N., and it originated from a number in the Netherlands. The fax was a kind of job offer.[5]

It came from a man unknown to Goldstone named Antonio Cassese, who identified himself as the president of the International Criminal Tribunal for the Former Yugoslavia (ICTY). President Cassese noted that his court was lacking a chief prosecutor, and he asked Richard Goldstone "whether you might be interested in fulfilling this demanding position." The president himself had no powers of appointment, but he made it clear that he wished to forward Judge Goldstone's name to the secretary-general of the U.N., who would in turn pass it along to the Security Council.[6]

On the face of it, the idea was preposterous.[7] Cassese's letter specified that "prosecutorial experience" was one of the "basic requirements" of the position. Yet Goldstone had never been a prosecutor of any sort, much less a prosecutor in an international court. Indeed, the bulk of his work as a lawyer and a judge had been in commercial work. He knew little of Serbia and Bosnia and Croatia, or of international law, or of the U.N., other than some appreciation for the global institution's support for his work in suppressing violence in his country.

The timing was particularly challenging because the letter from Antonio Cassese was actually the *second* job offer that Richard Goldstone received upon returning home from vacation. He had already spoken with Dullah Omar, the new South African minister of justice, who had told Goldstone confidentially that he was indeed one of the four sitting judges who would be named to the new Constitutional Court.

It should have been easy for Richard Goldstone to say no to Antonio Cassese, but in fact he wrote back immediately to say that he was tempted. "The prospect of sitting on the [South African] court is a most exciting one," he wrote to Cassese within hours. "Nevertheless the prospect of working with your Tribunal is one I would find difficult to refuse." He told Cassese that he had already set up a meeting that afternoon with Dullah Omar, and that since his judicial appointment was by the country's president he would also have to consult with Nelson Mandela: "Their views as to where my duty lies will obviously be paramount in coming to a decision."[8]

Behind the scenes, Noleen Goldstone was helping to shape her husband's thinking. After all, she argued, it would not be the worst thing in the world to get out of South Africa. Apartheid was over, but there were still a lot of angry holdouts among those who had served in the security forces, men who were perhaps even more dangerous now that they had been displaced. Richard Goldstone was a convenient target for their anger. Getting some distance from Afrikaner operatives might help the Goldstones sleep better at night.

In the meantime, an impatient Antonio Cassese followed up his fax with a phone call. In the musical cadence of his Italian-accented English, Cassese told Goldstone that he could not wait long for an answer. In a follow-up letter, the Italian made a direct appeal to what he imagined was the South African's eagerness for public attention. "Probably things can be worked out in such a way as to reconcile your legitimate interest in becoming a member of such an important national body [the Constitutional Court of South Africa] with the tremendous international exposure that the position of Prosecutor would entail."[9]

Despite the urgings of Cassese, his wife, and his friends, Goldstone was reluctant to turn his back on South Africa at such a critical moment. Then Nelson Mandela called.

The two men had developed their rapport when Goldstone was a high-ranking judge and Mandela was still outside of government as the leader of a resistance movement. Now it was a president who was speaking to a member of his extended government.

Overriding any objections, the president told the judge that he had already informed the secretary-general of the U.N. that Goldstone would take the position if offered. This was not just about Richard Goldstone. It was about the legitimacy of the new South Africa in the international arena. For years South Africans, representing the apartheid regime, had been blocked from appointments in the U.N. South Africa, moreover, owed an untold debt to the U.N. for helping end apartheid. This was the first prominent appointment offered since the transition, and it was imperative for Richard Goldstone to accept.[10]

But what, Goldstone inquired, of his appointment to the Constitutional Court? Don't worry about it, Mandela assured him. The cabinet had already met, and they were prepared to have Goldstone named to the court and then accept a leave of absence. Temporary substitutes would fill in while he worked in The Hague. When Goldstone confessed that he felt unprepared to serve as a prosecutor for an international court, the president brushed off the concern. "You're a clever chap," Nelson Mandela told him. "You'll learn it all very quickly."[11]

"Perhaps there are people who can refuse a direct and personal request from Nelson Mandela," Goldstone later recalled. "I am not among them." He called back Antonio Cassese and said yes.

The ICTY was formally established in May 1993. In the fourteen months since that date, it had had one chief prosecutor, and he lasted fewer than ten days on the job. The court was facing a crisis of confidence and credibility, and Cassese and his fellow judges were in a hurry. Richard and Noleen Goldstone had no more than a month to make their move to The Hague.

In the meantime, Goldstone started a crash course—or more accurately, several simultaneous crash courses—to try to acquire the basic knowledge about everything he did not know: the history of the Balkans and of the war that was still raging there; the body of law governing the prosecution of criminals at the international level; the ins and outs of the U.N. and this new-fangled entity, an ad hoc court established by the international community. Always enchanted by biography, he found a book on the life of Josip Broz Tito, the founding president of Yugoslavia, to be particularly compelling.[12]

In July 1994, the grinding war in the Balkans had been raging for three years, with the most intensive fighting since the spring of 1992 in the territory of Bosnia-Herzegovina. Blood had been spilled across nearly every part of the former Yugoslavia, a country that once prided itself both on its multiethnic character and on a socialist ethic that tried to balance the centralization of power with strong support for regional autonomy and identity.

Yugoslavia as a nation-state was born in the aftermath of World War I, in beautiful, rugged landscape that was at the crossroads of two great empires, the Austro-Hungarian and the Ottoman Turk.[13] The "land of the South Slavs," as its name meant literally, would finally give the people of this region the chance to follow their own destiny. The Serbs, Russian Orthodox by religion and clustered in the eastern half of the country, would, by virtue of an existing kingdom, have something of an upper hand in the new country. But by design they would share the land with other peoples: Roman Catholics clustered in Croatia, to the west, and Muslims, who were the majority in the multiethnic center of the country, Bosnia-Herzegovina.

World War II brought a violent shock to the political and social fabric of the country. Powerful political and military forces exploited existing religious and "national" differences, creating a bloody and angry legacy. In Croatia, the Nazis installed a puppet regime called the Ustaše, which turned the Third Reich tactics of slaughter and internment against the Serbs. Serbs loyal to their former king organized their own military organization, the Chetniks, that repaid Croatians in kind. Transcending these divisions, the anti-Nazi partisans emerged from the war as the strongest party. When it came time to form a postwar government, the leader of the partisans, Josip Broz Tito, became president-for-life and in many ways the embodiment of the new Yugoslavia.

Postwar Yugoslavia was a multiethnic federation, with six republics and two autonomous provinces, held together as a nation by the sheer force of Tito's personality and his vision of a socialist state that would avoid the horrors of Soviet-style centralization. Tito broke with the Soviets as early as 1948, and over the next thirty-two years he forged his own path in central Europe, several times modifying the political nature of Yugoslavia, but always privileging "Yugoslav" identity over the ethnic and religious loyalties that had torn the country apart during World War II.

Tito's death in 1980 was a blow, because there was no natural successor who had his authority and charisma. Still, the country maintained its reputation as a haven of multiethnic harmony, especially in 1984, when Sarajevo, the capital of Bosnia-Herzegovina, showcased its beauty and its history as the host of a successful Winter Olympic Games.

In the late 1980s, however, the fabric of the nation began to fray and then to unravel as local politicians used the emotional pull of ethnic nationalisms to secure their power bases. The first seat of unrest was among Serbians, who felt that they had in some ways lost the most when they gave up their historic kingdom to become part of the Yugoslav state. Murmurs of discontent began in Belgrade; they were nurtured and amplified by an ambitious politician, Slobodan Milošević, who parlayed a vision for a Serbian renaissance into a power base that by 1990 had eliminated the autonomous regions within Serbia, brought neighboring Montenegro under its influence, and was threatening to break up the Yugoslav federation. Nationalist movements also gained strength in Slovenia, Croatia, and to some extent within Bosnia as well, culminating in 1990 elections that put opponents of a united Yugoslavia into key positions in almost every corner of the country. Even the Muslims, who had been among the steadiest supporters of a "pan-Yugoslav" identity, increasingly felt that they had to assert their own interests in a partisan environment.

On the same day in June 1991, Slovenia and Croatia declared their independence. Serbia, ostensibly protecting the interests of ethnic Serbs who were a minority in the two breakaway republics, began military offensives. The land of the South Slavs descended quickly into war.

The war in what quickly became the *former* Yugoslavia proceeded with exceptional brutality and extensive suffering among the civilian population. Slovenia managed to achieve its independence and peace after a short conflict with Serbia, but the war in Croatia through the fall of 1991 wreaked havoc.

As the Serbs ostensibly tried to protect their ethnic kin within Croatia's borders, civilians were caught in the crossfire. Most dramatically, the Serbs shelled and virtually destroyed the city of Vukovar, including the bombardment of a busy hospital that attracted international condemnation. But it was the war in Bosnia-Herzegovina that fully captured the world's attention. Many Serbs, Muslims, and Croats lived in Bosnia, but no group constituted a majority. Any ethnic battle for territory was bound to embroil the republic as a whole.

Bosnia declared its independence in April 1992, but the political leadership of the Serbs of Bosnia had already decided that they wanted no part of the new nation. Instead, they initiated plans to create their own Bosnian Serb republic under the leadership of Radovan Karadžić, a psychiatrist who had skillfully exploited national anxiety to establish a personal power base. Creating a Bosnian Serb republic, however, was no easy matter, because there was no clearly defined Serbian swath of Bosnia. There was instead a complex jumble of towns, villages, and provinces, with varying proportions of ethnic and religious composition.

The war in Bosnia-Herzegovina that began in the spring of 1992 had a highly localized, personal character. The conflict began with the support of the JNA, which was once a multiethnic institution but was now a mostly Serbian force under the ultimate control of Slobodan Milošević. Soon thereafter, a network of regional and local paramilitary, militia, and police forces, loosely coordinated but operating under a master plan inspired by Karadžić, took over the heart of the fighting.[14] In April 1992, this array of Serbian forces began to round up Muslims in villages across eastern and northern Bosnia, expelling many from their homes, detaining others, and in some cases resorting to outright killings. The story of Ibro Osmanović and his province of Vlasenica was repeated many times over. Ethnic cleansing had arrived.

In May 1992, the JNA formally withdrew from Bosnia. Milošević wished to preserve the fiction that Yugoslavia was not interfering in the affairs of its newly independent neighbor. But many units of Serbian soldiers were reorganized and constituted the core of a new army of the Bosnian Serbs. The new army's leader was General Ratko Mladić, who had previously served in the JNA. With Karadžić as the political leader and Mladić as its chief military strategist, the Bosnian Serbs proceeded to take control of 60 percent of Bosnia-Herzegovina, driving more than a million Muslims from their homes.[15] As the fighting spread across the region, Muslims and Croatians also took up arms and organized fighting units, fueling a cycle of violence and revenge that uprooted long-standing relationships and sparked brutalities on all sides of the conflict.

By the summer of 1992, the war in the Balkans—and especially the suffering of the men, women, and children of the region—was making daily headlines around the world. Three developments draw particular attention. The first was the shelling and siege of the Bosnian capital of Sarajevo, a majority-Muslim city under attack from its surrounding mountains by Mladić's Bosnian Serb army. When sixteen civilians were killed and more than one hundred injured after a shell struck a square where Sarajevans were waiting in line for precious supplies of bread, a worldwide public outcry erupted.[16] Shells, sniper fire, and limited utilities and supplies made Sarajevo, previously a symbol of Yugoslavia's multiethnic glory, a symbol instead of the brutality of war.

The second development was the revelation, later in the summer of 1992, of the network of internment camps established by the Bosnian Serbs where Muslims like Ibro Osmanović were detained in the most primitive conditions and subjected to humiliation and torture. Television news cameras captured scenes of rail-thin, half-naked prisoners crowded together behind barbed wire.[17] Comparisons to the Nazi concentration camps were inevitable. The images drew the condemnation of world leaders. The plight of Bosnians became an issue in the 1992 presidential campaign in the United States, where candidate Bill Clinton castigated President George H. W. Bush for his inaction in the face of massive suffering.

No one was enduring more in the Bosnian conflict than the region's women. Horrific descriptions of rapes and assaults against women emerged from Bosnia, thanks in part to the efforts of human rights and women's rights organizations that sought out victims and provided a setting where they could tell their stories. It was becoming clear that these sexual assaults were more than brutal acts by individual soldiers. The accounts by journalists and NGOs suggested that rape was taking place on a massive scale as part of a planned and systematic attack on the dignity and the integrity of the Bosnian Muslim people. This third development spurred visceral outrage in the arena of world opinion.

Despite the public outcry, world leaders took only paltry actions to halt the conflict and protect the men and women of the former Yugoslavia. The U.N. Security Council condemned the fighting and instituted an arms embargo; this action hurt the Muslims, who possessed much less weaponry, significantly more than it hurt the Serbs or the Croats. NATO established a no-fly zone in the region, but this zone was violated with impunity hundreds of times. Later NATO also carried out some air strikes, but these attacks, widely derided as "pinpricks," failed to deter Serb advances. U.N. peacekeeping forces were deployed in the region, but they could not be effective because there was no peace to keep. Newly elected President Clinton faced the reality, once in office, that his generals were a lot less eager to commit U.S. troops in the mountainous terrain of central Europe than they had been on the open deserts of the Persian Gulf in 1991.[18]

Out of this climate of outrage and frustration emerged a new sentiment: if the crimes could not—at that moment—be stopped, there could at least be a mechanism to punish those responsible for the atrocities still ongoing throughout Bosnia and beyond. A Serbian journalist, Mirko Klarin, farsightedly suggested as early as 1991 that a court should be established to focus on war crimes in a conflict that was then in its infancy.[19] In October 1992, the U.N. Security Council established a Commission of Experts to amass evidence regarding possible war crimes in the former Yugoslavia.[20]

By early 1993, the brand-new U.S. ambassador to the U.N., Madeleine Albright, had adopted the issue as a personal priority. Fighting opponents from both inside her government and around the world, Albright took a lead in the historic movement to hold individuals accountable for the crimes now being perpetrated in the Balkans. Within the U.S. State Department, cautious bureaucrats urged a slow approach to moving a new tribunal forward, but Albright pushed for a fast track. At a February 1993 debate in the Security Council on a resolution that would set the process of creating a court in motion, Albright made an impassioned plea for swift and certain justice. "The lesson that we are all accountable to international law may have finally taken hold in our collective memory," she said. "This will be no victor's tribunal. The only victor that will prevail in this endeavor is the truth."[21]

On May 25, 1993, expressing its "grave alarm" at "reports of mass killings, massive, organized, and systematic detention and rape of women, and the continuance of the practice of 'ethnic cleansing,'" the Security Council created a new institution with a mouthful of a formal name: the International Tribunal for the Prosecution of Persons Responsible for Serious Violations of International Humanitarian Law Committed in Territory of the Former Yugoslavia since 1991.

It was a new thing under the sun, this international tribunal. There had been nothing like it since the trials at Nuremberg, nearly half a century earlier, where many of the leaders of Nazi Germany faced a court established by the Allied victors of the war. But history, law, and circumstances in the 1990s were vastly different from those that produced convictions at Nuremberg. This new international court would have to start from scratch in its new home in the Dutch capital of The Hague.

The ICTY had a statute, hammered out in the spring of 1993 by member states of the U.N., but nothing else.[22] The statute stated that the new court would try individuals for war crimes, genocide, and crimes against humanity. The goal was to avoid the trap of collective punishment by identifying specific men and women whose actions directly led to atrocities. Yet it was not at all clear how such an institution would function while war was still raging in the region. After all, as one ICTY participant recalled later, "there was no talk about getting all these people [in the Balkans] to sit around and sing 'Kumbaya.' No, this was more punitive and deterrence, and threatening to whack them over the head that you're going to be held to account for what you're doing."[23]

The creators of the ICTY answered the problem of creating a legal institution during wartime in a novel way: by declaring that the new criminal court was itself designed to help make peace. The general expectation in international law was that courts that crossed national boundaries should be established by treaty among the participating countries. But agreements between governments take time to negotiate and be approved, so Madeleine Albright and the other framers of the ICTY used an untested strategy to bypass the cumbersome treaty process. They created the court under the provisions of Chapter VII of the U.N. Charter, the section that gave the Security Council the authority "to maintain or restore international peace and security."[24] The text said nothing specific about the establishment of an international court to preserve order, but then again it did not say that the Security Council could *not* make a court one of its tools for keeping the peace. On this thin reed, the framers of the ICTY built the future of international criminal justice.

By the fall of 1993, the U.N. had named a full complement of eleven judges, a group of distinguished lawyers whose knowledge of international law was rich but whose experience on the bench was minimal. Antonio Cassese, elected president by his fellow judges, was a towering figure in the world of legal scholarship, particularly in the law of human rights, yet he had never previously served as a judge. Brilliant and mercurial, Cassese was intensely frustrated by the fact that the judges by themselves could do absolutely nothing except draft and approve the rules of procedure for the new court. Those rules were fascinating and important as landmarks in the development of international criminal law, but by themselves they could not bring a single case or even produce a single witness.

So the judges had to wait. What they needed was a prosecutor.

The statute of the ICTY made it clear that the Security Council itself would name the chief prosecutor, acting on nominations from the U.N. secretary-general. This arrangement put the prosecutor's appointment squarely into the arena of world power politics, and politics quickly took a toll on the process.

While all of the permanent members of the Security Council voted for the establishment of the tribunal, once it came into being they found themselves at odds about what its character should be. Beneath the high-flown rhetoric about the importance of justice, not everyone actually *wanted* the tribunal to succeed. These doubts affected the process of choosing the chief prosecutor, who would be the single most important actor in the new institution.

A candidate who emerged early in the process was M. Cherif Bassiouni, a professor of law from DePaul University in Chicago who was a dual citizen of Egypt and the United States.[25] Bassiouni was already hard at work chairing the U.N.-appointed Commission of Experts that was amassing evidence on war crimes in the region. He had proved himself adept at generating resources for that project, and his passion for the quest for justice was undeniable. Madeleine Albright, pleased with Bassiouni's competence and zeal, lined up behind him in the summer of 1993, but by fall it was clear that his candidacy was going nowhere.[26] The British, his principal opponents, were reported to be concerned that he would indeed derail efforts to negotiate a peace.[27] As Bassiouni's prospects faded, the Bosnian Muslims complained publicly that the great powers were discriminating against Bassiouni because he was Muslim by background.[28]

In October 1993 the Security Council finally did agree on a compromise candidate, formally naming Ramón Escovar Salom of Venezuela to the chief prosecutor's post. Escovar Salom, however, did not show up in The Hague to assume his post until February 1994. When he finally arrived, his tenure lasted only a few days. He abandoned the ICTY to assume the post of vice president in his own country. In that short time frame, Escovar Salom did take one significant action. He appointed a deputy prosecutor for the tribunal, which would turn out to be a helpful first step. At the broader level, however, the process had to start all over again.

Over the first half of 1994, at least eight other candidates came under consideration, but without agreement among the great powers. By June that year, the situation was becoming embarrassing. It had been more than a year since the ICTY was established, and the position of chief prosecutor remained vacant. There was a skeleton staff in the prosecutor's office, thanks to the efforts of the deputy, Graham Blewitt of Australia, and the help of the U.S. government. Yet the ICTY was well on its way to coming an afterthought, if not exactly a laughingstock. The Serbs even took advantage of the lull to institute their own prosecutions for war crimes, though there was little evidence to suggest that these trials were more than a fig leaf.[29]

Antonio Cassese saw his institution wilting on the vine, and he was determined to play as active a part as he could in securing its future. In June, he spoke with Roger Errera, a French judge with whom Goldstone had come into contact during his work on the Commission.[30] Errera mentioned to Cassese that Richard Goldstone might make a good candidate for the post. Amidst a welter of bad news in 1994, the relatively peaceful transition to democracy in South Africa was a beacon of hope. Perhaps one of the engineers of that transition would be good, substantively and symbolically, for the fledgling tribunal in The Hague. The fact that Goldstone was Jewish was a positive factor as well, since it would be hard to pin him with a religious bias in favor of the Christian Serbs and Croats or the Bosnian Muslims.[31] Cassese was persuaded.

As Cassese swung into action on behalf of Goldstone's candidacy, a trio of Americans was lining up behind him as well. U.N. ambassador Madeleine Albright had encountered Goldstone during his April 1993 U.S. tour, and now two active deputies, David Scheffer and John Shattuck, also became involved. Goldstone was an English speaker, familiar with the common law, yet he was also an African, removed from the fierce political battles of continental Europe and the permanent five members of the Security Council. While Cassese secured the support of Secretary-General Boutros Boutros-Ghali, the Americans were working on their Russian counterparts.[32] If Russia vetoed yet another candidate for the post, there was a very real chance that the ICTY would never get off the ground.

Nelson Mandela made the final difference. The secretary-general asked Mandela to make calls to key members of the Security Council, taking advantage of the moral stature of the former prisoner who had peacefully liberated his country.[33] In the summer of 1994, Richard Goldstone was not alone in his predicament. Boris Yeltsin also could not say no to President Nelson Mandela.

On July 8, 1994, by unanimous vote on resolution 936, the Security Council, appointed Richard Goldstone as the chief prosecutor for the ICTY.[34] It would be up to him to bring men like Dragan Nikolić, "the God, the stick, and the law," to justice.

To the extent that anyone was paying attention anymore, Richard Goldstone's appointment was greeted warmly, though with a dose of caution. "His brilliance, his ambition, and his sense of humor" emerged as his central qualities in the international media, as they recognized the importance of the Goldstone Commission to the transition from apartheid in South Africa.[35] From the United States, the *New York Times* columnist Anthony Lewis, who had briefly covered the Commission, wrote his congratulations. "Your appointment as chief prosecutor for the Yugoslav war crimes tribunal is some good news at last from that appalling conflict," Lewis wrote in a private letter. "I shouted when I read that story in our paper this past weekend."[36]

In The Hague, Antonio Cassese was crowing. "*Habemus papem*," the Italian declared to his press officer.[37] Goldstone was not a pope, but the president saw him as a savior of sorts for the ICTY.

Beneath the accolades, however, lay a strong streak of skepticism. One newspaper declared that Goldstone will have to be a "legal Houdini" to succeed in The Hague.[38] When Goldstone encountered the former British prime minister Edward Heath at a party in Cape Town shortly after the announcement of his appointment, Heath asked with disdain, "Why did you accept such a ridiculous job?" If people wished to murder one another in someplace outside of Britain, Heath went on, it was not really his concern.[39]

As part of his preparation, Goldstone read the famous opening address by Robert Jackson at the first Nuremberg trial in 1945. Jackson, on leave from his post as a judge of the U.S. Supreme Court, was serving as the chief prosecutor for the trial of twenty-four of the top Nazi leaders in the immediate aftermath of World War II. The horrors of war, Jackson told the Nuremberg judges, "make it hard to distinguish between the demand for a just and measured retribution, and the unthinking cry for vengeance which arises from the anguish of war. It is our task, so far as humanly possible, to draw the line between the two. We must never forget that the record on which we judge these defendants today is the record on which history will judge us tomorrow."[40] Heading north to Europe, Richard Goldstone was acutely conscious that he, like Robert Jackson, would now operate under the scrutiny of history. His responsibility extended not only to a new institution, but to a whole new development in world affairs: the movement to make criminal justice global. "What makes the task so daunting," he said shortly after his arrival, "is the responsibility of being so intimately involved in an endeavor, the success or failure of which will have repercussions for this movement."[41]

7 ▸ A PATCHWORK COURT

RICHARD GOLDSTONE ENVISIONED himself at the apex of a respected new institution, with the power of nearly 200 member states of the U.N. behind him. What he found instead was a poorly funded office constrained by the rules of a global bureaucracy and further hamstrung by the ambivalence with which the international community had created the first global criminal court. Yet he also discovered a small but zealous corps of men and women on a mission to right a massive wrong that was unfolding before the world's eyes. As it turned out, Goldstone had just the temperament to channel that zeal, and the political skills to navigate the ICTY through the choppy waters of global politics.

He may have seen himself as a new Robert Jackson, but the employees of the Office of the Prosecutor (OTP) who greeted Richard Goldstone on his first full day on the job in The Hague were hard-pressed to see him that way. What they saw on August 15, 1994, was a short, stocky, balding, bespectacled man in his mid-fifties, slightly uncomfortable in his unprepossessing suit, with a manner so understated that he seemed almost shy.[1]

"Shy" was not a word that hard-driving prosecutors associated with one of their own. There were forty men and women employed in the OTP when Goldstone arrived, twenty-two of them from the United States. There was Nancy Paterson, a veteran of the sex crimes unit in the office of the Manhattan district attorney. Terree Bowers had gone after drug dealers and corrupt officials in Los Angeles. Bill Fenrick had already spent eighteen months gathering evidence on war crimes in the Balkans for the U.N.-sponsored Commission of Experts. Prosecutors prided themselves on toughness and single-mindedness. As Richard Goldstone made his way through the offices, politely greeting lawyers and administrative staff with slightly awkward courtesy, it was easy to wonder whether this man was up to the task at hand.

The skepticism heightened when the office was turned upside-down for the new prosecutor's main agenda item for the day.[2] Floodlights and bulky cameras materialized in the hallways and offices. Marching into the middle of this scene came a face familiar to all of the Americans and many of the others: the famed television journalist, Mike Wallace.

Richard Goldstone's biggest appointment on his first full day on the job was with the press, for a segment on the American weekly newsmagazine *60 Minutes*.[3] Wallace, known for his hard-hitting investigations and abrasive interviewing style on the show, was personally on hand to grill Goldstone about whether his office would be able to achieve anything at all. The newsman and the newly arrived prosecutor staged a walk down the hallway, and they set up shop for a more formal discussion in the host's still-spartan office.

Goldstone had not arranged the interview, but the timing gave rise to misinformed speculation in a nervous office of lawyers. Over the past weeks, rumors of Goldstone's ambition had made their way from South Africa to The Hague via the international press. The notion that he had accepted the appointment as prosecutor to build his international reputation had taken root in the fertile soil of office gossip, and the presumed haste to set a date with *60 Minutes* seemed to confirm the worst. On the basis of his first day on the job, the OTP staff came away with a misleading impression: that their new boss was a polite showman who looked more capable of charming the world than pursuing criminals.

For his part, what Richard Goldstone saw on his first day in The Hague was an enthusiastic group of mostly younger men and women who had nowhere near the resources that they needed to undertake an enormous job.

Fortunately, he took an immediate liking to the man on whom he would most have to depend. Goldstone had made a preliminary trip to The Hague in July to get the lay of the land.[4] On that visit, Graham Blewitt, the deputy prosecutor appointed back in February, met him at Schiphol Airport. Heavy-set and slightly disheveled, a veteran of many years of chasing former Nazis accused of war crimes in his home country of Australia, Blewitt had no idea whether his new boss would want to overturn everything he had done, or even to fire him.[5]

As they approached the waiting car at the terminal curb, Goldstone asked if he could sit on the right side of the back seat, as he was hard of hearing in his right ear. Blewitt was only too happy to acquiesce, since it was his own left ear that functioned poorly. "I guess we are made for each other," Gold-stone declared. Blewitt was happy to take this as a good omen.[6]

The offices of the ICTY had been established in one wing of a building owned by Aegon, a Dutch insurance company. The solid-stone seven-story structure faced a barren concrete plaza, off a busy boulevard lined with the ubiquitous trams and bicycles of every Dutch city. The ICTY, in its growing pains, was a jumble. In many countries, a healthy physical separation kept space between police, prosecutors, and judges, who played very different roles in the legal process. At the ICTY, they all shared the same building, separated only by stairways and doors with special passcodes. The court also had no courtroom; construction would not be completed for several months.

As for his own OTP, Goldstone sized up its shortcomings quickly. Of the forty staff members, almost half were on loan from the United States, "sec-onded" to the tribunal by a sympathetic American administration aware that this new U.N. stepchild was squeezed for funds.[7] There were desks to go around, but other infrastructure was lacking. Although this was an "interna-tional" tribunal, twenty prosecutors were forced to share the single office phone line that could make calls outside of the Netherlands.[8] Throughout the office, there were some obvious mismatches in expertise. The historian cur-rently in residence, whose work would be crucial to developing the factual con-text for the charges that the OTP would bring, did not speak Serbo-Croatian, the common language of the Balkans. The office librarian's background was not in law, but in musicology.[9]

Goldstone firmly believed that the ICTY needed immediately a change in public perception. An institution widely mocked as a "fig leaf" for inter-national inaction and marked by the press as "doomed to fail" was unlikely to generate the resources it needed. Goldstone was anxious about facing Mike Wallace and his legendary toughness, but he did not regret spending his first day (and much of his first weeks) cultivating a relationship with the press. When he arrived at the ICTY, the OTP still shared press resources with the other branches of the tribunal. So Goldstone decided that for the time being he would serve not only as the chief prosecutor for the OTP, but also as its chief spokesperson.

He was relieved when Mike Wallace went easy on him. Goldstone confidently assured the newsman that he would leave no stone unturned to ensure that the ICTY functioned efficiently. "And if it doesn't function efficiently?" Wallace asked. "Well, then," Goldstone answered, "a lot of noise will be made about it."[10] It was not clear whether the prosecutor would be making the noise, or whether the noise would be made about him.

In the throes of one of its periodic budget crises, the U.N. had tried to launch the ICTY on a shoestring, and the organization was funding the tribunal in bite-sized chunks. The U.N. did not approve initial funds until December of 1993, seven months after the formal establishment of the court, and even then only for the shortest possible time period: $5.6 million for the first half of 1994. For the second half of the year, the U.N. acted a bit earlier, approving funds for July 1 onward by April, but they approved even less than the first installment, just $5.4 million. Fortunately, in the absence of robust support from the parent institution, some member countries, including Canada, Hungary, Ireland, Malaysia, Italy, and the United States, made direct voluntary contributions.[11]

In comparison to the task at hand, the investment of $20 million in U.N. and voluntary contributions during 1994 was painfully insufficient. An international court, built from scratch, needed everything. For physical space, it needed not only a courtroom and offices, but also a prison. The OTP required not only attorneys and paralegals; in the absence of an international police force, it also needed teams of trained investigators. Someone had to pay for elaborate security arrangements to protect judges, staff, witnesses, and the defendants themselves from the dangerous tentacles of the forces still at war in the Balkans. An international institution could not function without international travel. Then there were the mind-boggling costs of translation of documents and testimony, involving not only the court's two official languages (English and French), but also the common language referred to as Serbian, Croatian, or Bosnian, depending on where one's sympathies lay. Not least, the tribunal's budget had also to include the costs of fair and qualified legal representation for the defendants.

In short, the ICTY combined all the expenses usually divided among several branches of police, political, and legal institutions that supported justice in individual countries, with the special expenses of providing clarity and fairness in an international venue. The court's political founders were the only ones who thought that this could be done on the cheap. The *Christian Science Monitor* pointed out in August 1994 that the United States had spent $75 million just to prosecute the crime boss John Gotti, and that the investigation of the federal Iran-Contra scandal had cost $40 million. Yet the first international war crimes tribunal since Nuremberg had only $550,000 at its disposal for investigations into potentially 150 cases. A lawyer experienced in the field opined at the time that "the budget they put together last year was $20 million short of what they need for a minimally credible prosecution."[12]

Once in The Hague, Goldstone continued to suffer the petty harassments of the U.N. bureaucrats. A zealous official in the administrative office of the ICTY, the Registry, questioned every travel expense and reported on Goldstone's activities to U.N. headquarters. Eventually Secretary-General Boutros Boutros-Ghali himself personally quizzed Goldstone on the purpose of his trips.[13]

Even the U.S. government's good deed of seconded personnel for the OTP did not go unpunished. It turned out that there was a rule that any gift to the U.N. must be accompanied by an additional gift of 13 percent of the value of the contribution, ostensibly to cover the U.N.'s administrative costs. When this rule was invoked in relation to the twenty-two salaries that the American government was paying for OTP personnel, the U.S. government balked at what would amount to hundreds of thousands of additional dollars. The Americans threatened to pull the seconded personnel from The Hague if the government was compelled to make this additional contribution.[14]

The new chief prosecutor could not afford to lose the core of his staff in a single stroke. He decided to confront this problem in person, traveling first to Washington, D.C., where State Department officials were sympathetic and supportive to the tribunal's plight, but told Goldstone that their hands were tied. Republicans in Congress were already using the U.N. as a political battering ram against the Clinton administration; the U.S. government would never pay an additional "tax" on a move that was already out on a political limb. In New York, Goldstone brought his case to the U.N.'s Office of Legal Affairs and to the delegations of several key countries. His personal touch paid off. The U.N. backed off its demands for overhead—for two years—and the Americans stayed.[15]

Nevertheless, the incident suggested how much perseverance and relationship-building would be essential just to keep the wheels of justice turning at the ICTY. The U.N. had looked a lot more appealing from South Africa, when its rhetoric and good offices had provided support for opponents of apartheid. Now Goldstone found himself dependent on a bureaucracy with people from 186 nations. It struck him as 186 times more difficult than any bureaucracy that a single country could spawn.[16]

Petty battles over travel itineraries and computer software might have sapped the strength of others. After all, these matters were at a far remove from the gritty tragedies of the former Yugoslavia. The court designed to bring perpetrators to justice had not even issued an indictment, much less locked up anyone in its incomplete detention facility. Meanwhile, those who were supposed to be crusading for justice were reduced to begging for reimbursements.

The trivial tiffs frustrated Richard Goldstone, but he understood them in the context of a larger framework. He did not see the law as a towering abstraction set apart from everyday realities. He knew that men like Dragan Nikolić and Radovan Karadžić would not be tried in some antiseptic chamber, where the law was applied with clinical precision. They would instead be tried in the real world, where politics at every level would be part of the process.[17] In South Africa, the guardians of the apartheid regime had held most fiercely to the tenets of positivism, of law as a "black letter" enterprise that had simply to be read and applied. The opponents of apartheid had confronted the political dimension of law, understanding that courts did not stand alone in creating the circumstances where fairness and justice could thrive. If the OTP prosecutors would be able to build cases and make arrests, they would need the cooperation of bureaucrats and politicians. Goldstone approached with zest the prospect of securing that cooperation.

Before his arrival, the court had been on the defensive, reacting to criticisms of slowness and inaction. Goldstone mounted a campaign to project himself as a vigorous leader. He cultivated a strong working relationship with Christian Chartier, a former correspondent of France's *Le Monde* who was hired before his arrival as the ICTY's official press officer. Chartier formally reported to the president of the court and the registrar, but Goldstone strategically integrated him into the work of the OTP. He invited the press officer to the prosecution's daily staff meetings—the only invitee from outside of the prosecutor's office. "In order to know what he *can* say," Goldstone explained to his lawyer colleagues, "Christian must know all that he should *not* say."[18]

Understanding that the court needed a face, Goldstone offered his own, speaking in a manner that suggested that his remarks were virtually self-evident. Men have committed crimes and they will be held accountable, he told the press, just as criminals are held accountable in every civilized society in the world. "I have no doubt from my experience that there's only one way to stop criminal conduct in any country . . . ," he explained to the *Guardian*. "If would-be criminals think they're going to be caught and punished, they're going to think twice. It's no different in the international sphere."[19] Goldstone refused to give the press off-the-record insights or glimpses into the inner workings of the prosecutor's office, but he promised indictments in the coming months.[20]

Goldstone's American supporters appreciated the importance of the prosecutor's role in the media, but they were not convinced that he was fully up to the task. On one of Goldstone's first trips to Washington, D.C., Madeleine Albright arranged for him to undertake an intensive session in media training at the Pentagon. In practice sessions, his trainers told him to speak up, to lift his head higher, and to avoid saying "I think" because it suggested uncertainty. When he left the room believing that he was heading outside for a break, he was ambushed by a gaggle of faux reporters who thrust microphones in his face and tested his ability to think quickly on his feet and parry their thrusts.[21] Goldstone suspected that he would never be a mesmerizing public performer, but he learned to match his warm personal style with a more confident dignity. In the end, his refusal to overplay to the cameras projected a kind of moral stature that served him and the ICTY well.

As a part of his strategy, he adopted an identity that would affirm his gravitas: at the court and in the press, he asked to be known as "Justice Goldstone." He had not yet served for even a day as a justice of the Constitutional Court of his home country, but the title was a distinct improvement on the alternatives. A mere "Mr." Goldstone would look weak and diminished amidst the powerful forces around him. He initially suggested "Judge Goldstone," since he had held that title in South Africa for a quarter century, but Antonio Cassese and other members of the ICTY bench objected that this title could potentially undermine their own status as the actual judges of the tribunal. The moniker of "Justice Goldstone" sent a message of authority, and equally important, a message of independence.[22] As a "justice," he could be seen as accountable only to the law, not to the other people and institutions who might want to direct or curtail his efforts.[23]

Securing the cooperation of Western nations consumed much of Goldstone's time in his first months at the OTP. In the United States, enthusiasm for pursuing war criminals was tempered in parts of the administration by cross-cutting considerations. The U.S. military, for example, had extensive intelligence that could contain vital evidence to implicate high-ranking leaders in the former Yugoslavia, but the idea of sharing such evidence with an international body did not sit well with defense leaders, who worried about compromising their intelligence assets. Goldstone began discussions in the fall of 1994 to secure cooperation on sharing information with the ICTY. These conversations were the beginning of a long and painstaking process, but they led within five months of Goldstone's arrival to a remarkable arrangement. The U.S. government agreed to provide classified satellite imagery to the ICTY, as long as Goldstone and his staff created a series of safeguards to ensure limited access to the evidence, and with the understanding that any use of the evidence in legal proceedings had to be approved in advance.

In symbolic terms, the most important trip of the fall of 1994 was to the former Yugoslavia itself, a journey for which Goldstone depended heavily on U.N. and NATO cooperation.[24] Traveling with Graham Blewitt, he visited all three capitals: Belgrade in Serbia, Zagreb in Croatia, and Sarajevo in Bosnia-Herzegovina. In each city Goldstone sought permission for the ICTY to set up local field offices as regional headquarters for investigations. Without a local presence, the court's ability to acquire evidence would be severely limited. The two prosecutors tried to achieve this through meetings with high-ranking officials, but they made an upfront decision that they would not meet with the presidents of any of the countries.[25] There would be no front-page photograph of Richard Goldstone shaking the hand of Slobodan Milošević—or any other major political leader whom the ICTY might eventually investigate.

The leaders in each country predictably showed interest only in the collection of evidence against the other side. In Belgrade, Goldstone was taken to an official mortuary, where a curt and angry physician showed him albums with photographs of hundreds of mutilated corpses whom the doctor claimed were Serbian victims of atrocities committed by the Muslims. "Those are the crimes that you must investigate," the doctor insisted. "Whose dead bodies are they? And where were the crimes committed?" the prosecutor fired back. The doctor had no answers to these questions, but the Serbian press nevertheless crowed that hard evidence of Muslim war crimes had been turned over to the ICTY.[26]

Traveling in and out of Bosnia-Herzegovina in wartime was precarious. The Bosnian Serbs still controlled the mountains around the city of Sarajevo, and the airport was closed, so arrival by helicopter was the only option. Goldstone and Blewitt decided to hitch a ride to Sarajevo with U.N. special representative Yasushi Akashi, who was actually en route to negotiate with the Serbs to allow the airport to be reopened. Akashi tried to dissuade Goldstone from coming along, stressing that it was a highly volatile and dangerous situation. Goldstone insisted on making the trip. "I felt that it was unacceptable for me to send people on my staff to places that I would not visit myself," he said later.[27] As they boarded the helicopter in the Croatian city of Split, the pilot told the men not to bother putting on the flak jackets that they found on their designated seats. They should sit on them instead. "The bullets," the pilot explained, "come from below."[28]

Upon arrival in Sarajevo, their helicopter was surrounded by tanks to protect them from snipers. Goldstone found the city beaten but unbowed. More than two years of artillery fire had flattened whole neighborhoods, and Sarajevo's famous atmosphere of open-air cafés had been reduced to makeshift enclaves amidst the destruction. The ICTY delegation received a warm welcome. Goldstone admired the resilience and sense of purpose of the men and women he met there. The Bosnian Muslim authorities were eager to cooperate, and they backed their words up with actions. They believed, after all, that Serbian atrocities against their people would be the center of the ICTY's attention. The establishment of a field office for the OTP in Sarajevo, with the full cooperation of the Bosnian authorities, was the single tangible accomplishment of the trip.[29]

Goldstone returned to The Hague at the end of October with a renewed sense of purpose. He had had a firsthand glimpse at the costs of the war in the Balkans. While he did not have the chance to look Slobodan Milošević in the eye, he did have the opportunity to put Serbs, Croatians, and Muslims alike on personal notice that the ICTY was a force to be reckoned with, and that their actions were being watched. How seriously the warring parties would take this warning was a matter of debate. But Justice Goldstone could now bring the authority of firsthand experience to the ongoing battle for the prestige and legitimacy of the court.

The chief prosecutor's luncheon and travel schedule riled some of the staff back in The Hague.[30] They understood the delicate politics, but the leader's frequent absences created a leadership vacuum. Goldstone empowered Graham Blewitt, for all intents and purposes, to run the OTP.[31] The jovial Australian had little interest in taking center stage in the public eye, and he was happiest in trying to bring a sense of order and coherence to the work of the tribunal. He embarked on a not entirely successful quest to make the OTP a paperless office, taking advantage of the American-funded computer system and recent strides in data management technology. He started to assemble the teams of investigators and lawyers who would develop the cases. And Blewitt took upon himself the job of maintaining office morale, especially in presiding over Friday afternoon staff gatherings in The Hague's poor attempts at pubs.[32] Goldstone's frequent absences meant that inevitably the chief prosecutor "floated above" the day-to-day operations of the office, as one lawyer recalled. "He didn't have the time or the inclination to deal with day-to-day matters."[33] An undercurrent of frustration ran through the OTP in the first part of the fall of 1994, as some of the lawyers wondered whether their boss had a full handle on the magnitude of the task before them.[34]

For the Goldstones, husband and wife, living in The Hague provided a welcome change from the high tension of the previous five years in South Africa. The city had a calm and cosmopolitan atmosphere that had never been possible in apartheid-era Johannesburg or Cape Town. In addition to hosting the seat of the government of the Netherlands, The Hague had for the last century been home to a burgeoning number of international institutions, especially in the areas of international peace and global justice.

Despite the presence in the city of a diverse collection of ambassadors, judges, and other officials from around the world, The Hague had a well-earned reputation for being staid and a bit boring. The Dutch capital offered quiet lanes of brick houses, tree-lined parkways, a spectacular dune-strewn beach on the North Sea, and, in the center of town, the Mauritshuis, home to Vermeer's *Girl with a Pearl Earring* and Fabritius's *Goldfinch*. But the restaurant selection was limited, with some establishments closing their doors as early as 9:00 P.M.—quite a shock to first-time visitors from cultures where an "early" evening meal was unlikely to start before 10:00 P.M. Young people flocked to Amsterdam. The Hague was a more comfortable place for older people of steady habits.

This meant that The Hague suited Richard and Noleen Goldstone just fine. Noleen found an apartment for the two of them on Jozef Israëlsplein, a quiet square which they were pleased to learn was named for a nineteenth-century Jewish painter who was a leader in The Hague school of artists. By now, Glenda was married and living in South Africa, while Nicky had taken up residence in Israel, happily living out of the shadow of her father, the famous judge.[35] The Goldstones' social life, carefully cultivated by Noleen, connected them with members of the international community who could be useful to the chief prosecutor's work.

On October 2, 1994, *60 Minutes* aired the segment that included the interview that Mike Wallace conducted with Goldstone on his first day at the OTP. "In the year and a half since the U.N. voted to establish a war crimes tribunal," Wallace intoned in the introduction, "no one has been tried; no one has even been indicted. And the skeptics suggest that this whole tribunal, with its judges already on salary and its courtroom under construction, that this whole multimillion-dollar enterprise is not just an exercise in futility, but worse: that it's an exercise in hypocrisy."[36] Wallace portrayed the ICTY as an institution so blatantly underfunded that it seemed that its creators did not really want it to succeed. "The fact is that as the wanton atrocities continued in the former Yugoslavia, in makeshift offices in the headquarters of an insurance company in The Hague, the UN War Crimes Tribunal limped along, an underfunded, unwanted, stunted creation."

Richard Goldstone was pleased to see that, as the newcomer, he came off relatively well. Wallace gave Goldstone the chance to make a not so subtle plea to the great powers that he would need their help in actually locating and arresting those who were charged. Yet the *60 Minutes* segment, with its prominent visibility in the country that had been most supportive to date of the tribunal, was another reminder that the pressure was on for the prosecutor to deliver. Nothing could prevent the Security Council from pulling the plug on the ICTY if powerful governments lost confidence or simply had a change of heart.

8 ▸ BIG FISH, LITTLE FISH

Not Long after Richard Goldstone arrived in The Hague, the man who had most badly coveted his job showed up to offer his counsel. M. Cherif Bassiouni arrived at Goldstone's invitation to talk the new prosecutor through the findings of the U.N.-appointed Commission of Experts that he had chaired. In June 1994, shortly before Goldstone's appointment, Bassiouni had sent 65,000 documents, hundreds of hours of videotape, and a massive computer database from the commission's headquarters in Chicago to The Hague. The empty files and offices at the ICTY now brimmed with narratives of violence and suffering.

Bassiouni arrived for his meeting with Goldstone in the guise of a professor offering a lecture for a single, untutored pupil. The American scholar had been researching crimes in the former Yugoslavia for almost two years, and he was confident that he was significantly more knowledgeable than the mild-mannered South African he encountered in the old insurance building. Bassiouni claimed to be horrified to find that there was not even a map of the former Yugoslavia handy in the prosecutor's office. "Fortunately, I had brought maps," Bassiouni wrote later, "as well as the necessary information for him and his staff to get started with." This was nonsense, especially because members of Bassiouni's own investigative team were now working at the OTP. Nevertheless, Bassiouni showed no reluctance to dispense detailed advice about what he considered the obvious lines of prosecution that Goldstone and his office should pursue, building on the commission's collected documents.[1]

When Bassiouni arrived in his office, the new chief prosecutor listened respectfully and refused to bristle at his visitor's manner. Indeed, the two men became instant friends. Justice Goldstone was happy for advice from any place he could get it, and he was genuinely grateful for the commission's trove of materials. But the bulk of the commission's testimony was not immediately useful. 'They put together a good dossier, a good starting point," recalled Nancy Paterson, one of the American lawyers seconded to the OTP, "but so much of their information was hearsay, second hand, was not anything we could corroborate."[2] While the commission's documents included names of hundreds of alleged perpetrators, the direct connections between the specific crimes and the individuals who committed them were weak or nonexistent.[3] When it came to the "big fish," the commission had been oddly cautious. Its final report contained general language about the likelihood that political and military superiors directed campaigns of violence, but it scarcely mentioned the names of Milošević, Karadžić, and Mladić.[4]

In addition to the report from the commission, Goldstone and his staff were trying to make sense of another onslaught of information, mostly from the government of Bosnia. The Bosnians had their own list of 5,000 alleged war criminals, as well as a compendium of dozens of physical sites of mass murders that required analysis and follow-up.[5] Goldstone needed to figure out how best to organize the OTP to turn narratives of horror into evidence of guilt.

At the broadest level, there was a prior question: the nature of international criminal law itself. The courts of the United States, Great Britain, France, and South Africa were built on hundreds of years of precedent and practice. A trial of a thief or a murderer took place in the historical context of thousands of other such trials. The ICTY, on the other hand, operated in a legal vacuum. The tribunal had a legally binding statute, and its judges had created rules and procedures, but when it came to how exactly a criminal case should be built and what its legal foundation should be, the path was far from clear. The court had the bare outline of a roadmap in its founding documents, and it had the example of history.

When Richard Goldstone traveled to Nuremberg, Germany, to attend a conference on war crimes, he visited Room 600 in the famous building where, fifty years earlier, the most famous war crime trials in human history had taken place.[6] He took in the impressive paneling, the somber German architectural projection of authority. Because Room 600 was still a working courtroom, Goldstone regretted that he did not have the opportunity to stand in the spot where Robert Jackson had delivered his famous opening address.

In the dock in 1945 were twenty-one military and political leaders of the Nazi regime charged with dozens of counts of war crimes and crimes against humanity. They included some of the most infamous figures in Nazi Germany: Hermann Göring, Rudolf Hess, Joachim von Ribbentrop, and Albert Speer, among others. Conspicuously absent were the masterminds of Nazi aggression and the Holocaust, Adolf Hitler and Heinrich Himmler, who had escaped capture by committing suicide before the Allies could catch up with them. Robert Jackson made it clear in his address in November 1945 that the purpose of the trials was to "reach the planners and designers, the inciters and leaders without whose evil architecture the world would not have been for so long scourged with the violence and lawlessness, and wracked with the agonies and convulsions, of this terrible war."[7]

Nuremberg proceeded in a formal trial setting, with multinational participation. Although they had the political, legal, and military resources of four victorious nations arrayed against them, the prisoners also had recourse to legal counsel, and they had the opportunity to mount a vigorous defense. The results indeed suggested distinctions in standards of proof and degrees of responsibility: nineteen were convicted, three were found not guilty. Among those convicted, twelve were sentenced to death, while seven served terms in prison.

Yet there was no follow-up to Nuremberg for almost half a century. While the Genocide Convention of 1948 and the Fourth Geneva Convention of 1949 codified the strongest protections for civilians that the international community had ever created, no institutions were created to apply those laws. During the middle decades of the twentieth century, international courts were developed for other purposes: to adjudicate disputes between nations, and to provide individuals with recourse if their human rights were violated by their own governments.[8] Proposals to develop a court that might hold individuals responsible for war crimes or crimes against humanity went nowhere.

Two aspects of Nuremberg struck Richard Goldstone as particularly important. The first was that the proceedings had helped to establish the principle of universal jurisdiction: some crimes were of such magnitude and so contrary to the universal values of humankind that they transcended the normal legal boundaries of national borders. The second aspect of Nuremberg that Goldstone found compelling was the idea of individual criminal responsibility. No longer, after Nuremberg, could leaders take moral or legal refuge in the defense that their criminal acts were simply a fulfillment of their responsibilities to the nation.[9]

Important as these principles were, Goldstone also understood that, public perception aside, the ICTY was quite different from Nuremberg. In the aftermath of World War II, the Allies had occupied Germany and therefore had complete access to documents and witnesses that implicated the defendants, a striking contrast to the challenges of gathering evidence in a country still embroiled in war. On the other hand, the ICTY was a more genuinely international institution, with a stronger foundation in law and practice. Whereas Nuremberg was established by the winners of a war, the ICTY was founded by a unanimous vote of the Security Council of the U.N. It could therefore claim more genuine international authority and demonstrate global representation among its judiciary and its staff. The ICTY also had the advantage of a half century of further codification of international law, and the credibility of a formal statute and rules of procedure.

In September 1994, Goldstone met for the first time with the judges of the ICTY in their plenary session. In other circumstances, it might be seen as inappropriate—and sometimes outright wrong—for a prosecutor to meet in closed session with the judges before whom he would appear in court. But Goldstone considered the ICTY an exception, as did President Cassese. There were good reasons for breaking the usual rules that separated the functions of a legal system. The ICTY was a court-in-formation, and there were certain basic matters of law and structure and practice that needed to be ironed out. A quiet conversation between the principals might be more effective than sorting out these matters in the complex circumstances of a public trial. Furthermore, the tribunal operated under a mixture of rules adopted from different legal systems. The civil law system, familiar to Judge Cassese and other judges from continental Europe, drew less firm distinctions between the prosecution and the judiciary than did the English-based common law, allowing for freer conversation. In any case, Goldstone reasoned, in the fall of 1994 there were no ongoing trials, so no defendants' rights could be compromised right now by so-called ex parte communications.

The judges pressed Goldstone hard from the beginning about pursuing the Serbian leadership. Two others, besides Cassese himself, were most vocal. Georges Abi-Saab, like the court president one of the top law scholars in the world, had privately backed Cherif Bassiouni to be the ICTY's first prosecutor. He now made it clear that he expected Goldstone to pursue Milošević with at least the fervor that he would have expected from his longtime friend. The French judge, Claude Jorda, aligned himself with those who were telling Goldstone how to do his job; among other things, Jorda had been irritated that the international community did not appoint a chief prosecutor who spoke French. These early skirmishes presaged deeper conflicts to come.

The ICTY prosecutors had no paper trail and no clear route to establishing the responsibility of the commanders. By necessity Goldstone and Graham Blewitt adopted what they called a "pyramid" strategy. If the court could identify and try lower-level commanders who had direct responsibility for crimes committed in specific villages and regions, the prosecutors could assemble tighter, fact-based, winnable cases. The facts established in those cases would become part of the legal record establishing beyond doubt that war crimes and crimes against humanity had been perpetrated in the region. Lower-level figures might be persuaded to testify against their superiors. Successful prosecutions of "little fish" would then provide the basis for indictments against the men at the top of the pyramid.

The pyramid strategy struck even some of Goldstone's supporters as a timid approach to the inauguration of international criminal justice. Aryeh Neier, a human rights advocate who had supported the ICTY financially through his leadership of the Open Society Foundation, believed that prosecuting low-level figures was "wholly apposite" to the situation. Perhaps this would work in fighting organized crime in a domestic situation, Neier said, but "this was not a situation where plea bargaining was going to work."[10]

Meanwhile, a more immediate concern loomed. Goldstone had a date with the heart of the U.N. bureaucracy in New York. He was scheduled to appear in December before the Advisory Committee on Administrative and Budgetary Questions, known by its awkward acronym, ACABQ.[11] This was the committee that for all intents and purposes controlled the U.N.'s purse strings. In New York, Goldstone would have to beg for funds to continue the ICTY's work into 1995. As early as September, when he had been on the job for only a month, word was already filtering back to the prosecutor through the back channels of the U.N. system: If the OTP failed to issue a public indictment before December, the ACABQ might well recommend cutting off funding altogether.

In 1994, Ibro Osmanović was living in Sweden, having made his way out of Bosnia after detention in Sušica and his eventual release from the Batković camp in 1993. The OTP investigators reached him there and took a formal statement of what he saw and experienced in Sušica, and of what he knew about the actions of the commander of the camp there. Because Sušica was in eastern Bosnia, freed Muslims in that part of the country had an easier escape route to Germany and other countries outside the former Yugoslavia. OTP investigators also found Redjo Cakisić, who had been detained at Sušica at the same time at Osmanović, and who provided more details about the death of Durmo Handžić. They tracked down a woman named Zehra Smajlović who saw Nikolić beat and humiliate the prisoner Fikret "Cice" Arnaut.[12] The OTP also obtained crucial information from a former guard at Sušica, Pero Popović, who had first told his story to the *New York Times* in the summer of 1994.[13] The outlines of a narrative began to take shape. It might be challenging to build a case against Milošević, but the investigating team at the OTP was now constructing the story of Dragan Nikolić, the commander of the Sušica camp who had blood literally on his hands.

In October in The Hague, Goldstone and Blewitt assembled their core leadership team. Were they ready to go with an indictment on Nikolić? The OTP attorneys were hesitant. There were at least three powerful reasons that acting against Nikolić was a bad idea. First, the case against him was not really ready to go. Having a lot of interview statements was not the same thing as a fully developed basis for prosecution. Second, Nikolić was not in custody, and there was absolutely no prospect that he would be brought to The Hague any time soon.

Goldstone decided that he could dismiss those first two concerns with a single argument. Since it was likely true that the ICTY was not going to have Nikolić in its prison in the near future, there would be plenty of time for the OTP to fill in the gaps in the case in the period between the indictment and any future arrest. In other words, the OTP did not have to be trial-ready in order to issue an indictment.

The third argument against indicting Nikolić was harder to dismiss. Nikolić was the commander of a single camp in a single corner of Bosnia for a contained period during 1992. As such, he was the very definition of a "little fish."

Would indicting him only serve to confirm the suspicion that the ICTY was no more than a paper tiger?

Goldstone felt that he had to take that chance. After all, the story of Sušica, as experienced by Ibro Osmanović and the other witnesses, was a compelling microcosm of the experience of the Bosnian Muslims. The ethnic cleansing of the town of Vlasenica, the arbitrary detention, the midnight beatings, the rapes of women prisoners, and the callous killings of the weakened men— these reflected real experiences of real victims of Serbian atrocities. Although some of the attorneys argued that they were not yet ready to go, the chief prosecutor insisted that his office move forward with the formal charges.

On November 4, 1994, Judge Elizabeth Odio Benito, acting on behalf of the ICTY judges, formally confirmed the indictment of Dragan Nikolić on charges of persecution, murder, and grave breaches of the Geneva Conventions.[14] A warrant was issued for his arrest and was faxed to Pale, the self-proclaimed capital of the republic of the Bosnian Serbs. Everyone at the OTP knew that the warrant would be ignored.

Fewer than three months after Goldstone's arrival, an international court had issued formal charges of war crimes and crimes against humanity against an individual for the first time since Nuremberg. The prosecutor himself conceded later that the Nikolić case "was a most inappropriate first indictment for an international criminal court," but it was a start.[15]

The Nikolić indictment was not the only start. There was another "little fish" in the ICTY's waters, and this one was actually in a net.

In the winter of 1994, six months before Richard Goldstone came to The Hague, rumors began to fly among the Bosnian Muslims who had escaped their war-torn country and were now living in exile in Munich. Many refugees in Munich had come from the Prijedor region, in northwest Bosnia, and some of those had lived through the hellish conditions in Omarska, a notorious detention camp that had come to international attention in 1992. Now some people swore that that they had spotted around town a self-important figure known to former prisoners as the "Butcher of Omarska."

His name was Duško Tadić. Before the war, Tadić, a Serb, had owned a pub in Kozarac, a Muslim-majority town in the Prijedor region. When the Bosnian Serbs began their campaign of ethnic cleansing in the area, Tadić was on hand to help identify targets for the shelling of his town and identify

Muslim leaders as targets for detention or even execution. When the detention camps were established at Omarska and nearby Trnopolje, Tadić provided muscle and brutality. Without any formal position in the Bosnian Serb hierarchy, he acquired a reputation as a hands-on organizer and dispenser of terror and murder. According to one story, Tadić had once forced a man to drink motor oil and then bite off the testicles of an unconscious fellow prisoner. No one could say what he was doing in Munich, but his appearance sent a shiver of fear and anger through the Bosnian exile community.

A television producer managed to capture some footage of Tadić on a Munich street and turned the tape over to the German authorities. On February 13, 1994, the German police arrested Tadić outside his brother's flat, holding him under German law on suspicion of murder, aiding and abetting genocide, and causing grievous bodily harm.[16]

Through the spring of 1994, before Goldstone's arrival, Graham Blewitt tracked Tadić's situation from The Hague. Here was one live person, apparently responsible for brutal crimes in the region, who was now in custody but still out of reach of the ICTY. In the absence of a chief prosecutor, however, there was little that Blewitt could do. After his arrival, Goldstone decided to ask Germany formally to defer to the ICTY and to transfer Duško Tadić to The Hague.

In February 1995, the ICTY issued an indictment charging Tadić with thirty-four counts, including murder, rape, and torture. But it was not until March 31, 1995, that the Bundestag finally passed the law allowing for his extradition. In April 1995, Tadić was moved to The Hague, where he became the first prisoner to be housed in the ICTY detention facility in Scheveningen, a short ride from the seaside parkland where Richard and Noleen Goldstone sometimes bicycled through the dunes.

When Richard Goldstone arrived at The Hague, he found hundreds of letters, reports, and other correspondence waiting for him, urging the ICTY to make the prosecution of rape one of its highest priorities.[17] He was touched by these missives, often in broken English, that told horrifying stories and recounted the ways in which women's narratives had been dismissed and ignored by others.

In the 1990s, rape occupied a murky legal ground in the international sphere. Forced sex was a crime in every society during peacetime. In the context of war, however, rape had generally been seen as regrettable but inevitable, as an individual crime committed by individual men against individual women (and sometimes against individual men). The traditional view was that rape in wartime was not materially different from rape in peacetime—a personal crime for which individuals should be punished domestically, not as a war crime. Despite the well-known prevalence of sexual violence during World War II, rape played no part in the Nuremberg trials.[18]

In recent years, however, advocates for women had begun to see rape in wartime in a different light—not as an individual crime, but as an actual tool of warfare. Broader documentation of the horrors of military campaigns, reporting and commentary by feminist writers, and an expanding body of international human rights law all contributed to this new perspective. If rape was not just about sex but also about power, and if it was used to create fear and humiliation among the civilian population, then, many people began to argue, rape should be seen and punished not as an ordinary crime but as a violation of the laws of war. The public outcry over Bosnia brought this line of thinking to the highest circles of the international community. In its 1993 resolutions on Bosnia, and in the statute of the ICTY, the U.N. Security Council described rape as a war crime and as a crime against humanity.[19] Responsibility could theoretically be attributed not only to the actual violator, but also to the political and military leaders who tolerated or even encouraged sexual violence as part of their overall strategy.

The ICTY judges took this process a step further. When they wrote the court's rules of procedure, they determined that in the case of rape there was no need for corroboration of the victim's testimony by another eyewitness, that consent was not a permissible defense against a rape charge, and that the prior sexual conduct of a victim was not admissible evidence.[20] Still, the actual legal basis of prosecuting rape as a war crime remained uncertain. What would be the actual difference in court between prosecuting rape as an ordinary crime and as a war crime? What evidence would be necessary, and who would bear the burden of proof? How high up the chain of command could rape charges be sustained?

A determined movement of individuals and organizations outside the ICTY kept up a steady drumbeat of pressure to call attention to these questions. NGOs, including Physicians for Human Rights, the Jacob Blaustein Institute, and Amnesty International provided documentation of crimes committed against women in the Balkans, as well as offering Goldstone and his fellow prosecutors advice on how best to approach these issues legally.

Typically, Goldstone approached this problem not as a matter of theory but as a matter of practice. The letters from women around the world had a common theme: the ways in which their complaints and accounts had so frequently been dismissed and ignored by male policemen, judges, and other guardians of the law.[21] At the ICTY, he realized that he was in danger of repeating the pattern. The band of ICTY investigators was almost all men, a kind of club of professional policemen accustomed to a shared environment of insular male jocularity. "In just about every country they came from, there was a very macho, anti-feminist attitude," Goldstone recalled later. "It was nothing malicious. It was just rooted in their cultures."[22] One Friday afternoon, Goldstone joined the investigators for their weekly beer, where he heard the men trading sly and demeaning jokes about women. He clinked his glass and reprimanded them, asking the African men in the group pointedly how they would feel if similar jokes were being told at the expense of blacks.[23]

An allegation of sexual harassment within the OTP stirred Goldstone to stronger action. He created a new position within the office—gender affairs adviser—and recruited an American lawyer who had recently arrived in the office named Patricia Sellers to the position. Sellers's first task was internal—to figure out how to create a climate of mutual respect and equality between the genders within the office. If the OTP was going to be successful in investigating and prosecuting gender crimes, it would have to set its own house in order. The atmosphere in the ICTY was not only very masculine, but peopled with professionals "who had been used to working mainly with males too in their home jurisdiction," Sellers recalled. "Also, they assumed that it was normal for men to be in charge. They also felt it was absolutely normal in the crux of our job—when a war occurred—that they were to look for 'who killed the dead bodies,' not where there was sexual violence. They essentially transferred their domestic police outlook to the international arena."[24] Sellers proved skillful at changing the atmosphere at the OTP, and her role quickly expanded to include developing an overall strategy for prosecuting gender crimes across the OTP's caseload.

Women's rights and gender crimes were not at the center of Richard Goldstone's attention before he came to The Hague. As a judge in South Africa, his rulings had not always shown the greatest sympathy to women's perspectives. But he understood quickly at The Hague that his success as a prosecutor would be intimately tied to how much justice the women of Bosnia would receive. If rape was recognized—and proved—as a war crime, the ICTY would be striking a novel blow for justice for women everywhere.[25]

By the end of 1994, just over four months into his term as chief prosecutor, Richard Goldstone could point to tangible progress at the ICTY. One indictment had been filed. One defendant was in custody (though it would take four more months before Duško Tadić arrived in The Hague). These steps were enough to convince the ACABQ in December to increase its appropriation to the ICTY, although it would not be until July that the budget for 1995 was finalized.[26] The New York Times, once skeptical about the tribunal's achievements, published an editorial urging that the ICTY continue full-speed ahead.[27] Yet with a dozen ongoing investigations stretching the OTP staff thin, the real challenges for the Goldstone and the ICTY had only just begun.

9 ▸ THE PAPER TIGER

BY THE BEGINNING of 1995, the gap between the ICTY's modest achievements and the expectations for the tribunal remained large. So Richard Goldstone's initial successes as prosecutor did little to ease the pressures on him and the court. Indeed, the prosecutor discovered that the existential threats to the ICTY, masked in the flurry of activity in the fall of 1994, were more powerful than ever. Over the course of 1995 and into the first half of 1996, Goldstone felt the burden of carrying the tribunal on his shoulders as he parried one crisis after another.

The first crisis began with the restless judges. As the calendar turned from 1994 to 1995, they were determined to turn up the temperature on the prosecutor, whom they felt should be more aggressive in pursuing charges against the Serbian leadership.

The nine men and two women on the ICTY bench had been elected in the fall of 1993 by a vote of the U.N. General Assembly.[1] Some were distinguished scholars of international law or human rights, such as Georges Abi-Saab, an Egyptian who had spent most of his career in Geneva, teaching international law and playing an active role in the emerging U.N. human rights structure based in the Swiss city. Others had served as judges in their own countries, like Ninian Stephen of Australia, who had moved nimbly between judicial, executive, and diplomatic posts over the course of his career. The United States, which had supported the creation of the ICTY so strongly, had successfully pushed for the election of Gabrielle Kirk McDonald, the first African American woman to be appointed as a judge in Texas, and only the third black woman to serve as a federal judge anywhere in the country. Four of the eleven, including Abi-Saab, hailed from majority-Muslim nations, a fact of significance to the Bosnians. By design, there were no judges from any part of the former Yugoslavia itself.[2]

In early 1995, Antonio Cassese began to assert himself even more strongly in relation to the work of the OTP. Cassese had been elected president by his fellow judges in November 1993, and in that role he saw himself not only as a judge (he served on the appeals chamber) but also as the man responsible for the overall direction of the ICTY.

In fact, things had started well personally between Richard Goldstone and Antonio Cassese. Thrilled to have a prosecutor in place at last, Cassese had made the Goldstones feel at home in The Hague. Goldstone realized that after a year of waiting "anyone with two legs and two eyes would have been warmly welcomed," but he was still gratified by the lunch that the judges gave in his honor at the Promenade Hotel and by the social invitations that he and Noleen received from the court president.[3] Richard and Noleen began to spend a lot of time with Antonio Cassese and his wife Silvia. Professionally, the men shared a passion for using the law on behalf of the underdog. Personally, Silvia's background as a Jewish survivor of the Holocaust gave the couples an added bond.[4]

Temperamentally, it seemed sometimes as though their roles at the ICTY were reversed. Cassese, impulsive, unpredictable, visibly zealous, and given to showy rhetoric, seemed more cut out for the role of a prosecutor.[5] Goldstone's streak of passion ran below the surface, and his style of commonsense understatement seemed more in tune with the role of a judge.

The two men were collaborators, sharing a single-mindedness about the success of the tribunal, but they were also competitors. Each man aspired to be the "face" of the ICTY in the press. In this competition, Goldstone was the clear winner. At this stage, it was the prosecutor who was gathering evidence and developing the tribunal's storyline, so the press naturally saw Goldstone in the leading role. When the BBC mistakenly referred to Goldstone as the "head" of the ICTY, Cassese stormed into the tribunal's media office and ordered the press secretary to call London immediately and order a retraction.[6] Their competitive spirit spilled over into more trivial matters as well. On one occasion, the two men were together in New York to report to the U.N. One observer remembered Goldstone's smile of triumph after he managed to secure a place on a trans-Atlantic Concorde jet and arrive back at the tribunal hours ahead of Cassese.[7]

In early 1995, their differences over strategy and tactics took a more serious turn, and it began to fray the professional side of their relationship.[8] At Cassese's invitation, Goldstone had attended plenary meetings of the judges during the last months of 1994. The prosecutor had found their impatience to move forward understandable and manageable.[9] He was happy to receive the documents and suggestions that they were sending to the OTP in writing. He explained to them as clearly as he could the steps that the OTP was taking, and he politely but firmly drew lines when he felt that the judges' suggestions were shading into thinly veiled orders.

The primary issue was clear: Why had the prosecutor not made more progress in going after Milošević, Karadžić, and Mladić? Goldstone patiently described his method of building the cases against the leadership from the ground up. Many of the judges were unconvinced. "With a little luck," Cassese said sarcastically, "in fifteen years, after you have mounted the entire military hierarchy, you might manage to trap a general."[10]

As a show of good will, on January 27, 1995, Goldstone submitted to the judges a program of projected indictments for the period of February through June 1995. He promised at least one indictment every month, beginning with Duško Tadić and others in February. This document was itself a significant concession by the prosecutor, but Goldstone could not in good faith promise that indictments of the three main leaders were immediately forthcoming. Cassese and the other judges were unappeased, saying that "we all felt that the [planned] indictments were not congruent with the extreme seriousness of the crimes."[11]

Behind the scenes, Cassese—with Abi-Saab and Jorda as his principal collaborators—began to conduct a campaign to undermine Goldstone within the U.N. Cassese sent a "report on the judges' unhappiness" with the prosecutor's strategy to the U.N.'s Office of Legal Affairs, and then to Secretary-General Boutros-Ghali. Cassese and Abi-Saab followed up their written report with an in-person, off-the-record meeting with the secretary-general in

New York. Their agenda: to report in person on the chief prosecutor's alleged foot-dragging on the "big fish," and to discuss the prosecutor's contract and whether or not Richard Goldstone should remain in the position.[12] It was likely that the judges were taking the extraordinary and unethical step of trying to get an independent prosecutor fired.[13]

At first, Richard Goldstone took no action in response to the judges' extracurricular meetings, either because he did not know about them or because he decided to pretend not to know. He was not worried about losing his job. He had been appointed by the fifteen member states of the U.N. Security Council. The secretary-general did not, in fact, have the power to fire him.

Whether driven by the judges' pressure or his own sense of mission, Goldstone did act with urgency during the first months of 1995. On February 13, the OTP announced the indictments of Duško Tadić and twenty other individuals for crimes committed in the Prijedor region.[14] Meanwhile, his best team of lawyers and investigators was quietly digging deeply into the cases of Karadžić and Mladić, focusing on events in 1992 and 1993. At that time the political and military leaders of the Bosnian Serbs had been visibly on the scene, especially in and around Sarajevo, when hundreds of Muslim civilians had died from artillery fire and snipers operating from the mountains around the city. The U.S. Central Intelligence Agency provided in the winter of 1995 some key photographic evidence and other documents that might help to pin these actions on the Bosnian Serbs. Even with this boost, the OTP prosecutors told their boss that they could work only so quickly in preparing legal charges that might actually stick in court.[15]

Antonio Cassese seemed constitutionally incapable of sitting back and letting the prosecutor do his work. In March 1995, the court president took matters into his own hands. In doing so, Cassese not only put himself on a collision course with Richard Goldstone; his actions threatened the integrity of the entire tribunal.

First, Cassese went into the business of directly gathering and soliciting evidence, a task decidedly outside of the court president's job description. In early March, he spoke with a Bosnian lawyer living in Geneva who passed along information about witnesses to the events in Omarska and who had spoken to a Swiss television reporter. When Cassese was interviewed by an Israeli filmmaker, Ilan Ziv, he used the occasion to ask Ziv about interviews that he had conducted with witnesses to crimes committed by a Serbian named Dušan Vučković. He had his assistant place a call to Kenneth Roth, the executive director of Human Rights Watch, asking for information about the ongoing trial of Vučković in Serbia; he then went on to ask Human Rights Watch for twenty packets of reports on violations of the laws of war in Croatia and Bosnia. He solicited similar information from the Helsinki Committee for Human Rights and from the International Committee of the Red Cross. He met with an American professor, Paul Rice, to ask for his thoughts about how to handle issues of "hearsay" with respect to the thousands of victim statements that could potentially come before the tribunal.[16]

Then, a complex legal matter presented the court president with the opportunity to increase his direct pressure on Goldstone with regard to strategy. As the judges of the ICTY had been impatient, so too was the Muslim-led government of the embattled state of Bosnia-Herzegovina. The territory that the Bosnian government held was reduced and fragmented, but anger at the Bosnian Serbs, with whom they were still at war, remained high. Unconstrained by an international statute and global political considerations, the Bosnian government had itself quietly begun constructing its own legal investigation into war crimes committed on its soil by Karadžić and Mladić.

Goldstone knew that a trial in a court in Bosnia of two of the biggest fish would permanently undermine the ICTY. The international court could succeed if and only if the ICTY was the only legitimate venue to try the most powerful perpetrators. It was worse that the Bosnians were contemplating a trial in absentia, whose proceedings would be widely regarded as a show trial and would cast an indirect shadow over the ICTY. It had been difficult enough to build the credibility of the Hague tribunal; it would be impossible if chasing down the war criminals in the Balkans became a free-for-all.

On March 17, Goldstone came to Cassese with a plan. Rather than indict Karadžić and Mladić right away, he would instead formally ask the judges to request that Bosnia-Herzegovina fulfill its legal obligation to "defer" to the international tribunal when it came to trying the leadership. When Goldstone brought the matter to Cassese, the president exploded. A deferral order was exactly the kind of halfway measure that the court president detested. Cassese told Goldstone that he wanted an indictment *now*.[17] The president told the prosecutor he could not understand why it was necessary to bring a deferral application against Karadžić, "as there was such an abundance of evidence on which to indict him on a charge of genocide." Cassese made reference to a 1991 statement allegedly made by Karadžić "to the effect that if there was to be a war, then you Muslims will cease to exist." Cassese told Goldstone that this statement was "even stronger evidence than that which had been available against Hitler on the planning of a genocide."[18]

Asking the Bosnians for a deferral, Cassese insisted, would only make the tribunal look weak. Goldstone refused to give in. He knew that his team needed at least several more weeks before the indictment would be solid, and they really needed months. But he told Cassese that if the judges refused to grant a date to hear the deferral request, he as prosecutor would have no choice but to engage in an unseemly tug-of-war with the Bosnians and his own judges in the public media. Two could play the game of threatening to go public.

The president believed that he had the upper hand. "Governments, international organisations and world public opinion at large will perceive the application for deferral of the two 'big shots' as a roundabout and indeed devious way of going after top leaders," Cassese wrote to Goldstone as a follow-up to their meeting. "Outsiders will immediately ask themselves: why has the Prosecutor not issued an indictment against these top leaders, given that the Office of the Prosecutor has been active for at least one year?" Cassese went on to comment directly on the whole prosecutorial strategy. Conceding that the prosecutor was theoretically independent, Cassese nevertheless believed that the president was "empowered to ensure the smooth running of the whole Tribunal." With that authority, he claimed that "it is not inappropriate of me to set out to you, in private and confidentially, my views on the results of your prosecutorial activity. . . . We are a unique international institution consisting of various bodies, all working for the same goals and all concerned about our achieving the aims set out in our Statute." That said, Cassese went on to complain about Goldstone's changes in plans since his initial program of action in January, and especially that all that the judges really had in front of them were "possible indictments against minor thugs."[19]

At this point, Richard Goldstone's patience with Antonio Cassese came to an abrupt end. This was no longer just a matter of turf wars between the judiciary and the OTP, nor was it simply a matter of Goldstone's pride and independence as a professional. What concerned Goldstone in March 1995 was this: the president of the ICTY, by his repeated pressure and insistence on indicting Karadžić and Mladić, was directly implicating the two top leaders in crimes throughout Bosnia. If Cassese had already made up his mind, then he was not an impartial judge. And if the judges of the ICTY were not impartial, then the whole enterprise was threatened.

On March 22, 1995, Goldstone wrote to all eleven of the tribunal's judges detailing his complaints about their conduct, saying that "in my view, the perception, and the reality, of judicial impartiality is essential to the credibility and success of the tribunal. But it appears that while trying to serve the interests of the Tribunal some judges may have created the impression that they lack impartiality."[20]

Goldstone's March 22 letter did not detail Cassese's actions. Instead, he emphasized more generically that some of the tribunal's judges were in the habit of expressing opinions about the identity of those responsible for the crimes in the Balkans. Goldstone also described the ways that judges were collecting evidence from governments and NGOs. "I believe that it is inappropriate," the chief prosecutor wrote, "in both civil and common law traditions, for judges to express such opinions and engage in such activity. In the context of an historic judicial body that must exemplify the highest standards of all traditions, such conduct will surely undermine the Tribunal's ability to conduct trials that are universally regarded as fair."

Then Goldstone dropped the bombshell: "If the conduct continues, my office may be bound to disclose it to the defence, and some judges may find it appropriate to disqualify themselves from hearing particular cases." This was an extraordinary threat. The prosecutor was saying that he would be willing to compromise the success of his own trials if the judges did not change their behavior. His ethical obligations left him no choice.

Goldstone took the precaution of pulling together a thorough dossier of materials about Cassese's actions during the early months of 1995.[21] He included copies of the letters that Cassese had sent to him describing his efforts to solicit evidence. He related that Cassese had directly expressed his "complete lack of confidence" in the top associates in the OTP, and that "he has accused me of failing to give any leadership and in failing to turn around a hopeless strategy." Goldstone noted that Cassese had questioned his competence at the U.N. and had undertaken to provide reports to the secretary-general evaluating the prosecutor's work. "If actions of this kind are designed to put pressure on me," Goldstone wrote, "they are quite improper. In some jurisdictions they might even be regarded as criminal." He described his conversation with the court president about Cassese's belief in the evidence against Karadžić for genocide, and he outlined "the professional and moral duty I may have" to disclose the president's predilections. "I may find myself in a position where, if I did not do so, I would be compromised and become a party to proceedings which were unfair and not in accordance with justice."

Putting all of this in writing to eleven judges was a calculated risk. Goldstone clearly wanted Cassese to be reined in, which required strong and unambiguous language. But he also did not want to create a situation where one of them would be compelled to resign. He chose a tone of moral indignation, rather than (for the most part) legal recrimination, but he backed up his charges with significant and specific documentation. Goldstone had no doubt that the future of international criminal justice as a whole was at stake.

In the meantime, Goldstone continued to seek a way to align more closely with the judges—finding a way to go after the "big fish" while at the same time preserving the integrity of his office. He met with Vasvija Vidović, the Bosnian government's representative in The Hague, to persuade her that the OTP prosecutors were making substantial progress on indicting Karadžić and Mladić and to convince Bosnia to drop its own efforts at prosecution. Vidović would not roll over. She said that her government would be happy to defer to the ICTY, but on one condition: the judges of the tribunal would need to make the request for the Bosnians to drop their own proceedings formal and public.[22]

This time when Goldstone went to Cassese to discuss deferral, the prosecutor was determined to reach a compromise. He still was not ready to issue an indictment, but he offered an alternative. In advance of the public hearings on deferral, the OTP would make a public announcement that Radovan Karadžić and Ratko Mladić were formally under investigation. While this news would hardly be surprising, it would constitute a form of public pressure on the Bosnian Serb leadership.[23] When he proposed this arrangement to Antonio Cassese, the court president reluctantly acceded.

On April 24, 1995, two key events constituted a turning point for the tribunal. As he promised, Richard Goldstone told the world that his office was preparing charges against Radovan Karadžić and Ratko Mladić, two of the three most wanted men in the Balkans conflict. He gave no timetable, however, for a decision on or a public release of any possible indictment.[24] On the same date, the German government sent Duško Tadić, the lone Serbian suspect actually in custody, by helicopter to The Hague. On April 26, 1995, Tadić appeared in the ICTY's lone courtroom, a somehow diminished figure in a yellow T-shirt and a brown leather jacket. He looked to one American observer "like everyman, the guy next to you on the bus or at the ball game, ill-qualified to carry all the weight of the violence at Omarska."[25]

The twin events—the announcement of the pursuit of the big fish and the presence of a little fish in the ICTY's custody—eased the immediate pressure on Richard Goldstone from Antonio Cassese and his fellow judges. Goldstone had in fact carried the day, proceeding at his own pace and following his own strategy. He had managed in the end to do so without public confrontation with the men and women who were, after all, his partners in the pursuit of justice at the tribunal.

In early May, the ICTY judges summarily dismissed Goldstone's complaints about their behavior, adamantly defending Antonio Cassese. On May 2, ICTY vice president Elizabeth Odio Benito wrote to Goldstone announcing that the judges were "astonished" by his letter of March 22, 1995, and that they considered the allegations to be "wholly unjustified and providing no conceivable ground for disqualification." Goldstone's correspondence, they informed him, "reveals a misconception on your part of the role of the President of this international Tribunal."[26] The judges, in other words, stood by Cassese's conviction that he, as president of a new and untried court, had both the right and the obligation to transcend ordinary judicial boundaries in the service of assuring the ICTY's success. Richard Goldstone believed that he was protecting the fledgling institution in a more important way: by taking every measure to ensure that its proceedings would be without bias and above reproach.

The announcement of the investigations of Karadžić and Mladić, however, had taken some of the steam out of the conflict. Goldstone later maintained that his personal relationship with Cassese remained intact throughout this period, a claim that is difficult to believe given the strong language exchanged in what even Goldstone called a series of "horrible letters." The point, as Goldstone saw it, was that he had stood up for the integrity of the tribunal at a moment when it was most vulnerable. He had weathered what turned out to be only the first crisis of 1995.

Through the rest of the spring, Goldstone whipped the OTP into a frenzy of activity. When the Serbian army shelled the Croatian capital of Zagreb on May 2, a Serbian general, Milan Martić, went on television to claim responsibility. At 9:00 A.M. the next morning, Goldstone turned to Graham Blewitt and his colleagues and asked whether the OTP could mount an immediate investigation. "Here's a neat, single incident," Goldstone said. "It looks like a war crime. Shouldn't we show the world how important it is to have an up-and-running war crimes office?"[27] The Martić case became the ICTY's first real-time investigation, which would later lead to the general's arrest and conviction. While the Martić case was proceeding, Graham Blewitt urged other OTP teams to bring their work to fruition, leading to a flurry of indictments submitted to the judges for confirmation. By the end of June 1995, the OTP had indicted more than forty individuals in four situations: Prijedor, Keraterm, Bosanski Šamac, and Brčko.[28]

Indeed, so many indictments and investigations were now on the books that privately some of the prosecutors themselves began to wonder whether they had gone after too many "little fish" too quickly.[29] One American prosecutor wryly referred to the OTP's indictment philosophy as the "whiff of suspicion" standard.[30] The lawyers wanted to develop the strongest cases. The chief prosecutor wanted to keep the tribunal alive. These two imperatives sometimes pulled in different directions.

On the investigation of Karadžić and Mladić, however, Goldstone was more cautious. At the beginning of July, he told the *Washington Post* that he hoped to decide by the end of the year whether or not to indict the Bosnian Serb leaders. The decision, he said, "will be reached on the basis of accumulated evidence, not by the political climate."[31] Events of that month would drastically change that calculation.

Dražen Erdemović was a one-man microcosm of the complexities of Yugoslavian identity. A Croatian by ethnic background, he was born in the city of Tuzla, a Muslim-majority enclave in the Serb-dominated region of eastern Bosnia. He completed his mandatory service in the JNA, the Yugoslavian national army, over the final sixteen months that his country of birth could be said to be a nation. He was mustered out in March 1992, just weeks before the war in Bosnia destroyed the final filaments of Yugoslavia.[32]

With the war in full swing, Erdemović, a married man at age twenty-one, struggled to fit in. In July 1992 he was called up to serve in the army of his new country, Bosnia-Herzegovina, but after a few months there he joined the paramilitary Croatian Defence Council near his hometown of Tuzla. By late 1993, Erdemović wanted out of his war-torn country, but getting the right papers was a challenge. He moved from Tuzla to the self-styled Republika Srpska, territory that the Bosnian Serbs controlled, because he knew someone there who promised that he could take Dražen and his wife to Switzerland. But the man he knew broke his promise, and Erdemović, as a Croatian in what was effectively a Serbian country, had few options for work and security. He joined the army of the Bosnian Serbs in April 1994.

By July 1995, three months after Richard Goldstone had announced publicly that the OTP was investigating Karadžić and Mladić, Dražen Erdemović was serving in Eastern Bosnia in a reconnaissance unit of sixty men under a commander named Milorad Pelemiš. On the night of July 10, his unit was ordered to take up a position outside the city of Srebrenica, the largest Muslim town in the region. After a protracted battle in 1992, the U.N. had declared Srebrenica, along with the towns of Tuzla and Gorazde, to be "safe areas"—Muslim enclaves surrounded by territory held by the Bosnian Serbs. The U.N. deployed peacekeepers as a safeguard for the beleaguered Muslims.

When Erdemović's unit entered Srebrenica on the morning of July 11, there was no fighting, and there were no peacekeepers in sight. The city was practically a ghost town. There were scarcely any residents on the streets, only a few older men and women. Erdemović and his men were under orders to tell all residents to gather at the city's main soccer field. When they encountered one younger man on the street, however, Lieutenant Pelemiš gave a peremptory order. Erdemović's stomach tightened as one of the men in his unit, named Zoran, calmly slit the man's throat and left the body in plain view on the street in the center of the town.

A few hours later, Erdemović was near the entrance of the town. A convoy of Bosnian Serb military vehicles passed by. On one of the jeeps, Erdemović saw a familiar figure in fatigues, an older, powerful-looking man with broad features and prominent chin. General Ratko Mladić had arrived in Srebrenica.

Erdemović's unit left town that day without further incident, but five days later, on July 16, they were sent to a farm in a place called Pilice, just a few miles from Srebrenica. Early in the morning they were ordered to take up a position in a meadow behind the farmhouse; they were deployed, with their weapons, in a line. Soon, a bus pulled up to the farmhouse. Armed guards pushed a group of ten men off the bus. They were in ragged civilian clothes and blindfolded, but Erdemović could see that they ranged in age from teenagers to old men who could scarcely walk. He knew, too, that they were Muslims, and he was told that they were from Srebrenica. The blindfolded men stumbled into the meadow, stopping around twenty meters from Erdemović and his fellow soldiers. At an order from the ranking officer on the scene, Dražen Erdemović and his comrades shot and killed all ten of them.

Another ten men were pushed into the field, and then another. The soldiers fired another volley of bullets, and then another. Another bus arrived, and then another. Erdemović protested. The commanding officer asked him whether he wanted to join the blindfolded men. So Erdemović continued to pull the trigger. One Muslim man made an impassioned plea to Erdemović, saying that he had personally helped save many Serbs from violence earlier in the war. Erdemović wanted to spare his life, but the officer insisted that there could be no witnesses.

By 3:30 P.M., when the last bus left Pilice, Erdemović had long since lost count of how many men he had killed. He did not want to know.

When Dražen Erdemović left Pilice, the world was just beginning to understand and take in what had happened over the past week in and around Srebrenica. For months the Bosnian Serbs had been massing forces in the area and restricting the flow of supplies into the Muslim enclaves. By early July, Serbian troops were mounting a direct offensive, and the civilian population of Srebrenica was in flight. The Dutch peacekeepers, under the pressure of the Serbian advance, surrendered or withdrew. Shortly after Erdemović saw Ratko Mladić at the entrance to the city, the general proudly announced that Srebrenica was a gift to the Serbian nation, and that the time to take revenge on the Muslims had arrived. The next days were an orgy of massacre, rape, and terror in the vicinity of Srebrenica, an area that was no longer by any definition safe. How many were dead? How many were displaced? On July 16, the reports were still sketchy, and the Serbs were telling a mendacious story of a purely military triumph. But it was becoming obvious that the scale of death and destruction at Srebrenica was unparalleled even in the four-year history of the brutal war in the former Yugoslavia.

At the ICTY, the reports from Srebrenica in the summer of 1995 hit painfully hard. For a year the investigators and the prosecutors had been carefully building their cases, seeking to establish the principle of accountability for mass violence. On the one hand, the tribunal was supposed to deliver justice after the fact, to punish the perpetrators. Another important reason to invest in international criminal justice was to protect against future crimes. "We need to combat discrimination through justice because it is the only way to break the spiral of violence and deter such conduct in the future," Richard Goldstone had told one reporter at the beginning of July 1995.[33] Certainly that was the hope and the conviction among many in the OTP. Even while news reports of Serb pressure on Srebrenica were leaking out in the early summer of 1995, OTP prosecutor Minna Schrag was telling friends confidently that the Serbs wouldn't dare commit further atrocities with the whole world watching.[34]

The appalling and undisguised nature of the attack on Srebrenica sent a message from the Bosnian Serbs to the ICTY and to the world. When Mladić boldly entered the city, he let Serbian television announce his triumph and hint at the massacres that were already beginning to take place. The Bosnian Serb general was thumbing his nose at the international tribunal and at the world community at large.[35]

Srebrenica changed Goldstone's outlook on the investigations into Karadžić and Mladić and made delay untenable. Two weeks after telling the press that he expected the investigation to last another six months, he asked Mark Harmon, who was leading the prosecution team, to present everything he had to the assembled lawyers of the OTP. The prosecutors, of course, had no evidence about the Srebrenica massacre itself. No one knew yet with any certainty what had happened there. But the lawyers nevertheless had a lot to say about what had happened in Bosnia since 1992: the detention camps, the shelling of Sarajevo, the destruction of sacred sites, ethnic cleansing.

It was a stormy meeting. "Goldstone really pushed on Karadžić and Mladić, to the point of rebellion," one OTP staff member recalled later.[36] Nevertheless, a majority of the lawyers in the room voted for delay, to send Mark Harmon and his team back to work further on the evidence and the charges. Even Goldstone's loyal fellow South African, JJ du Toit, then doing investigations on the Karadžić and Mladić cases, was one of those who felt that it was too soon, that the OTP did not have a case beyond "reasonable doubt" at that time."[37]

Goldstone retreated to his office with Graham Blewitt. Privately, the two men likely knew that the majority had the better of the argument, in strictly legal terms. But Goldstone was concerned about the risk to the ICTY if it was silent in the face of Srebrenica. The idea of the law proceeding at its own pace, untainted by external considerations, was a luxury that the tribunal simply could not afford. He decided to overrule the majority and proceed as quickly as possible.[38]

On July 24, 1995, two weeks after the massacres in Srebrenica began, Richard Goldstone submitted a fifteen-page indictment to Judge Claude Jorda, one of the judges who had been most eager to see the leadership in the dock. The indictment charged Radovan Karadžić and Ratko Mladić with genocide and crimes against humanity stemming from ethnic cleansing in Bosnia, the shelling and sniping of Sarajevo, and the taking of U.N. peace-keepers as hostages. It contained no mention of the events in Srebrenica, which were still unfolding. Judge Jorda did not delay. Less than twenty-four hours later, on July 25, he confirmed the indictment and issued arrest warrants for the Bosnian Serb leaders.[39] Two of the three biggest fish were now officially fugitives from international justice.

The news brought the kind of boost that Richard Goldstone was hoping for. "What is happening is serious business," wrote Anthony Lewis in the *New York Times*. "Serious for the Bosnian Serb leaders and for standards of fundamental human rights in the world. A legal process that not many believed could work is working."[40] Other observers greeted the news skeptically if not with outright hostility. "The price of making negotiations impossible by issuing arrest warrants for one side can be terrifyingly high," A. M. Rosenthal wrote in the *Times* on the same day as Lewis's words of praise. "Without peace talks, the ever-deeper Western involvement can bring Europe to where it stood 81 years ago this week—at the cusp of a world war."[41]

In New York, Boutros-Boutros Ghali was furious, peevishly complaining that he was not consulted about the indictments beforehand. Goldstone parried the U.N. secretary-general's thrusts, explaining that prosecutorial independence required him to act according to the evidence and without widespread consultation.[42] The idea that the prosecutor had acted without regard to political considerations was absurd, but maintaining that posture was an imperative in the game of legal diplomacy that Goldstone had to play.

Meanwhile, there was another investigation to launch—into the events of Srebrenica itself. It would be a race to see what the ICTY could learn before the Serbs managed to destroy the evidence.

Richard Goldstone at Brandeis University, November 2009. *Mike Lovett/Brandeis University.*

The main quadrangle of the University of the Witwatersrand. *Photo by Daniel Terris.*

Albert Jacobson, Richard Goldstone's maternal grandfather. *Courtesy of Richard Goldstone.*

Goldstone (center) at an event as president of the SRC at the University of the Witwatersrand, 1961. Vice-Chancellor William Sutton is second from left. *Courtesy of Richard Goldstone.*

Richard Goldstone (left) with a fellow international student on his trip to attend a student conference in Nigeria, 1959. *Courtesy of Richard Goldstone.*

Richard and Noleen Goldstone's wedding, 1962. *Courtesy of Richard Goldstone.*

Opposite: Richard Goldstone receives his BA from the University of the Witwatersrand, 1959. *Courtesy of Richard Goldstone.*

Richard Goldstone with his brother, David. *Courtesy of Richard Goldstone.*

Richard Goldstone (third from left) with friends in the 1980s. At left are Godrey Pitje, a prominent attorney, and his wife Molly. At right are Isaac Meletse of NICRO and his wife Elsie. Noleen Goldstone is at far right. *Courtesy of Richard Goldstone.*

"(Gold)stone Is Going Up!" cartoon in the *Sowetan* newspaper, 1992. *Courtesy of Richard Goldstone.*

The Sondela Brewery gate, near the site of the 1990 Sebokeng tragedy, 2013. *Photo by Daniel Terris.*

Certificate naming Goldstone as an Honorary Fellow of Hebrew University, 1988. *Courtesy of Richard Goldstone.*

Richard Goldstone and Nelson Mandela, date unknown. *Courtesy of Richard Goldstone.*

The International Criminal Tribunal for the Former Yugoslavia (formerly the Aegon Insurance Building) in The Hague. *Courtesy of the ICTY.*

Dragan Nikolić, the first man indicted by the ICTY, in court, November 1994. *Courtesy of the ICTY.*

The opening session of the ICTY, November 1993. *UN Photo.*

Goldstone (left) with judges of the ICTY. To Goldstone's right are Gabrielle Kirk Mc-Donald and ICTY president Antonio Cassese. *Courtesy of Richard Goldstone.*

Richard Goldstone addresses the ICTY judges regarding the indictment of Dragan Nikolić, November 1994. *Ed Oudenaarden/AFP/Getty Images.*

General Ratko Mladić at the closing arguments of his trial at the ICTY, December 2016. *Courtesy of the ICTY.*

Goldstone (top right) and other members of the Constitutional Court of South Africa. Justice Albie Sachs is top row, third from left. *Courtesy of Richard Goldstone.*

The U.N. Fact-Finding Mission on the Gaza Conflict in 2009. Left to right: Christine Chinkin, Richard Goldstone, U.N. high commissioner for human rights Navi Pillay, Hina Jilani, and Desmond Travers. *UN Photo/Patrick Bertschmann.*

Richard Goldstone (center) walks with Hamas deputy Ahmed Bahr (second from left) and members of his delegation as they visit the Palestinian parliament building that was destroyed during Israel's December 2008–January 2009 offensive in Gaza City, June 2009. *Mohammed Abed/AFP/Getty Images.*

Goldstone presents the Gaza report to the HRC in Geneva, September 2009. Christine Chinkin and Desmond Travers are in the background. *UN Photo/Jean-Marc Ferré.*

Goldstone with former Israeli ambassador to the U.N. Dore Gold, one of his fiercest critics, at an event at Brandeis University after the release of the Gaza report, November 2009. *Mike Lovett/Brandeis University.*

Goldstone in his robes in his role as chancellor of the University of the Witwatersrand. *Courtesy of Richard Goldstone.*

Richard, Kitty, and Noleen Goldstone, 2013. *Photo by Daniel Terris.*

10 ▸ THE BARGAINING CHIP

IN THE SUMMER and fall of 1995, an even more potent challenge to the future of the ICTY emerged. The threat came, ironically, from progress toward peace. As a process opened to end the war in the Balkans, some negotiators saw the ICTY as an obstacle. Men under threat of indictment, after all, might be unwilling to settle for a deal that could land them in prison. As the push toward peace intensified, so did the pressure on the ICTY.

Yet the relationship between justice and peace was not a one-way street. The existence of the tribunal itself shaped the negotiating environment, creating avenues for discussion that did not exist before. That fall, Richard Goldstone played a vital role both as a defender of his institution and as an actor who propelled the peace drama forward.

The diplomat who loomed large in Goldstone's vision in 1995 was Richard Holbrooke, the assistant secretary for European and Canadian Affairs in the U.S. Department of State, who became the driving force in global efforts to find a solution to the conflict. Holbrooke was famous for his outsized ego and his blunt, take-no-prisoners style of diplomacy. In his Yugoslavia mission, Holbrooke was driven to succeed not only because of his commitment to peace, but because bringing the war to an end would enhance his own credentials and his hopes for eventually becoming the U.S. secretary of state.

Since 1991, many negotiating efforts led by Western diplomats had led to ceasefires, sometimes for months at a time, but in the absence of international determination and pressure, the warring parties continued to slip back into violence. By the summer of 1995, however, several factors were combining to prepare the ground for more serious peace negotiations. For one thing, the military landscape had shifted. As recently as 1994 the Bosnian Serbs had controlled more than 70 percent of the territory of Bosnia-Herzegovina, while Serbia proper controlled the Croatian province of Krajina. By July 1995, however, separate ambitious offensives by the Croats and the Muslims had made a serious dent in Serbian gains, reducing their control to less than half of Bosnia, and pushing them out of Krajina altogether. With diminished morale among their troops and diminished support from Milošević in Serbia, the Bosnian Serbs began to feel vulnerable, and therefore more open to peace talks.

In addition to the military situation, external pressures were mounting. The events at Srebrenica in July shocked the world by the sheer scale and audacity of the Serbian brutality. Western governments came under increasing criticism from the global human rights community and their own publics for letting the violence continue unabated. Within the U.S. government specifically, support for playing a more decisive role in the Balkans was gaining momentum. In July 1995, Assistant Secretary of State John Shattuck made a dramatic visit to Srebrenica, where he was one of the first senior officials to give an eyewitness account of the aftermath of the massacre.[1] Following Shattuck's report, Holbrooke intensified his efforts, both to pressure the Serbs to ratchet back their attacks on civilians, and at the same time to try to bring all of the parties to the negotiating table. The ICTY—and Richard Goldstone's latest actions—were at the crux of the discussions.

On August 28, 1995, an artillery shell exploded in a crowded square in central Sarajevo, killing thirty-eight shoppers at the local market.[2] Although the Serbs tried to deflect the blame for the August shelling (claiming that the Muslims had fired on their own people in order to gain international sympathy), the incident finally pushed Western governments into action. NATO for the first time implemented a series of sustained and punishing air strikes on Serbian targets in an effort to relieve the pressure on Sarajevo.

On August 30, 1995, two days after the Sarajevo shelling, Holbrooke was in Belgrade talking with Slobodan Milošević. The Serbian leader was eager to consolidate his own gains and power, but the global condemnation of the Bosnian Serbs meant that he was now paying a price for his alliance with Karadžić, their political leader. For his part, Holbrooke had a new card to play. Karadžić was now under an arrest warrant issued by an arm of the U.N. Holbrooke frankly told Milošević that there was no way that an indicted war criminal could attend and participate in an international peace conference. If the Serbian leader wanted peace talks, he would have to go forward without his Bosnian Serb ally. Milošević made a show of objection and bluster. He told Holbrooke that the Bosnian Serbs were an essential part of any talks, that without them an agreement would fall apart, that a comprehensive approach was necessary. Holbrooke remained implacable. He insisted that the United States would not compromise on the question of the war crimes tribunal.[3]

Following the NATO bombings and the September negotiations, the parties agreed to gather at the beginning of November 1995 at Wright-Patterson Air Force Base, outside of Dayton, Ohio, to try to hammer out a deal. Richard Holbrooke and a representative of the European Union, Carl Bildt, would serve as the principal facilitators. Karadžić would not attend.

In October, even as Goldstone fretted about what the peace talks might bring, the ICTY received a rhetorical boost from a higher authority: the president of the United States. Bill Clinton, speaking in Nuremberg, made a public declaration that the tribunal was "non-negotiable."[4] Still, as the Dayton talks approached, speculation increased that Western powers might bargain away the tribunal if Milošević insisted that this was one price for peace.

In late October, Goldstone issued a preemptive strike in the press. He made a public call for any agreement reached at Dayton not only to leave the ICTY intact, but to make cooperation on arrests an essential part of the accord. If the people of the Balkans wanted peace, then their governments should have to help bring the perpetrators of mass atrocities to justice. It is nonsensical, Goldstone said, to expect that hundreds of thousands of victims could forgive and forget. "To suggest that politicians have a right to forgive on behalf of these people has to be refuted," Goldstone said. "Who has the moral right, or the political right, to forgive on their behalf?"[5]

Two days later, with the talks at Dayton already under way, Goldstone made this position formal. He wrote to Madeleine Albright, still the tribunal's most vocal supporter in her post as ambassador to the U.N., asking that the U.S. government make the surrender of indicted suspects a condition for any peace accord.[6] Albright was supportive, but she was not in Dayton, and it quickly became clear that the fate of the tribunal was a subject of vigorous discussion within the American administration. "We're going to do as much as is realistic," one anonymous official told the *New York Times*. "We're not going to take on a mission that may be unachievable and may make it hostage to the larger peace settlement."[7] Unattributed public statements like this understandably put the chief prosecutor on edge.

Goldstone recognized that if the ICTY was going to survive, then he must play an active role, even while maintaining the posture that he as prosecutor was simply following the timetable of the regular course of justice. Inside the OTP, he pressed the staff hard, urging the completion and submission of more indictments to the judges for confirmation. The prosecutor knew that fresh charges would command the attention of the respective governments.

On November 7, one week into the Dayton process, the ICTY indicted three Serbian officers for war crimes and crimes against humanity stemming from the notorious incident in which the JNA, the Yugoslavian national army, had shelled a hospital near the city of Vukovar in Croatia in 1991. By issuing an indictment at this time focused on the JNA, Goldstone sent a message that even though Slobodan Milošević was at Dayton, the actions of military forces under his authority were still under the microscope.[8]

The public announcement of the Vukovar indictments, which addressed one of the most memorable atrocities of the Balkans war, kept the ICTY in the frame while all eyes were on Dayton. The new charges also highlighted a problem. In the nearly two years since the OTP had begun its investigations, all of the individuals indicted thus far had been Serbs. Serbian political leaders were complaining bitterly that the ICTY was no more than an instrument of anti-Serb bias. If the tribunal was going to maintain its credibility and its relevance at Dayton, it would have to be seen as dispensing justice fairly among perpetrators from all sides.

At the same time as the Vukovar indictments, the OTP delivered a stack of papers related to three other situations to the office of Judge Gabrielle Kirk McDonald. They were the culmination of an investigation of officers in the army of the Bosnian Croats, known as the Croatian Defence Council. The indictments charged the officers with crimes against humanity stemming from the ethnic cleansing of local Muslims in the Lašva Valley in central Bosnia in 1993.[9]

Almost alone among the OTP staff, Richard Goldstone had the privilege of crossing the security barrier to the floor that housed the judges' chambers. In early November, he used this privilege to pay a visit to Judge McDonald. Making a direct appeal to a judge to deliver a certain outcome on a certain date was a calculated risk, but the stakes were high, and the prosecutor couched his visit in terms of the values of the institution as a whole. He told the judge that he knew that his office had delivered a mountain of paperwork to her, but he emphasized that it was vital that she confirm the indictments as quickly as possible. Without charges against Croatians, the prosecutor indicated, the future of the tribunal would be in doubt. McDonald understood very well her job as a judge, and the interference of the prosecutor in her decision-making was not altogether welcome, but she also understood the situation of the prosecutor and of the court. Besides, the evidence against the Bosnian Croat officers was reasonably strong. Working quickly, McDonald confirmed the Lašva Valley indictments on November 10, allowing the process to move forward. Goldstone's choreography of the dance between politics and justice paid off.[10]

With the Vukovar indictments making headlines and Lašva Valley establishing a sense of balance, Goldstone could focus on the public unveiling of a third crucial investigation, the one that was most important of all. Over the past three months, the OTP had been working feverishly to try to collect evidence on the massacres in and around Srebrenica. Nothing was as important to the ICTY's relevance as holding accountable the men who had ordered the worst single atrocity in Europe since World War II.

For all its boldness and scale, Srebrenica was nevertheless difficult to investigate. The OTP had limited ability to send personnel to the area, which was controlled by the very Bosnian Serb forces that had committed the violence. Much of the investigators' work involved the painstaking process of accumulated detail. "We didn't find any smoking gun documents," remembered Glyn Morgan. "There wasn't a signed order from Radovan Karadžić saying, 'Kill all the Muslims!'" Instead, investigators relied on the tedious collection of data like fuel records that proved that military vehicles were in and around Srebrenica.[11]

With limited access to the sites on the ground, Goldstone desperately needed evidence from the air. He knew that reconnaissance photos from U.S. satellites and planes could show the sites of mass graves in the fields and farms in the region.[12] It was a matter of urgency. There were strong indications in the fall of 1995 that the Bosnian Serbs were working feverishly to remove and scatter the bodies of victims in order to be able to deny that mass killings even took place. The OTP made numerous requests to the U.S. State Department for photos from the air, but the pace of response was frustratingly slow. Goldstone grew concerned that the Bosnian Serbs might succeed in erasing the physical markers of Srebrenica, just as Dražen Erdemović's commander had been determined to leave no witnesses in the killing field at Pilice.

On October 30, 1995, Goldstone wrote a detailed letter to the U.S. Department of State complaining about the pace of the U.S. response. He took care to praise the United States as the most reliable friend of the tribunal, but he said that the Americans had recently been providing only open-source material and deflecting or ignoring his requests for more specific forms of information. Goldstone's letter was intended to be confidential, but it ended up in the hands of the Washington Post, which published excerpts in early November, in the midst of the first week of the Dayton talks.[13]

The State Department bristled, considering Goldstone's account a "highly inflated accusation."[14] One spokesman huffed that there were legitimate security reasons why not everything that the United States collected could be shared with the international community.[15] Privately, Goldstone heard from friends in Washington that the public disclosure of the prosecutor's complaints was an irritant, and a boost for those who would like to see the U.S. distance itself from the tribunal's efforts. A day later, another spokesman was more conciliatory, volunteering that if the U.S. government had pertinent information it would find a way to get that to Justice Goldstone.[16]

On November 14, Goldstone called a press conference in The Hague for another preemptive strike. He said publicly that any deal in Dayton that could include amnesty for the leaders of the Bosnian Serbs would be "abhorrent," and he made a direct threat that he himself might well resign from the ICTY if that outcome were to come to pass.[17] The threat to resign received widespread attention in the international press, and annoyed even Goldstone's friends in the American government, who had been busy assuring him that the United States would never agree to any such arrangement.[18] The prosecutor was aware, however, that his own allies in the U.S. government were not necessarily the ones with the final word on the negotiations.

Two days later, on November 16, Judge Fouad Riad confirmed the OTP's new indictment against Radovan Karadžić and Ratko Mladić, charging them with genocide and other crimes in connection with the events at Srebrenica.[19] The two principals were not in Ohio, so they could not be arrested. Goldstone maintained the public posture that the timing was coincidental, that the indictments simply were submitted when they were ready.[20] Even in hindsight, Goldstone maintained this position, but Graham Blewitt proved more forthcoming. As Blewitt later told one historian, "We wanted to make sure that we were going to be part of the Dayton solution, whatever came out of it, that we were going to be part of the deal."[21]

At the time that the Srebrenica indictment became public, Richard Goldstone was already in Washington, D.C., making a frantic series of rounds at the State Department, the Department of Defense, and other agencies. David Scheffer and John Shattuck accompanied him, presenting a united front between the ICTY and two of its most fervent proponents in the State Department. Goldstone positioned himself in these discussions as a firm advocate of his tribunal who was also willing to make accommodations to reality as long as the basic principle of criminal accountability was preserved. Having no role in the direct negotiations, Goldstone did not go to Dayton himself.

The Dayton process dragged on for three agonizing and chaotic weeks, nearly collapsing several times.[22] For its first two weeks, one of the stumbling blocks was that the leader of the Bosnian Muslims, Alija Izetbegović, insisted that he would not sign any accord that did not include the immediate surrender of Karadžić and Mladić to the ICTY.[23] While such a provision would have been excellent for the tribunal, it went nowhere in Dayton. Even if he were inclined to support such an agreement, Slobodan Milošević claimed that he would be powerless to compel his Bosnian Serb allies to turn themselves in. Izetbegović reluctantly conceded the point.[24]

With frantic last-minute shuttle diplomacy by Richard Holbrooke, the warring parties agreed on a peace deal on November 21, 1995.[25] Bosnia-Herzegovina would remain a divided country, with the Serbs governing almost half of the territory, under the auspices of a weak federal government with mandatory representation from all three ethnic groups. A new constitution would aim to establish the rule of law and a path to reconciliation in the region.

The ICTY survived the Dayton Accords, but with a series of compromise clauses that threatened to undermine its effectiveness. Formally, the accord emphasized the strict obligation of all the competent authorities in Bosnia-Herzegovina—the Muslims, the Croats, and the Serbs—to cooperate with the tribunal. At the last minute, however, negotiators eliminated a crucial clause. An earlier draft had stated that the various authorities must cooperate with the tribunal "and its orders." The final agreement settled for the vaguer language that all parties must cooperate "with the tribunal"—full stop.[26] In other words, complying with the tribunal's *orders* could be considered optional.

Furthermore, the accord provided little detail about how alleged war criminals would be apprehended and brought to justice. The agreement called for a new NATO Implementation Force (IFOR) that would be deployed in the region to help keep the peace, and it specified that this force would indeed have the authority to arrest any indicted war criminals that it encountered. But the agreement did not say that NATO *must* arrest suspects. The parties agreed only that NATO *could*, at its discretion, make such arrests. Even then NATO was authorized only to apprehend those whom its forces happened to encounter. There was no provision for taking proactive steps to capture the accused. It was hardly a promising formula for bringing the fifty indictees to justice.[27]

The new Bosnian constitution also gave Karadžić and Mladić plenty of space in which to operate. The document included a provision that convicted war criminals would be barred from holding public office, and that even those indicted would be ineligible for leadership positions if they took measures to evade capture.[28] Radovan Karadžić, in other words, would be eventually edged out of Bosnian politics. But the timetable was uncertain, and in the meantime he and Mladić would remain at liberty and in charge.

Publicly, Richard Goldstone chose to make the best of it. He and Antonio Cassese issued a joint statement that welcomed the accords, saying that the two ICTY leaders trusted that the agreement would be fully and rigorously implemented.[29] They noted that the agreement now bound the Serbian government and the Bosnian Serbs, for the first time, to cooperate with the tribunal's investigations, and they emphasized that the agreement provided no amnesty for those accused of violations of the laws of war. Cassese and Goldstone hoped, in other words, that the compromise language of the agreement would be interpreted in the light most favorable to the tribunal by those who would have the responsibility for implementation. In the end, the tribunal emerged from Dayton intact, and that in itself was a significant victory.

In retrospect, the Americans involved in the talks insisted that there had never been any real danger that justice might have been traded for peace. Richard Holbrooke painted himself as a steadfast friend of the tribunal in his account of the Dayton peace process, and Goldstone's friend David Scheffer likewise insisted that "no such deal was ever contemplated at Dayton."[30] Perhaps so, but given Holbrooke's determination to reach a deal, it seems at least possible that matters could have taken a different turn. One close observer of the process recalled later that Holbrooke considered the tribunal a "pain in the neck" and that it was common knowledge that he had intimated to Milošević that the Serbian leader would not be prosecuted if a successful peace deal could be worked out.[31] Goldstone's shrewd campaign of indictments and publicity during the fall created facts on the ground that made it difficult to use the tribunal as a bargaining chip. David Scheffer put it clearly some years later: "Goldstone influenced the Dayton talks, for the better."[32]

In later years, Goldstone went further, making the case that the existence of the ICTY was itself a key factor in allowing the Dayton talks to happen at all. He argued that the indictments of Karadžić and Mladić, far from being an obstacle, actually made the accord possible. Had the Bosnian Serb leaders been free to participate in Ohio, Goldstone argued, the Bosnian Muslims might well have refused to participate, dooming the process from the start. And even if all the parties had shown up, it is unlikely that anyone could have persuaded the Bosnian Serbs to make the necessary concessions to move forward.[33]

Rather than being a hindrance, the pursuit of justice had arguably created the conditions for the pursuit of peace. Now the prosecutor had to hope that the pursuit of peace following Dayton would lead to conditions for the fuller realization of justice.

At the end of 1995, the fighting on a large scale stopped. As Richard Goldstone had feared, however, the weaknesses in the Dayton Accords' language did in fact hamper the tribunal's work. In January 1996, Goldstone and Graham Blewitt began a multicity campaign to secure the cooperation they needed for access to mass grave sites and for assistance with arrests. U.S. secretary of defense William Perry promised Goldstone that NATO troops would escort ICTY investigators to the sites, but the prosecutor wanted more. If NATO did not provide twenty-four-hour monitoring of the graves, the Serbs would have ample opportunity to tamper with the evidence. In Brussels, Goldstone and Blewitt met with George Joulwan, the senior NATO commander, who insisted that the new NATO contingent, IFOR, could not possibly take responsibility for guarding grave sites on top of its other duties.[34] That kind of assignment, Joulwan said, was a police responsibility, and IFOR was not a police force. The same went for making arrests: a job for police, not for a military organization whose first priority was to prevent war from breaking out again.

It looked to Goldstone like a repeat of a continuing pattern. Western governments pledged support for the tribunal on paper, but had little appetite for providing the resources to make the court a living reality. So Goldstone moved his argument up the ladder. He also met in Brussels with Javier Solana, the secretary-general of NATO, who had already been public in support of General Joulwan's cautious position.[35] But after meeting with Goldstone, and after critical articles in the media, Solana made concessions to the prosecutors. Three days after saying vaguely that NATO would cooperate "to the extent possible" with the ICTY, the secretary-general and Admiral Leighton Smith, the U.S. commander of NATO-led operations in Bosnia, promised that NATO would in fact take concrete steps to prevent the Bosnian Serbs from destroying grave sites near Srebrenica.[36]

From Brussels, Goldstone headed to Washington, D.C., where the tribunal's supporters in the State Department assured him that they were doing their best, but that the Defense Department remained reluctant to pressure NATO on the issue of arrests.[37] The Americans did promise more access to aerial imagery from their planes and satellites.[38] Nevertheless, two months after the signing of the Dayton Accords, Duško Tadić was still the only accused in ICTY custody. Even with NATO troops on the ground, Karadžić, Mladić, and dozens of others were still at large, and the leaders moved with impunity throughout the territory still controlled by the Bosnian Serbs—sometimes thumbing their noses at NATO by broadcasting their appearances on local television.

On March 1, 1996, Richard Goldstone took an urgent call from a woman who identified herself as a correspondent for ABC News.[39] Vanessa Vasić-Janeković was a freelancer based in Belgrade; on the phone she was so upset that Goldstone could barely make out her words.[40] Finally he came to understand that the journalist had in her possession a videotape of a man who had confessed to taking part in the massacres on a farm called Pilice near Srebrenica. The man had described on film the sequence of busload after busload of Muslim men being executed in the field behind the farmhouse. Some weeks later, he told her, he had been shot and wounded in a quarrel with his commanding officer, and he had now come to regret the crimes that he said he was compelled to commit. The problem, Vasić-Janeković sputtered, was that her tapes had been seized by the Serbian police. The man whom she interviewed was on the run, and she was worried about him. His name was

Dražen Erdemović, the Croatian soldier who had enlisted in the Bosnian Serb army.[41]

Goldstone called Graham Blewitt, and the two men canceled their dinner plans and huddled in the Goldstones' apartment. They had never heard of Erdemović, who was, after all, a low-level soldier. If what the journalist was telling them was true, however, Erdemović would be the first person in the Bosnian Serb army willing to provide a firsthand account of the atrocities in and around Srebrenica the previous July. The two prosecutors had reason to be worried. Erdemović was in Belgrade, and the regime of Serbian leader Slobodan Milošević had been highly protective of their allies, the Bosnian Serbs, throughout the war. There was no reason to think that the Serbs would allow Erdemović to remain free, and there was further the chilling possibility that he would not be allowed to remain alive to tell his story.

It was not clear, however, what the prosecutor could do about it. The Serbians had a formal responsibility under the Dayton Accords to cooperate with the tribunal, but Erdemović as an individual was not under indictment. Goldstone had no particular legal leg to stand on. So he resorted to the tool that he had wielded skillfully in the past: the power of publicity. On Sunday morning, at the chief prosecutor's request, Graham Blewitt sent a blizzard of faxes. Some went to the Serbian authorities asking, preemptively, that Erdemović be turned over to the ICTY so that he could be "questioned." Others went to members of the press, alerting them that a compelling potential witness had been identified in Serbia.[42]

In Serbia, Erdemović was desperately trying to find a safe way to turn himself in. He tried to surrender at the U.S. embassy in Belgrade, but he was turned away. The Serbian police finally caught up with him on Sunday, March 3, in the city of Novi Sad. They announced that they were holding him themselves on suspicion of having committed war crimes. Taking an ostensible moral high ground, the Serbs insisted that they would handle Erdemović without any help from The Hague.

Goldstone could see only two plausible outcomes to this situation, neither of them particularly palatable. In one scenario, the Serbs would go ahead and put Erdemović (who was, after all, a Croat by birth) on trial. If so, they would seek to blame him and other low-level soldiers for events in Srebrenica. The Serbs would deflect blame for atrocities from the political and military leaders, and they would set a precedent that would echo the meaningless Leipzig trials that the Germans conducted after World War I.

The other scenario was the one that Vanessa Vasić-Janeković feared: Erdemović would simply disappear and never be heard from again.

On March 7, Goldstone formally asked one of the ICTY judges to request that the Serbs hand Erdemović over to the tribunal.[43] Pilice was already on the radar of the ICTY's investigators. Aerial photographs showed evidence of a mass grave site behind the farm, and IFOR troops, following the agreement with NATO, had helped to protect the vicinity. Now Goldstone informed his supporters in the U.S. State Department that a potential eyewitness to events at Pilice was within the tribunal's grasp. Two weeks after the Serbs arrested Erdemović, the obscure farm was thrust into the international spotlight when Madeleine Albright insisted on visiting the site while on a trip to the Balkans. Reporters watched and recorded the scene as Albright encountered a badly decomposed body, one of more than a thousand buried at the site. "It's sickening," the ambassador said. "It's the most disgusting and horrifying sight for another human being to see."[44] Albright was standing in Bosnia, but her unstated message was intended for Milošević in Belgrade: the Americans were keeping an eye on how the Serbs would handle Dražen Erdemović.

On March 28, Judge Fouad Riad conveyed the ICTY's formal request to the Serbian government that Erdemović be transferred to The Hague. On March 30, to Goldstone's surprise, the Serbians did an about-face and complied.[45] The Serbs continued to insist they intended to prosecute Erdemović themselves, but they agreed to send him to the Netherlands, on a supposedly temporary basis, to tell his story as a witness. The Serbs doubtless knew that there was no way that Richard Goldstone would deliver Dražen Erdemović back to Belgrade.

The intense pressures on the ICTY were taking their toll on Richard Goldstone. Back in the summer of 1994, The Hague had seemed like a pleasant respite from the turmoil of South Africa. Richard and Noleen would enjoy the charms of a European capital and the unfettered liberty from the heavy security that had protected them from the threats of apartheid supporters during the work of the Goldstone Commission.

By late 1995 and early 1996, The Hague was no longer quite the haven it once seemed. The numerous threats to the very existence of the ICTY weighed heavily on the prosecutor, and the demands of the travel schedule often left him exhausted. During the stressful period of the Dayton negotiations, observers thought he looked haggard and careworn, juggling a raft of responsibilities. He still maintained his composure and his calm demeanor, but colleagues found him just a little more short-tempered, a bit frayed around the edges.[46]

Aside from the political threats to the tribunal, he was still constantly fighting the budget battles. Even after the horrors of Srebrenica, the U.N. still kept a tight lid on spending. The General Assembly was now providing funds in three-month increments, which meant that as soon as one installment was approved, Goldstone already had to start begging for the next one.[47]

The carefree life without round-the-clock protection was gone too. Ever since the prosecutor publicly announced the investigation of Karadžić and Mladić in 1995, the Goldstones had had twenty-four-hour security, courtesy of the Dutch government.[48] The Bosnian Serb leaders had long and powerful tentacles, and no one was taking any chances. Dutch security was a bit less onerous for the Goldstones than in South Africa. In his home country, with fewer resources to spare, security often consisted of two guards on duty for full days on end, so Goldstone had often found himself staying at home to give their protectors a few hours off. The Dutch, more professionalized, worked in shifts, with their restaurant meals paid for by the government. That made things a bit easier, but it was still not the same as a life outside the zone of security.[49]

Nelson Mandela had originally given Goldstone a leave of two years from the Constitutional Court. In early 1996, the end of that period was in sight, and the prosecutor was beginning to look forward to returning home and donning the deep green robes of a judge again. When the tribunal was in danger of being negotiated away, he had threatened to resign, but he would much rather walk away with dignity at the end of his term of service. His friends and supporters in the U.S. government and the NGO community, however, did not want to let him go. They, more than anyone else, understood and appreciated the role he had played in keeping the tribunal afloat, especially during Dayton. Almost every public argument against the ICTY had gained some traction—except for criticism of Richard Goldstone himself. Indeed, Goldstone's reputation in the international community was flying high. Once again, there was open speculation that he might be a strong candidate to succeed Boutros Boutros-Ghali and become the first Jewish secretary-general of the U.N.[50]

In early 1996, Aryeh Neier of the Open Society Foundation spearheaded a campaign to extend Goldstone's term of service at the ICTY. The effort involved high-level supporters in the U.S. government, including Secretary of State Warren Christopher and President Bill Clinton. More locally in The Hague, Goldstone received a flurry of calls from friends in the NGO and government communities urging him to stay on as prosecutor, insisting that the tribunal could not afford to lose him now. Goldstone thought that he had an easy answer for them: the president of his country had put a time limit on how long he could shirk his duties on the Constitutional Court. So Neier opened a new line of communications, directed at Nelson Mandela himself. The prosecutor's supporters succeeded in persuading the South African president to extend Goldstone's leave for an additional three months, until the beginning of October 1996. They were eager to buy a little time.[51]

When Mandela agreed to the extension, Goldstone agreed as well. With this arrangement in place, Goldstone realized that he did not want to leave the question of his successor to chance, or to the whims of international politics. The best exit strategy, after all, would be to have a new, well-qualified prosecutor ready to step in.

He talked the matter over with Noleen. The couple agreed on three things. First, it was obvious that the next prosecutor would need to have a greater background in criminal law than Richard himself brought to the post. For these past two years, perhaps, this was not so crucial, because when he arrived trials were still a long way off, and the tribunals needed a political touch. With the prospect of more arrests, and more trials, a credible court would need someone at the helm who could more confidently oversee the legal strategy. Second, the next prosecutor should be fluent in French as well as English. Goldstone recognized that his own limited skills in French had occasionally handicapped his work.

Third, the next prosecutor should be a woman. Even if the principle of diversity were not involved, the evolving emphasis on gender violence in the former Yugoslavia made it important that the prosecution represent as ably and visibly as possible the interests of the women victims. A woman prosecutor would provide strong public leadership, and would also be best positioned to continue Goldstone's efforts to bring gender balance and sensitivity to the work of the prosecutor's office itself.[52]

It was Noleen who brought up a Canadian judge whom the two of them had met at a conference in South Africa some years before. Louise Arbour was smart, capable, had a background in criminal law, was bilingual in French and English, and had a sterling reputation. Arbour had a distinguished record as a legal scholar on criminal law and had spent a term as a judge on the Ontario Court of Appeal. She was not a household name in international legal circles, to be sure, but then the number of women at the top levels of international law were few and far between. On a trip to a conference in Canada, Goldstone paid a visit to Toronto, and found that Arbour would, in fact, be interested in the post.

At his next meeting with Boutros Boutros-Ghali, Goldstone suggested Arbour as his successor. The secretary-general, still wary of the prosecutor and his independent streak, was suspicious. What do the Americans think of this? he demanded, knowing of Goldstone's close ties to the U.S. State Department. So Goldstone turned to Madeleine Albright, who hosted a lunch for Arbour in New York. The Canadian impressed the Americans, and then, at a separate meeting, the Russian delegation; with that combination, her appointment was assured.[53] In February 1996, the Security Council formally named Louise Arbour as the next chief prosecutor for the tribunals, effective at the beginning of October.[54]

11 ▸ IN THE DOCK

I N OCTOBER 1995, the time should have been ripe, at long last, to begin the trial of Duško Tadić. The international media was watching closely. The new U.S. cable television network, Court TV, was hyping Tadić, looking for a sensational international counterpart to the O. J. Simpson trial in Los Angeles that had recently captured the attention of the American public. "I have been saying to anyone who will listen, and every reporter who called me about the Simpson trial, that this trial in The Hague is the real trial of the century," said Court TV founder Steven Brill.[1] Richard Goldstone knew that out of respect for the court's sober image he was obliged to play down the titillating aspects of the media attention, but he was also keenly aware that a prurient interest in the tribunal's affairs was much preferable to no interest at all. Television ratings, after all, could play their part in opening governments' pocketbooks.[2] "America's media supremos believe they have finally found the man to keep the nation hooked on courtroom television," declared the British newspaper, the *Guardian*.[3]

Then a pocketbook issue set back the Tadić trial. The defendant appeared at an October 1995 hearing looking "pallid and clearly sleepless" in the glass booth. Tadić's legal team told the judges that it was short of cash, $78,000 in arrears to be precise, and the shortfall was interfering with the lawyers' ability to prepare the defense.[4] Furthermore, in an ironic twist, Tadić's lawyers said that the Bosnian Serbs were not cooperating with *them* any more than they were cooperating with the prosecutors. The defense needed potential witnesses friendly to Tadić back in his home province of Prijedor, and the authorities there were impeding access.[5]

The three judges on the Tadić trial chamber were reluctant to start a trial with a defense claiming that it was underfunded. Like Goldstone, they were fully aware that any perception of a "stacked deck" against the defendants would sully the reputation of the tribunal. They granted a postponement of the start of the trial to May 1996. The "trial of the century" was on hold again.

The postponement of the Tadić trial was a blow to Goldstone, who was then struggling to maintain the credibility of the ICTY in the run-up to the Dayton peace talks. The chief prosecutor had a Plan B. Like any Plan B, it was inferior to Plan A, but it was better than waiting passively. Goldstone understood that nothing could make the public case for the tribunal better than the stories of the men, women, and children who were exposed to violence in the former Yugoslavia. Even before the postponement of the Tadić trial, he had decided to use the court's rules and procedures to broadcast the narratives of the victims in another case, the case of Dragan Nikolić. Goldstone invoked Rule 61.[6]

On October 9, 1995, Richard Goldstone was not exactly resplendent in his black robe, but he was properly dignified. His head remained uncovered. British barristers wore wigs in court, but this tradition had long since elapsed in South Africa, and he saw no reason to adopt the practice for this courtroom in The Hague. Flanked by two of his OTP colleagues, Grant Niemann and Theresa McHenry, he read from a prepared text.

Before him, at the center of the courtroom, the three judges listened attentively. They were somewhat more resplendent, in red and black robes that provided the only real flash of color in the courtroom. Claude Jorda presided, flanked by Fouad Riad and Elizabeth Odio Benito. In front of them and beneath their bench was a phalanx of court officials and stenographers, armed with a panoply of microphones, computer monitors, and keyboards.

Everyone in the courtroom had a headset. Out of sight, but very much present, a cadre of translators prepared to move the proceedings back and forth between English, French, and the languages of the Balkans. Before the breakup of Yugoslavia, those Balkan languages had a common name: Serbo-Croatian. Now the business of translation itself was embroiled in the conflict. The ICTY relied on the acronym BCS (Bosnian-Croatian-Serbian) to identify a single tongue, but nevertheless finding the right translator for each witness would become a sensitive process.[7]

The audience for this theatrical scene sat in a dim, tiered gallery, separated from the actors by a massive plate-glass wall. Visitors listened in on headphones, even if no translation was necessary. The audience entered the court through metal detectors in a specially constructed security booth on the plaza, in front of the imposing entrance to the old insurance company building.

Everything was in order when Judge Jorda pronounced in French that the hearing was open and requested that the registrar please introduce the case.[8] Judges, prosecutors, stenographers, translators, guards, and visitors were all accounted for. Everyone was in place—that is, with one exception. On the right-hand side of the courtroom, the table reserved for the defense was empty. There was no accused.

From the prosecutor's podium, Richard Goldstone explained to the court why this was so. Eleven months ago, Judge Odio Benito had confirmed the indictment of Dragan Nikolić on charges of murder, torture, and persecution, stemming from his term as camp commander at Sušica in eastern Bosnia. Although a warrant was issued for the arrest of Mr. Nikolić, he had not yet been apprehended, despite the best efforts of the tribunal. He was believed to be at large in territory controlled by the Bosnian Serbs, and there was no real prospect that they were going to turn over one of their own to the ICTY.

Mr. Nikolić was not in The Hague, but others who were at Sušica were present at the tribunal. They were the survivors, the witnesses. Among them was Ibro Osmanović, who had watched in horror as Dragan Nikolić forced a bayonet down the throat of Fikret "Cice" Arnaut.

The procedure in the high-tech courtroom in October 1995 was a halfway measure, a special type of hearing created by the judges of the tribunal, known as Rule 61 by its number in the ICTY's rules of procedure.[9] The rule, created before Goldstone arrived in The Hague, had been a compromise between those judges who wished to allow trials in absentia and others who felt that fairness demanded that the accused be there in person to face the charges.[10] Under Rule 61, there would be no trials in absentia. Instead, if an indicted individual could not be arrested, the prosecutor or the judges would have the option to initiate a special hearing where the testimony of witnesses could be heard in open court. This hearing would not result in a verdict or a sentence. But it would serve, if the evidence was strong enough, as the basis for the judges to issue an international arrest warrant for the accused.

It was far from perfect, but Richard Goldstone was determined to make the best of it. Rule 61, he said, was a way of making sure that the evidence against a perpetrator could not be buried while the defendant was at large. "I have laid much emphasis upon the rights of an accused and of the primary right to a trial in person," Goldstone told the judges. "However, there can be no justification at all for ignoring the rights of the victims and their families. They, too, have a right to be heard. . . . The failure by the accused to come forward and stand trial and the complicity of any UN member state or de facto administration should not be allowed to effectively close the mouths of those victims."[11] At long last, the stories of those who suffered in Bosnia would become part of the formal public record for the larger purposes of law and of history.

Privately, the prosecutor was more ambivalent about the Rule 61 hearings. Whatever pains he took in his public remarks to differentiate this from a trial in absentia, the empty chair at the defendant's table threatened to tell a different story: a procedure without a defendant might highlight the tribunal's impotence.[12] Furthermore, the ICTY risked exposing the witnesses to reprisals back in Bosnia.

After his opening statement, Goldstone turned over the proceedings to OTP lawyers Grant Niemann and Theresa McHenry. Over the next five days, they led thirteen eyewitnesses through testimony that painted a gruesome picture of the ethnic cleansing of the town of Vlasenica and the horrors of detention in Sušica, where Dragan Nikolić declared himself "the God, the stick, and the law." They described the murders of Durmo Handzić and seven other Muslim men, the brutal beatings administered to others, the torture of Cice Arnaut, and the unlawful imprisonment of thousands. Most of the witnesses came forward and testified openly, despite knowing that the Bosnian Serbs might seek to exact retribution on them or on their extended families. One witness gave his testimony under the cloak of confidentiality, his identity screened from the visitor's gallery by a curtain.

The prosecutors guided most of the witnesses through their testimony, but the judges intervened as well. The rules permitted the ICTY judges to ask questions directly of witnesses and to explore avenues of inquiry not necessarily brought forward by the lawyers. Elizabeth Odio Benito played a particularly active part. When one male witness mentioned briefly the conditions of women in Sušica, Odio Benito pressed him for details. The judge also took over from prosecutors to delicately guide a female witness through a string of follow-up questions about sexual violence in the camp.

On October 20, 1995, after the testimony was concluded, the three judges issued a formal review of the indictment. For each of the charges, they affirmed that witness statements provided compelling evidence for pressing forward, and they duly issued the ICTY's first international arrest warrant. All member states of the U.N. were now under a legal obligation to arrest Dragan Nikolić and turn him over to the tribunal, and the court would alert Interpol accordingly.[13] All this was what Goldstone expected and hoped for when the Rule 61 hearing was initiated.

The judges, however, went further. After confirming the charges as presented, the panel took the extraordinary step of issuing what they called an "invitation" to Richard Goldstone to amend the indictment. Noting that witnesses told of instances of rape and sexual assault at Sušica, the judges remarked that these allegations did not seem to relate solely to isolated instances. With that in mind, the judges said, "the Prosecutor may be well-advised to review these statements carefully with a view to ascertaining whether to charge Dragan Nikolić with rape and other forms of sexual assault, either as a crime against humanity or as grave breaches [of the Geneva Conventions] or as war crimes."[14]

It was a novel approach—one Goldstone himself would never have dared to suggest to the judges—but coming from the judges themselves, it provided an opening and a catalyst for further action. The initial surprise gave way to doubt, and more questions. Did the prosecutors really have the evidence to back up charges of sexual assault? When composing the original indictment, Goldstone and his team had been hesitant about overreaching. Now they had heard Judge Odio Benito teasing out the stories of women in the camp in the courtroom, and the full trial chamber had practically chided the prosecution for *not* including rape in the original indictment. The door was open for a more fundamental legal consideration of rape as a tool of war.

Richard Goldstone had made gender crimes a point of emphasis in his first year at the ICTY, beginning with the installation of Patricia Sellers as gender adviser. Yet he was also aware of the challenges involved in trying individuals for rape at the tribunal. At a personal level, witnesses in rape cases were often both at physical and psychological risk. At a legal level, the standards for determining when rape was a war crime had never been developed. In fact, there was not even a settled legal *definition* of rape in the international context. While the prosecutor prided himself on taking steps to bring gender to the forefront of the ICTY's work, he was not inclined to press forward heedlessly.

Patricia Sellers, with her special responsibilities for gender issues, took the lead in drafting a motion that Goldstone submitted to the judges in May 1995 focusing on the protection of witnesses in cases involving gender crimes in connection with the case against Duško Tadić. The indictment included a charge that Tadić himself had committed rape in the Omarska camp, and that other sexual violence had taken place under his authority. The motion asked the judges to allow victims to be given pseudonyms in an indictment and in the process of giving evidence—including being able to testify anonymously in court. The motion, granted by the judges in August, promised confidentiality to victims who would come forward.

The next month, Goldstone deflected a second, private "invitation" on this issue from another of the powerful women on the ICTY bench. In November 1995, Judge Gabrielle Kirk McDonald reviewed the Lašva Valley indictments against five Bosnian Croats. The charges focused on the internment of Muslims, as well as on the destruction of Muslim villages. When Goldstone, under pressure from the Dayton process, came to see her, McDonald took the opportunity to offer some pressure in reverse. Although reluctant to tell the prosecutor directly what charges he should bring, the judge went out of her way to hint to Goldstone that the materials that the OTP provided on Lašva Valley had ample documentation regarding sexual assault. Without being precise, McDonald managed to let Goldstone know that she was following up on Odio Benito's invitation in the Nikolić case to be more aggressive about charging crimes of sexual violence. As with Nikolić, however, the Goldstone did not want to rush to make changes in the Lašva Valley cases that might not hold up in court. The process left a frustrated McDonald wondering how deep the prosecutor's commitment really was to bringing gender crimes charges. "I let them know that I was not happy with their representation," McDonald recalled later. "They came up with all kinds of excuses. I remember that Richard came to me later and apologized, but there was no change in the charges."[15]

Despite his disinclination to make the prosecution of rape a crusade, Goldstone was methodically building the OTP's capacity and looking for an opportunity to bring charges of gender crimes where they had the best chance of success. Rather than focusing on bringing rape charges in *every* case, he saw an opportunity to make a more important mark. He asked Patricia Sellers to focus her attention on a single case, one against a group of Serbian men for whom rape and the enslavement of women was not simply another brutal act. Sexual violence was their calling card.

The girl had a name, but for her own protection she was called in court documents only "FWS-87." In April of 1992, she was fifteen years old when war came to her village. She had grown up in Trošanj, a village of Muslim families on the outskirts of a larger town called Foča in southeastern Bosnia. When Bosnian Serb forces began forcing Muslim families in surrounding towns out of their homes, and when rumors talked of beatings and worse, the girl and her family abandoned their home and camped out in the woods, where they hoped to avoid the worst of the violence.[16]

The Bosnian Serbs caught up with the girl and her family in July when they overran Trošanj and the surrounding territory. The men and the women were split up, and the girl was taken to a rooming house in a nearby town. There a soldier she knew only as "Pero" ordered her to take off her clothes and raped her. Soon after, she was interrogated by four other soldiers, who wanted to know whether she was a virgin. Without affect, she answered that she had been a virgin—until a few minutes ago. She did not have the strength to look anyone in the eye.

She was taken to Foča High School, where she had been a student until April. The classrooms were stripped of desks and chairs and were lined instead with mattresses. At night the soldiers came for her and the other girls who were imprisoned there. Sometimes they took her to the Partizan Sports Hall, which they forced her to clean before they assaulted her. She could not remember all of the men who abused her while in Foča, but she could identify one man who raped her at the sports hall. He was a commander, and his name was Dragoljub Kunarac.

Then came two grim months at a place in the town of Miljevina known only as Karaman's house, where she was locked up as a house slave for three Serbian soldiers. After that, without explanation, she found herself moved to the house of a soldier named Radomir Kovač. She gradually understood that Kovač owned her. He liked to make her and another girl undress, climb on a table in his disheveled living room, and dance to American hard rock, while he toyed with his pistol and occasionally pointed it at them. When they complained, Kovač marched the girls down to the river and threatened to kill them on the spot, but instead he returned them to the apartment and further exploitation.

In February 1993, Kovač sold the girl to two soldiers from Montenegro for 500 deutsche marks. They took her to Podgorica, their country's capital, where they forced her to work in a café and turn her earnings over to them. Shortly before her sixteenth birthday, she managed to scrape together enough money to escape by bus.

Her movements after her escape from Montenegro were not part of the public record, for her own protection and for the protection of her surviving family. What was known about FWS-87, however, was that she was brave enough to tell her story, first to investigators from the Yugoslavia tribunal, and much later in Courtroom 1 at the ICTY in The Hague.

Over the course of 1995, a team at the OTP began to develop a case focused on the events in and around the town of Foča. With the help of NGOs, they tracked down women victims who managed to make their way out of the Balkans: to Germany, to Sweden, to Turkey, some even to the United States. They heard, dozens of times over, stories like the one told by the girl known as FWS-87. And they heard of victims whose stories would never be told, like a twelve-year-old who was also held in the house of Radomir Kovač and who had not been heard from in the three years since.

A portrait emerged of Kunarac, Kovač, and other Bosnian Serb soldiers and paramilitaries in the Foča region. That they were exploitative, cruel, and brutal was obvious, but the pattern of violence was more than a matter of individual cruelty, or the satisfaction of sexual urges. Forced sex for these men was part and parcel of their military campaign in the region, whose goal was the elimination of Muslims from the area, consolidating and unifying a Serbian Bosnia. It was not an orchestrated campaign with orders issuing neatly down the hierarchy from headquarters. But it was a campaign nevertheless— a chaotic, unpredictable onslaught against Muslim women serving as an instrument of terror. Who among the Muslims, after all, would want to return to Foča, the site of such savagery?

The campaign, in Serbian terms, was a success. By 1995, there was no Foča. The buildings of the town still stood, but its Muslim population was long since scattered. Foča was no longer on the map. In its place was a town with a provocative Serbian name, Srbinje ("the place of the Serbs").

In June 1996, Richard Goldstone filed an indictment in what would, stubbornly, still be called the Foča case. The charges focused exclusively on crimes of sexual violence, including rape and enslavement. Eight men, including Kunarac and Kovač, were charged with gender crimes both as war crimes and as crimes against humanity. The full emphasis of the Foča trials would be on forced sex as a method of terrorizing and defeating a civilian population. The story of the girl called FWS-87, along with many others, would not be hidden from public view. It would instead be part of the public record, used both to punish the perpetrators and to demonstrate to a wider world that justice was coming to the aid of those victims who, in previous centuries, might simply have been neglected or ignored.

Under Richard Goldstone's leadership, the world's first prosecutions of gender crimes as systematic atrocities went forward.[17] The prosecutor himself was not the crusader or the catalyst. Much of the credit for these developments belonged properly to the staff of NGOs who advocated tirelessly for women victims, to journalists who made those stories part of the global public discussion, and to the women judges who used their authority to prod the prosecution to adopt a bolder legal strategy. Goldstone's patient approach sometimes exasperated advocates for women who found him too cautious, or who believed that his hesitations unconsciously betrayed his lack of commitment to the issue. Yet, in the end, Goldstone's methods laid the foundation for a legal process, pressed forward by Patricia Sellers, that proved remarkably effective. The OTP not only brought gender crimes indictments; over the course of time, they made them stick. Goldstone's thoroughness, political skills, and timing provided an important complement to the zeal of the advocates.

May 7, 1996, was a brilliant spring morning, and the tulips were in bloom in The Hague. The quiet plaza outside the ICTY was a frenzy of cameras and microphones under canvas tents. Nearly 400 journalists had descended for the biggest day in the tribunal's short history.[18] The judges, with Gabrielle Kirk McDonald presiding, were in their customary red and black. The court recorders, the guards, and the translators were at the ready. The visitors' gallery was packed. The trial of Duško Tadić was finally ready to begin.[19]

This time, unlike at the Rule 61 hearing for Nikolić, the defendant was present. Tadić, who had looked scruffy and worn at his initial hearing more than a year ago, was dressed on this day in a sharp navy suit and tie. The curious omission now was at the prosecutor's table: the one expected person who was not in sight was Richard Goldstone.

The chief prosecutor was watching the proceedings on television, from his office just steps away from Courtroom 1. He had decided that he did not want to steal the moment from the prosecuting team that had worked so hard to prepare for this day. He would let Grant Niemann, who was leading the case for the OTP, make the opening statement and kick off the ICTY's first trial.[20]

For those who thought of Richard Goldstone as a man hungry for attention and publicity, it was a curious choice. Why would Goldstone pass up the chance to issue the 1990s equivalent of Robert Jackson's "stay the hand of vengeance"? Some critics thought that it was precisely because of the shadow of Jackson that he stayed away. Goldstone was worried, they surmised, that his speech would be unfavorably compared to that of his American predecessor. Perhaps so, but from this day forward, it would be that much harder to argue that Richard Goldstone was a man driven by playing to the cameras.

Goldstone had, however, been a strong proponent of having cameras in the courtroom.[21] In its first two years, the ICTY had scant opportunity to have a direct impact on minds and lives of the people of the former Yugoslavia, those who had the largest stake in its proceedings. Now, with the judges' approval, television cameras in the courtroom would provide gavel-to-gavel coverage, not only on Court TV, but via a service called Internews back to the Balkans. Hundreds of thousands of people in Serbia, Croatia, and Bosnia would have The Hague beamed into their living rooms, in their own language. If the ICTY was to play a role in the process of healing the wounds of war and bringing a more stable peace to the region, it would begin with the trial of "the butcher of Omarska."

The chief prosecutor also played a key role in creating the circumstances for the kind of fairness that he believed would help build credibility in the court. The shortfall in funds for the defense had caused a delay of six months, but Goldstone chose to address an even more important liability for his opponents. Tadić's lawyer, Mikhail Wladimiroff, had been working alone. Worse, Wladimiroff, who lived in the Netherlands, was trained and practiced in the Continental law tradition. In Dutch courts, defense lawyers did not cross-examine witnesses; that job was left to the investigating judge. But the ICTY rules gave the edge to common law practice in the court-room: Duško Tadić needed a lawyer on his team who could hold his own in the rough-and-tumble environment of the adversarial system.

Some months earlier, Goldstone had raised this problem with Mark Ellis, the director of the American Bar Association (ABA)'s Central and Eastern European Initiative. Ellis had asked Goldstone how the ABA could be helpful to the tribunal. The prosecutor answered promptly: shore up the defense. So with Goldstone's blessing, the ABA provided funds to Tadić's defense, and, even more critically, Ellis helped recruit an experienced British barrister, Stephen Kay, to be a part of the Tadić team. The defense team was still vastly outnumbered by the resources in the OTP.[22] By helping to level the playing field, however, Goldstone had nevertheless made his own colleagues' job more challenging.[23]

Grant Niemann, the Australian senior attorney at the OTP, took the floor instead of Richard Goldstone on day one of the Tadić trial. Over three methodical hours, Niemann laid out the case against the sometime local parking officer.[24] Critics of the tribunal complained that the first defendant was a little fish, but from the point of view of the prosecution, there were advantages to this. Duško Tadić was not at some distance from the violence in Prijedor, insulated from responsibility by a complex chain of command. Niemann was able to describe scenes where Tadić himself was alleged to have beaten and tortured Muslim men and women under his absolute control during his on-again, off-again presence at the Omarska camp. The prosecutor mentioned a string of eyewitnesses who would be able to speak to Tadić's direct involvement in violence directed at the Muslim population, as part of a pattern of persecution that stretched across the country.

Defense attorney Mikhail Wladimiroff spoke more concisely. His argument, in brief, was twofold. First, Duško Tadić was not in fact present at the incidents described by the prosecution. And second, if it was established that he *was* present, he was there merely as an observer, and not as an actor.

The cameras rolled, and the Tadić trial moved forward over the next several months. Goldstone had high hopes, both in the effectiveness of the prosecution's legal case and in the trial as a public relations boon for the tribunal. There were setbacks on both fronts.

Before the trial ever got started, the prosecution was forced to drop a key charge against Tadić. A young woman held at Omarska had told ICTY investigators that Tadić had forced her to have sex with him. Agreeing to testify under the shield of confidentiality, she was identified on the prosecution's list as "Witness F." Days before the trial, after hours of conversation and preparation, Witness F told the prosecutor that she was too frightened, that she was unwilling to testify in open court. Without her, the prosecution had no choice but to drop the charge of rape as a war crime. Goldstone's team offered all the assurances and protection that they could, but they could not and would not compel a reluctant victim to testify.[25]

A different and more strategic choice, however, threatened to make the Tadić trial irrelevant as a public demonstration of international justice. After the opening statements, the prosecution spent four days questioning a young British historian named James Gow. From a legal point of view, this was all very sensible. Through Gow, the prosecution entered into the record the long and complex history of the descent into war in the former Yugoslavia, and the particular events that led to violence in Bosnia and finally in the Prijedor district where Duško Tadić lived. This was, after all, the first trial, and if the prosecution was going to bring charges of war crimes, then it was going to have to prove legally that a war was indeed taking place, what its nature was, and how the events at the Omarska camp fit into the larger picture.[26]

If Gow's testimony made sense as legal strategy, it was a disaster in terms of public relations. Viewers who turned on the Tadić trial—whether on Court TV or in Bosnia—were not tuning in for a history lesson. Even the judges got impatient. "Could you please fast-forward a couple of centuries?" Gabrielle Kirk McDonald later remembered asking.[27] To make matters worse, Gow did not always demonstrate authoritative command of the material. It did not take long for the interest of the global media to flag. Following Gow, the prosecution called a series of "policy" witnesses who filled in the details of the structure and actions of the Bosnian Serbs and their allies across the border in Serbia proper.[28]

Again, as legal strategy, Niemann had good reasons for proceeding in this fashion. Part of the prosecutor's problem was that the judges had refused to clarify for the prosecution exactly what the standard of proof would be for conviction. Everyone was operating in unfamiliar territory. The judges were reluctant to create abstract language around standards of proof without hearing the evidence. So the prosecutors, in the absence of guidance, felt that they needed to err on the side of overkill to make sure that they were leaving no stone unturned in establishing Tadić's guilt. In addition, this broader context would be helpful in terms of creating a record on which future trials could build. As public theater, however, it was terrible. By mid-June, nearly a month into the trial, no eyewitnesses had yet been called, and scarcely any of the witnesses had so much as mentioned Tadić's name. The visitors' gallery was virtually deserted, and the trial had disappeared from the international press.[29]

Richard Goldstone felt a sense of deflation as the opportunity for public attention faded away, but he was not inclined to interfere with what he recognized was a defensible legal strategy. "You can't micro-manage a trial if you're not really steeped in it," he explained later. He conceded that Gow was "an unbelievably boring witness" and that this was a "tactical error." His preference would have been to call more eyewitnesses earlier, but overruling Niemann went against the chief prosecutor's philosophy of trusting his subordinates. He let the Tadić case proceed at its ponderous pace.[30]

Once the prosecution did get started on eyewitnesses in June 1996, its case moved forward in fits and starts. The courtroom echoed with some compelling and disturbing accounts of the horrors of life in Prijedor and at Omarska. Yet, other aspects of the case proved embarrassing to the prosecutors, especially when key confidential witnesses changed or withdrew their stories. These reversals meant that some of the most serious charges against Tadić were unlikely to stand up to proof in the court of law.[31]

Later commentators would complain that Tadić was a "scapegoat," that his trial was "less an example of individual responsibility than collective guilt" and "a token gesture" for a court that "was built to flounder."[32] Despite the early challenges of the Tadić trial, Goldstone had an apt response. "How can one say that a man like Tadić is a little fish?" he asked. "Here is somebody who carried out multiple murders, rapes and acts of torture against his neighbors. If he had carried out these acts in the United States he would have been called one of the worst criminals of the century."[33]

In the summer of 1996, there was a welcome problem at the ICTY: a traffic jam in the tribunal's only courtroom. Every day possible, Gabrielle Kirk McDonald was presiding over the Tadić trial. But not every day was possible. One day, the Tadić trial had to give way to the formal courtroom appearance of two Bosnians Muslims who had been turned over to the ICTY to stand trial in a case focused on a camp in Čelebići.[34] Another day the court announced the confirmed indictments in the Foča sexual violence case. And in mid-July, the Tadić trial had to shut down for almost two weeks to make way for another sensational proceeding: a Rule 61 hearing in the case of Radovan Karadžić and Ratko Mladić.

The Rule 61 hearings for Karadžić and Mladić had a special purpose. It was a way of counteracting the embarrassing fact that for seven months they had eluded arrest, even with 60,000 NATO forces in the region. Over the course of two weeks in July, the empty chairs for Karadžić and Mladić were center stage in the ICTY courtroom. Almost a year to the day after he shot dozens of Muslim men at Pilice, Dražen Erdemović took the stand to describe his part in the events at Srebrenica. In May, he had pleaded guilty to murder and associated war crimes; he would be sentenced in November. In the meantime, he was the star witness in the proceedings, a man who was willing to describe, in excruciating detail, how he came to be part of a swath of violence that had taken the lives of untold thousands.

It had been almost exactly two years since the Security Council appointed Richard Goldstone as prosecutor at the ICTY. A man of action and optimism, Goldstone had hoped for much more to be achieved in two years than had actually come to pass. Yet the important thing was this: in the summer of 1996, the ICTY was still standing. The testimony of Dražen Erdemović was living witness to the possibilities of the tribunal. A man would face punishment for his part in a horrifying massacre. And he would also help make the case against two of the architects of the Balkan atrocities. Justice, with all of its imperfections, was being served.

12 ▸ RWANDA

O N APRIL 6, 1994, two countries in southern Africa stood at dramatically different historical moments. In South Africa, Richard Goldstone was helping to lay the groundwork for the first democratic elections in his nation's history. In Rwanda, Prime Minister Agathe Uwilingiyimana heard shocking news that portended the disintegration of her country.[1]

A phone call at 8:30 P.M. informed the prime minister that the president of Rwanda, Juvénal Habyarimana, had just been killed in a plane crash. The circumstances were suspicious. The head of the prime minister's security detail told her urgently that she should move from her house in the Kiyovu neighborhood of the capital, Kigali, to a more secure location.

Agathe Uwilingiyimana was a success story, a woman of only forty who was born to farming parents and had challenged traditional gender roles at a young age, becoming a teacher of mathematics and chemistry. While still a science teacher, she founded a self-help organization for rural women that brought her to the attention of government officials and earned her a post in the Ministry of Commerce. She became active in politics, joining an opposition party, and ended up as minister of education in a power-sharing scheme under President Habyarimana. In 1993, the president named her as the first woman prime minister in the history of Rwanda.

By background a Hutu, the majority in Rwanda, the prime minister was known for her opposition to ethnic favoritism. As an education official, she had opposed quota systems and supported merit ranking, positions that put her at odds with powerful Hutu leaders who had been fanning the flames of rivalry with the minority Tutsis in the country.

On the night of April 6, Uwilingiyimana refused to leave her house, choosing instead to try to reach members of the cabinet by telephone and address the crisis. One man she could not reach was Théoneste Bagosora, the head of the Rwandan military and the man most responsible for securing the safety of the city in the wake of the death of the president.

The situation in Kigali quickly deteriorated. The prime minister's house was guarded by ten Rwandan policemen and half a dozen U.N. peacekeepers from Ghana. Reports reached the house that soldiers were blockading streets and that units of the Rwandan presidential guard were moving through a nearby neighborhood targeting government ministers. Uwilingiyimana phoned the headquarters of the Rwandan U.N. peacekeepers and asked for reinforcements. The situation was urgent enough that the security detail moved the prime minister and her family into hiding in a home next door. Four jeeps of Belgian peacekeepers had arrived at the compound by 5:00 A.M.

Shortly after 7:30 A.M., the advancing soldiers opened fire on the prime minister's compound. They disarmed the security detail, murdered the Belgian peacekeepers, and then moved in on the home next door where Uwilingiyimana and her family had taken refuge. There were loud voices and gunshots. Soldiers argued about whether the prime minister should be killed or taken to military headquarters.

By mid-morning, Agathe Uwilingiyimana's naked, bullet-ridden body was lying openly in the garden outside her house. A bottle was shoved into her vagina. She never made it to military headquarters, where the man in charge, Théoneste Bagosora, was presiding over the start of a genocide.

Richard Goldstone had been named prosecutor of the Yugoslavia tribunal in mid-July 1994, just days after the Tutsi-led Rwanda Patriotic Forces swept into Kigali, bringing the genocide to an end. With the precedent of the ICTY already in place, there were already calls for a similar tribunal to be created for justice in Rwanda.

To some extent, the motivation was the same. As with the former Yugo-slavia, civilians bore the brunt of the violence in Rwanda, and the international community had failed to act on the chances that it had to prevent or at least slow the pace of the atrocity. An after-the-fact tribunal would not bring back to life the 800,000 dead, but a court offered one route to establishing the truth and holding the killers accountable.

The movement to create a tribunal had gained momentum as early as August 1994. Members of the new Rwandan government, a coalition of Tutsis and Hutus who had opposed the genocide, at first insisted that they were prepared to try and execute thousands of individuals who perpetrated the violence.[2] Yet the prospect of thousands of rapid trials was hardly realistic in a country whose entire judicial system had just been destroyed. John Shattuck, the American official who had played a key role in the establishment of justice for the Balkans, traveled to Kigali and worked to persuade the government to support an international tribunal.[3] The Rwandans agreed, as long as the international community promised to deliver justice quickly and efficiently.

Goldstone was still finding his feet in the OTP at The Hague, but he made sure to enter the conversation about the situation in Rwanda. After all, there was a powerful argument that the best course forward was simply to expand the mandate of the Yugoslavia tribunal to include the situation in the beleaguered African nation. Same judges, same prosecutor, same investigators, same courtroom. From the standpoint of efficiency, it might be much easier than starting from scratch.

When the U.S. State Department's David Scheffer put this argument to Goldstone in September, the prosecutor thought that it was a good idea.[4] He was keenly aware that it had taken more than a year for all the pieces to be in place at the ICTY, and the first indictments had not yet been issued. How much longer might it take to start from scratch with a tribunal in sub-Saharan Africa, where the infrastructure was weaker than in continental Europe? Besides, Goldstone had his private reasons for supporting a joint court. An institution charged with conducting trials for two situations would presumably be better positioned to garner the financial commitments it needed for success.

The idea of a fully integrated joint tribunal did not survive the process of international politics. The Rwandans were not enthusiastic about having their situation subsumed into the existing court, with cases to be tried thousands of miles from the scene of the crimes. The scenario echoed a colonial mindset, with resources and the seat of power firmly planted on European soil.

There were, however, strong legal reasons to join the two courts in some fashion. International criminal justice, if it was going to be credible and effective, needed consistency. If two international courts proceeded along separate legal journeys, confusing and contradictory rulings might undermine the whole project. If, for example, one court ruled that commanders were responsible for war crimes committed by their subordinates, while in a similar circumstance the other tribunal let the military leadership off the hook, international criminal justice would begin to look less like law and more like chaos.

The United States, having first supported a joint tribunal, floated a proposal in September that recommended two tribunals with two different prosecutors.[5] Richard Goldstone told David Scheffer that he strenuously objected to the idea of separate prosecutors for the two tribunals.[6] This would be financially wasteful, create unnecessary bureaucracy, and undermine consistency. In addition, a second international prosecutor could emerge as a rival, creating an unhealthy competition between two OTPs for money, resources, and attention.

So a compromise was born: a new court based in Africa, but sharing certain resources and practices with its sister tribunal in Europe. Trials would be in Africa, but in the context of the rule of law as a global endeavor. The two tribunals would be independent U.N. institutions, but they would share two crucial features. First, they would have a common appeals chamber, based in The Hague. Appeals of rulings from both courts would be heard by the same judges, and the legal principles would have the same force in both tribunals. Furthermore, the two tribunals would share a chief prosecutor. The OTP, however, would be divided geographically. For the Rwanda tribunal the main investigative and legal work of the prosecutor would be done from an office in Kigali, at a great distance from the chief prosecutor's main office in The Hague.

With the Security Council ready for a vote at the end of October 1994, the government of Rwanda suddenly balked.[7] As it happened, Rwanda was currently serving a term as a member of the Security Council, and it would therefore have a vote on the matter. The heart of the issue was the death penalty, which was ruled out by the proposed statute of the new tribunal in deference to a strong but not universal international consensus. The Rwandans, recovering from the hand-to-hand slaughter that had enveloped their country, believed that only executions would satisfy their citizens' hunger for punishment and justice. Having supported a tribunal for almost three months, they now did an about-face. Even after a delay of the vote by a week for extended discussions, the Rwandan government was unpersuaded.

On November 8, 1994, Security Council resolution 955 created the new International Criminal Tribunal for Rwanda (ICTR).[8] The ICTR would have jurisdiction over crimes committed in Rwanda between January 1 and December 31, 1994. The resolution passed 13-1, with Rwanda itself as the only negative vote. Article 15 of the Statute specifically stated that the chief prosecutor of the Yugoslavia tribunal would serve as the chief prosecutor of the Rwanda tribunal. Richard Goldstone now had two jobs.

Goldstone traveled to Rwanda immediately to launch the OTP's work in Kigali. Rwanda at the end of 1994 was still a country in shambles, in the process of frantic ongoing patchwork to piece together the roads, the buildings, and the institutions that had been destroyed so rapidly earlier in the year. That tragedy on such a vast scale should have happened on his own continent and in his own era shook Goldstone deeply. He had witnessed the aftermath of violence in his own country on many occasions—after Sharpeville, after Soweto, and before him in a Johannesburg courtroom—but the scale and immediacy of suffering in Rwanda dwarfed anything he had seen. Or smelled. Even six months later, a lingering odor of death blew through the breeze in Kigali.[9]

Yet he also felt a keen sense of purpose in returning to his own continent to bring the promise of law and justice. He did not know what to expect from the Rwandan leadership, following their vote against the tribunal at the U.N. But he found that his reception in Rwanda reflected his origins. He was an African, and one known to be almost a personal emissary of Nelson Mandela. When he met the new president, Pasteur Bizimungu, the two men dispensed with formal handshakes in favor of a hearty African embrace. Even in this fractured country, Goldstone felt that in some way he had come home.

He also found the Rwandans readier to cooperate than he had anticipated. They pledged their assistance in establishing an office for the prosecutor in Kigali, a home base for investigations. Goldstone believed investigations and prosecutions at the ICTR would be "much easier" than at the ICTY. "The war is over," he told one reporter, "and we shall be immediately able to investigate top leadership because we know who they are."[10] The prosecutor and the Rwandan government agreed to disagree about the death penalty. Goldstone adopted the posture of the attentive listener, ready to learn and to absorb. The Rwandans still planned to conduct their own trials, theoretically of lower-level perpetrators. This was permitted under the ICTR's statute, but what was left unclear was how exactly to decide which accused would be tried in the local courts, and which in the international setting. The prosecutor postponed points of controversy. He could not afford to alienate his hosts.

Once these niceties were completed, the challenges of establishing a prosecutor's office at a distance, in a neglected part of the world, and without sufficient resources, began to catch up with him. If the Yugoslavia tribunal was a stepchild of the international community, then the Rwanda tribunal was the stepchild of a stepchild. Neglect had replaced exploitation in the history of Western treatment of Africa.

It was hard to imagine that the funding issues would be more acute than those he faced with the Yugoslavia tribunal, but they were. The U.N. had created the new tribunal without appropriations, a reflection both of ambivalence and of the organization's ongoing fiscal crisis. Once again, Goldstone was willing to use his diplomatic contacts and reputation to raise funds from outside the U.N. system, but once again the U.N. bureaucracy seemed bent upon thwarting him. When he raised some start-up funding from Switzerland, the U.N.'s Office of Legal Affairs berated him for begging directly from governments. Goldstone reminded his U.N. contacts that Switzerland was not a member of the U.N., so there was no reason to stand on ceremony.[11]

Naturally the U.N. had not allotted funds for furniture or equipment for the prosecutor's office in Kigali. Goldstone spent an unreasonable amount of time trying to solve this problem. He finally received a phone call from Kofi Annan, then a U.N. under-secretary-general. Annan had good news and bad news. The good news was that he had turned up some unused furniture in a U.N. warehouse in Brindisi, on the heel of Italy. The bad news was that the U.N. could not afford to send the furniture to Kigali. So the chief prosecutor had to spend some of his capital with the U.S. State Department to help commandeer an American transport jet to haul the tables and chairs southward.[12] John Shattuck helped to organize a donors' conference in Kigali in early 1995, but the fragmentary and uncertain basis of the funding inevitably slowed down the tribunal's progress.

Even more difficult, however, was the challenge of establishing a powerful and effective office of investigations from so far away. Over the course of his tenure as prosecutor, Goldstone traveled to Kigali every six weeks or so.[13] But these rushed visits lasted only days at a time, not nearly enough for him to put any real stamp on the development of the office. Furthermore, despite being chief prosecutor, he had a limited say over the leadership of the Kigali operation. Under the ICTR statute, the deputy prosecutor for the tribunal was to be named by the secretary-general of the U.N., after consultation with the chief prosecutor.[14] By the end of 1994, Boutros Boutros-Ghali and Richard Goldstone had already been at odds, so Goldstone was not surprised that the required process of consultation was no better than pro forma.[15] In January 1995, Boutros-Ghali named Honoré Rakotomanana of Madagascar as the deputy prosecutor, and Andronico Adede of Kenya as the registrar, the chief administrator for the tribunal.

Hiring the rest of the staff was even more difficult. It was far easier, Goldstone discovered, to attract well-qualified investigators and prosecutors to work in The Hague than it was to persuade them to pull up stakes and move to Kigali, where the security situation was still precarious and the only housing available was in two badly damaged hotels.[16] Furthermore, the Rwandans had their own political calculations. The tribunal desperately needed French speakers, as French was widely spoken in Rwanda, a former Belgian colony. But the Rwandan government, furious at the French government for its refusal to provide assistance at a key moment in the genocide, objected strenuously to providing job opportunities for French citizens. The Belgian government, for its part, actively prohibited its citizens from working at the tribunal, clearly a violation of accepted international practice.[17] There were limited qualified applicants from other Francophone countries in Africa. By August 1995, nine months after the tribunal's establishment, the Kigali office still had fewer than a dozen staff members.[18]

It did not help that the deputy prosecutor and the registrar were incompetent as managers.[19] Their hiring practices were lax, and their budget management was almost nonexistent. Rakotomanana, the deputy prosecutor, was laid-back and personable, but he did little to inspire the confidence that Goldstone had in Graham Blewitt in The Hague. There was in-fighting among the personnel, and a desperate grab for personal gain that the deputy was not able to check. There were no budgets or accounting procedures. One employee received a double salary, told no one, and then requested a large personal advance and disappeared. Even so, his contract was extended. The registrar, Adede, tried to seize control of the situation, but his dictatorial style alienated staff and contributed to the dysfunction.

The situation was complicated by the fact that the U.N. had decided to locate the seat of the court not in Rwanda but instead in the city of Arusha, in neighboring Tanzania. This would give the judges and court staff a bit more breathing room from the threat of political interference from the Rwandan government, but it had the distinct disadvantage of fragmenting the tribunal's operations and contributing to a sense of remoteness from the prosecution offices.

Richard Goldstone was aware that not all was right in Kigali, but inevitably Rwanda commanded relatively little of his time and attention between visits. He had his hands full in The Hague. When the deputy prosecutor told him that, yes, there were certain challenges, but that he had the situation well in hand, Goldstone was happy to believe him and not press the matter further.[20] Besides, back at the ICTY, his team was complaining that the Rwanda tribunal was a distraction from the many demands more immediately at hand.[21]

For most of Richard Goldstone's tenure as chief prosecutor, the OTP in Kigali was little better than a work in progress.[22] The Rwanda situation, however, had some distinct advantages for prosecution that helped to offset its drawbacks. Goldstone's political skills helped him make the most of those advantages. Despite its many weaknesses, in some ways the Rwanda tribunal leapfrogged over its ICTY sibling as it began to come to terms with the legal dimensions of genocide.

Rwanda was in shambles, its people reeling from death and loss, but from a prosecutor's point of view, a relative peace meant that work could be done. The first substantial investigation for the new tribunal involved a mass grave site in the prefecture of Kibuye. The killing in Kibuye had been intensive and concentrated, in both time and location. There were thousands of bodies in four sites across the area: the Catholic Church in the Home St. Jean area, the stadium near the main traffic circle in the center of town, a second church in an area called Mubuga, and a string of fields in a place called Bisesero.[23]

As with Yugoslavia, speed was of the essence if the tribunal was going to acquire credibility. When the chief of investigations for the ICTR told Goldstone proudly that he would be able to put together strong cases against top leaders within eighteen months, the prosecutor rebuked him sharply. If you don't have indictments within eighteen *weeks*, Goldstone said, then you won't even be here eighteen months from now.[24] By April 1995, four months after the tribunal was established, Goldstone was telling the international media that his office had identified 400 suspects whom they were investigating.[25] But it would not be until December 1995 that the first Rwanda indictments, focused on the situation at Kibuye, were confirmed by the judges.[26]

Compared to the former Yugoslavia, it should have been easier to find and arrest those accused of crimes in Rwanda. Unlike the Bosnian Serbs, there was no governmental or military authority to shield them. Most had fled the country, but in theory there should have been no safe haven for them elsewhere in Africa or anywhere else in the world.

The international community, however, showed no particular resolve. As early as the summer of 1994, for example, the French were insisting that their hands were tied regarding the arrest of suspects, giving the technical reason that the 1948 Genocide Convention had not been formally integrated into French law.[27] Once the tribunal was formally established, the United States, with Madeleine Albright's leadership, pushed for a follow-up Security Council resolution that would require U.N. members to detain Rwandan suspects and to cooperate with the prosecutor's office.[28] But by the time the resolution was adopted in February 1995, the language had been watered down (with France again playing a key part). The resolution merely "urged" governments to do their best.[29]

Legally, the situation was somewhat delicate. The list of wanted individuals was amorphous and variable, a collection of names informally floated by the Rwandan government, by human rights organizations, and by the OTP itself. Many of the wanted individuals were living in refugee camps in neighboring countries, such as Zaire (now the Democratic Republic of the Congo), where Hutu leaders were reorganizing and creating new, smaller reigns of terror among the hundreds of thousands of displaced Rwandans.

The good news was that other African countries were detaining genocide suspects. Sometimes it was at the request of the Rwandan government, at other times because these individuals were causing new problems within the refugee camps. By early 1996, jails in Cameroon, Zaire, Zambia, and Belgium, among other countries, were holding individuals suspected of crimes in Rwanda. But with the U.N. having only "urged" cooperation with the ICTR, the process of transferring these individuals to the custody of the international court got bogged down.

On his visits to Rwanda, Goldstone made side trips across the African continent, asking officials for their cooperation.[30] The relationship with the ICTR was complicated by Rwanda's continuing ambivalence. With Rwanda still publicly calling for more authority to conduct its own domestic trials, other African nations were hesitant to cooperate fully with the international prosecutor. Some were quite public about it. Kenya's Daniel arap Moi said explicitly in 1995 that not only would he not cooperate with the ICTR, he would not even permit its investigators to enter the country.[31] Goldstone had to send him a public letter reminding Kenya of its obligations as a member of the U.N. Other countries were less overt about their resistance than Kenya, but they were deft at deflecting direct requests from the ICTR prosecutor.

Despite these challenges, the Rwanda tribunal succeeded, within eighteen months, in an achievement that would take its sister tribunal for Yugoslavia many years: it had in custody one of the top military leaders who orchestrated the mass violence. It did not come easily.

In early 1996, Théoneste Bagosora, was living in Cameroon, in West Africa. In April 1994, Bagosora's presidential guard had rampaged through the affluent neighborhoods of Kigali, targeting government ministers and others suspected of opposition to the regime, and eventually killing and maiming the body of Prime Minister Uwilingiyimana. A U.N. Commission of Experts had identified Bagosora as a key player in the lead-up to the genocide. From a base in neighboring Zaire, he had smuggled thousands of weapons into Rwanda via the Seychelles Islands, arming both the government soldiers and extremist Hutu factions who would be at the apex of the violence.

In January 1996 the government of Belgium formally asked Cameroon to detain and extradite Bagosora, on charges that he ordered the killing of the ten Belgian soldiers who had been guarding the prime minister's compound on the night that the genocide began. The Cameroonian authorities did arrest Bagosora along with another suspect, setting off a three-way tug-of-war. Once the Rwandan authorities learned that Bagosora was in custody, they insisted that the colonel should be sent to face charges in his home country first.[32] Bagosora, through his lawyer, made clear that he would be happy to be questioned in Belgium. Anything was better, as far as he was concerned, than being sent into the custody of Rwanda, where he would almost certainly face the death penalty.

Richard Goldstone stepped actively into the fray and met with the entire Rwandan cabinet in Kigali. The chief prosecutor told the assembled ministers that he would rather shut down the tribunal himself than yield important suspects to a Rwandan justice system that barely existed.[33] Goldstone was outnumbered in the room, but he had a trump card: as with the ICTY, the ICTR specifically had primacy over Rwanda and any other national jurisdiction. Goldstone proposed a face-saving compromise. Cameroon would send Bagosora to the ICTR, while sending a less significant second suspect arrested with him to Rwanda for trial.[34] Goldstone also allowed it to be understood that he wished to avoid such confrontations in the future, and that he would not, by and large, stand in the way of Rwanda's ongoing efforts to proceed with its own trials. It was not exactly a promise that he would not interfere, but the discussion was left at a vague enough level that the Rwandans agreed to let Bagosora face trial in Arusha.[35]

Securing Bagosora took the better part of another year. On at least two occasions, the ICTR sent a U.N. plane to the Cameroonian capital of Yaoundé only to return empty-handed as the authorities stalled and kept their options open.[36] Bagosora was not transferred to Arusha until early 1997, by which time Richard Goldstone had left the tribunal, and his trial did not begin until 2002. Nevertheless, securing one of the top leaders of the genocide was a major coup for the young Rwanda tribunal, evidence that despite its structural shortcomings, it had the potential, more quickly than its counterpart in The Hague, to hold the "big fish" accountable.

As it turned out, the first trial held in Arusha focused neither on the Kibuye massacres nor on Théoneste Bagosora. Instead, the man on trial was a *bourgmestre*, the mayor of a community called Taba. His name was Jean-Paul Akayesu. His arrest in Zambia in October 1995 gave the small ICTR prosecutor's staff a focus to their work. By February 1996, Akayesu became the first man in custody to be charged by an international court with the crime of genocide.[37]

As mayor, Akayesu had extensive political powers in his district. When the violence broke out in early 1994, Akayesu did not participate directly at first, and even offered some initial resistance to local efforts to attack the Tutsi population. But within ten days of the start of the massacres Akayesu had become an active participant, helping chase down Tutsis trying to escape, identifying intellectuals and other local leaders for the Hutu militia to kill, and allowing local police to rape and abuse Tutsi women who had sought shelter and safety at the municipal offices. He remained in office through June 1994—in other words, through the full horror of the genocide. At least 2,000 Tutsis died in Taba during his period of leadership.[38]

With full access to witnesses at in the Taba area and with the accused in custody, the prosecutor's office in Kigali amassed considerable direct evidence against Akayesu. From The Hague, Goldstone helped coordinate the process of solidifying the legal case against the ICTR's first defendant. One of the challenges involved proving the charge of genocide. It was obvious to all that hundreds of thousands of Tutsis had been killed by their Hutu countrymen. Proving this legally as genocide was less obvious.

Under the U.N. Genocide Convention, genocide was not simply mass killing. The killing had to be undertaken with intent to destroy a national, ethnic, racial, or religious group. Was the Tutsi population, in fact, a group under one of those four categories? A case could be made that they were not. After all, like the Hutu, they were Rwandan citizens. It was notoriously difficult to draw a racial distinction between Hutus and Tutsis, who shared a language (Kinyarwanda), religious beliefs (most were Catholic), and common values. The two peoples did not fit most understandings of separate ethnic groups, which generally connoted some significant difference in history or culture. Yet the Tutsi were indeed slaughtered because they were Tutsi. Was there room in the definition of genocide to accommodate the Rwandan situation?[39]

Goldstone put the staff of the ICTY in The Hague at the disposal of the understaffed Kigali office of the ICTR to work out an innovative approach to the problem. Ethnicity, they argued, could be *created* as well as it could be inherited. In Rwanda, the Belgian colonizers had, in effect, codified some loose distinctions between peoples within their colony. The Belgians had eventually created a system where families were legally defined on one side or another of an artificial ethnic divide. What began as a colonizer's tool of "divide and conquer" became an embedded fact of life in an independent country, with identity as either a Hutu or a Tutsi determined by birth and enshrined in laws. It did not matter, the prosecutors argued, whether Tutsis were biologically or culturally distinct from Hutus. They were a separate group in political and legal terms. When Tutsis were targeted for death, it was on the basis of this group identity. This was the essence of genocide.

The Akayesu case broke new ground in another area as well: the prosecution of gender crimes. The original indictment of Akayesu included genocide, but it did not include rape. As at the ICTY, a woman judge was not content to let crimes of sexual violence go unnoticed and unpunished. Judge Navanethem Pillay of South Africa, one of the three judges on the Akayesu trial, was as active as Elizabeth Odio Benito had been in the ICTY trial of Dragan Nikolić. Hearing witness testimony in the prosecution's case about the rape of women by policemen under Akayesu's authority, Pillay went on the offensive, questioning the witnesses more intensively about these incidents, and openly inviting the prosecution to amend the original indictment. With the judge's encouragement, the prosecution took the unusual step of amending the Akayesu indictment in mid-stream, at the point that it closed its presentation of the case.[40] By this time, the rape charge at the ICTY against Dusko Tadić had been withdrawn. So Jean-Paul Akayesu became doubly notorious. Not only was he the first individual to be convicted of genocide, but he was the first to be tried and found guilty of rape as an integral part of his genocidal acts.

In July 1996, Goldstone took a four-week leave to return to South Africa for the ratification of the constitution. By the time he returned to The Hague, there were only a few weeks left in his term, and with a successor in place, he began to withdraw from longer-term decision-making, which could be left to Louise Arbour.[41] The frustrations over the paucity of arrests by the NATO forces in the Balkans continued, as did his concern over the chaotic management of the prosecutor's office in Kigali, but he recognized that at this point there was little further that he could do about these chronic problems.

By September 1996, the Yugoslavia tribunal had seventy-five individuals under indictment, including Karadžić and Mladić. Of those seventy-five, seven were in the custody of the tribunal. In Rwanda, fourteen were under indictment, and three in custody in Arusha. The OTP had grown from a shoestring unit to a full-fledged investigative and legal operation with branches on two continents.[42] In Courtroom 1 in The Hague, Dusko Tadić was beginning to present his defense. In the lone courtroom in Arusha, the trial of Jean-Paul Akayesu was starting.

Among the lawyers and staff who had worked for him, there were mixed emotions about Goldstone's imminent departure. There was grudging admiration for his efforts outside the office, tempered by resentment of his skills as a "political animal." Some of the prosecutors, on the other hand, keenly felt a sense of drift in Goldstone's approach to leading the office, a feeling that opportunism and improvisation had trumped strategy. Goldstone's task, as the chief prosecutor himself reflected on it, had been to get the tribunals on their feet under difficult circumstances. When the staff at the ICTY threw him an affectionate going away party at the end of the month, he felt with some satisfaction that he had achieved that goal. Asked several years later what was the "major mistake" he made as a prosecutor, Goldstone answered without hesitation, "Absolutely none. That's an easy one." He could not think of a single thing that he would have done any other way.[43] Still, he conceded that when it came to the larger question of whether or not the tribunals constituted a success, "the jury is still out."[44]

13 ▸ GLOBETROTTER

In FEBRUARY 1995, Richard Goldstone had been particularly happy to get away from The Hague for a few days. Progress on the indictments for the ICTY was stalled, and the prosecutor's battle with the court's judges was heating up. So the long flight from Amsterdam to Johannesburg proved a welcome respite. Even better was the reason that he was making the trip. On February 14, 1995, the new Constitutional Court of South Africa was to be officially opened by President Nelson Mandela. A new era of law and justice was beginning in Goldstone's native country. Goldstone himself was attending in his formal role as a member of the Court's first bench, yet his presence was anomalous. While he was in The Hague, his seat was being kept warm by Sydney Kentridge, one of the senior statesmen of South Africa's anti-apartheid legal community.

The Constitutional Court had adopted as its symbol the concept of "justice under a tree," an African trope that represented humanity as a sheltered collective under the embracing branches of the law. At the ceremony, and later on the bench, the judges donned forest-green robes to echo this theme, and Goldstone found it a "moving experience" to wear his for the first time. The ritual echoed the diversity of the nation. Judges could choose to be sworn in in any of country's eleven official languages, with or without their hands on the sacred text of their choice. Goldstone took his oath in English, with his hand on a Bible. For all the pageantry, Nelson Mandela remained the center of the occasion. "The last time I appeared in court was to hear whether or not I was going to be sentenced to death," Mandela told the gathering. "Fortunately for myself and my colleagues we were not. Today I rise not as an accused, but on behalf of the people of South Africa, to inaugurate a court South Africa has never had, a court on which hinges the future of our democracy."[1]

The Court's first order of business was a groundbreaking case: to decide whether the death penalty would make the transition from the apartheid regime to the new polity. The day after the formal opening, the judges sat for the first hearings in *S. v. Makwanyane*, an appeal of a 1993 case in which the defendants had been sentenced to death for murder. The case, focusing on the legality of capital punishment, promised to be a landmark first test of the human rights principles embedded into the interim constitution that had given birth to the new South Africa.[2]

Richard Goldstone did not take part in the *Makwanyane* case or the other cases of the Constitutional Court's first eighteen months. He did, however, take a three-week break from The Hague a year later to participate in an even more momentous procedure: the Constitutional Court's certification of the permanent constitution of the Republic of South Africa. As of 1994, the country was operating under an interim constitution that was the result of negotiations between the apartheid regime and the anti-apartheid parties. The document called for the drafting of a permanent constitution that would be certified formally by the Court. On July 1, 1996, Goldstone began sitting with his colleagues for ten intensive days of hearings on a document that had been approved in May by the Constitutional Assembly. In September, he and the other judges unanimously rejected the May 1996 version, citing shortcomings in human rights protections and autonomy for the republic's provinces. In October, the Constitutional Assembly met again to revise the document.

By November of 1996, when the Constitutional Court met to consider the revised version, Richard Goldstone had concluded his service in The Hague and was back in Johannesburg as a permanent member of the bench. On December 4, 1996, the Court formally certified the revised version as adopted by the Assembly earlier in the fall. "We, the people of South Africa," the preamble began, "Recognise the injustices of our past; Honour those who suffered for justice and freedom in our land; Respect those who have worked to build and develop our country, and Believe that South Africa belongs to all who live in it, united in our diversity." Goldstone was particularly gratified that the Constitution articulated among the broadest human rights protections anywhere in the world. Its Bill of Rights used the concept of "inherent dignity" as a touchstone, and it specifically included such far-reaching provisions as the right to privacy and rights to housing, health care, food, and water. Of course, expressing rights was going to be a great deal easier than securing them for the nation's citizens. The Constitutional Court was designed to play a central role in bringing rights to life.[3]

Six of the Court's eleven judges, like Richard Goldstone, had been judges before 1994. The other five had years of legal experience, but had never before sat on the bench. Goldstone naturally knew very well the other holdovers. But he also had long associations with some of the "newcomers," including Arthur Chaskalson, the Court president, and Ismail Mahomed, who had been a colleague at the Johannesburg bar.

The Court adopted a style suitable to its role in a new democracy. In many Supreme Courts, including the United States, judges were seated according to seniority. This practice made no sense in South Africa, since all eleven had entered this particular bench at the same time, and it would certainly not do to give precedence to those who had served as judges in the old regime. Rather than fixed places, the judges rotated among seats, making every effort to promote a spirit and a look of diversity and equality, even though seven of the eleven justices were white in the black-majority country.

In the years after Goldstone began to sit, he participated in a series of landmark decisions that set the tone for the nation. He was with the majority in two cases that upheld equality on the basis of sexuality: in 1998, the Court struck down sodomy laws, and in 1999, it ruled that same-sex couples had the same rights as heterosexual couples when immigrating to South Africa.[4] In 1999, the Court ruled that prisoners could not be denied the right to vote.[5] In 2002, the Court made global headlines when it ordered the government to provide AIDS medicine and other services to HIV-infected people across the country.[6] The case, brought by an NGO called the Treatment Action Campaign, was a major test of the human rights character of the South African Constitution, since it rested on the provision that citizens of the republic had a right to access to health care. It was also a reprimand to the man who had by then succeeded Nelson Mandela as South Africa's president, Thabo Mbeki. Mbeki had earned global scorn for his public skepticism about the scientific consensus around the nature of the AIDS virus, but the Court's order compelled his government to implement a policy based on medical science.

Richard Goldstone did not push himself forward as a leading voice on these cases. He became on the court a consensus-builder, a calm but decisive voice who was eager to see the Court's business advanced efficiently. "He liked to talk things through," recalled Kate O'Regan, who served with him. "If he could see a forward way towards an agreement he would grab it, but he wouldn't push about it. He never lost his temper. He was very calm, very steady." He also retained his strong self-confidence. "He has no personal anxiety about being wrong," O'Regan said. "He just doesn't have it."[7]

Service on the Constitutional Court also enabled Goldstone to build a relationship with Albie Sachs, another Jewish South African lawyer who had acquired an international reputation. Sachs had left South Africa as a young man in the 1960s, going into exile to work with the ANC to combat the apartheid regime from abroad. He became one of the leading thinkers of the anti-apartheid movement, helping build its strong commitment to human rights, and playing an integral role in the early stages of drafting a new constitution for South Africa. Sachs had paid a steep personal price for his commitment. A bomb planted in a car in Mozambique in 1988 by the South African security police cost him his right eye and most of his right arm.

In contrast to Goldstone, Sachs was a flamboyant speaker, writer, and personality. He loved big ideas and sweeping statements, and he relished his new role on the Constitutional Court as an opportunity to inspire a public commitment to the principles of justice. He enjoyed the melodramatic, and he was pleased to be a public face for the Court in international forums.

Goldstone and Sachs became friends during their years on the Court. They respected each other's commitments and achievements, but each man could not entirely suppress his skepticism about the other's style. Sachs confessed that "before I knew [Goldstone] on the court I saw him as rather a dry figure, a little bit grey.... He could have been a good manager of a store, a financial operator, a whole lot of things." But Sachs came to appreciate Goldstone's wit and understated manner. "I saw a totally different side of Richard. Suddenly the man in the grey suit becomes . . . not the clown, but he used humor at key moments to soften debates, to score a point in a very helpful way." Regarding Goldstone's judgments, Sachs said that "you won't find memorable phrases in his writing," but that he was "focused in a very attractive way."[8] For his part,

Goldstone admired his colleague's flair, but he was amused by Sachs's preference for the grand gesture. Goldstone characterized his own opinions as full of "short sentences and short judgments," shorn of legal philosophy and direct. Sachs, by contrast, "wrote in a flowery style with punchy first lines and last lines, and so on."[9]

Both men relished the limelight, and a genial competition ran beneath the surface of their friendship, much as Goldstone had competed with Antonio Cassese at the ICTY. On the court itself, Goldstone and Sachs both worked fast, and each admitted to keeping an eye over his shoulder about how quickly the other was delivering the drafts of his judgments. In the international arena, Goldstone was taken more seriously and had the larger reputation among the movers and shakers in the political and legal wings of the international community. Sachs and his colorful history, by contrast, cut a larger figure in the media and in activist circles. Their hunger for attention seemed not, however, to damage the bond between them. Years after Goldstone left the Court, Sachs delivered a passionate defense of Goldstone's character at a time when he most needed public support.[10]

Goldstone's careful style of argument and his flexible pragmatism made him an invaluable contributor during the period when the Court was trying to find its feet. A typical and important case arose in 1997.

Shortly after he became president, Nelson Mandela had issued a Presidential Act that, among other things, commuted the sentences of categories of female prisoners who were at the time the mothers of children under the age of twelve. John Peter Philip Hugo, who was serving a fifteen-year prison term, brought suit. As the father of a young child whose sentence was not commuted, Hugo argued that he was the victim of gender discrimination, which was outlawed under the South African Constitution. The lower court agreed with Mr. Hugo and ordered Mandela to amend the Presidential Act. The government appealed to the Constitutional Court.

The majority judgment in *President and Others v. Hugo*, as written by Richard Goldstone, had to contend with two large issues.[11] The first was whether the president's constitutional power of pardon was judicially reviewable. This was an early test for the new nation, both in defining the role of the president, and providing a framework for the separation of powers between branches of government. Goldstone, speaking for his colleagues, dispatched of this issue quickly, effectively delivering the commonsense answer that under the Constitution the president was not above the law. True to his international background and to the Constitution, which permitted judges to draw on foreign sources for inspiration, Goldstone borrowed liberally from the law of the United States, Germany, Canada, and other Western nations in coming to this conclusion.

The substantive issue was more challenging, because it asked, in effect, just what the meaning of equality was going to be in the new South Africa. The prisoner, John Hugo, argued that it meant that men and women should be treated the same. Either he and all men with young children should be released along with the women, or else the order should be struck down for all. But Goldstone did not agree. His argument rested on the observable fact that the *starting point* for men and women in South Africa (as in just about every society in the world) was not identical. Given women's greater role in childrearing, the social benefit to the children of the nation from the release of incarcerated mothers was bound to be greater than releasing fathers. Furthermore, the pragmatic Goldstone also accepted the president's argument that releasing all the men with young children, who outnumbered women by more than fifty to one, would have a destabilizing effect on the country as a whole. Goldstone declared the president's order to be "not inconsistent" with the interim constitution (which had been in effect at the time of Mandela's order). All but one of his fellow justices, including all of the women, agreed. John Hugo would remain in prison.

Beyond his work on the bench, Goldstone received the occasional assignment to return to his investigative role. In 1997, President Mandela asked him to look formally into charges that a member of the TRC, a lawyer named Dumisa Ntsebeza, had played a part in a 1993 incident in which four students had been killed at the Heidelberg Tavern in Cape Town. Goldstone's inquiry cleared Ntsebeza, and he went so far as to recommend that the accuser be charged with perjury.[12]

Goldstone also took on a number of external roles that drew on his long-standing commitments and associations. He served for seven years as president of World ORT, and he was named chancellor of the University of the Witwatersrand, a mostly honorary position that he occupied for twelve years. At Brandeis University in the United States, he helped to establish and lead an annual institute for international judges.[13] As one of the leading figures in international criminal justice, he received and accepted many invitations to give lectures and attend conferences, expounding on lessons that he had learned in

The Hague. In 2000, he seized on an opportunity to weigh in formally on the most important development in the Balkans since the war in Bosnia.

The region of Kosovo had been an "autonomous province" of Yugoslavia under Tito. Nestled on the country's southern border, the majority of its population was ethnically Albanian and Muslim by religion, but governed by the Serbian minority. Under Slobodan Milosević tensions in the region heightened, as the Albanian groups formed nascent nonviolent political organizations to fight for equal rights and potential independence, and as the Serbs tightened their grip. Ethnic conflict in Kosovo was neglected during the negotiations that led to the 1995 Dayton Accords, and as a result the simmering tensions in the region came to a boil in the years that followed. By 1997, many Albanian Kosovars were losing patience with nonviolence, and the Kosovo Liberation Army (KLA) began to operate as a guerilla movement with independence as its ultimate goal. Armed conflict accelerated in 1998 and 1999, and Serbia responded with increasing measures of violence and repression. A failed set of negotiations in the French town of Rambouillet in March 1999 left the Albanian Kosovars vulnerable to further Serbian reprisals.[14]

Four years after the war in Bosnia, Western powers were still smarting from their failure to protect the region's vulnerable Muslim population from mass violence and ethnic cleansing. In 1999, the U.N. was no more effective than it had been in Bosnia. With Russia and China reluctant to support intervention in another country's "internal affairs," the body was paralyzed. So Western Europe and the United States undertook an independent response. In March 1999, NATO forces began a seventy-eight-day campaign of air strikes on targets in Kosovo, and eventually in Serbia proper, designed to hit Milosević hard and to deter further attacks on the Albanian Kosovars.

The air campaign was both a painful failure and a striking success. In the short run, it stiffened Serbian resolve. The Serbs accelerated their campaign of ethnic cleansing and displaced as much as 90 percent of the Kosovar Albanian population. More than 800,000 fled across the border to Albania, and nearly 600,000 were internally displaced. In June 1999, however, Milosević capitulated. The U.N. established a protectorate in Kosovo, checking Serb power and violence.

The NATO air campaign raised many troubling questions. Most important was the question of whether NATO had the right to conduct the war against Milosević at all. Even if the cause of protecting a vulnerable population was just, did a regional group have the right to conduct a military campaign against a sovereign nation, outside of the purview of the U.N.? What kind of precedent would this set for the future?

In August 1999, the government of Sweden decided to address these questions by establishing an independent commission to examine the Kosovo situation and the NATO intervention. Given his background in the region, Richard Goldstone was a natural choice to chair the commission, along with Swedish diplomat Carl Tham.[15] Goldstone and Tham assembled a team of leading thinkers from around the world, including Canadian Michael Ignatieff and Americans Richard Falk and Martha Minow.

For Goldstone, the chance to jump back into the fray of issues of protecting civilians from harm was irresistible. The Kosovo Commission met five times, worked quickly, and issued its report in mid-2000. Its conclusions spread the blame around. Serbia was responsible for the preponderance of the violence, although the KLA, which also targeted Serbian civilians, did not escape unscathed. The commission was also tough on the quality of the Western countries' response, saying that they prepared poorly, failed to coordinate effectively, and did not foresee the consequences that their actions would have for civilians in Kosovo. By far the Kosovo Commission's most important statements, however, focused on the legal and moral basis of the NATO intervention.

One finding was easy. NATO's military campaign was clearly illegal under international law. The U.N. Charter was explicit. Countries could resort to military action only in self-defense, or with explicit authorization by the Security Council. The Kosovo campaign fit neither of these criteria. The campaign was in violation of international law, and the commission said so directly.

The Kosovo Commission, however, refused to concede that the legal answer was the end of the story. Richard Goldstone's willingness to operate at the fungible borders of law, politics, and morality helped to drive toward an argument built on the conviction, as the commission put it, that "the moral imperative of protecting vulnerable people in an increasingly globalized world should not be lightly cast aside by adopting a legalistic view of international responses to humanitarian catastrophes." Three factors weighed heavily: the Kosovo intervention had no other purpose besides rescuing a vulnerable population; all measures at the Security Council had been exhausted; and, finally, the military campaign actually worked, by driving Milosević to the bargaining table.

With these factors in mind, Goldstone's commission came to a novel conclusion: the NATO campaign was "illegal but legitimate." Yes, it violated the letter of international law—and this was no small thing—but it respected the spirit. One of the underlying purposes of law was to shield ordinary people from extraordinary harm. "The effectiveness of rescue initiatives," the commission concluded, "would seem to take precedence over formal niceties."[16]

Goldstone foresaw and understood the dangers in this labored formulation. For one thing, the principle that "rescue" could take precedence over formal legal procedures was naturally open to abuse. After all, the Germans had invaded the Sudetenland under the pretext of rescuing ethnic Germans (and the Russians would use the same argument when moving troops into Georgia in 2008). So the report spent a great deal of text qualifying this conclusion, and trying to limit the cases for its application. "Illegal but legitimate" was the best that the international community could do in 1999, but the commission's hope was the Kosovo case would stimulate more broadly accepted principles for the future. One of its suggestions was that the rules of the Security Council be modified so that ten members could override a veto when humanitarian considerations were at stake. This suggestion was a tall order, as implementation required revising the U.N. Charter, but it indicated the commission's frustration with the U.N.'s paralysis in the face of catastrophe.

The Kosovo Commission's report played a vital part in creating momentum for the pursuit of a new international principle: humanitarian intervention. In the years that followed, other groups heeded its call for more sustained articulation of how legal and moral norms might be balanced. By 2005, a global movement had coalesced around another, related formulation. Nations of the world, said the U.N. in 2005, have a "responsibility to protect" vulnerable populations. Debate continued about whether it was legitimate to take military action in the absence of a blessing from the Security Council, but a widespread consensus developed around the rhetoric—if not the practice—of "protection."[17]

Richard Goldstone knew that the formulations of the Kosovo Commission created challenges, but he was happy to see moral convictions at least share the stage with the principle of sovereignty. For this reason Goldstone found the Iraq War, initiated in 2003 by the United States, so deeply troubling. The 1991 Gulf War had been carried out in an international coalition, in defense of a sovereign nation, the country of Kuwait. The reasons behind the 2003 war were less convincing: the threat that Iraq harbored weapons of mass destruction, for example, turned out to be hollow. One of the other reasons that the United States gave for the prosecution of the war was to protect ordinary Iraqis from their dictator, Saddam Hussein.

Goldstone worried that this pretext for the U.S. invasion threatened to deliver a fatal blow to the principle of protection of vulnerable populations, just as it was gathering momentum. Given his close working history with the Americans in his work in South Africa and The Hague, he found it painful to speak out against the United States, but he became a vocal and public critic of the Iraq War. The U.S. actions in Iraq, he said, did not have "anywhere near" the justifications for the Kosovo strikes, and he added that U.S. president George W. Bush's claim that he was protecting the Iraqi people was "disingenuous" and "very much an afterthought."[18]

The principle of "responsibility to protect" continued to have a fraught history in the subsequent years. Formally invoked by the U.N. with regard to Libya in 2008, it led to the overthrow of Muammar Qaddafi, but also to chaos and violence throughout North Africa. Yet the Kosovo Commission's report continued to stand out as a document that rejected complacency and despair. However imperfect their formulations, Goldstone and his fellow commissioners helped to create an ethic of responsibility even at the most cynical and self-interested levels of global engagement.

By 2003, Goldstone was ready for a change from his work in South Africa. His health was excellent and his work habits remained formidable, but he saw outlets for his energies and contributions beyond the Constitutional Court. Two New York City universities were wooing him with offers of a visiting professorship, and the idea of living in Manhattan appealed to both him and Noleen. At the age of sixty-five, with almost a quarter century of service as a judge, he was guaranteed a full pension; in strictly financial terms, he had no incentive to remain on the bench, especially since his nonrenewable term would be ending within two years.

When he announced his retirement, some of his colleagues and friends were baffled. "I couldn't understand why teaching law students was as important as continuing to work on South Africa," one fellow judge recalled.[19] Others felt that by leaving before completing his term he was defaulting on a responsibility to the nation. Characteristically, Goldstone betrayed no hesitations. He was leaving on his own terms, and without regrets. "I wasn't getting the satisfaction from [serving on the court] that I thought I would get from teaching," he recalled later.[20]

The Court hosted a celebration where his colleagues on the bench toasted his contributions to South African law and society. He was hailed for "his uncanny ability to work quickly and yet lucidly; how he was always ready to give his view, regardless of how difficult or complex the problem might be; the value he placed upon collegiality; and his formidable debating skills and his sense of humor."[21] With tributes behind them, Richard and Noleen Goldstone departed from South Africa for a life as peripatetic wanderers in the academic world.

Harvard, Yale, Stanford, Georgetown: the law schools of the United States opened their arms to Goldstone and his intimate knowledge of the still-new world of international criminal justice. He found that he loved the classroom. He peppered his lectures with anecdotes from his experiences, and he was moved and uplifted by the idealism and the incisive curiosity that he found in so many American law students. Richard and Noleen also came to relish the chance to resettle themselves anew once every few months. Over the past decade, they had acquired friends across the United States, and their long-term stays in Cambridge, New Haven, and a half dozen other academic locales widened their social circles even further.

The academic life gave Goldstone further opportunity to hone his thinking about international criminal justice broadly, and also to become an even more prominent commentator at conferences and in the press. Even a decade after the establishment of the Yugoslavia and Rwanda tribunals, the cloud of skepticism around their purpose and effectiveness had not dispelled. Goldstone's talks tended to lay out, in straightforward language, the process by which the tribunals had been built, and their accomplishments in the face of challenges.

Goldstone also emerged during this time as a strong critic of the United States, even beyond the Iraq War, as the administration of George W. Bush pursued the "war on terror" and turned away from a spirit of multilateralism in world affairs. From his early days in South Africa, he had looked to the United States for inspiration on issues of rights and justice, but he was dismayed to see what he considered an erosion of human rights protection as America responded to the attacks of 9/11. He was particularly vehement in protest against the Bush administration's justification for the use of torture as a weapon in the fight against terrorism. If the United States so baldly swept aside basic rights protections, he believed, it would embolden other countries to follow suit.[22]

He also bemoaned the American refusal to join the new International Criminal Court (ICC). The United States, under Bill Clinton, had played a leading role at the 1998 conference in Rome where the ICC's founding statute was drafted. Clinton did put his signature on the Rome Statute shortly before he left office, but George W. Bush quickly withdrew presidential approval, and the question of membership of the ICC was never put before the Senate. American critics of the ICC argued that the Court would become a political tool, used to put U.S. soldiers and even political leaders on trial for spurious reasons. Goldstone scoffed at these fears, explaining whenever he had the chance the complex safeguards built into the Rome Statute, and arguing that American credibility as a world power depended on participating on an equal basis in vital global institutions.[23]

Beneath this critique of U.S. policy, however, Goldstone was well aware of the weaknesses of the very global institutions that he defended. Shortly after he began his new career in the classroom he trained his investigatory sights on the largest international organization of them all.

Richard Goldstone had worked for the U.N. in The Hague, and he was intimately acquainted with its challenges. In 2004, he joined a three-person commission that focused on the U.N.'s single largest initiative of the previous decade, the Oil for Food Program (OFP) in relation to Iraq.[24]

After the 1991 Gulf War, the U.N. had established economic sanctions against Saddam Hussein's regime in an effort to compel Iraq to destroy its weapons of mass destruction and to allow international inspectors to verify these actions. The problem with sanctions, however, was that they ended up hurting ordinary Iraqis more than the regime itself. So, in 1996, the U.N. established the OFP. The idea was that Iraq would be permitted, under strict guidelines, to sell its oil overseas in order to pay for shipments of food, medicine, and other vital supplies that were supposed to aid ordinary Iraqis. The sums involved were enormous; between 1997 and 2003, Iraq sold $64 billion in oil under the program.

By 2003, however, it had become clear that something was amiss. Stories were emerging in bits and pieces of kickbacks, sweetheart deals, and political interference. With the amount of money at stake spread out around the world, the opportunities were rife for corruption. The U.N. came under pressure to take action. Secretary-General Kofi Annan named a commission, led by former U.S. Federal Reserve chair Paul Volcker, to investigate. Annan invited two other members, a Swiss lawyer named Mark Pieth, and Richard Goldstone.

Goldstone worked intensively on the investigation from April 2004 through December 2005, aided by the fact that he was in residence in New York City for most of the period. The OFP had involved thousands of companies from countries around the world, either in the sale of oil or the provision of goods, so the process of investigation was complex and labor-intensive. The commission hired ninety staff members from twenty-eight countries to conduct the work. Goldstone's training as a commercial lawyer prepared him for the intricacies of the complex financial transactions, and he understood well the political trade-offs inside the U.N. system.

The most delicate aspect of the investigation involved the secretary-general himself. Goldstone was friendly with Kofi Annan, who had been head of U.N. peacekeeping forces while Goldstone was at the ICTY, and it pained him to see his fellow African enmeshed personally in the scandal. But the evidence available to the commission showed clearly that Kofi's son Kojo had taken advantage of his U.N. contacts to secure work with Cotecna, a Swiss inspections company that was bidding on contracts under the OFP. The question lingered: How much did Kojo's father know about these efforts, and when did he know it?

There was no way to get to the bottom of this issue besides talking directly to Kofi Annan himself. Goldstone told Paul Volcker that the task was too delicate to leave exclusively to the paid staff, that at least one of the commissioners should be present in person. Since he had taken on the OFP assignment, Goldstone had carefully avoided speaking with Annan, taking pains not to get close when they attended functions at the same time in New York and elsewhere. But Volcker asked Goldstone to be the one to represent the three commissioners at the meeting. "The questioning of Kofi Annan was one of the most difficult experiences that I have ever been through," he recalled later. "What was particularly unpleasant was seeing a father's grief at the lies his son had told him."[25] Kojo had told his father that his employment at Cotecna had long since ended, but the OFP investigators showed the secretary-general documents proving that his son's association had persisted. Kofi Annan denied any knowledge of Kojo's direct involvement. Goldstone believed him. His memorandum to his fellow commissioners made this case, even over the objection of the OFP investigators who were present with him for the interview.[26]

The OFP Commission's report, as it came out in parts over the course of 2005, presented a damning picture. Saddam Hussein had masterfully gamed the system, enabling the Iraqi regime to make money on kickbacks and fees from both the sale of oil and the provision of the humanitarian goods. "Lax oversight" by the U.N. itself let it happen. Indeed, the individual whom Kofi Annan put in charge of the whole program, a Cypriot named Benon Sevan, himself stood accused of mismanagement and personal benefit. Kofi Annan was faulted for his general responsibility for the U.N.'s shortcomings, but the report exonerated him from personal corruption. The commissioners recommended a series of concrete steps, including the appointment of a chief operating officer for the U.N. as a whole, designed to improve the efficiency and the effectiveness of the organization.

Looking back from the vantage point of a decade later, Goldstone believed that "the most important aspect of the report is that it saved Kofi Annan's reputation," and by extension the reputation of the U.N. In other words, problems with management at the U.N. were not news; a report of corruption at the pinnacle of the organization might have done lasting damage. The corruption, Goldstone aptly pointed out, was mostly outside of the U.N., and was also permitted to fester thanks to the indifference and incompetence of the U.N.'s member states, including the United States and the countries of Western Europe.[27] The report suggested that those who pointed fingers at the U.N. would do better to look into the mirror.

The work of the OFP Commission ended up reflecting many of the hallmarks of Goldstone's philosophy and style. He believed in public accountability, even for those organizations (like the U.N.) whose mission was vital but whose public support was fragile. At the same time, he understood, there was no real alternative to the U.N., with all of its imperfections, as an instrument for preserving the global order. So he helped shape the report in such a way to highlight its shortcomings without undermining its foundation. In the end, relatively few of the major recommendations were implemented, and the U.N. remained susceptible to mismanagement at many levels. But Goldstone was willing to live with the shortcomings of the U.N.'s bureaucracy in a world in which there was no reasonable alternative to its role in promoting peace and stability.[28]

14 ▸ CAST LEAD

MIRELA SIDERER DID not like to "deal in politics."[1] She was a physician, a gynecologist, trained in her native Romania, who had moved to Israel in 1984. On May 14, 2008, she was examining a patient as usual in a clinic on one of the upper floors of the Hutzot Mall in Ashkelon. This city of 120,000 hugged Israel's Mediterranean coast, its southern edge less than three miles from the border of the Gaza Strip. Throughout the winter and spring of 2008 rockets fired from Gaza had been landing in and around Ashkelon. But Mirela Siderer felt secure in her office. It was, she thought, a protected place.

Her clinic was not a protected place. In the middle of a busy Wednesday, without any warning, a Grad Katyusha rocket struck the mall. The ceilings and walls of the upper-floor clinic collapsed, and Mirela Siderer found herself trapped under debris. She lost consciousness, and when she came to, she saw her left arm bleeding. It felt like a ball of fire was spinning inside her face, and she realized that her teeth had been knocked out. A few feet away, she could see her patient, her abdomen cut open and her intestines exposed. Fighting her own pain, Siderer did her best to keep her patient calm until a rescue team arrived to bring them both to the hospital.

At least sixty people were treated for injuries from the rocket strike on the mall. Israel's Code Red system, which was supposed to give people at least a short window of warning of a rocket fire, had been turned off; there had been too many disruptive false alarms in recent weeks. So when the rocket hit, the mall was full, the damage extensive. Israeli prime minister Ehud Olmert called the attack "entirely intolerable and unacceptable" and vowed to "take the necessary steps so that this will stop."[2]

It took six operations to restore Mirela Siderer to a semblance of health. A year later, she still had a piece of shrapnel lodged in the left side of her back, too near to her spine to remove safely. But the worst, she felt, was her psychological state. She had studied medicine to help people, not caring whether they were from anywhere in Israel, or from Gaza, or from anywhere in the world. "What was my crime?" she wondered. "What did I do wrong to deserve this?"

At 1:45 A.M. on the morning of January 6, 2009, Muhammad Fouad Abu Askar, a resident of al-Fakhura Street in the Jabaliyah refugee camp in the northern part of the Gaza Strip and a member of the Hamas political organization, received a telephone call.[3] A brusque male caller, speaking in accented Arabic, identified himself as a member of the Israel Defense Forces (IDF). The caller told Abu Askar that he and his family should evacuate his residence at once.

Abu Askar swung into action, rousing the nearly forty members of his family and hustling them outside their makeshift residence. He sounded a warning to his neighbors as well. At 1:52 A.M., a missile from an F-16 fighter jet crashed into the Abu Askar home. No one was hurt or injured.

During the daytime on January 6, the Abu Askars retrieved furniture from their damaged residence and were looking for temporary accommodations in the neighborhood. By mid-afternoon, foot traffic clogged al-Fakhura Street, much of it coming in and out of a school building that was now being used by the U.N. as a shelter for more than 1,600 residents of Gaza. Newly arriving residents of the shelter were hauling their belongings down the street on donkey carts.

At 4:00 P.M., a series of explosions rocked the neighborhood. Residents ran for shelter, but in the immediate vicinity of al-Fakhura Street, it seemed as though there was nowhere to hide from the burst of mortar fire. Four shells fell within a radius of 100 meters. After two minutes, the explosions ended, but human screams from all sides of al-Fakhura Street penetrated the silence.

One of the shells landed in the courtyard of the al-Deeb house, nearly adjacent to the damaged Abu Askar residence. Nine members of the family were killed instantly, and two others died later of their wounds. Of the eleven members of the family who died, four were grown women, four were girls.

At least twenty-four more people died from the impact of the other three shells, including two sons of Abu Askar, nineteen-year-old Khaled and thirteen-year-old Imad. The shelter in the school run by the U.N. was untouched, but its residents and staff were profoundly shaken. Had one of the shells fallen fifty meters to the north, the casualty toll could have been in the hundreds.

Israeli military spokesmen explained that their forces had fired into al-Fakhura Street in response to mortar fire from the vicinity of the school. "They shot back to save their own lives," said Ilan Tal, a brigadier general.[4] By the Israeli account, the incident demonstrated that Hamas was callously putting its own civilian population at risk by staging military operations from densely populated neighborhoods. That very day, Hamas rockets had landed in the Israeli border town of Sderot, and, more alarmingly, in the city of Gadera, halfway between the Gaza border and Tel Aviv. Khaled and Imad Abu Askar, said the Israelis, were "Hamas terrorist operatives," and therefore legitimate targets of the mortar fire.

January 6, 2009, was the tenth day of the fighting in the Gaza Strip, in an operation known in Israel as "Operation Cast Lead." By this date, as many as 640 residents of Gaza had died, perhaps 150 of those civilians.[5]

The fighting came on the heels of nine years of rocket fire from Gaza into southern Israel. By Israeli accounts, more than 12,000 missiles fell on Israeli soil between 2000, when the outbreak of violence known as the "Al-Aqsa Intifada" began, and December 2008.[6] Of the 1,100 Israelis who died in Palestinian attacks during that period only a small number were killed by missiles from Gaza.[7] But the rockets made fear constant in the lives of Israelis in the southern sector of the country. They left permanent scars on the lives of people like Mirela Siderer.

For nearly six months in the second half of 2008, the Israelis and the Palestinians observed a ceasefire in Gaza. The barrage of missiles mostly stopped, but the ceasefire produced no substantive progress on broader issues between the parties. When the six-month end date for the ceasefire arrived on December 19, 2008, Hamas renewed its rocket fire in earnest.

Israel responded with Cast Lead, an operation that took its name from a children's song for the Jewish holiday of Chanukah, which was being celebrated as the conflict began.[8] Cast Lead began with eight days of aerial bombardment, followed by a ground invasion. The stated goal of the operation was to stop the rocket attacks into Israel. The campaign included considerable military activity in areas where many Palestinian civilians lived and worked. There was no choice about this, the Israelis said. Because Hamas had chosen to locate rockets and other military activities among its civilian population, Israel had to take its fight directly to those neighborhoods.

The attack in al-Fakhura Street, in conjunction with others in recent days, roused the concern of world leaders. "These attacks by Israeli military forces which endanger U.N. facilities acting as places of refuge are totally unacceptable and must not be repeated," the U.N. secretary general, Ban Ki-moon, declared. "Equally unacceptable are any actions by militants which endanger the Palestinian civilian population." In the United States, president-elect Barack Obama broke his silence on the Gaza conflict, telling reporters, "The loss of civilian life in Gaza and Israel is a source of deep concern for me."[9]

The intensity of the conflict sparked a steady stream of outside commentary. Supporters of Israel took to the airwaves to remind the world that no country could tolerate years of missiles attacking its civilian population without a strong and targeted military response. Human rights groups raised cries of alarm about the extent of the tragedy among Gaza's civilian population.

In Geneva, the U.N. Human Rights Council (HRC) called a special session that began while the fighting in Gaza was still at its peak. After three days of debate, on January 12, 2009, the HRC adopted resolution S/9-1, "The grave violations of human rights in the Occupied Palestinian Territory, particularly due to the recent Israeli military attacks against the occupied Gaza Strip." The resolution strongly condemned the ongoing Israeli military operation, demanded an immediate end to Israeli attacks and the withdrawal of its forces from Gaza, and called on the international community to protect the Palestinian people. The HRC also decided to dispatch an international fact-finding mission "to investigate all violations of human rights law and the laws of war by the occupying power, Israel, against the Palestinian people in Gaza."[10]

In Johannesburg, Richard Goldstone agonized over the headlines from the Middle East. He was at home in South Africa for a brief stint between his overseas teaching commitments. He had spent the fall of 2008 at Harvard Law

School teaching a class on comparative constitutional law and South Africa's Bill of Rights.[11] For spring 2009, he had no semester-long obligations. Instead, he would take some vacation, and then spend several weeks in The Hague as the inaugural "peace philosopher," a new visiting position created by the city in collaboration with local academic institutions. He was looking forward to his first sustained period in the capital of the Netherlands since his departure from his chief prosecutor position in 1996.

Goldstone paid close attention to the television coverage of the conflict in Gaza, which he followed mostly on the BBC, CNN, and the English-language Al-Jazeera network.[12] The images that flashed across his screen touched him deeply for several reasons. There was, first of all, his lifelong attachment and connection to Israel, embedded in his memory through key milestones: the celebration of Israel's independence when he was nine years old; his first trip to Israel while in college; the elation of Israel's victory in the Six Day War in 1967. While serving as the leader of World ORT, his frequent trips to Jerusalem gave him a steady sense of belonging in the place he thought of as the Jewish homeland. In recent years, his institutional ties to Israel were strengthened after he was named to the board of governors of Hebrew University, the premier Israeli institution of higher education. He had family ties to Israel as well. His daughter Nicky was now living in Canada, but the decade that she spent in Israel had left its mark on her, and her passion for all things Israeli was contagious within the Goldstone family.

Goldstone also viewed the events in the Middle East through the prism of his experience as an advocate for human rights and for international humanitarian law. The fear and suffering both within Israel proper and within the Gaza Strip troubled him deeply. After his experiences in South Africa, in the Balkans, in Rwanda, it was impossible for Richard Goldstone simply to shrug his shoulders. If the violence against civilians on either side of the border was by design, then someone should be held accountable. And even if the violence was not by design, were military commanders among the Israelis and the Palestinians doing enough to ensure that civilian suffering was at a minimum? Random or disproportionate strikes in civilian areas could also be considered war crimes. That winter, Goldstone was one of sixteen global human rights figures who signed a letter, drafted by Amnesty International, saying that events in Gaza had "shocked us to the core" and calling for a U.N.-backed investigation. The commission, the letter said, "should have the greatest possible expertise and authority: a mandate to carry out a prompt, thorough,

independent and impartial investigation of all allegations of serious violations of international humanitarian law committed by all parties to the
conflict."[13]

On January 19, 2009, the Israelis and the Hamas leadership in Gaza agreed
on a new ceasefire, and Operation Cast Lead came to an end. Depending on
whose estimates were more accurate, somewhere between 1,166 and 1,444
Palestinians died during the three-week campaign. During the same period,
thirteen Israelis died in the conflict. Of those nine were soldiers involved in
the ground operation in Gaza; four others, including three civilians, were
killed within Israel by the continuing rocket fire from Gaza during Cast
Lead.[14] Those figures did not include the deaths and injuries suffered by
Israelis like Mirela Siderer in the rocket attacks that had preceded Cast Lead.

In February 2009, Richard and Noleen Goldstone headed from South
Africa to New Zealand, where they embarked on a three-week cruise in the
southern Pacific. Their ship was docked in Adelaide, Australia, on March 9,
2009, when a message arrived from Navanethem Pillay, the U.N. high commissioner for human rights, the U.N.'s most senior human rights figure. Pillay
was a fellow South African, one of the first non-White women to practice law
in Goldstone's native country. In 1995, she had been named as one of the first
judges of the ICTR while Goldstone was serving as its chief prosecutor.[15] She
served on the panel that presided over the Akayesu trial, and she became president of the ICTR after Goldstone left the prosecutor's post. A message from
Navi Pillay was bound to get Richard's immediate attention.

Pillay was inquiring whether Goldstone would be willing to head a fact-
finding mission to Gaza to investigate acts of violence during the recent Israeli
campaign. Goldstone replied immediately, saying that he was honored to be
considered. He had some practical considerations, but also some pressing
questions. Would he be permitted to take into account the rocket fire from
Gaza while considering the Israeli military actions? "I would need to be
assured," he said, "that the investigation would be even-handed." He also wondered whether there was any prospect that Israel would cooperate with the
process.[16]

He talked it over with Noleen at dinner the next night. Noleen remained
his most trusted counselor in many difficult decisions, but this offer required
relatively little discussion. Goldstone could see from the title of the special
session itself that before the HRC had met it had already decided that "grave
violations of rights" had been committed. The resolution gave all its attention

to the harm done by the "occupying power, Israel" to the Palestinian people. Not a word addressed any possible violations by Hamas or other Palestinians.

This was an easy call. There was simply no way that Goldstone could accept leadership of a mission with such a one-sided mandate. It violated every principle of fairness that had animated his entire career. He wrote back to Navi Pillay to decline the offer.

Pillay persisted, appealing to Goldstone's conscience and to their friendship. She managed to reach him by telephone on the cruise ship to push the point personally. The Middle East was still a tinderbox, she told him. Somehow, there had to be a fair way to bring the principles of international law, which they both cared about so deeply, to bear on the conflict there. Besides, she said, the current president of the HRC was a reasonable fellow. In short, Pillay said, would Goldstone come to Geneva simply to provide the HRC with some quiet advice?

To this modest request from an old friend, it was hard to say no. Besides, as he thought about it more, the possibilities opened up before him. By the time that the Goldstones returned to South Africa after the cruise, Richard was already thinking about the impact that he might be able to make on a situation that seemed, on the face of it, to be "unwinnable." One South African friend found him "excited" about the challenge and the opportunity that the investigation presented. It was a chance for him to get back into the arena, at the center of the world's attention, and to make a difference in a way that he, perhaps alone in the world, could make.[17]

Martin Uhomoibhi, the Nigerian president of the HRC, looked more the scholar than the diplomat. Trim, bespectacled, natty in a bow tie, he welcomed Richard Goldstone into his Geneva office with a warm smile and professions of admiration.[18]

Nigeria held the rotating presidency of the HRC, and Uhomoibhi was not going to be shy about exercising the authority of the office. Yes, he acknowledged right from the beginning of their conversation, the January resolution establishing a fact-finding mission for Gaza was seriously flawed. Of course he could understand why a respected judge could not possibly accept it. On the other hand, Uhomoibhi continued, it seemed like a lost opportunity for the cause of international justice. After all, what use were the laws of war and human rights if they were applied only selectively around the world? Did Justice Goldstone not agree?

Justice Goldstone did indeed agree, since applying justice equally had been one of the cornerstone principles of his career. But any application of justice had to be built on a foundation of fairness.

Out of curiosity, Uhomoibhi countered, what would a better mandate look like? Did the justice have some thoughts on how the HRC might have better conceived the mission? Taken slightly aback, the visitor fumbled for words. The mandate, Goldstone started, should be extended to include both the Israelis and their Palestinian antagonists, and it needed to incorporate a full sense of the run-up to the Gaza conflict.

The ambassador thrust a blank legal pad and a pen across his desk. Write it down, he urged. What would be a better mandate?

Goldstone thought for a moment, then filled in the first lines on the sheet in unpracticed, hurried script. The fact-finding mission, he wrote, should "investigate all violations of international human rights law and international humanitarian law that might have been committed at any time in the context of the military operations in Gaza in 2008–2009 whether before, during, or after."

Uhomoibhi perused the paper carefully, raised his head, and looked Goldstone squarely in the eye. "Very well," he smiled. "We will fill in the exact dates, and THIS will be your mandate. The Council's resolution specifically empowers the president to establish the mission, and *these* will be your terms." He paused. "You will accept?"

Goldstone asked for a night to think it over, but even as he and Uhomoibhi were exchanging pleasantries on his way out the door, he suspected that he had been outmaneuvered.

It was precisely because the investigation was so difficult and delicate, and because the situation in Israel was personal to him, that Goldstone felt a special responsibility. For decades Israel had been treated as a human rights pariah by those who sought to undermine its legitimacy. The aftermath of Gaza provided an opportunity to give Israel a fair shot, to bring it into the community of nations by judging its actions by universal standards, alongside a scrupulous consideration of the actions of the Palestinians.

Yes, there were plenty of others who had the qualifications to lead the mission, but Richard Goldstone represented a unique combination of experience in international justice, a reputation for fairness, and a demonstrated commitment to the well-being of Israel. His prior connections to Israel would be criticized in some quarters as a conflict of interest, but this was just the point. With Richard Goldstone at the helm, he believed, Israel would have sufficient confidence in the mission's objectivity to cooperate, to let its soldiers and leaders tell their side of the story, and therefore to bring Israel's point of view into the center of the global conversation.

On April 3, 2009, Martin Uhomoibhi announced the establishment of the fact-finding mission in Geneva, with Richard Goldstone at his side. Goldstone would chair the mission, which would include three other members: Christine Chinkin, a British law professor; Hina Jilani, a Pakistani human rights activist; and Desmond Travers, a retired Irish military professional. "Let me assure you that accepting this position was not an easy decision," Goldstone told the press. But he felt a deep concern for peace in the Middle East and for the victims on all sides. "What does it mean for you personally," a reporter asked, "as someone from your background who is now heading a UN investigation of a conflict related to Israel, a Jewish State?" "Well it certainly came to me as quite a shock as a Jew to be invited by the President to head this mission," Goldstone responded.[19]

There had been many international investigations of Israel in the past, and there were several others that were under way in the spring of 2009 regarding Operation Cast Lead. By April, some had already issued reports. Human Rights Watch had published *Rain of Fire*, which argued that the IDF's use of the chemical white phosphorous in densely populated areas of Gaza constituted a war crime.[20] The Israel Intelligence Heritage and Communication Center released a document offering evidence that Hamas used civilians as human shields, and that its operatives fired rockets from within residential neighborhoods.[21] U.N. secretary-general Ban-Ki Moon had commissioned a separate, more targeted investigation focused on the damage done specifically to U.N. facilities in Gaza during the conflict.[22]

Under Richard Goldstone's leadership, the new U.N. Fact-Finding Mission on the Gaza Conflict commanded special attention from the start.* It had often been easy for supporters of Israel to dismiss other reports as the product of investigators with obvious biases against Israel. It would be dif-

---

* The word "Mission" is capitalized from here forward when it refers to the formal body under Goldstone's leadership that conducted the fact-finding in Gaza.

ficult to make that same claim about findings over the name of Richard Goldstone.

Difficult, but not impossible. Within days of the announcement of Goldstone's leadership of the Mission, supporters of Israel were already launching a robust preemptive critique. Before Goldstone had taken a single action, several individuals emerged to dismiss the Mission as biased and wrong-headed. They would maintain a steady drumbeat of hostility to the Mission through the publication of its report and long beyond.

There was Alan Baker, a British-born lawyer who had been an international law expert with the IDF and then Israel's ambassador to Canada. Ten days after its formation, Baker called the Mission "just another UN fact-finding farce, I'm afraid."[23] Avi Bell, a professor of international law at Bar-Ilan University and the University of San Diego, insisted that Richard Goldstone should start by investigating Hamas first and by acknowledging forthrightly that "Hamas's repeated and explicit targeting of Israeli civilians constitutes prima facie acts of terrorism." In other words, according to Bell, Goldstone could gain credibility only by announcing certain anti-Palestinian conclusions up front.[24] Then there was Hillel Neuer, the executive director of UN Watch, an organization established to monitor the anti-Israel and anti-Semitic tendencies of the U.N. Neuer was an uncompromising critic of the HRC. Two years earlier, he had given a speech before the body in which he called it "criminal"; his address was sufficiently strong that it was struck from the records of the proceedings.[25] Now UN Watch issued a statement claiming that while "we do not impugn the motives of Mr. Goldstone . . . his own statements raise serious questions about whether he is aware of elementary facts about the council's record and intentions, and therefore, serious questions about whether he appreciates the consequences of his actions."[26]

The intensive focus, in this period shortly after the Mission's formation, remained on the HRC itself, which critics argued was a poisonous hotbed of anti-Israel sentiment. The critics insisted that no side deal that Richard Goldstone had cut with the president of the HRC could change the original mandate. "Clearly the United Nations or any other body presuming to investigate Israel's actions must come with clean hands," said Alan Baker in the *Jerusalem Post*. Goldstone's Mission, like its predecessors, was "doomed to fail."[27]

The critics had a point. Human rights at the U.N. had a checkered history. Eleanor Roosevelt took a leading role in the creation of a nonbinding Universal Declaration of Human Rights at the dawn of the organization in

1948. The U.N. then established a Commission on Human Rights (CHR), which helped bring the rhetoric into reality, through a series of treaties like the International Covenant on Civil and Political Rights and the International Covenant on Economic, Social, and Cultural Rights in 1966. But by the end of the twentieth century, the CHR had been tarnished. Some of the world's worst abusers of human rights, such as North Korea, managed to get themselves voted onto the fifty-two-member group. In 2003, CHR members elected Libya, governed by the notorious dictator Muammar Qaddafi, as its chair. With so much cross-cutting politicking, the CHR tended to avoid any tough look at specific situations in specific countries—except when it came to Israel, whose alleged abuses appeared regularly on its agenda.[28]

Under attack for its deficiencies, the CHR was disbanded in 2006, and the new HRC was established as a successor institution. The new council was designed to be more effective and fairer. It had slightly fewer members (forty-seven instead of fifty-two), its election procedures were changed to make it easier to mount a campaign against obvious human rights violators, and countries that joined had to pledge to open their own national practices to the scrutiny of the HRC. In its first years, observers did detect some improvements, but one pattern persisted. Between 2006 and 2008, the HRC devoted four of its special sessions to Israel; the entire rest of the world merited only three special sessions during those three years.[29]

The January 2009 resolution condemning Israel alone for its actions in Operation Cast Lead was put forward jointly by Cuba, Egypt, and Pakistan.[30] Thirty-three countries voted in favor, including China, Nigeria, Qatar, Russia, and Saudi Arabia. Only Canada voted against. Most of the European members of the HRC—including Great Britain, France, and Germany—abstained.[31] As a result of this one-sided resolution, several leading human rights figures turned down an invitation to lead the Mission, citing the bias of the mandate. Most prominent among these were Mary Robinson, the highly respected former president of Ireland and former U.N. high commissioner for human rights, and Martti Ahtisaari, the former president of Finland. So by the time that Navi Pillay had turned to Richard Goldstone in early March, there was a sense of urgency, if not desperation, to find a credible leader.

Goldstone was well aware of the hypocritical geopolitics of human rights at the U.N., but he had also always believed that meaningful change happened by engagement, not through avoidance. Throughout his career he had acted on the conviction that tainted politics and institutions could be challenged through one crucial asset: his independence.

Thanks to his conversation with Martin Uhomoibhi, Goldstone now had a mandate that would permit him and his fellow Mission members to look at violations of international law by both Israelis and Palestinians. Goldstone knew quite well that this revised mandate was in a grey area in formal terms. Uhomoibhi was not about to put the new language to a vote of the entire HRC; he and Goldstone knew that it would not pass that test. On the other hand, the two men made their intentions known in the widest public arena, and none of the HRC members voiced any objection. The countries' silence amounted to tacit agreement to allow the Mission to proceed in the even-handed manner that Goldstone had articulated.

Goldstone and his fellow Mission members now had the freedom to write the truth as they saw it. They had full powers to scrutinize both Israeli and Palestinian actions, and there was really nothing that the countries that sponsored the original, one-sided resolution could do about it. The Mission members could follow wherever the evidence might lead.

The critics who relentlessly attacked the HRC's mandate, then, were really challenging something else: the integrity of the Mission's leader. While professing great respect for Goldstone's reputation and experience, the critics were effectively announcing their skepticism that the justice could produce, under these conditions, a truly independent report. Attacking the mandate was, indirectly, the first salvo in what became a concerted effort to undermine the credibility and legitimacy of Richard Goldstone himself.

Goldstone met right away with the Palestinian representative in Geneva, Ibrahim Khraishi, who pledged his government's cooperation. At the same time, Goldstone requested an in-person meeting with Aharon Leshno-Yaar, Israel's ambassador to the U.N. in Geneva. Leshno-Yaar refused, explaining that he had not been authorized by his government to hold such a meeting. Goldstone speculated that the ambassador's hesitation was merely because there had been a recent change of government in Israel. Within the last week, Benjamin Netanyahu had replaced Ehud Olmert as prime minister, and perhaps Leshno-Yaar did not wish to be out in front of the new administration on a sensitive subject.[32]

On April 3, 2009, Goldstone wrote Leshno-Yaar reiterating that the Mission would be unbiased, and that "it is also clearly necessary to take into account all relevant contextual facts that might be relevant to assess the actions that were taken by Israel in response to the attacks." He went on to emphasize that "it is my earnest wish that the Mission should visit the areas that were effected [sic] by the rocket attacks and, if possible, to meet with some of the victims of those attacks, to ascertain the physical damage caused by them, as well as the effect that they had on an ongoing basis upon the civilian population in the effected [sic] areas of Israel." He added that it would also be important to have access to relevant Israeli government and military officials.[33]

Four days later, on April 7, 2009, Goldstone received an unambiguous reply: Israel will not cooperate. The reason, once again: the "grossly politicized" and "hopelessly one-sided" resolution of the HRC. The ambassador stressed Israel's respect for Richard Goldstone personally and his letter acknowledged Goldstone's long-standing commitment to the welfare of Israelis and Palestinians alike, but he said that the Mission head's commitment to impartiality could not change the resolution's legal basis. The answer was no.[34]

The Israeli response weighed heavily on Richard Goldstone. There was, first of all, the practical concern. Without cooperation from Israel, it would be difficult to get the full story behind what happened before and during the conflict in Gaza. The Mission would not have access to the thinking behind Israeli political and military decisions. Equally important, it would not have a full understanding of the impact of attacks from Gaza on the Israeli civilian population. The Mission would have to extrapolate a lot of information from public records and published sources. But Goldstone had another, deeper concern. A principal reason that he had accepted the Mission was to help bring credibility to the Israeli narrative in the context of the U.N. If the Israelis refused to cooperate, this would be difficult, if not impossible, to achieve.

Goldstone could not bring himself to believe that Israel would stick with its decision. The problem of the mandate seemed like a smokescreen. It was a matter of politics, of negotiation, and he had succeeded in this arena before. Given his authority as a giant of international justice and his Zionist credentials, he believed that he would succeed again. Eventually, however, Aharon Leshno-Yaar sent another letter to Goldstone that emphasized that Israel was conducting its own investigations of Cast Lead and reaffirmed that the government had no intention of cooperating with him.[35] By the time that Goldstone received that letter, in July 2009, it was too late, he felt, to walk away from the Mission.

Later he wondered aloud whether he would have accepted the offer to head the Mission had he known in advance that the Israelis would refuse to cooperate.[36] After many years of success, the failure to persuade the Israelis to cooperate was one of Richard Goldstone's few major diplomatic failures. "He miscalculated," one Israeli observer put it. "He thought that his stature would enable him to be the bridge. It left him only with the cliff."[37]

15 ▸ GAZA

THE MEMBERS OF the Mission met together for the first time in Geneva in the first week of May 2009.[1]

Christine Chinkin was a feisty defender of the rights of women worldwide. Born and trained in the United Kingdom, she held an academic post at the London School of Economics, but she had extensive experience as an investigator and consultant on women's issues and the laws of war in the international community. As early as 1991, she published a groundbreaking essay that brought feminist analysis to the forefront of the study of international law.[2] She had worked previously for the Office of the United Nations High Commissioner for Human Rights (OHCHR) on issues of human trafficking, and her consulting work had taken her to central Africa, Kosovo, and Peru, among other locales. Well-known in international legal circles, Chinkin was unafraid to ruffle feathers, and she had shown a willingness to challenge the actions of Western nations acting on behalf of human rights.[3] Just a year earlier, she had coauthored a report for the U.N. with Desmond Tutu regarding a 2006 incident in Gaza, which concluded that Israeli shelling had potentially constituted a war crime.[4]

Hina Jilani also brought to the Mission a focus on the rights of women and girls. The daughter of an outspoken critic of Pakistan's military dictatorship, Jilani was a founder of her country's first all-women law firm, as well as Pakistan's first legal aid center. Working on human rights issues in Pakistan was a dangerous occupation, and for nearly two decades the Pakistani government had kept her under twenty-four-hour surveillance. Outside Pakistan, she had served as a special representative for the U.N. for human rights defenders, and she had participated in an inquiry, at the behest of the Security Council, into the situation in Darfur. "I am a very laid-back person," Jilani once said, "but one thing I can't tolerate is injustice. That makes the adrenaline run, which makes me get up and take action."[5]

Desmond Travers brought a markedly different profile. A career military officer with the Irish Army, his work in the Middle East began early, with a posting in Cyprus in the 1960s. After the 1986 war in Lebanon, Travers volunteered to come to the region as a military observer, and he lived with his family in northern Israel for the better part of two years. His work took him to both sides of the border, and he found himself detained both by Lebanese and by Israeli forces at different points of his tour of duty. His international experience also included command of peacekeeping troops in Croatia and Bosnia, so he and Richard Goldstone shared a connection with the Balkans.[6]

It fell to Richard Goldstone to mold this disparate group of individuals into a team. "I could count on one hand the number of times when I have had a similar experience of cohesion, a sense of purpose, where everyone understood where they were within an organization and what it was about," Desmond Travers remembered.[7] They had at their disposal a staff of seventeen, under the leadership of Francesca Marotta of Italy, the longtime head of investigations in the OHCHR.

In Geneva, Goldstone and the other Mission members issued a public call for voluntary submission of evidence to the Mission, and they began to catalogue the information that they would need: public reports, satellite data, and the testimony of professionals and civilians from both Israel and the Palestinian territories. They consulted early on with NGOs with operations on the ground in Gaza. Because Israel had effectively barred journalists from entering Gaza during Cast Lead, NGOs, with their immediate access to people and communities, were indispensable sources of eyewitness accounts. The Mission's reliance on information from NGOs, however, would later become a matter of dispute, as critics complained that this evidence was being gathered by organizations with an anti-Israel bias.[8]

The Mission members also decided that their revised mandate allowed and indeed required that they consider a broad range of issues related to the Israeli-Palestinian conflict. The mandate encouraged the Mission to look at the pattern of rocket fire by Hamas into Israel over the preceding several years, hence turning their attention to potential violations of international law by Palestinian actors. But the Mission members determined that the rocket fire—and Israel's response to it—were also inextricably linked to a broad spectrum of other events and developments. It was impossible to understand the events in Gaza, they agreed in Geneva, without also understanding what was happening with Palestinians in the West Bank. Events in the West Bank were also linked to developments within Israel proper, particularly the question of how the Israeli authorities treated those who expressed disagreement with government policy toward the Palestinians. By the time they finished four days of internal discussions, they decided to include and examine, over the next four months, a sweeping set of issues in the Israeli-Palestinian conflict since the second intifada began in September 2000.

The next step, as far as Richard Goldstone was concerned, was to travel to Gaza to hear directly from people on the ground. With the help of the Swiss, who maintained direct relations with Hamas, Goldstone secured the cooperation of those whom the Mission referred to in its later report as the "Gaza authorities." The Mission's first visit was scheduled for the end of May 2009, just days after Goldstone formally received the MacArthur Prize for International Justice in The Hague.

It was always a borderland. The Hebrew Bible mentions ancient Gaza as a corner of the Canaanite Empire, and ever since Jewish sages have argued about whether it really could be considered part of the land of Israel. Its tiny territory hugged the coast of the Mediterranean at the northeast corner of the Sinai Peninsula, a small city surrounded by rich farmland, the last outpost of greenery, supported by deep wells, before the desert climate of the northern coast of Africa. When the ancient Egyptians took it over, they built an enormous fortress impressive enough to appear on royal friezes across the Nile.[9] Then came a seafaring group, the Philistines, whose name, slightly transformed, came to represent a land and later a people. Palestine, in its various modern meanings, owed its identity to this contested territory.

The cosmopolitan port offered access to the Mediterranean to the tribes of the inland kingdoms of the Middle East. The Nabateans, who built the magnificent city of Petra in the mountains of modern-day Jordan, helped make Gaza rich. Wealth also meant trafficking in human beings, and Gaza was a principal slave market in the centuries before the Christian era.[10] When Alexander the Great laid siege to Gaza City in 332 B.C.E., his forces took advantage of the area's loose subsoil to dig tunnels as a way into the heart of the city. (More than two millennia later, tunnels still played an outsized role in the affairs of the area.) Following Alexander's conquest, Gaza became "thoroughly Hellenized," the Greek influence persisting even after the Romans took over the region and extending through Gaza's transformation into a Christian city after Constantine became the Roman emperor.

When the Muslims conquered the southern Mediterranean in the seventh-century C.E, Gaza became a crucial crossroads between two kingdoms. Under the Mamluks and later the Ottomans, Gaza City thrived as a seaport, a locus of commercial activity but little political power. Twelve centuries of Muslim rule were interrupted only for the period between 1100 and 1187, when European Crusaders secured the area and built an outpost there.

Even before modern-day Zionism brought large numbers of Jews from Europe to Palestine, there was a tiny indigenous Jewish community in Gaza, numbering perhaps 100 families by the early nineteenth century. During that period, the Jews of France took an interest, supporting the Gaza community's synagogue and school. Gaza lay outside the plans for Theodore Herzl's colonization movement, and the Jews there remained isolated and vulnerable, even after the 1917 Balfour Declaration and the establishment of the British Mandate after World War I.

When violence broke out between Arabs and Jews throughout Palestine in 1929, the Jews of Gaza found themselves under siege. On August 24, 1929, rumors of trouble were rippling through the Jewish community, but most of them, unwilling to violate the Sabbath, stayed in the city. A crowd gathered threateningly, stones began to fly, and shouts of "Itbah al-Yahud!" ("Slaughter the Jews!") were heard. But a courageous group of Arab policemen worked to smuggle the Jews out of town in ambulances, and a group of Arab locals stepped in to provide additional protection. Gaza turned out to be the only place in Palestine where Jews were attacked without suffering a single casualty.[11] Following 1929, however, the pressures of living as a tiny minority in the area were too intense, and the Jewish community pulled up stakes and moved north within Palestine, never again to live in Gaza City. Jews did begin to acquire farming land on the outskirts on a small scale as early as 1930 and on a larger scale in the 1940s, as Zionists began establishing *kibbutzim*, farm collectives, in the area. The 1947 U.N. partition plan for Palestine, however, designated Gaza as an Arab region, and Jewish settlers there found themselves an embattled minority.

The 1948 Arab-Israeli War created Gaza in its contemporary social and political form. Two hundred thousand Arab refugees poured into the area from the surrounding farms, and from as far away as central Palestine. The population tripled; by the end of the war, Gaza, which represented 1 percent of the land area of mandatory Palestine, now had more than a quarter of the area's Arab population. The negotiated peace created the modern Gaza Strip, forty kilometers along the coast and just thirteen kilometers across at its widest point. The Strip came, uncomfortably, under the administration of Egypt, ruled by a military governor, and supported by the new United Nations Relief and Works Agency for Palestine Refugees, which established a massive network of camps. Set up to provide temporary shelter, the camps became a permanent feature of the Gaza cityscapes.

Cycles of violence have swept through Gaza ever since. Palestinian guerilla fighters used the territory as a base to launch fatal attacks against Israeli settlements in the southern half of the new country. In the wake of the Suez Crisis in 1956, Israel seized the Strip and undertook its first occupation of the territory. Hundreds of Palestinians died during the assault and the occupation, and some accounts claimed that civilians were killed indiscriminately by Israeli troops. Israel returned Gaza back to Egypt in early 1957, only to reoccupy it a decade later in the aftermath of the Six Day War.

Under Israeli administration, restrictions on movement, evictions of people from their homes, and crackdowns against suspected terrorists put daily pressure on the Palestinian population. Yet at the same time, the economic circumstances of the residents of Gaza improved considerably under Israeli rule. Although the territory did not have open borders, the creation of three guarded gateways in the early 1970s allowed the number of Gazans working in Israel proper to increase more than eightfold in just five years.[12]

Geographically isolated from the Palestinian community on the West Bank, and from the political base of the Palestinian Liberation Organization (PLO) in Tunisia, Gaza also became a hotbed for internecine conflict. The PLO had a foothold in Gaza, but it competed for Palestinian hearts and minds with an Islamist movement, under the leadership of Sheikh Ahmed Yassin, beginning in the early 1980s. The Islamists had little interest in the larger question of negotiating Palestinian liberation with the Israelis. When they reorganized themselves in 1987 under the name Hamas, their charter uncompromisingly rejected any legitimacy for the Israeli state.

Gaza was the initial site and the inspiration for the first intifada, between 1987 and 1992, when Palestinians faced off against Israeli troops with stones as their principal weapons. During the second intifada, starting in 2000, however, the violence spiraled. Hamas and other Palestinian militant groups, now well armed and well organized, launched a devastating series of suicide bomb attacks against nearby settlements and within Israel, some of them originating from Gaza. Israel responded with punishing counterattacks by air and by land, often stirred into action in defense of beleaguered Jewish communities on the edges of the Gaza territory.

In 2005, led by Prime Minister Ariel Sharon, Israel decided that it had had enough of Gaza. Without any negotiations or discussions with the Palestinian leadership about the political and economic future of the territory, Israel withdrew its troops and forcibly removed the Jewish settlers from the agricultural communities that had been established there in the 1970s. The political administration of Gaza now belonged to the Palestinians, though Israel still controlled the access to the territory by land and by sea, as well as its airspace.

Hamas won a surprising victory in the Palestinian legislative elections of 2006, and then consolidated its power with a military takeover of Gaza in 2007. The Islamists established their own political and economic structures, separate from those of the Palestinian Authority, and began to depend on economic support from outside forces, such as Iran. Firing missiles smuggled in through tunnels from the Sinai Desert in Egypt, the Gaza authorities sought to maintain the pressure on Israel by demonstrating their ability to touch the lives of its civilian population.

The Hamas regime managed the internal affairs of Gaza, but Israel continued to control its external connections. Legal and political figures debated whether this situation still constituted an occupation. Israel, having withdrawn its people and its troops, maintained that its occupation had come to an end in 2005. But Palestinians, citing Israel's exclusive control over access by land, sea, and air, insisted that Gaza's circumstance remained occupation in another form. Similarly, Israel claimed credit for continuing to allow vital goods and services to cross the borders; what other country, Israelis asked, would do so much for a people whose leaders were publicly committed to the destruction of their neighbors? On the other hand, Israel's tight restrictions on border crossings were leaving thousands of Palestinians without access to basic supplies.

This was Gaza in 2009: 360 square kilometers, just over twice the size of Washington D.C. It was bounded on one side by the Mediterranean Sea and on the others by a seventy-two-kilometer-long fenced border patrolled by Israeli and Egyptian soldiers. There were three checkpoints: two maintained by Israel at Erez and Nahal Oz, the third by Egypt at the southern city of Rafah. Gaza was home to more than 1.5 million people, at an astonishing density rate of more than 4,000 people per square kilometer. Gaza residents were no longer permitted to cross through the checkpoints to work in Israel, and the unemployment rate was more than 40 percent. Most Gazans depended for their livelihood on aid from the outside world. Hamas was the principal political authority, but its control was limited. There were dozens of other groups—many of them heavily armed—that had their own power bases and often enough weaponry to threaten both the Hamas regime and Israeli civilians outside of Gaza proper. More than half of Gaza's residents were under the age of eighteen. Born in the waning years of the twentieth century or the first years of the twenty-first, most had lived their entire lives in the cramped confines of this zone of insecurity.[13]

Three days before the Mission left for Gaza, in the first days of June 2009, Richard Goldstone bolted upright in the middle of the night. He had just been kidnapped by Hamas, and he knew that there was no one to rescue him. In fact, he discovered, everyone in Israel was rejoicing.[14]

Even outside of his dreams Richard Goldstone was anxious about traveling to Gaza.[15] He had lived under threat of death before, but he had never traveled to a territory controlled by a designated terrorist organization. He would be a Jew in a heavily armed place where hatred of Israel and hatred of the Jewish people went, for many, hand in hand.

The Israeli government refused permission for the Mission members to enter its territory. They could neither visit the border towns to collect evidence related to Hamas rocket attacks nor pass through Israeli territory en route to Gaza. So the Mission members and their staff entered via Egypt and the Rafah crossing.[16] An extensive Egyptian security escort accompanied the Mission's white U.N. SUVs all the way from Cairo to the border, where the group then placed itself in the hands of Hamas personnel. Goldstone tried to maintain his sense of humor, but conversations on the long ride across the desert were clipped and tense.

As the Mission made its way into and around Gaza, Richard Goldstone was powerfully moved by the impact of the remaining effects of Operation Cast Lead. He had absorbed the statistics and the postconflict journalistic accounts of the destruction, but now he saw firsthand the piles of rubble, the collapsed concrete buildings, the treacherous craters on the roads, the thousands of people still living in makeshift tents. Most of all, he witnessed the physical harm done to the people of Gaza. He was struck by the numbers of ordinary people limping around the streets of the cities, with disfigured faces or missing limbs. The aftermath of death he was prepared for. The throng of the walking wounded staggered him.[17]

After weeks of trepidation, he was encouraged by the reception that he received from the dignitaries of Hamas and from the people of Gaza. He noted similarities in temperament and feeling between the Gazans and Israelis whom he had met on earlier visits to the region.[18] Goldstone had discussed with his fellow Mission members whether or not they should meet with the Hamas leadership. Doing so was technically a violation of U.N. protocol, since Hamas had seized power in Gaza and had no internationally recognized political authority there. But the Mission members felt that this was a necessary step, since Hamas cooperation would be essential to their fact-finding activities.

Soon after the Mission's arrival, they met with Ismail Haniyeh, the de facto prime minister of Gaza, as well as other Hamas officials.[19] Goldstone found Haniyeh warm and welcoming, a man of laughing eyes and a gregarious personality, and he thought Palestinian cooperation "admirable," even though he knew that Haniyeh was engaging in "diplomatic puffery."[20] "I'm very aware that you're Jewish," Haniyeh told Goldstone with a smile. "I have no objection, no objection at all." Goldstone pressed Haniyeh directly on the question of rocket fire into Israel. Haniyeh blithely claimed that this had nothing to do with him, that the missiles were under control of the al-Qassam brigades, the military wing of Hamas, and other independent groups. Goldstone chose not to argue with Haniyeh about this patent fiction. The Mission leader then asked whether Haniyeh would help arrange meetings with the leaders of the various military factions. The Hamas leader promised to try, but it was unlikely that he tried very hard. Meetings between the military leaders in Gaza and the Mission members never took place.[21]

The four Mission members divided into teams of two to visit the locales that their staff had identified as significant sites for investigation. Mission staff had already been on the ground in Gaza for weeks, visiting sites, speaking with victims, and consulting with representatives of the U.N. and NGOs. Those staff members had pinpointed approximately three dozen specific incidents that they felt warranted in-depth attention. In traveling through Gaza, Goldstone paired most often with Hina Jilani. Together they traveled through the streets in conspicuous white U.N. vehicles, escorted by members of the Hamas security forces.

Later, critics of the Mission would insist that the field investigation was compromised because the Hamas presence meant that victims could not speak freely.[22] The Mission members, however, insisted at the time and long afterward that Hamas operatives were not present for the interviews, and that they posed no obstruction to the process of gathering evidence during their visit. "We talked about the possibility of intimidation," Christine Chinkin recalled, "but it wasn't something that as far as I was aware of it we were experiencing."[23] In any case, evidence collection was not the principal purpose of the Mission members' visit. Most of the witnesses had previously been interviewed by members of the U.N. team's staff; the visit itself was primarily designed to provide the members with firsthand experience, rather than new knowledge.

On one trip, Goldstone and Jilani made their way through the crowded Gaza City streets to the outskirts of the Jabaliyah refugee camp. The Mission's head dressed casually: khaki pants, a white shirt without a tie, sunglasses (but no hat), and a mobile phone on his belt. They headed toward the al-Maqadmah mosque, in the al-Alami housing project. The two-story structure, relatively new, had been built as a tribute to one of the earliest leaders of Hamas, Ibrahim al-Maqadmah, who was killed in an Israeli strike in 2003. The mosque was the epicenter of one of the incidents in Operation Cast Lead that the Mission had identified for closer scrutiny.

Palestinian sources had given the following account. On January 3, 2009, between 5:00 and 6:00 P.M., hundreds of men had gathered on the upper floor of the mosque for evening prayers. A large group of women gathered below in the building's basement. The worshippers were facing eastward toward Mecca, away from the entrance, when an explosion rocked the building. The force of the blast blew one of the two wooden doors of the building off its hinges. The door flew across the prayer area to the opposite wall. A noisy and terrifying chaos ensued, as those worshippers who were unhurt rushed to assist those who were bleeding and in pain. At least fifteen people, all of them inside the mosque at the time, died; more than forty were injured.[24]

After the end of the Cast Lead operation, the Israeli government had issued a statement in response to allegations that the mosque had been attacked. The government said that its own internal investigation revealed that "it was discovered that as opposed to the claims, the mosque was not attacked at all." Any casualties, the Israelis said, must have been caused by some other attack not involving the mosque. In any case, the report continued, those who died were not civilians, but Hamas operatives. The government provided no details about either its inquiry or the sources of its information. It was a blanket denial. "The mosque is still standing unharmed," the report concluded bluntly.[25]

Five months later, when Goldstone visited the site, there was no rubble around the entrance, and the mosque was indeed in operation, but the Mission members could clearly see that the idea that it was standing "unharmed" was preposterous. The entire front of the building had been reconstructed because of the damage. The entrance to the mosque had been raised from street level, and a newly built wooden ramp allowed worshippers to gain access. The officials of the mosque met the U.N. party and showed them what remained of the crumbled concrete stairs beneath the temporary ramp. New wooden doors adorned the entrance. Around the doorframe, both inside and outside of the building, Goldstone could see dozens of small metal cubes buried deep into the concrete.[26]

The sheikh of the mosque, ninety-one-year-old Moussa al-Silawi, greeted the visitors and delivered a passionate speech. He was present on the evening of January 3 and he heard the explosion, but he could see nothing, because he was blind. As his son Moteh was helping him from the damaged building, the sighted people around him gave him frantic reports. He heard first that he had lost his son, Ibrahim, himself a father of seven children. Then a nephew. Then his grandson, Muhammad. "Where is Islam?" the sheikh asked. "Where is honor? Where is justice?"[27]

The sheikh's son, Moteh al-Silawi, had been leading prayers that evening, and he showed Goldstone where he was standing, at the far side of the mosque, looking back toward the doorway. He said that he saw fragments falling like rain at the doorway of the mosque, and then described the chaos of bodies and limbs he had to step over as he guided his father to safety. Then he noticed that a fragment of metal had pierced his own hand. He showed Goldstone the scar. "We must have our rights," Moteh insisted. "The criminals who perpetrated these crimes must be held accountable."[28]

After their tour of the inside of the mosque, Goldstone and Jilani took a short walk in the surrounding area of the refugee camp. There was no other visible damage in the immediate area of the mosque—in or around the housing units, or the nearby hospital. Whatever happened at al-Maqadmah mosque appeared to have been confined to the neighborhood of the building itself, rather than the epicenter of a pitched and confusing battle scene. "It is that sort of conduct that is absolutely unacceptable," Goldstone said a few months later. "I put myself in the position of how Jews would feel if they were attacked in a synagogue when it was full of worshippers."[29]

Mission staff took further photographs of the damage for later analysis, along with further statements from witnesses to the incident. Goldstone and his colleagues would have to weigh the evidence of damage that they saw with their own eyes, the reliability of the testimony of eyewitnesses, and the relevance of the medical documentation regarding the deaths and injuries to worshippers. In the absence of Israeli cooperation, the only counternarrative available to the Mission was a bare and unverified public statement denying even that the mosque was damaged.

From Jabaliyah the U.N. vehicles took Goldstone and Jilani to Zeytoun, a more rural area south of Gaza City. Here there were groves of olive and fig trees, chicken coops, and agricultural land, but there were very few houses— only piles of bulldozed rubble, and some tents propped forlornly among the unused garden plots. The area had been home for generations to the extended al-Samouni family, for which the particular neighborhood was named. It was the site of another significant incident that the Mission was probing.

The story, as the Mission had heard it from local sources, was this.[30] On the morning of January 4, 2009, the Israeli ground invasion reached the al-Samouni neighborhood. Soldiers entered a number of the houses before dawn. According to local Palestinian witnesses, a soldier shot and killed one homeowner, Ateya al-Samouni, even though his arms were raised and he was holding his ID and Israeli driving license in his hands. Over the course of the morning of January 4, the soldiers ordered families out of their various houses, telling them that they should all gather in the home of Wa'el al-Samouni, one of the largest in the area. By the end of the day, more than

100 members of the extended family had crowded into the house, with scarcely any food, water, or milk for the several infants.

Early the next morning, January 5, a handful of the men, including Wa'el al-Samouni, went outside for firewood. In the dim predawn light, they could see Israeli soldiers stationed on the rooftops of the nearby homes. Then . . . an explosion. One of the wood-gatherers, Muhammad Ibrahim al-Samouni, died on the spot. The others managed to retreat inside the house. Within five minutes, there were more explosions, including at least two, maybe three direct hits on the house itself. Twenty-one members of the family died; the youngest was two-year-old Azza. After the strikes, many surviving members of the family gathered themselves and walked to Gaza City, but some were left behind. Red Cross workers found four children trapped in a house with the corpses of their mothers.[31] Family members said later that Israeli soldiers prevented ambulances from reaching them in order to assist and evacuate the wounded. The al-Samouni family members remained in Gaza City for two weeks, unable to go back to their homes until the ceasefire on January 18. When they returned, they found that Wa'el's house, most of the other homes in the neighborhood, and the small mosque had been demolished. The stench of death was overwhelming.

Saleh al-Samouni, the father of Azza, walked Goldstone around what remained of the neighborhood. He showed Mission staff where he and the other men seeking firewood were standing when the first projectile struck. They were in full sight, he said, of the Israeli soldiers who were on the rooftops of the nearby houses. Saleh led the group into the still-standing home of his dead father, Talal. There Goldstone cringed when he saw the crude graffiti on the living room walls. He could read the English: "Arabs need to die." "1 is down, 999,999 to go." "Make war not peace."[32] A staff member translated the Hebrew under a black Star of David: "The Jewish people are alive."

Wa'el al-Samouni's house was no longer standing, but he greeted the Mission members at the home of one of his cousins. Wa'el walked Goldstone around the courtyard, whose walls were lined with twenty-three photographs in somber black frames. The two men stopped by each portrait, Wa'el telling the Mission head, with the help of the translator, a little about each family member that he lost—their relation to him, an anecdote, a remembered gesture. The pain of loss affected Goldstone deeply. As Wa'el completed the tour, neither man could contain his emotion, and the two clasped each other in a tearful embrace.

In the immediate aftermath of the incident, a spokesman for the IDF had denied that civilians were targeted.[33] Since that date, there had been no further Israeli government statement on the issue, nor had any investigation into the incident been announced. So the Mission had no access to any other interpretation of these events.

Goldstone and the other Mission members spent a total of four days in Gaza. The Mission head struggled to maintain his poise in the face of the suffering that he encountered. For many years, he had absorbed a sense of the fragility of the state of Israel, surrounded on all sides by hostile neighbors. In Gaza, he felt palpably the vulnerability of men, women, and children who had, after all, nowhere else to go. Seeing Israeli power through Palestinian eyes drove a painful wedge through him.

From his days visiting prisoners in apartheid South Africa, Richard Goldstone had believed that direct encounter with victims provided an important outlet, a signal to them and their neighbors that the outside world was taking their suffering seriously. For the investigator—for Richard Goldstone himself—the direct encounters with the sheikh at the mosque and with Wa'el al-Samouni gave him a depth of insight and emotional understanding of the situation in Gaza that thousands of pages of reports could not convey. The emotional impact of the encounters with victims and survivors inevitably created an even stronger moral imperative toward accountability. A holy building had been struck, dozens of members of a single family had become casualties in a single day, and the pain of the survivors was vivid and immediate. It was natural for any investigator to feel that *someone* had to be responsible, and the scale of suffering in Gaza suggested strongly that responsibility did not lie simply with the actions of a few rogue soldiers. The images and conversations from those four days in June would remain vivid for Richard Goldstone from afar as the Mission continued to gather evidence and come to its conclusions.

Three weeks later, Goldstone and the Mission members were back in Gaza, this time with the more limited purpose of presiding over two days of public hearings. Goldstone made the hearings a personal project. The proceedings directly applied the lessons he had absorbed from South Africa and The Hague—that making public the stories of suffering was an essential element both of accountability and of eventual reconciliation. Nearly every witness had previously spoken to the Mission's investigators, who could collect better evidence privately than in front of microphones and cameras. But

Goldstone hoped that the hearings would magnify the Mission's impact and contribute to mutual understanding.[34]

Over two days, the Mission heard from more than twenty witnesses in a secure U.N. facility in Gaza City.[35] Sheikh Moussa Al-Silawi recounted his version of the explosions at the al-Maqadmah mosque. Wa'el and Saleh al-Samouni brought their twenty-three photographs to the hearings and told their version of the events in Zeytoun. Ziad Al-Deeb, a university student, was wheeled into the hearing room. He related that eleven members of his family were killed in an explosion at Jabaliyah on January 6, 2009; his own legs were sliced off by the blast. The Mission members also heard from doctors and social workers who testified to the broader impact of the conflict on the Gaza population: the overwhelmed hospitals, the decimated infrastructure, the damage to an already feeble economy.

Goldstone also wanted to hold a set of hearings in southern Israel, the better to hear directly from victims of rocket fire from Gaza. Since the Israeli government made this impossible, he decided to schedule two days of testimony in Geneva in early July.[36] He made a special plea to Israeli organizations to send representatives to testify there and arranged for the U.N. to pick up the travel expenses for those for whom the cost of travel might be a barrier.[37]

Mirela Siderer came to Geneva to relate her experience as a victim of the 2008 missile strike on her clinic in the mall in Ashkelon. She apologized for the way that she looked and for her labored breathing, the results of her injuries. "I have no understanding of terrorism," she told the Mission members. "I want you to understand that. I have no understanding of killing children, killing women, ordinary people, innocent people, but nevertheless I do have a great deal of sorrow for all of the victims, for the children and the women on the other side. They too are innocent. This has to stop. It has to stop."

"We understand the emotion that you are suffering," Richard Goldstone said from the chair. "Please don't apologize for it. We extend our deepest sympathy to you."

The Mission heard, too, from Israelis who spoke to the broader impact of the rocket attacks. The mayor of Ashkelon, Benny Vaknin, narrated his many attempts over the years to build social and economic cooperation with counterparts in Gaza, before the second intifada made these overtures impossible. The Mission members heard from Noam Bedein, the head of a media center in Sderot, the town on the Gaza border that had borne the brunt of the missile fire over the previous decade. Bedein showed a video, *What Does It Mean*

Having Fifteen Seconds to Run for Your Life?, featuring footage of Sderot children running for shelter on the first day of school. "Fifteen seconds to run for your life," Bedein told the Mission members. "This is normal routine now in Sderot."

Noam Shalit, the father of kidnapped solider Gilad Shalit, made an impassioned plea for the release of his son. On June 25, 2006, the younger Shalit, newly inducted into the IDF, was kidnapped by Hamas operatives who had snuck into Israel from Gaza via cross-border tunnels. His abduction became a cause célèbre in Israel and in the Jewish community around the globe, as Hamas held the Israeli soldier without permitting him contact with his family or the outside world. By the time of the Mission hearing, Shalit had been in captivity for more than three years, and efforts to negotiate his release had come to naught. Noam Shalit used his testimony at the hearings to speak directly and forcefully to the Palestinian community. "People of Gaza," Shalit said, "like many of you, we are suffering the consequences of the decisions and failures of others. . . . As a parent speaking to a multitude of parents I ask you to understand my family's anguish."

Speaking for his fellow Mission members, Richard Goldstone assured Shalit that "all four of us are parents. Some of us are grandparents so we can empathize with what you and what your family are going through."

It was not clear that either the Gaza or the Geneva hearings had any significant public impact. The press coverage was minimal, and the broadcasts back to Israel, the West Bank, and Gaza commanded little attention. Still, Goldstone regarded the effort as important. The Mission had, at least, made an effort to bring Israeli voices to the forefront, and to communicate the real and pressing suffering of Israeli victims. Even some of Goldstone's harshest critics agreed. By inviting Israeli victims to testify alongside Palestinians in Geneva, said UN Watch, "Goldstone introduced something new to the UN," adding that the Mission chair deserved "particular credit" for including Noam Shalit in the proceedings.[38]

In the first week of August in Geneva, Richard Goldstone, the other Mission members, and the key staff members hammered out the details of their report. There were hundreds of pages of text to consider, principally drafted by Francesca Marotta and other staff members of the investigating team.

For Goldstone, the heart of the report was the scale of civilian suffering among both the Palestinian and the Israeli populations. There could be no doubt that the conflict—before and during Operation Cast Lead—had severely harmed men, women, and children who had no direct part in military operations. The scale of the suffering did not by itself prove that any party had violated international law. But the duration and the scale of human misery in Gaza, the West Bank, and Israel did require, in Goldstone's view, a sharpened attention to the decision-making process behind military actions.

The Mission members found that on the basics of the report, there were relatively few areas of disagreement among them. "One of the things that was most remarkable," said Christine Chinkin, "was our ability to maintain an equilibrium between the four of us. There was no sense of any divide between the group." There were skirmishes over particular word choices and passages, but there were only three battles over significant points of emphasis.[39]

The first involved whether or not the report should mention the kidnapped Israeli soldier, Gilad Shalit. Chinkin and Jilani argued against it. There were thousands of Palestinians in Israeli prisons, they argued. To take up the single case of an Israeli being held by Palestinian forces invited the criticism that the Mission was showing special favor to the Israeli cause. Goldstone argued forcefully for including the Shalit case. Shalit was kidnapped, not arrested, and his Hamas captors were making no pretense that holding him was in any way part of a process of legitimate justice. His father had testified powerfully at the Mission's hearings in Geneva. On substantive grounds, it was only right that the report should call for his release. The argument on political grounds was at least as powerful. If the report was going to have a chance at being accepted in Israeli circles, Goldstone knew, then it had at the very least to acknowledge the case that had become a major public issue in Israel over the past three years. The other Mission members reluctantly agreed.

The second disagreement involved the overall tone of the report. While the Mission had assembled considerable evidence for its conclusions from firsthand visits, personal testimony, documents, and public records, Goldstone believed that many of its conclusions might look different if they had had access to the Israeli perspective. He argued that in many places the text should be more conditional, using phrases like "it appears that" or "the evidence indicates," rather than stating conclusions as established fact. The other members were unconvinced, fearing that such language would dilute their report to the point that it had little meaning and little impact. In the main, Goldstone conceded the point. Better perhaps to have a strong report that might overstate at some points than to issue a document that said little of anything at all.[40]

Finally, the Mission members battled over what exactly their recommendation should be regarding the follow-up to the report. If they were suggesting that war crimes had likely been committed, then who would do something about it? The other three Mission members had an answer: they should recommend that the Security Council immediately refer the situation in the Middle East to the prosecutor of the ICC.

Richard Goldstone found himself in the ironic position of resisting an immediate referral to the ICC. After all, no one had done more than he to establish international criminal justice, and his work at the Yugoslavia and Rwanda tribunals had led directly to the creation of the ICC itself. But a principal reason for establishing such courts, as he saw it, was to try to push countries around the world to take full responsibility for the misdeeds of their *own* leaders and soldiers. He urged that the report give both the Palestinians and the Israelis an opportunity to conduct their own credible investigations, using the Mission's report and evidence as a starting point. If they failed or refused to do this, then and only then should the ICC take up the matter.

On this issue, Goldstone held firm. If the other three insisted on an immediate referral, he said, then he would issue a public dissent on this point. In fact, none of the group wanted a dissent—it would weaken the report fatally.[41] In the face of Goldstone's stand, the other members backed down. The report would recommend first and foremost that the parties undertake a serious investigation of themselves.

After the gathering in Geneva, Richard and Noleen Goldstone headed home to Johannesburg for a short stay. There were continued email exchanges regarding minor edits, but the Mission's work was mostly done. By the third week in August, the couple was en route to New York, where Richard would spend the fall as a visiting professor at Fordham Law School. He had moments of nervous anticipation about the release of the report, but he had faith that his own goodwill, his long-standing history with Israel, and his strong attachment to fairness would persuade the public to give the Mission's conclusions a fair hearing. "I think that the truth is always helpful," he told a reporter during his stay in South Africa. "If the truth makes all sides a little bit uncomfortable, that's not a bad thing."[42]

16 ▸ THE GOLDSTONE REPORT

THE DOCUMENT THAT would make Richard Goldstone the most hated man in the Jewish world was released on September 15, 2009, as U.N. document A/HRC/12/48, the *Report of the United Nations Fact-Finding Mission on the Gaza Conflict*. It weighed in at 452 pages, including its annexes.[1] The names of all the Mission members were listed in the second paragraph, but given the prominence of its lead author the document quickly acquired a public moniker: the Goldstone Report.

Its text spoke from the perspective of "the Mission," a phrase that cut against the grain of its lawyerly language and sometimes evoked a disembodied voice from outer space. Its tone was mostly legalistic and bureaucratic, with occasional bursts of emotion—a moment of sympathy for the victims, or barely concealed impatience at the intransigence of one or another of the parties.

The Mission members and their staff reviewed more than 300 reports and submissions, amounting to more than 10,000 pages, in addition to interviews with victims, site visits, analysis of 30 videos and 1,200 photographs, forensic analysis of weapons and ammunition remnants, and testimony at the public hearings in Gaza and Geneva.[2] The Mission bemoaned the lack of cooperation by the Israeli authorities, and it extended its thanks to "the people of Gaza for their warm welcome, their humanity and their hospitality in spite of such difficult and painful circumstances."[3]

The document described the painful toll of the Israeli-Palestinian conflict. More than 7,000 Palestinians and almost 1,500 Israelis had died between 1987 and 2008. Suicide bombers alone killed 542 people in Israel. On the West Bank, Israelis built what the report called, echoing the Palestinian terminology, the "separation wall."[4] In Gaza, following the takeover by Hamas in 2007, Israel imposed a crushing economic blockade. The report devoted more than one hundred paragraphs to the impact of the blockade on the availability of food and nutrition, on water and sanitation, on housing, on physical and mental health, and the disproportionate impact on the women and children of Gaza. The Mission made a case that understanding Operation Cast Lead required a broader understanding of the background issues in the Israeli-Palestinian context. Yet the pressures of time and space inevitably meant that the report's treatment of these enormously complex circumstances was superficial at best. The weakness of these sections later made an easy target for critics, who used them to characterize the Mission's overall methodology as slapdash.

When it came to the origins of the 2008–2009 Gaza conflict, the Mission went out of its way to take no sides. The Mission did not fault the Palestinians for resorting to military action in order to pursue their right to self-determination. Nor did it fault the Israelis for responding to the barrage of missiles with military force. The Mission, instead, focused on *how* each side chose to fight the battle.

The rockets fired over eight years from Gaza, the Mission members said unequivocally, deliberately spread terror among the Israeli population. More than 8,000 rockets were fired into Israel during this period—before, during, and after the 2008–2009 conflict. The report noted by name the four Israelis (two Jewish, one Bedouin, one Druze) killed in rocket fire. Drawing on testimony in Geneva, submissions to the Mission, and telephone interviews with Israelis, the report detailed the psychological impact of rocket fire on the communities in southern Israel, citing one NGO's statistic that as many as 94 percent of the children in the border town of Sderot showed signs of post-traumatic stress. The Mission also dwelt on the damage to property, the impact on social and economic life, and the constant disruption to schools, which it termed an abridgment of the Israeli children's right to education.

Goldstone and his fellow Mission members rejected the recent, half-hearted statements by Hamas that its military wing did not mean to target civilians. After all, the al-Qassam brigades specifically claimed credit for each of the Israeli civilian deaths. "The Israelis began this tension and they must pay an expensive price," the Mission quoted one Hamas militant. "They cannot leave us drowning in blood while they sleep soundly in their beds." Many of the rockets landed nowhere near military targets. Moreover, firing rockets with such poor rates of accuracy toward population centers indicated reckless disregard for casualties. The Mission concluded that Hamas and the other Palestinian groups firing into Israel made no distinction between civilian and military targets, a violation of the laws of war.

It is unlikely that this conclusion was what Cuba, Egypt, and Pakistan had in mind when they sponsored the original HRC resolution calling for an investigation into the actions of "the occupying power Israel." For the first time, an official U.N. report stated that there were strong indications that Palestinian groups had committed war crimes.

So, too, said Goldstone and the other members, did the Israelis. At the center of the report, 157 pages provided a "factual and legal" examination of thirty-six individual incidents that took place in Gaza between December 27, 2008, and January 18, 2009. (The section on Palestinian rockets attacking Israel comprised twenty pages.) All of these incidents involved actions allegedly taken by the IDF in which Palestinian civilians came to harm.

During the first minutes of the operation on December 27, 2008, ninety-nine policemen and nine members of the public were killed in an aerial attack on a graduation ceremony for a Palestinian police academy. The Israelis argued that, under Hamas, the police forces were very much integrated into the overall security apparatus and were therefore legitimate military targets. The Mission rejected this view. It accepted the characterization of Hamas authorities (actively disputed by critics later) that the Gaza police were limited to enforcing the law within the territory and were therefore decidedly not combatants.

The same principle applied to attacks on two hospitals in January 2009. The Mission concluded that the Israeli forces targeted the hospitals with artillery fire, including shells containing white phosphorous. The Israelis, in their public statements, had suggested that Hamas fighters cynically used hospital buildings as bases of operations, thus making those buildings legitimate targets for attack. But the Mission concluded that in the two incidents that they examined there was no evidence that the hospitals housed military personnel.

Therefore Israel had failed to take feasible precautions to protect these sensitive civilian sites.[5]

The shelling of al-Fakhura Street on January 6, 2009, which killed the sons of Muhammad Fouad Abu Askar and twenty-two others, represented to the Mission an example of an indiscriminate attack on the civilian population. Goldstone and his fellow Mission members argued that the use of a mortar shell—inherently inaccurate—was a crude tool to use in a densely populated area, and that the Israeli commander who ordered the strike had plenty of time to consider other options that would have had less dire consequences. Therefore, they concluded, the shelling of al-Fakhura Street represented a failure to take adequate precautions to preserve the lives of civilians, and this was a violation of international law.[6]

The al-Fakhura Street incident and others also triggered discussions of the principle of proportionality. Even if an attack was appropriately aimed at a military target, there was a further question under international law about whether the means used to carry out the attack were "proportional" to the situation. Proportionality was notoriously difficult to assess. Just how much force was legal under international law in a certain situation required an intensive analysis of a mass of details, and even then the question of how much force was permissible was open to dispute. For some outside observers, the stark imbalance in the numbers of casualties in Cast Lead (nearly one hundred Palestinian casualties for every Israeli casualty during the conflict itself) was itself evidence of the Israeli government's disproportionate use of force. The Mission did not, by and large, focus its own analysis on proportionality. In avoiding the subject, however, it lost an opportunity to use the Cast Lead situation to explore the complexities of a difficult but essential principle of international law.

The Mission gave substantial attention to a series of attacks that produced no direct civilian casualties but in its opinion constituted attacks on the livelihood and well-being of the people of Gaza as a whole. These included the destruction of the Gaza Strip's only flour mill, the destruction of farms housing more than 100,000 chickens, and the destruction of one of Gaza's main wastewater treatment plants, causing a vast outflow of raw sewage into surrounding neighborhoods.[7] In the case of the flour mill and the chicken farms, the Israelis said that these were sites of intense fighting, and that damage done to food supplies was an unfortunate outcome. The Israelis denied hitting the water treatment plant altogether. The Mission, relying on its site visits and interviews with Palestinian sources from the area, said that there was no evidence to support the Israeli claim that these outlying structures were important military sites. They left no doubt that they considered these actions violations of the Geneva Conventions and, in effect, war crimes.

The Mission devoted its most intensive scrutiny to eleven incidents that it described as "deliberate attacks against the civilian population."[8] Prominent among these were the incident of the al-Maqadmah mosque and the deaths of the twenty-four members of the al-Samouni family. It also examined seven incidents in which Israeli soldiers were said to have deliberately or recklessly shot and killed Palestinian civilians. Some of these instances, the Mission members said, were willful killings. Furthermore, the Mission said explicitly, individuals could and should be held responsible for these criminal acts.

Cumulatively, the descriptions of the thirty-six incidents represented a searing indictment of the Israeli conduct of the Gaza conflict. The tales of suffering and trauma raised difficult questions about just how far a democratic nation could and should go as it sought to protect its own citizens from present and future harm. While some later critics would carp about the Mission's reliance on certain NGOs for information, there was little dispute about whether the Mission's report had accurately captured the *impact* of Cast Lead on the people of Gaza. There were quibbles over details, but the evidence-gathering function of the Mission would remain essentially unrefuted.

The narratives themselves, however, were only half the story. The other half, as the Mission told it, was the motivation. The harm that came to the civilians of Gaza, according to the Mission members, was no accident. It was deliberate and systematic, not a matter of carelessness, but a matter of Israeli government policy.

The Mission's explosive argument that Israel deliberately intended to punish the people of Gaza in Operation Cast Lead rested on three main pillars.[9] First, the Mission could find no legitimate military reason for actions taken by the Israeli forces in many of the thirty-six incidents; in the absence of a military purpose, the members concluded, the harm that came to civilians must have been intentional. Second, the Mission unearthed what they argued was a pattern of public statements by Israeli political and military leaders, principally in the aftermath of the 2006 war against Hezbollah forces in Lebanon, that suggested that targeting civilians would henceforth be a necessary tactic in the fight against Israel's enemies. Third, the Mission relied on the accounts of

Operation Cast Lead by current and former Israeli soldiers who were part of a group called "Breaking the Silence"; the group had published several dozen narratives criticizing IDF tactics in June 2009.

The incident of the al-Maqadmah mosque illustrated the Mission's first line of argument. The Mission looked around the site, interviewed witnesses, and could not find any indication that the mosque had been used for military purposes or that there was a legitimate military target even in the area. The IDF did not provide its own explanation of what they knew about the area and denied that the mosque was even targeted. The Mission in this incident and many others discounted the possibility of accident. It argued that because the Israelis had complete control of the Gaza airspace they therefore possessed very detailed intelligence capabilities. Since the IDF had such extraordinary access to information, the Mission suggested, it was not plausible that to imagine that there would be many errors when it came to choosing targets.

Furthermore, Israel liked to brag about the precision of its high-tech weapons. The Mission quoted one Israeli official as saying after Operation Cast Lead that 99 percent of the strikes on Gaza hit their targets. With that level of accuracy, the Mission said, the chances of multiple errors with civilian casualties should be extraordinarily low. It meant, said the Mission, that what was struck was meant to be struck. If a missile blew the doors off the al-Maqadmah mosque, the Israelis must have been aiming for the doorknobs. The Mission applied this same logic to nearly all of the incidents that involved missile strikes from the air.

The analysis of the destruction of the Gaza food supply followed a similar pattern. The flour mill and the chicken farms, lying exposed and well outside the urban areas, had no obvious strategic importance from a military point of view. Four months after the conflict, the Mission members who visited these sites had found no evidence that these were sites of military operation by Palestinian groups. In the absence of any such evidence, and in the absence of any explanation from the Israeli government, the Mission concluded that the intent of these operations was to inflict collective punishment on the people of Gaza.

When it came to the facts of the incidents in Gaza, the Mission had a great deal of specific information on which to draw. In analyzing the motivation behind these incidents, however, the Goldstone Report mostly asserted a negative. It used the absence of evidence to the contrary to prove its case, a method of argument that was obviously vulnerable to error if further facts became available. The Mission sought to bolster its case by relying on indirect commentary by Israeli officials and soldiers.

In 2006, Israel had fought a small bitter war against the Shi'ite group, Hezbollah, which had been building a military stronghold in southern Lebanon for years. Hezbollah began to fire missiles into northern Israel, striking among many other places the major city of Haifa. The IDF struck back, with a fierce air and ground attack designed to uproot Hezbollah from the area. But the Hezbollah forces had carefully embedded their rocket launchers and their military operations in and around villages in southern Lebanon, and also within the capital city of Beirut. So the Israeli counterattack necessarily had a strong and direct impact on civilians in that region. A particularly intense battle took place in the Beirut neighborhood of Dahiya, where the IDF virtually destroyed the entire quarter in order to uproot the Hezbollah operations there.

In the wake of the Lebanon war, some Israeli military and political leaders articulated what came to be known as the "Dahiya doctrine." The central premise was that it was no longer possible to draw a clear distinction between the fighting forces of terrorist groups and the civilian population that aided and abetted them. If Israel was attacked, then it would strike back hard, and would not hesitate to punish civilians in pursuit of its military goals. In essence, this line of argument suggested that the venerable principle of distinction between military and civilian targets was no longer valid in an era of guerilla tactics by nongovernment forces.

The Mission argued that the Dahiya doctrine, though developed in response to the war in Lebanon, was implemented in the war against Hamas in Gaza. In support of this premise, it quoted public statements by Israeli officers.[10] "What happened in the Dahiya quarter in 2006 will happen in every village from which Israel is fired on," said Major General Gadi Eisenkot, the head of the Israeli Northern Command, in 2008. "We will apply disproportionate force on it and cause great damage there. From our standpoint, these are not civilian villages, they are military bases. . . . This is not a recommendation. This is a plan. And it has been approved."

None of the Israeli military figures quoted in the Goldstone Report made their statements while in positions of command in relation to Operation Cast Lead. This weakened the link between those statements and actual events in Gaza, but Goldstone and his fellow members believed that they did not have to determine whether Israeli military officials were directly influenced by these writings. What the Mission saw on the ground, it said, proved that what was prescribed as the best strategy was in fact put into practice.

If military leaders did not comment directly on Gaza, Israeli political leaders did. On January 6, 2009, Deputy Prime Minister Eli Yishai called the ongoing Operation Cast Lead "a great opportunity to demolish thousands of houses of the terrorists, so they will think twice before they launch rockets."[11] The Mission used Yishai's statement to make the case that Israel used the Hamas tactics of embedding military operations in civilian areas as an excuse to treat all Gaza civilians as legitimate military targets.

Selective quotation of political and military leaders made for evidence of uncertain value. On the one hand, some of the direct quotations did come from highly placed members of the Israeli establishment. On the other hand, even casual observers of Israeli politics were well aware that leaders of the party in power often made public statements at odds with government policy. In addition, overstatement and inflamed rhetoric were staples of Israeli political discourse. So it was difficult to know how much weight to put on the quoted statements, and how much connection to draw between public discourse and official practice.

The third pillar of the Goldstone Report focused on Israeli intent rested on accounts collected by a NGO called "Breaking the Silence."[12] Founded in 2004 by a group of soldiers who had served in some of the toughest areas of the West Bank, Breaking the Silence collected and published hundreds of narratives by veterans who had served in the occupied territories. "Cases of abuse towards Palestinians, looting, and destruction of property have been the norm for years," the organization's website explained, "but are still explained as extreme and unique cases. Our testimonies portray a different, and much grimmer picture in which deterioration of moral standards finds expression in the character of orders and the rules of engagement and are justified in the name of Israel's security."

In June 2009, Breaking the Silence published a collection of fifty-two testimonies of soldiers who served in Operation Cast Lead.[13] Analyzing these testimonies, the Mission members deduced what they called two Israeli "policies."[14] The first was summarized succinctly: "Shoot in case of doubt." Soldiers testified that they were encouraged, in a threatening situation, not to hesitate. Better to err on the side of hitting an innocent person than to hesitate and expose oneself, one's comrades, or one's countrymen to danger. "In urban warfare," one soldier summarized this attitude, "anyone is your enemy. No innocents."

The second policy, according to the Mission, was a rigid enforcement of "red lines." If the IDF made clear that no one should pass beyond a certain point in a street, for example, then the soldiers had clear and unambiguous orders to open fire if anyone crossed that line. In one instance, according to one soldier's account, a Palestinian mother and two children, after being ordered to leave their house, turned left instead of right. When they inadvertently crossed one of these red lines, an Israeli opened fire, killing all three on the spot. "From our perspective," said the soldier telling the story, "[the marksman] did his job according to the orders that he was given."

While it seems a stretch to use the word "policies" to describe these practices, the Mission described the soldiers' testimonies as part of a pattern. Rather than erring on the side of protecting civilians, the Mission charged, Israel consistently encouraged its forces to err on the side of protecting themselves and eliminating any possible terrorist threat. It was this attitude that encouraged soldiers to overreact and led directly to the shooting deaths of many Palestinian civilians. In the incidents that it had specifically investigated, the Mission identified thirty-four Palestinian civilians who "lost their lives owing to Israeli fire intentionally directed at them."[15] By identifying these practices specifically as policies, the Mission appeared to be making sure that the incidents they described could fall within the ambit of the ICC.[16]

The report devoted thirteen pages to a consideration of whether and how the Palestinian authorities exposed their own citizens to danger.[17] Here the Mission admitted the limitations of its own investigating powers. In introducing the subject, the report noted that "those interviewed in Gaza appeared reluctant to speak about the presence of or conduct of hostilities by the Palestinian armed groups," apparently out of fear of retaliation against witnesses and their families by those very groups. As a result, the report was diffident about its conclusions here. The Mission conceded that it was very possible that Hamas did indeed booby-trap houses and use mosques for military operations or use ambulances to facilitate the movements of its forces. The members insisted, however, that they had no evidence at their disposal to point to specific instances of any of these practices.

Goldstone and the Mission acknowledged the Palestinians' deliberate confusion of military and civilian operations, but they considered the Israeli response a massive overreaction. Israel, they said, chose to interpret everything and everyone within Gaza as "supporting infrastructure" and therefore a legitimate target. The fragile protections for civilians in a time of war were destroyed.

The Mission even had a theory about why. Israel, it said, wished to punish the Gaza population for its resilience and for its apparent support for Hamas, and possibly with the intent of forcing a change in such support.[18] The report provided no evidence for this motivation. Nothing in the statements that it quoted from the generals and political leaders, for example, touched either on the question of Palestinian "resilience" or on the possibility of forcing Hamas from power. Yet the Mission said that it "considers this position to be firmly based in fact, bearing in mind what it saw and heard on the ground."

"The Government of Israel has a duty to protect its citizens," Richard Goldstone acknowledged in his public presentation of the report in September. "That in no way justifies a policy of collective punishment of a people under effective occupation, destroying their means to live a dignified life. This contributes to a situation where young people grow up in a culture of hatred and violence, with little hope for change in the future."[19]

On the matter of intent, then, the Goldstone Report made some far-reaching claims, but it is also important to recognize what it did *not* do. The Mission never made the argument that in Operation Cast Lead Israel was waging war out of hatred for the Palestinian people. Richard Goldstone had prosecuted Serbian leaders for targeting Muslims and Hutu leaders for targeting Tutsis, but the charge against the Israeli leadership was different. Even when the Mission accused the Israelis of encouraging direct violence against Palestinian people, the report emphasized tactical and strategic reasons, not ethnic hatred. Israel stood accused in the Goldstone Report of a very serious set of war crimes, but with the intent to punish the Palestinian people, not to obliterate them.

Only twice did the report focus on the possibility of crimes against humanity—that is, actions that might be construed as a large-scale or systematic attack against a civilian population.[20] It suggested that the long-standing blockade of Gaza might constitute the "persecution" of the Palestinian people.[21] It also indicated that Hamas rocket fire into Israel, since it had no military purpose whatsoever, might be construed as a war on the Israeli people.[22]

In presenting his report publicly to the HRC in September, Richard Goldstone commented that "it has been my experience in many regions of the

world, including my own country, South Africa, that peace and reconciliation depend, to a great extent, upon public acknowledgement of what victims suffer. That applies no less in the Middle East. It is a prerequisite to the
beginning of the healing and meaningful peace process." He made it clear that
he believed that the suffering of Israeli and Palestinian civilians was the product of misguided and cruel decisions by individuals in leadership positions.
Holding those leaders accountable, he also believed, was a way to avoid the
"collective guilt" that often poisoned the well of reconciliation between
divided peoples. He maintained a firm and optimistic belief that the Mission's
report—*because* it faced the conflict honestly—offered a chance to create a
positive dynamic in the Middle East. "People of the region should not be
demonized," he offered. "Rather, their common humanity should be
emphasized."[23]

17 ▸ OUTRAGE

W<small>HEN THE GOLDSTONE</small> Report made its public debut, the first headlines in the mainstream press emphasized balance. "Inquiry Finds Gaza War Crimes from Both Sides," reported the *New York Times* in a page one story on September 16.[1] A spokesman for Hamas categorically denied that Hamas rockets had been aimed at Israeli civilians. The Israeli ambassador to the U.N., Gabriela Shalev, promised that her nation would review the report, while reiterating the objection to the original mandate.

By the next day, however, the Israeli promise to reflect had already turned to outrage. The government of Israel was "nauseous and furious," said one of its spokespersons. Just two days old, the report was already "one of the most disgraceful documents in the long collection of shameful documents put out by the United Nations."[2] A raucous chorus—principally Jewish commentators from Israel and the United States—joined in swift and highly emotional condemnation. Israeli president Shimon Peres accused the report of "making a mockery of history" and a spokesman for the prime minister called the report "conceived in sin and is the product of a union between propaganda and bias."[3] "Biased UN body. Biased mandate. Biased panel," said the American Jewish Committee's David Harris. "Three strikes and you're out."[4] "All

I can say is it's a good thing that the United Nations wasn't around during World War II," said Max Boot. "I can just imagine its producing a supposedly even-handed report that condemned the Nazis for "grave" abuses such as incinerating Jews, while also condemning the Allies for their equally "grave" abuses such as fire-bombing German and Japanese cities."[5] "At the U.N., Terrorism Pays," declared Ehud Barak, who had been Israel's defense minister during Operation Cast Lead.[6] Barak declared himself "outraged," and his pain was evident in his response to the report in the *Wall Street Journal*. Israel, the former minister said, "doesn't need the Human Rights Council, Richard Goldstone, or anyone else to teach us how to maintain the human rights principles that are our lifeblood."

The problem was that the Goldstone Report was worse, as it turned out, than Israel's supporters in the Jewish world had feared. They had expected Israel to be criticized for the suffering of the civilian population of Gaza. Now they saw in the Mission's conclusions something much deeper: a fundamental critique of two of Israel's most hallowed institutions, its army and its legal system. The Goldstone Report questioned the integrity of Israel's national values.

The character of the IDF was a particular point of pride for Israel and its supporters. The IDF, with its roots in the struggle for independence, had come in national life to represent the determination of the Israeli people to provide the robust sense of security that Jews as a persecuted minority had never enjoyed. It was a citizens' army, in which (until recently) nearly all Israelis served, and in which they continued to serve for two decades or more as reservists after they were mustered out. Israelis took pride not only in the strength and efficiency of their army, but also in its moral character.

In more recent years, the IDF had formalized a code of ethics, with the active participation of some of the country's most distinguished philosophers (most of whom were themselves reservists or veterans). That code placed a high premium on avoiding civilian casualties and was accompanied by an intensive training program that reached soldiers and officers at all levels of the hierarchy. Few other military forces in the world made such an extensive effort to integrate the language of ethics into their culture.

Equally importantly, Israelis took enormous and justified pride in their legal system. Since the 1980s, the Israeli Supreme Court had played an active part in overseeing and ruling on just how far the nation's army could go in combatting its enemies. Under the leadership of its visionary president, Aharon

Barak, the court issued rulings that curtailed the IDF's use of torture, restricted certain forms of search and seizure, compelled the government to reroute the security barrier in the West Bank, and created conditions for the use of targeted assassinations.[7] These restrictions on the military did not always make the Supreme Court a popular institution in Israel, and the court's leadership had often been criticized for compromising the country's security. Even those Israelis who criticized the court, however, would note with pride that there were few other nations in the world whose army was subject to such strict civilian oversight.

Furthermore, Israel had a well-established process for after-the-fact investigations of military actions. Commissions had issued stinging public critiques of military leaders for their neglect or refusal to protect civilian lives, most notably in the wake of a massacre of civilians during the 1982 war in Lebanon. The IDF had an internal process for investigations of allegations that was outside of the chain of command, and this process was also subject to oversight by the civilian courts. On paper, this process compared favorably to the practices of other democracies, and it was without question more transparent and thorough than anything that existed among Israel's various Arab neighbors. Israel's own investigations, said one spokesperson, are "a thousand times more serious than the Goldstone Report."[8]

It was unimaginable to many in the Jewish community that Israel—this democratic jewel, this modern fulfillment of an ancient moral vision—could deliberately rain pain and terror on innocent people. Beset by enemies though Israel was, the very idea that it could make war against the Palestinian people was profoundly offensive.

The Goldstone Report was so forceful on the question of Israeli intent that even some of Israel's most trenchant internal critics distanced themselves from its conclusions. One of the premier human rights organizations in the country, B'Tselem, had a long history of advocating for the rights of Palestinians. B'Tselem staff were on hand in Gaza in the aftermath of Operation Cast Lead, and Mission relied heavily on the NGO's assistance in identifying incidents and setting up interviews with victims. The NGO was on record as early as February 2009 with a critique of the military's system of investigating its own abuses.[9] Yet B'Tselem's director, Jessica Montell, could not bring herself to a full endorsement of the Goldstone Report. She castigated the IDF for its refusal to undertake serious investigations, but she said that the facts presented in the report do not support the "far-reaching conclusion" that the actions in Gaza constituted an actual overall policy designed to punish the Palestinian people.[10]

The most fervent supporters of Israel reacted to the report's charges with a vehemence whose heightened tone seemed almost maniacal. From the cauldron of hurt and anger spewed a series of personal attacks on the man whom supporters of Israel blamed for this assault. One columnist dubbed Richard Goldstone an "obsequious Jew" called in to "dance to the tune of the Gentile landowner," an "assimilated and gentile-groveling Jew" and a "deceived collaborator."[11] A Jewish lawyer in South Africa termed him a "quisling."[12] The vice president of an Israeli college said that Goldstone "resembles those who collaborated with the Nazis because they believed the Nazi propaganda that the Jews are guilty and hence must be dealt with through the Final Solution." "You are not one of our own," said David Altman. "You are far from us, you do not belong to us, and you are not welcome among us."[13]

Prominent figures in Jewish life joined the fray. From Harvard University, law professor Alan Dershowitz dubbed Richard Goldstone an "evil, evil man." It is as though, Dershowitz said, a Jew had written the notorious nineteenth-century anti-Semitic tract *The Protocols of the Elders of Zion*.[14] Even Shimon Peres, the president of Israel and a man with a reputation for his efforts at peacemaking, leapt to his country's defense. "Goldstone is a small man," Peres said, "devoid of any sense of justice." Peres was no lawyer, but that did not stop him from terming Goldstone "a technocrat with no real understanding of jurisprudence."[15]

Most often, however, Goldstone was saddled with the longtime label for critics of Jewish or Israeli behavior: he was, said his opponents, a "self-hating Jew." Others went further, accusing him of "perpetrating a blood libel." Just as a non-Jew could be anti-Semitic, said Israeli finance minister Yuval Steinitz, "a Jew can also be anti-Semitic and discriminate against and despise and hate our people."[16]

Within weeks of the release of the report that bore his name, Richard Goldstone became a symbol of betrayal in the Jewish world. His upbringing as a Zionist in South Africa, his years of service to World ORT, his position as a member of the board of governors of Hebrew University now only fueled the fury of his critics, who excoriated him for providing comfort to terrorists and undermining the security and even the very existence of the state of Israel. His critics included some cranks, to be sure, but they also included the man with the highest official position in the Jewish world.

"We face three major strategic challenges," declared Israeli prime minister Benjamin Netanyahu in the fall of 2009. "The Iranian nuclear program, rockets aimed at our citizens, and Goldstone."[17]

Amidst this torrent of criticism, some Jewish voices came to the report's defense. "We [Israelis] don't see what the rest of the world saw," said one commentator in the *Jerusalem Post*. "that those thousands of thousands of rockets on Sderot caused a tiny fraction of the death and destruction we caused in Gaza at the same time."[18] Amira Hass, a reporter for the left-leaning Israeli newspaper *Haaretz* who was known for her coverage from the Palestinian territories, was more straightforward: "The Goldstone Commission's findings are in line with what anyone who didn't shut his or her eyes and ears to witness testimony already knows."[19]

In the *New York Times*, columnist Roger Cohen, who had first covered Richard Goldstone while reporting on the war in the former Yugoslavia, called the Mission head "a measured man." "The Israeli response to his findings," Cohen says, "strikes me as an example of the blinding effect of exceptionalism unbound. Ordinary nations have failings."[20] Former U.S. president Jimmy Carter affirmed that the criticism of Israel in the Goldstone Report was justified. Bestowing the ultimate Carter compliment, he called the report's author a "devout Jew."[21] Being called "devout" by the evangelical world leader gave Richard Goldstone a rare chuckle in the fall of 2009.

In the United States, a group of liberal rabbis who had loosely organized on behalf of the people of Gaza offered a small anchor of support for Goldstone within the organized Jewish world. "I am devastated by these findings," declared Rabbi Brent Rosen, one of the founders of Fast for Gaza. "The moral implications of this report should challenge us to the core. And I am deeply, deeply troubled that the primary response of our Jewish communal leadership is to attack the source of the report while saying absolutely nothing about its actual content."[22]

Jewish supporters of the report admitted their reluctance to criticize Israeli actions, but their initial reaction also showed an understanding that even in the strongest democracy the gap between principles and realities on the ground could grow. Soldiers could dutifully nod in ethics training sessions and still "go wild" on the battlefield. Courts could issue courageous rulings on some matters while overlooking the destruction of rights and lives in others. In the Mission's narrative, the IDF's splendid code of ethics had been betrayed by an actual practice of collective punishment. Readers sympathetic to the report built on an underlying assumption that a democratic nation was inherently messy. High standards and noble actions could coexist with tarnished ideals and unvarnished brutality. Moral stature and moral accountability could go hand in hand.

Public commentators in the Arab and Muslim worlds showed no such scruples or ambivalence. They by and large welcomed the report, generally ignoring the accusations of war crimes against Hamas, and the documentation of human rights violations by the Palestinian Authority in the West Bank. "We did not intentionally target civilians," said Ahmed Yousef, a Hamas adviser. "We were targeting military bases, but the primitive weapons make mistakes."[23] Hamas supporters expressed concern that the balance of the report was pernicious, that it "held the executioner [Israel] and the victims [the Palestinian people] on the same level."[24] For others in the Arab world, it was clearly a source of inspiration that a U.N. body had placed blame at the highest levels of the Israeli government. "Goldstone knows, as many of us already do," said Ramzy Baroud, going well beyond the text of the report, that the civilian casualties from Operation Cast Lead were the result of "very much a political decision made at the highest levels by the likes of Olmert, Livni, Barak and other serial criminals who have tormented Palestinians for too long."[25] If the report provoked any serious self-scrutiny in the Palestinian community or the Arab world, it was not evident in the public commentary.

Richard Goldstone also received some expressions of support from prominent figures in the international law and human rights community. Mary Robinson, the Irish political and human rights figure who had turned down the opportunity to chair the Mission, weighed in on Goldstone's side. The mandate that he negotiated was a reasonable one, Robinson said, and the report that the Mission created must therefore be taken seriously.[26]

Still, with a Jewish community charged at a fever pitch, the sentiment against the Mission ran strong. An intensive public relations campaign undertaken by the Israeli government and organizations in the Jewish world maintained a steady flow of invective through the fall of 2009. Whatever else might happen, the Goldstone Report was not going to die for lack of attention.

Publicly, Richard Goldstone maintained his cool. The four Mission members had decided in advance that he as head would serve as the sole public face of their work. As critics leapt to savage the report, Goldstone penned a series of op-eds that took both Israel and Hamas to task for their unwillingness to make serious efforts to investigate their own actions. "Absent credible local investigations," he pronounced immediately after the report's release, "the international community has a role to play. . . . Western governments in particular face a challenge because they have pushed for accountability in places like Darfur, but now must do the same with Israel, an ally and a democratic state."[27] The next week, as critiques poured in, he weighed in to ask, "Who's Being Unfair?" He rejected the charge that the Mission had devoted disproportionate attention to Israel's actions. "The factual inquiries we were called upon to make relating to a severe three-week military operation from the air, sea and land were far more complex than the comparatively unsophisticated launch of thousands of rockets into Israel as acts of terror."[28] He pointed out that many of the critics appeared never to have read the report carefully. Opponents quarreled with its conclusions, he complained, without ever bothering to examine the Mission's account of specific cases and circumstances.[29] He also emphasized that the Mission had never pretended that any of its allegations were "proven"; their work was intended only as a prelude to more systematic investigations where actual guilt or innocence could be assessed.[30]

Amidst these moderate reiterations, a distinct tone of frustration and anger crept into Goldstone's responses. He clearly took offense at the charges of "self-hatred" and treachery that his Jewish critics had launched. "For most of my adult life, I was criticized by white South Africans for daring to speak out against the policy of the then-South African government. I was accused by a white person of being a traitor to the white minority in South Africa," he said. He added that he would have thought the history of the Jews as a persecuted people was "an absolutely compelling reason for all Jews to speak out against injustice and the violation of human rights."[31] As the level of invective increased, Goldstone uncharacteristically responded in kind, charging in one interview that by focusing on his Jewishness his critics were exhibiting a "form of racism." Underlying anger at the Israeli response led him to overstatement. Explaining to Bill Moyers that the Mission had focused on thirty-six specific incidents, Goldstone elaborated, "It could have been 3600."[32] Eventually, he tried to turn the tables, insisting that he was himself operating within the animating principles of Jewish tradition. "It's crucially important for Jews particularly to stand up for Jewish values," he said. "I don't think that this is happening sufficiently."[33]

Between these media appearances, he taught his classes at Fordham Law School that fall with the same methodical demeanor he had always maintained on the bench and in the classroom. Yet privately the toll was already unlike anything he had ever experienced. He had weathered intense criticism before, but mostly from those outside his moral universe. It was a badge of honor to be lambasted by the supporters of apartheid in South Africa, or by the architects of ethnic cleansing in the Balkans. It was quite another matter to be a target of fanatical wrath among your own people. Richard Goldstone's friends were used to hearing him talk openly—perhaps sometimes a little *too* candidly—about the issues of the day in which he was involved. In the aftermath of the report, his friends found him reluctant to reveal much more than he was saying publicly about the Gaza report.[34]

The report created a fissure in the Goldstone family, which itself became part of the public story. In the fall of 2009, Nicky Goldstone and her husband Adam Dodek were living in Toronto with their son Ben, and Nicky's ardent Zionism was undimmed. Now her beloved father was the infamous author of a blistering attack on her beloved nation. The conflict tore her apart.[35]

Nicky's first instinct was publicly to defend her father. Interviewed for Israeli Army Radio, she claimed that the report would have been even harsher if Richard Goldstone had not been the head of the Mission. "My father took on this job because he thought he is doing the best thing for peace, for everyone, and also for Israel," she said. As the reaction to the report gained momentum in the Jewish world, however, she was more drawn to Israel's defense. She drafted a public statement that she sent privately to Richard and Noleen, which she described as "both in defence of my father, in defence of Israel and for my own healing from the tear in my soul that comes from hearing my father described as a nazi, an anti-semite and an enemy of the State of Israel." She resisted the Mission's conclusions. "Let me be clear what I think of the report," she said. "I personally expected that the IDF would have gone in, blown up the tunnels, Hamas bases and that being pretty much what they have done. . . . Now, having read every page of the report and being a true lover of Israel, I should say that I still defend Israel and stand by the IDF." Yet she went on to suggest "that every Israeli should read the report in its entirety." As she had as a child in South Africa, she now again had to live with the consequences of having Judge Goldstone for a father. "I will not always agree with what he says and does but I will always love him . . . just like I do not always agree with everything Israel does."[36] Nicky never published the statement. Her father responded by thanking her for a "beautiful letter" that "makes me cry."[37]

In conversations and meetings with her parents, Nicky's anguish spilled over into rage. She told her father that she was furious that he had allowed himself to be used by those who seek to destroy Israel. She was equally furious at Noleen for enabling him. And she was angry at herself. She believed that she of all people should have been the one to dissuade her father from taking on this Mission, way back in March when he was considering whether to accept the post.[38]

Nicky made an impromptu trip over the Yom Kippur holiday in October 2009 to confront her own sins in the land of Israel. She made her way to the town of Sderot along the Gaza border, walking anonymously among the people who for almost a decade had faced the constant threat of rocket fire. She visited the Western Wall. She met with old friends who had served in the IDF. When she returned to Canada, she was calmer, but her anger was unabated.

For Richard, the continued intensity of Nicky's response was a heavy blow. If Alan Dershowitz called him an "evil, evil man," it simply diminished Goldstone's respect for Alan Dershowitz. But it was harder to dismiss Nicky's anger, and painful to contemplate the cost that his public stance was taking within his own family. Alongside anger and defiance entered feelings of regret.

On September 29, 2009, Richard Goldstone returned to Geneva to present formally the report of his Mission to the HRC.[39] The HRC began its consideration of the report with statements and questions from its members, as well as comments by Israel, Palestine, and by NGOs. Much of the discussion restated well-rehearsed positions from countries and organizations either praising the Mission's work or criticizing its basis.[40]

Another appearance brought a jolt of emotion and surprise for Richard Goldstone himself. It came as part of a presentation by UN Watch, the NGO that had been criticizing the Mission for months before the release of the report. The NGO brought to the floor a middle-aged woman with short, fair hair, glasses, and a face subtly puffed from multiple surgeries to a slightly unnatural roundness. "My name," she told the HRC in accented but clear English, "is Dr. Mirela Siderer. I am a gynecologist living in Ashkelon, Israel."

Reading from a prepared text, she addressed herself directly to the Mission head, sitting across from her in the chamber. "Judge Goldstone, in July you invited me to testify." She came to Geneva that month, she told the story of the bombing of her clinic in Ashkelon, and Goldstone himself wrote to tell her afterward that her testimony was "an essential part" of the Mission's activities. Now she had read the report, and she plaintively asked the Mission head, "Why did you ignore my story?" Her name appeared in the report text only once, in paragraph 1640. Israeli victims, she complained, received only cursory discussion.[41] "I feel humiliated," Siderer told the HRC.

Goldstone had taken pride in the public hearings in Geneva and saw them as an important way to give Israel victims their due. Now a witness from those hearings had turned against him, and he acknowledged that this hurt. "I'm clearly upset that she was humiliated by the report," he admitted to the chamber after Dr. Siderer had stepped down. Stumbling a bit, Goldstone nevertheless insisted that she had been treated in the report as fairly as any other witness.

Jewish and Israeli responses to the report hit Goldstone hard, but he was equally distressed by another, opposite line of argument in presentations at the HRC. One by one, representatives of the countries present took the floor to praise the report exclusively for its focus on Israel and without regard to the report's attention to the actions of Hamas. Furthermore, some of those representatives chose to insist that the Mission's finding amounted to a charge of "genocide" against Israel. Goldstone publicly refuted this language during the session, saying that he was "saddened" by this "misuse of the report." He could see that he was losing control of the narrative. The polarized politics of the region were swamping the Mission's careful compilation of evidence.

The September presentation left open the question of how exactly the HRC would act on the report. The Mission had recommended that it endorse the findings and forward them for further action to the General Assembly and the Security Council. Any such action would clearly give the report more weight and credibility in the international community, as well as lead to potential further consequences. But the submission of the report did not come in a vacuum. The Israelis and the Palestinians were talking in the fall of 2009 about the possibility of further negotiations, and a key player in this process was the United States of America. The Americans feared that any further formal adoption of the report would jeopardize efforts at resuming talks. Israel had already said so explicitly, with Prime Minister Netanyahu calling any potential endorsement of the report "a fatal blow to the peace process."[42] In the wake of the presentation of the report, the United States mounted a fierce lobbying effort to quash its endorsement.[43]

For many of the countries at the HRC, the question was, what do the Palestinians want? The answer was not self-evident. Hamas was in charge of the Gaza Strip, but this group, without international recognition, was not represented in Geneva, where only the PLO had the authority to speak for all of the Palestinian people. At the HRC hearing on September 29, PLO representative Ibrahim Khraishi called the report "professional and unbiased," praised its documentary aspects, and put the Mission's findings in the context of what he called a long line of "massacres" perpetrated against Palestinians. Khraishi was one of the speakers who termed Israeli actions over the years a form of "genocide."[44]

On October 1, 2009, however, the Palestinians made an abrupt switch. The PLO suddenly announced that it was now supporting a delay in the consideration of the Mission's report, perhaps until the next regular session of the HRC, which would not be held until early 2010. It was clear to all what had happened. The Americans had pressured the Palestinians to back away from the report, and Mahmoud Abbas, the Palestinian president, had given in to that pressure. Arab commentators speculated that the United States was trying to kill the report altogether. "The Americans wanted something to finish it," an anonymous Arab diplomat told the *New York Times*. "The compromise is to defer it."[45]

A week later, however, the Palestinians changed their mind. In the wake of the Palestinian Authority's announcement that it supported the delay, street protests broke out. Hundreds demonstrated in Ramallah, near the seat of the Palestinian Authority's government, furious at what they saw as an act of treachery. There were calls for Abbas to resign. In Gaza, where members of Abbas's Fatah party were a beleaguered and threatened minority, posters appeared on the walls saying that Abbas should be consigned to "the trash heap of history."[46] The internal pressures were too strong, and the PLO was forced to admit its "mistake." On October 13, the PLO formally requested that the HRC convene a special session dedicated exclusively to the Goldstone Report. That session was duly scheduled for October 15 and 16, 2009.

The abrupt about-face created a crisis for Richard Goldstone. For the special session, Pakistan drafted a resolution that enjoyed sponsorship from several groups of countries. The three-page resolution was a laundry-list critique of Israel and its treatment of the Palestinians, with several paragraphs devoted to Jerusalem and access of Palestinians to holy sites, and with several others devoted to the siege of Gaza and other actions of Israel as the "occupying power." The draft resolution endorsed the report, but said not a word condemning the actions of the Palestinians.

The draft distressed the Mission head. The lopsided text threatened to undo his efforts to assure balance in the Mission's work, and it would provide further ammunition for the critics who claimed that the whole exercise was predetermined by politics. Goldstone went public with his concerns, saying that "the draft resolution saddens me" and directly calling on the HRC to modify the text.[47] In the course of debate on October 16, Pakistan orally added a clause "*condemning* all targeting of civilians" and stressing the need for accountability. It was hardly a radical revision of the resolution, which still said nothing explicit about Palestinian actions per se. The resolution as amended passed. The HRC had now formally welcomed the report, endorsed its recommendations, and forwarded it for consideration by the General Assembly. Twenty-five countries voted in favor, six (including the United States) voted against, and eleven abstained. The nations in support included China, Cuba, Qatar, and Saudi Arabia. Only one European country—Russia—supported the resolution; nine either opposed it or abstained.[48]

The absence of Western support damaged the resolution's credibility, but Richard Goldstone was determined to make the best of it. After all, the HRC had accepted the Goldstone Report in its entirety. That meant, as far as he was concerned, accepting both the strong critique of Israel and the very serious charges against Palestinian actors. Goldstone chose to see this "first" within the U.N. system as a tangible step toward balanced accountability in the Middle East and beyond.

Amidst the political rhetoric and the angry diatribes, a few voices stood for a more reasoned, dispassionate consideration of the Goldstone Report and its implications. The most penetrating responses came from thoughtful Israelis who rejected the report's most extreme conclusions, but understood that Israel's continued occupation of the West Bank and its wars in Gaza had created nearly unbearable moral and legal dilemmas.

David Landau, the former editor of *Haaretz*, called the Goldstone Report a "wasted opportunity." The issue, as far as he was concerned, was not that Israel intended to punish the Palestinian people; Landau rejected that argument outright. Instead, Landau had hoped that a credible, independent examination of Cast Lead and the occupation could have raised more difficult questions. How should a modern nation act when fighting a weaker foe embedded in a civilian population? And what happens when the strong side begins to exploit its military might? "When does negligence become reckless-ness," Landau asked, "and when does recklessness slip into wanton callous-ness, and then into deliberate disregard for innocent human life?" By laying so much stress on the "fundamental premise, that the Israelis went after civil-ians," Landau complained, Goldstone "shut down the argument before it began." Richard Goldstone, by virtue of his credibility and authority, could have "stirred the conscience of the nation," building widespread concerns within Israel at the wide disparity among Israeli and Palestinian casualties during Cast Lead. "Instead, by accusing Israel—its government, its army, its ethos—of deliber-ately seeking out civilians, he has achieved the opposite effect."[49]

The most incisive and thoughtful critique of the report came later in the fall, published in the *New Republic* as "The Goldstone Illusion" by a distin-guished Israeli philosopher.[50] Moshe Halbertal had himself participated in the creation and shaping of the code of ethics for the IDF. "Since I'm deeply involved in the issue—I don't think I have a particularly apologetic posture— I really wanted to learn from this," Halbertal said later. "I don't care whether he had a mandate or not, or why us, or whether it's an effort to persecute our side. . . . You have to say, OK, here comes an observer. We might want to learn from him."[51] Halbertal positioned himself between two poles of Israeli opin-ion. He rejected the view of the "radical left" who believed that "since a struggle necessarily involves the killing of innocent civilians, there is no jus-tifiable way of fighting it." Providing security for Israeli civilians was a basic obligation of the state. Yet he also rejected the argument of the "radical right" that all responsibility lay on the shoulders of the Palestinian authorities. "The killing of our civilians does not justify the killing of their civilians," he said. "Civilians do not lose their right to life when they are used as shields."[52]

For Halbertal, the main shortcoming of the Goldstone Report was that the Mission proved unable to shed light on the complexities of asymmetri-cal warfare. Like Landau, Halbertal insisted that he had genuinely looked for independent guidance for Israel on how to balance the fight against terrorist group with protection of civilian life. He focused first on the Mission's charge that Israel had not observed the principle of distinction between military and civilian targets. Noting that many Hamas fighters in Gaza wore no uniforms, Halbertal mocked the Mission's conclusion that they had no evidence to prove that Hamas did this in order to shield themselves from attack. "Did

Hamas militants not wear their uniforms because they were inconveniently at the laundry?" the philosopher wondered sardonically. The Mission had also concluded that the Israeli air strike on Gaza police was an unjustified attack on a civilian target. Halbertal believed that the Mission had not pushed hard enough to figure out exactly what military role these officers might have played, and that therefore the conclusion represented "a misunderstanding of the nature of such a conflict."

The principle of proportionality, Halbertal conceded, was notoriously difficult to apply: "I must admit that I do not know the formula for such a precise calculation." But he faulted the Goldstone Report for failing to wrestle with the issues in their fullest complexity.[53] In the incident on al-Fakhura Street, for example, Palestinian civilians had died as the result of Israeli mortar fire. Halbertal faulted the Mission for failing to take into account the obligations of the army to look out for its own soldiers. "It is wrong to give the commanding officer a blank check to shoot anytime his soldiers are at probable risk, but he must be given the means of protecting them as well." Since the Mission had addressed "occasions of deep moral struggle, because they are matters of life and death," Halbertal was particularly disappointed that its report failed to provide guidance for "this new kind of micro-war," where "every soldier is a kind of commanding officer, a full moral and strategic agent."

Halbertal did credit the Mission with some important findings "that no honest Israeli can ignore," especially with regard to cases of civilian deaths, "some of which sound like cold-blooded murders," and with regard to the destruction of civilian infrastructure. The philosopher cited the case of the al-Samouni family as one to which "Israel will have to provide answers." He also was disturbed by the wanton destruction of homes, farms, and other resources that directly touched the lives of the Palestinian people. "When it comes to human life, the army does everything possible to minimize collateral harm," Halbertal said later. "When it comes to private property the levels of care that should be applied are lowered to a problematic degree."[54]

The Israeli philosopher argued that the Goldstone Report—by focusing on intent—had stifled debate where it was needed most. His own response was thoughtful and nuanced, yet in the end he succumbed to the temptation to reject the report as a whole, rather than hailing it as an imperfect contribution to an important discussion. The Goldstone Report, he concluded in the end, is a "terrible document" that "offers no hope in sorting out the real issues." Halbertal's dismissal indicated that the inflamed environment had warped the responses of even the most measured observers.

By late fall 2009, the outcry over the Goldstone Report had begun to quiet. Richard Goldstone completed his semester of teaching at Fordham and headed home to Johannesburg, eager to escape the global spotlight and the wrath of large swaths of the Jewish community. He was disappointed that many of the most penetrating questions asked by the Mission had been drowned out by the cacophony of competing voices, but he held out hope that a new year would bring more opportunities for more reasoned follow-up. He also held out hope that a return to South Africa—although only for a short break—would offer a respite. In this he was profoundly mistaken.

18 ▸ BAR MITZVAH

Nowhere was the Goldstone Report more bitterly de-
nounced than in his native South Africa. A palpable sentiment of betrayal
spread through the South African Jewish community. If anything, the Zionist character of the country's Jewish community had intensified since the
years of Goldstone's upbringing.[1] No Jewish community in the world, on a
per person basis, had more generously supported Israeli causes. Where
once Jews had fled the dubious privileges of apartheid for the United States,
Israel was now, according to the South African Zionist Federation, the number one destination for Jews who emigrated from South Africa.[2] Richard
Goldstone's national and global prominence had been a point of pride for
South Africa's Zionists, and he had been feted many times over since the
early 1990s at Jewish communal events. Yet in 2009, he was the one of their
own who had "smeared" Israel—and by many people's lights, the whole
Jewish people—with accusations of violence and malice.

The week after the report's release, the heads of the two major South Afri-
can Jewish organizations issued side-by-side broadsides in the *South Africa
Jewish Report*. Avrom Krengel, the current chairman of the South African
Zionist Federation, unimaginatively called the Mission's report a "modern

day blood libel" and pronounced that Richard Goldstone and the other authors should "hang their heads in shame." The head of the SAJBD, Avrom Krengel's brother Zev, held back a little in his commentary. He speculated that without Goldstone's presence on the Mission, "the final report would have been even more damning." He then proceeded to emphasize that his organization categorically rejected the document's conclusions.[3]

Avrom Krengel felt a particularly strong impulse to undermine Richard Goldstone's moral authority. The personal attacks on the South African judge were "wholly deserved," he insisted later. "A report by the other three members would have meant little. This international figure put his name and credibility on this report with no evidence to back it up. . . . That has real ramifications. The Israeli army in the next war was going to expose itself to much more damage."[4] The South African Jewish religious establishment soon followed. Warren Goldstein, South Africa's chief rabbi, published a lengthy dissection of the report in October, although like many others he did not challenge in detail its factual findings. The rabbi, who also held a PhD in law from the University of the Witwatersrand, called the Mission "a disgrace to the most basic notions of justice, equality, and the rule of law."[5]

Even before the Goldstone Report, the politics of the Middle East had already crept into South Africa's national conversation. The ties between the ruling ANC party and the Palestinian cause dated back to the 1960s. The ANC, opposing apartheid, and the PLO, representing Palestinians living since 1967 under occupation in the West Bank and Gaza, saw themselves as aligned in common cause against colonialist powers. These ties strengthened after 1967, when Israel openly courted the friendship of the apartheid regime as one of its few allies on the African continent. Since the ANC came to power in 1994, the South African government had publicly tilted toward support for the Palestinian people, while still maintaining strong economic ties with Israel.[6]

The two leading heroes of the transition to democracy in South Africa, Nelson Mandela and Desmond Tutu, had shown strong sympathy with the Palestinian plight. Mandela was unapologetic about praising and meeting with Yasser Arafat, although he also had many friendships and allies in the Jewish community of South Africa.[7] Archbishop Tutu, revered around the world for his inspiring leadership of the TRC, had in recent years become a more polarizing figure among South African Jews. On more than one occasion he had compared the Israeli occupation to the conditions of South African apartheid, and he had lent his extensive moral authority to critiques of

Israeli policy. Indeed, Tutu, along with Christine Chinkin, had himself previously conducted an U.N. investigation of an incident in Gaza, the 2006 shelling of a row of houses in the neighborhood of Beit Hanoun that killed nineteen Palestinians.[8] While many Jews believed that Israel was judged more harshly than other countries, Tutu appeared to believe that many gave Israel a free pass on moral matters. "I think the West, quite rightly, is feeling contrite, penitent for its awful connivance with the Holocaust," he told the press in the wake of the Goldstone Report. "The West is penitent, the penance is being paid by the Palestinians."[9]

The year 2009 had already been particularly trying for South Africa's Jewish community.[10] In January, while Operation Cast Lead was in full force, Fatima Hajaig, the country's deputy foreign minister, had spoken at a pro-Palestinian rally and blamed the United States for supporting Israel. The United States, she said, "is in the hands of Jewish money, and if Jewish money controls their country, you cannot expect anything else." Zev Krengel's SAJBD demanded and received an apology, but the incident sparked Jewish concern that a senior government official could voice such blatant anti-Semitism and still retain her job. Further incidents followed. One of the country's top union officials, Bongani Masuku, repeatedly said that his organization would target Jewish organizations and was quoted as vowing to "make life hell" for Zionists.[11] In August, pro-Palestinian protestors loudly called a South African-born Israeli soldier a war criminal when he came to speak at Goldstone's alma mater, the University of the Witwatersrand. The protestors demanded the soldier's arrest.[12]

The threat of arrest was not idle. South Africa was a party to the ICC, and the country's own laws required accountability for war crimes and crimes against humanity committed by South African citizens. Indeed, Richard Goldstone's own prominent position in the field of international criminal justice had played a significant part in cementing his nation's own fidelity to these principles. South African law was friendly to the concept of universal jurisdiction.[13] The Goldstone Report itself encouraged individual countries to take up prosecution of crimes committed in Gaza, especially in the event (as they expected) that the Security Council and other international bodies failed to take action. "It is the view of the Mission," the report said, "that universal jurisdiction is a potentially efficient tool for enforcing international humanitarian law and international human rights law, preventing impunity and promoting international accountability."[14]

Earlier in 2009, two South African civil society organizations, the Media Review Network and the Palestinian Solidarity Alliance, made a request to the National Prosecuting Authority to investigate more than seventy South African citizens who had served in the IDF. The groups had assembled their own 3,500-page dossier alleging that at least some of these soldiers served in Gaza and had participated in atrocities. The Goldstone Report itself cited this specific request, apparently with favor, as an example of the ways that national authorities might pursue violations of the laws of war within their own courts.[15]

In the fall, while Richard Goldstone was teaching in the United States and traveling to Geneva to present formally the report, his South African friends were keeping him abreast of the situation in his home country. At social occasions in the Johannesburg Jewish community, the Goldstone Report was on everyone's lips, and Richard's old schoolmates Benas Levy and Geoffrey Mansell found themselves in the awkward position of defending Richard's integrity.[16] What shocked them most was how easily and casually their friends and neighbors called Richard Goldstone's report "anti-Israel" and even "anti-Semitic," as though its tone were the same as an angry charge of "Jewish money" controlling a Western democracy. Goldstone's friends were themselves upset by the report—Mansell believed that it contained "grotesque errors" and he told Goldstone so directly—but he and Benas Levy were horrified by the feeding frenzy that they saw among their neighbors and friends.

In and around Johannesburg, the critique of the Goldstone Report began to take on a new dimension: a reexamination of the South African career of its principal author. When Richard Goldstone's work in The Hague had been a source of pride for South Africa's Jewish community, he had been hailed for his courage for his record as a liberal judge and the leader of the Goldstone Commission. Now that his Gaza report had changed the equation, letters in the Jewish press began to excoriate Goldstone as a "Nat Boetie," a judge who had willingly done the bidding of the National Party and the apartheid regime.[17]

The door was now open for all of those who had mistrusted or resented Goldstone's success to emerge into public. In October 2009, South African journalist R. W. Johnson asked in a prominent article, "Who Is Richard Goldstone?"[18] Johnson's answer: Goldstone has always been a self-seeking lawyer who curried favor with the powerful. He accepted an appointment on the bench from the apartheid regime, but when he saw that the winds of change were blowing, he ingratiated himself with the ANC by issuing reports against the government. This "icon of political correctness," Johnson suggested, wrote the Gaza report because he was still seeking approbation, in this case seeking to "pander to anti-Zionist opinion."

In late 2009 and through the first months of 2010, zealots with ready access to the trampoline effect of the internet followed up on R. W. Johnson's broadside. A Jewish Johannesburg lawyer named Ayal Rosenberg took it upon himself to become Richard Goldstone's nemesis. Rosenberg, a man in his forties in 2009, had lived for a time in Israel shortly after his graduation from Wits law school in 1985. In Israel he served in the legal division of the IDF, and then as a criminal lawyer. Rosenberg claimed that Richard's father Ben Goldstone had worked for his own father at the firm Gerber-Goldschmidt.[19] He purported to remember Ben coming to his father's house and bragging about Richard's close connections with John Vorster, P. W. Botha, and other leading lights of the apartheid government. Rosenberg's account of Ben Goldstone's connections was pure fiction, but scrupulousness about the facts was not his strength. He preferred instead to intersperse quotations and anecdotes from classic philosophy and literature amidst his broad but careless investigations into Richard Goldstone's record as a judge.[20] In another time, Rosenberg's scattershot critique might have been restricted to a small circle of friends and acquaintances in South Africa. But his half-truths about the Goldstone record along with other half-truths unearthed by other self-styled investigators become the natural fodder for blog posts, journalists, and eventually even academic commentators. Repeated in summary form and without sources, the stories about Goldstone's record as an "apartheid judge" entered the public discourse.

The nuances of the facts mattered little in an environment where undermining Goldstone's moral authority was the overriding goal. His record was not so much picked apart as selectively mined. Each instance when the judge felt that he could not on legal grounds overturn an unjust outcome became, in the retelling two decades later, an act of affirmative support for apartheid's cruelties. Goldstone's role as a judge had required a delicate moral balancing act, where he sought as much space as possible for justice within a patently unjust system. His compromises became easy fodder for historical second-guessing.

The South African accounts eventually found their way to Israel. In 2010 *Yedioth Ahronoth*, Israel's largest daily paper, published a front-page exposé highlighting Goldstone's death penalty record and a catalogue of other cases.[21] "Judge Richard Goldstone forgot just one thing," said the lead writer on the story, "to look long and hard in the mirror and to do some soul-searching before he rushes to criticize others." Goldstone's opponents were quick to seize on the story. "You know, a lot of people, German judges, say we just followed the law," opined Alan Dershowitz. "That was Mengele's defense and that was what everybody said in Nazi Germany. 'We just followed the law.' When you are in an apartheid country like South Africa, you don't follow the law."[22]

Richard Goldstone did not shy away from his own record. Apparently, he said defiantly, his efforts were considered good enough by Nelson Mandela to appoint him to the Constitutional Court in the new South Africa. "I have been judged by my fellow South Africans and by President Mandela for my role both during and after apartheid," he wrote, "and I find it curious that no one in Israel ever raised the issue except to laud me, prior to my Gaza report."[23] The historical record backed him up. Critics could nitpick about individual decisions, but any fair-minded and informed observer would have to conclude Goldstone's career in the challenging apartheid environment was distinguished by a fierce and effective commitment to principles of equality and human rights.[24]

As the attack on Goldstone's reputation mounted, leading lights from the South African legal community came to his defense. In early 2010, the *South African Jewish Report* published a long letter from Arthur Chaskalson and George Bizos, whose commitment to anti-apartheid activities extended as far back as the Rivonia trial of Nelson Mandela and others in 1963. Quoting a 1997 report of South Africa's TRC, they argued that Goldstone and the other liberal judges "were influential enough to be part of the reason why the ideal of a constitutional democracy as the favoured form of government for a future South Africa continued to burn brightly throughout the darkness of the apartheid era."[25]

In the winter and spring of 2010, Richard and Noleen Goldstone were based in Washington, D.C., where Richard was teaching at Georgetown Law School. The close proximity of the law school campus to the Capitol made for a lively interchange between law and politics, the intersection where Goldstone was on firmest ground. Connections to the foreign policy establishment in Washington offered stimulating conversations about the continuing development of the laws of war and human rights in the global setting. Yet it had been only a few months since Goldstone was, almost personally, the target of an angry resolution of the U.S. House of Representatives in the wake of the Gaza report.[26] He was now more keenly aware of the fickle and impulsive nature of the American political process.

The Goldstones, however, had something to look forward to: a family event back home in South Africa. Glenda's middle son, Sean, would become at age thirteen a bar mitzvah, taking his place as an adult among the Johannesburg Jewish community. The ceremony was scheduled for early May, just after the end of the Georgetown semester.

Richard and Noleen now had four grandsons, in whom they took enormous pride. Glenda's three boys, Jason, Sean, and Jordan, were showing both academic promise and the kind of prowess in team sports that had eluded their grandfather during his teenaged years. When in South Africa, the retired judge and his wife were frequent cheerleaders on the athletic field sidelines. Nicky's eight-year-old son Ben was growing up in Canada; one of the advantages of the older Goldstones' long stints in the United States was easy access to this branch of the family. With Glenda and Nicky living thousands of miles apart, and with their parents' peripatetic lifestyle, there were relatively few opportunities to bring the whole family together. So the Goldstones were looking forward to the upcoming celebration with special anticipation.

The event loomed even larger in importance because the Goldstone family had been enduring a private tribulation, in addition to Richard's public excoriations. In May 2009, Glenda had been diagnosed with breast cancer. So while the world focused on her father's actions and statements on Operation Cast Lead, Glenda was undergoing six months of debilitating chemotherapy, supported by her husband Julian Brener, a contractor, and visits whenever possible by Noleen. The bar mitzvah would provide a welcome distraction both from Glenda's health problems and from the global controversy in which they had become enmeshed.[27]

The first indications that the bar mitzvah might not go smoothly came early. In January 2010, before the Georgetown semester started, Julian and Richard paid a visit to Siggi Suchard, the rabbi of Beth Hamedrash Hagadol, the synagogue in suburban Sandton where Glenda's family were members. Rabbi Suchard admitted that the controversy was putting the synagogue in an awkward position. He affirmed the grandfather's right to attend the ceremony, but he suggested that Richard refrain from accepting the special honor of reciting an *aliyah*, the blessing before the reading of the sacred scripture.[28]

Richard paused before responding. The rabbi, after all, was proposing that the synagogue withhold a traditional honor, a quiet omission that would nevertheless be conspicuous in its absence. Another man might have taken deep and rapid offense and responded with justified anger. Goldstone chose to put himself in the rabbi's shoes; he had some feeling for the pressures that the synagogue might face. Besides, the sheer spiritual value of Jewish ritual had long since diminished for him. He agreed to skip the *aliyah*. He did not wish his notoriety to distract from Sean's celebration.

In the broader South African Jewish community, however, leaders were not content to let the matter rest there. When Avrom Krengel learned that Richard Goldstone would be present at the bar mitzvah, he swung into action. For Krengel, it felt profoundly wrong for the man who had struck such a vicious blow at Israel and the Jewish people to participate as a member of the Jewish community as though nothing was out of the ordinary. Goldstone's actions had put him beyond the pale of Jewish life, Krengel believed. Why should he be allowed to rest easy, when he had so blatantly imperiled the well-being of others?[29] Krengel was himself a member of Beth Hamedrash Hagadol, so he felt a special obligation to this particular Jewish community.

Krengel tested the waters with other leaders, including Chief Rabbi Warren Goldstein, but he wanted the Zionist Federation, with its mission focused on Israel, to take a lead. In April 2010, approximately three weeks before the date of the bar mitzvah, Krengel let board members of the synagogue know that the Zionist Federation would mount a peaceful protest outside the building on the occasion. One possibility was that the protestors would form a human chain around the building, in order to prevent Richard Goldstone from attending.[30]

Richard and Noleen heard the news of this planned protest in a call from Glenda. In contrast to Nicky, their older daughter had borne Richard's notoriety with comparative calm. Without the sustained experience in Israel, Glenda did not share her sister's personal anguish. Glenda was angry and frustrated, but she told her parents that she and Julian had talked it over, that they would figure out a way to weather the storm. There was no reason to give in to anyone who wanted to interfere with this sacred family occasion. They wanted both of her parents to be there for their grandson.

Richard and Noleen, however, were not convinced. After six months of relentless attacks, they understood better than anyone the intensity of the opposition to the report. After world figures had called Richard evil, a quis-ling, and compared him to the Nazis, there was no reason to expect that a protest outside the Sandton shul would be mild or respectful. There was, to the contrary, every reason to expect that the event would manifest the special kind of hatred that people reserved for those whom they considered traitors. Husband and wife talked it over. They appreciated Glenda's willingness to stand up for them, to defy the protesters on Richard's behalf, but their hearts sank when they considered how the anger and the publicity would likely over-whelm what should be a day of celebration. The day should belong to Sean Brener, not to Richard Goldstone. Reluctantly they informed Glenda—and Rabbi Suchard—that Richard would not attend the ceremony.

The synagogue had wanted to keep this arrangement quiet, but on April 14, 2010, the news broke in the *South African Jewish Report*.[31] It quickly went national and then international, featured on the front page of the *New York Times*.[32] Richard Goldstone, the world learned, had been "effectively barred" from his grandson's upcoming bar mitzvah. The press reported that this was the outcome of "negotiations" between the Zionist Federation, the synagogue, and the family. The judge confirmed the story. "In the interests of my grand-son," he said, "I've decided not to attend the ceremony." Avrom Krengel refused to elaborate on his organization's position, piously proclaiming that "we understand that there is a bar mitzvah boy involved." A different South Afri-can Zionist Federation official released a disingenuous statement claiming that her organization was actually trying to protect the Goldstone family from a "barrage of protestors."[33]

The story of the bar mitzvah shone a harsh light on the impetus of many in the Jewish community to turn every aspect of Jewish life into a test of unqualified support for the state of Israel. No prominent critic of the report had thus far gone on record to argue that the assaults on Goldstone's personal character had gone too far. Standing up for Israel had become in many quar-ters a handy rationale for character assassination, with the explicit approval of many of the most prominent figures in the Jewish world.

As the story spread, expressions of outrage and support poured in from around the world. Thirty-seven U.S. rabbis signed an open letter applauding the Goldstone Report as "an ugly truth that is so hard for many Jewish people to face," and regretted that he did not feel welcome at his home synagogue.[34] An op-ed in the *Los Angeles Times* called the personal attacks on Goldstone "a brand of hatred that represents a direct assault on Jewish values of tradition and justice and conscience."[35] In South Africa, Justice Albie Sachs, Goldstone's former colleague on the Constitutional Court, broke his silence. Sachs had until now refrained from reading the report, saying that he wished to preserve his neutrality in the event that he might one day be useful in a mediating role in the Israeli-Palestinian conflict. Of Jewish background but with a thoroughly secular outlook, Sachs used the occasion of a major address to the Cape Town Press Club to complain that the undue pressure on Goldstone had produced an undue result, and that intolerance had triumphed. "I could not believe," Sachs said, "that political anger against him—which people had every right to express—had evolved into an uncontrolled and unconscionable rage that sought to violate the spirit of one of the most sacred aspects of formal Jewish tradition."[36]

Over the next several days, Avrom Krengel and other South African Jewish leaders backpedaled furiously, presenting the protests as a kind of spontaneous combustion that was outside their control. Krengel insisted that there was no intention to bar Justice Goldstone from this special occasion, implying that public protests were not an act of personal pressure but a harmless form of protected speech. The justice could attend if he wished, Krengel seemed to be saying, but we Jewish leaders could not be held accountable if our angry constituents felt the need to have their voices heard.[37]

Rabbi Suchard wrote to Richard Goldstone privately to reiterate that "the shul *per se* will welcome the bar mitzvah and not relate to your presence," in effect reminding Richard of their previous agreement that he would have no formal role in the ceremony. The rabbi cited Maimonides to remind his congregant that "in Jewish law, one who causes harm to a fellow Jew and puts them in danger, especially to a country . . . could jeopardise their position in the world to come." Even while much of the Jewish world was recoiling at the treatment of Goldstone by his synagogue, his own rabbi was telling him that, in effect, he was going to hell.[38]

Chief Rabbi Warren Goldstein, who had fanned the flames by attacking the report on both legal and religious grounds, now tried to claim the high ground. "It is simply a question of decency and compassion to the bar mitzvah boy not to ruin his day," he opined. A few days later, Goldstein penned a pious paean to the concept of the "open synagogue" as "a place of holiness" that "should never become an arena of politics, division, and pain." But the chief rabbi left all of his commentary in the realm of abstraction, refusing to place any blame on the organizers of the planned protest.[39]

Still in Washington, D.C., Richard Goldstone was particularly disgusted at the Jewish leaders' repeated pattern of using their talk of freedom and openness to score political points against his report. Nothing the South Africans had said assured him that they would take any action to ensure that the bar mitzvah could proceed without incident. Talk of "open synagogues" rang hollow.[40] Chief Rabbi Goldstein's remarks upset him enough to make a reply of his own. "I was dismayed that the chief rabbi would so brazenly politicise the occasion of my 13-year-old grandson's bar mitzvah to engage in further personal attacks," he wrote in the South African newspaper *Business Day*. "His rhetoric about 'open synagogues' simply does not coincide with how my family and I have been treated."[41]

After a week of escalating press coverage, Avrom Krengel and his partners began looking for a way out. Instead of being seen as stout defenders of Israel and the Jewish cause, the South African Jewish community was being pilloried around the world for intolerance. The Zionist Federation turned to a prominent leader of the Jewish business community, Brian Joffe, who undertook a kind of shuttle diplomacy between the organizations, the synagogue, and the family.

Joffe called Goldstone in Washington, D.C. Would the judge be willing to meet with the leaders of the South African Jewish community in order to hear their perspective and to explore their concerns about the report? Of course, Goldstone answered. He would never have had any objection to doing so—if only they had made that simple request.[42] The business leader brokered a deal. The Zionist Federation would guarantee that there would be no protest. Richard Goldstone would attend the bar mitzvah. And the judge would sit down with Jewish leaders on the Monday after the Saturday ceremony for a full and frank discussion.

Given that everyone involved claimed that they could not control the passions of unspecified others, Goldstone decided to take precautions. When he spoke to Gill Marcus, a longtime friend who was now the head of South Africa's Reserve Bank, she offered to arrange security.[43]

On Saturday May 1, 2010, Richard Goldstone sat in the front of the packed hall at the Sandton synagogue. Armed bodyguards hovered as unobtrusively as possible, but everyone in the building could see them. Richard and Noleen Goldstone entered without incident, and the congregants were, on the surface at least, welcoming and polite. Goldstone permitted himself the pleasure of patriarchal pride in the presence of his daughter and his grandsons.

Sean chanted, as was the custom, from the portion of the Torah, the Hebrew Bible, that was assigned to this particular Sabbath on the Jewish calendar. The portion was a section of Leviticus that included chapter 24, verse 19: *If a man inflicts a wound on his fellow, as he did, so shall it be done to him; a break for a break, an eye for an eye, a tooth for a tooth; just as he will have inflicted a wound on a person, so shall it be inflicted upon him.*[44]

Richard Goldstone was not called to the altar to give an *aliyah*. There was no reason to press the point. After the service, Rabbi Suchard led a rousing version of the *hora*, the communal dance for every joyous Jewish occasion. Richard stayed firmly in his seat and smiled nervously. He did not want to take a chance of offending anyone by jumping into the fray. As it turned out, Rabbi Suchard himself made his way to Goldstone's seat and insisted that Richard take his hand and join the winding line of dancers.

Sean Brener's bar mitzvah took place without disruption or violence, but the events soured his immediate family on the Jewish community. Glenda and Julian Brener left Beth Hamedrash Hagadol, joining instead another local congregation where they could leave behind the unpleasantness of the spring. After the ceremony, Sean Brener himself more or less walked away from Jewish practice. Before the bar mitzvah, he had attended Jewish services regularly, but he abandoned that habit afterward. "He's still anti-shul and anything to do with religion," Julian Brener said five years later. "That's basically what came out of it."[45]

On Monday, May 3, 2010, Richard Goldstone headed to the board room of a law office in downtown Johannesburg to fulfill his end of the bargain. Fifteen members of the Jewish community, led by Avrom Krengel, bore down on him. He had faced worse.[46]

Krengel seemed to view the very fact that the meeting was taking place as a triumph. It was his chance to compel Richard Goldstone "to face the wrath of the community."[47] Krengel read a long statement that reiterated many by-now familiar complaints. Goldstone read his own response, in which he steadfastly denied that he was a "Jewish pawn" serving the interests of opponents of the state of Israel. Indeed, he showed some willful naïveté about the document's broader public reception. "I am not aware that the UN Gaza report has or is being used to delegitimise Israel by questioning her right to exist as a member of the international community," he told his fellow South African Jews. "I would object to any such use being made of it."[48] Seven months after the release of the report, Goldstone still seemed surprisingly unaware that his objections to misuse of the report would count for little. As head of the Mission, he could exercise influence over the document's text, but he had little control over its reception in the wider world.

Following the prepared statements, the Jewish leaders peppered Goldstone with questions, though it became obvious fairly quickly that few in the room had actually read the report. "It was really an inconclusive discussion, but a friendly one," Goldstone remembered later.[49] "I won't say that he changed any minds, but he took away the sting," said Gilbert Marcus, who had attended the discussion as Goldstone's lawyer.[50] From Goldstone's point of view, the encounter was, if not pleasant, at least relatively civilized, and thoroughly unremarkable. Goldstone found it amusing that the Zionist Federation was claiming victory in forcing the confrontation. He was always happy to sit down for a reasoned conversation, even with his most implacable opponents. Their crowing, Goldstone remembered later, "was almost childish in a way."[51]

For a moment, it seemed as though the incident of the bar mitzvah in the spring of 2010 would break the fever of the Jewish community, that some decorum would be restored to the discussion of the Goldstone Report. There were signs that even some of Goldstone's fiercest critics understood that things had gone too far. The process of discrediting the messenger was beginning to discredit the Jewish world itself. The peaceful resolution of the issue in Johannesburg suggested an opportunity for chastened dialogue.

Then, three days after the meeting with Krengel and others in Jerusalem, *Yedioth Ahronoth* published its front-page "exposé" on Goldstone's record as an apartheid-era judge, and the whole cycle started up all over again.

The Goldstone bar mitzvah incident exposed just how badly the Jewish community had twisted itself out of shape in defense of Israel. Highly placed Jews compared Goldstone to the worst perpetrators in human history, and then Jews professed surprise when some of their own took the next logical step: attempting to bar this villain and traitor from Jewish life altogether. The Goldstone Report had indeed made strong accusations against Israel. In response, however, many Jews around the world abandoned one of the deepest values of their tradition: the value of reasoned debate. Jews were not alone in this tendency. The attacks on Richard Goldstone came in an era when reasoned debate was suffering in all quarters, and where extreme voices were dominating public discourse.

Later in 2010, the American Jewish activist and writer Letty Cottin Pogrebin published an essay under the title, "The Unholy Assault on Richard Goldstone." There is a Hebrew word, Pogrebin said, for what the personal attacks on Goldstone amounted to: "They put him in *cherem*, a condition some call 'Jewish excommunication,' though in this case that's an understatement. Someone in *cherem* is not just persona non grata in the eyes of our religious arbiters, he is totally cut off from the Jewish community." For Pogrebin, this treatment of a Jewish man who had dedicated himself to the cause of justice was a source of intense shame—not for Richard Goldstone but for the Jewish community that ostracized him. The rabbis who attacked Goldstone, she said, surely knew how much this violated Jewish values. Tradition holds that God destroyed the First Temple and exiled the Jews for seventy years because of sexual immorality, murder, and idolatry among his people. "But the Second Temple," Pogrebin continued, "was demolished for only one reason—*sinat chinam* (baseless hatred), Jew hating Jew, an infraction so severe that it merited an exile of two thousand years."[52]

19 ▸ RETRACTION

W͏HILE THE PERSONAL attacks on Richard Goldstone were reverberating in South Africa and around the world, the response to the Mission's work was setting in motion a dynamic of debate that would eventually shift the ground on which Richard Goldstone and his coauthors' report had stood. Over the course of 2010 and the beginning of 2011, a series of developments combined to undermine his faith in the full extent of his report's original conclusions.

First, subsequent investigations brought to light new information, which Goldstone used to shape and justify a changed perspective. In addition, he was moved by private conversations with erstwhile adversaries who spoke to his conscience and his underlying values. Third, the controversy of the past eighteen months was taking its toll on his family. Finally, Goldstone began to resent the ways that politically motivated actors across the spectrum had used the report selectively to their own advantage. Together, these developments contributed to a change in Richard Goldstone in 2010 and 2011, leading eventually to a public declaration that would shake his detractors and supporters alike. These developments also illustrated the profound challenges faced by international justice in an environment of inflamed passions.

Following its initial investigations in 2009, the IDF continued to look into Operation Cast Lead, and the Ministry of Foreign Affairs released a series of additional findings. These updates provided brief summaries of the investigations under the overall leadership of a branch of the IDF called the Military Advocate General (MAG). Brigadier General Avichai Mandelblit, the chief MAG since 2004, had been appointed by the minister of defense, rather than by the chief of the general staff of the army, with the idea that the MAG was then legally independent from the chain of command and therefore freer to render impartial judgment. The MAG oversaw criminal investigations and directed prosecution of offenders.[1]

Israel issued updates on its Cast Lead investigations in January and July of 2010.[2] These reports, and additional announcements made in the form of press releases, presented more detailed accounts of the Israeli version of some of the key incidents described in the Goldstone Report.

The mortar strike in busy al-Fakhura Street where at least twenty-four Palestinians died, the Israeli government now explained, was a justified response by a commander to an immediate threat to the safety of his troops. The deaths of a large number of civilians on the street were "regrettable," but the MAG concluded that the response was not out of proportion, given the immediacy of the threat to the Israeli soldiers.

The MAG also determined that the IDF had had no intention of striking the al-Maqadmah mosque, where Richard Goldstone had seen the squares of tungsten steel embedded in the walls. The commanders planning the strike, according to the new account, had no idea that there was a mosque in the vicinity, because the building had no minaret or other telltale signs of a religious structure. In the wake of the Mission's investigation, the captain and the two officers who fired the missile had been reprimanded and temporarily suspended from operational activity. But the MAG concluded that just because the negligence of some officers led to at least fifteen civilian deaths did not "alter the good faith of the senior commanders in seeking to abide by the key norms of distinction and proportionality."

About the incident that so deeply affected Richard Goldstone, the blasts that killed twenty-one members of the al-Samouni family, the Israeli government said nothing for a long time. The first military investigation, conducted before the Goldstone Report was released, had concluded that there was nothing out of the ordinary in the strike. But in November 2009, after the release of the Mission's report, the IDF chief of staff ordered a special command investigation to review the incident. By July 2010, the Israelis were saying that this initial command investigation had led to a criminal investigation, but no details were forthcoming.[3] In October 2010, nearly two years after the incident, news reports revealed that senior army officers, including a commander of the Givati Brigade, were under possible criminal investigation for ignoring reports of civilians in the area. No firm conclusions, however, had yet been reached.

The results of the further investigations of these three incidents, then, were marked by inconsistency and inconclusiveness. The official Israeli accounts of these incidents shifted considerably, and in all three cases no one had yet been held accountable for significant civilian casualties. The investigations revealed new information, and they also advanced legal arguments whose foundation was that it was very difficult to second-guess the actions of battlefield commanders in a time of fast-moving conflict.

The Israeli investigations did erode one key pillar of the Goldstone Report: its description of a pattern of attacks on the food supplies for the people of Gaza. The Mission had concluded, on the basis of eyewitness testimony, that the flour mill had been destroyed by an air strike. But the Israeli investigation described a fierce ground battle in the area of the mill on the day in question. The mill was located at a strategic high point, and while the Israeli soldiers fighting the battle did not know for sure that Hamas fighters were holed up there, the IDF argued that it was a legitimate target in the middle of a battle. The MAG concluded that Israeli tank shells—rather than an air strike—destroyed the structure. This was not, in the Israeli account, collective punishment, but simply another cost that Hamas imposed on its own people by operating within sensitive areas.[4]

When it came, however, to the question of the destruction of private housing, the Israeli findings were less convincing. The Goldstone Report had charged that the widespread destruction of private houses was carried out "unlawfully and wantonly" in Gaza during Operation Cast Lead and that these actions therefore amounted to a grave breach of the Geneva Conventions. Without providing any significant detail, the IDF's internal investigations were said to reveal that, in essence, it was all a matter of military necessity. Booby-trapped buildings and ambushes put Israeli soldiers in danger, so destruction of houses was often the best way to protect soldiers' lives. But the Israeli reports did not respond at all to the charge in the Goldstone Report that Israeli soldiers actually destroyed a great deal of property during the three days that they were *withdrawing* from the Gaza Strip. Military necessity could not explain the destruction of homes in areas where the Israeli forces had already subdued Palestinian resistance.

By March 2011, the Israeli government had conducted approximately 400 command investigations in relation to the conflict in Gaza. These covered the full range of incidents discussed in the Goldstone Report, and dozens of others large and small. These investigations had obviously consumed tens of thousands of hours, at the least, in the process of self-scrutiny.[5] Yet more than two years after Operation Cast Lead, only three criminal cases had been submitted for prosecution, producing a grand total of two convictions. In the months shortly after the operation, an Israeli officer was convicted of stealing a credit card from a Palestinian civilian. He was sentenced to seven and a half months in prison. At the time of the Goldstone Report, he was the only Israeli soldier who had been held criminally accountable for actions during Cast Lead.

The second conviction involved a situation in which two soldiers forced a nine-year-old Palestinian boy to search bags that they suspected of being booby-trapped. This meant, in effect, that the soldiers were using the boy as a human shield, putting his life at danger in the service of their own. This was a clear violation of the laws of war. In November 2010, the soldiers were convicted, as a result of which they were demoted and given prison sentences of three months each. The sentences were suspended.

The third case was the most serious. It involved the prosecution of a soldier for "manslaughter of an anonymous person" in an incident at a place called Juhr ad-Dik on January 4, 2009. The Goldstone Report had found that Israeli soldiers opened fire at that spot on unarmed Palestinian civilians, killing two women, Majda and Rayya Hajaj. The Israeli investigators said that they could not confirm the deaths of the two women, but they announced that there *was* evidence to suggest that someone—a young man—was indeed shot by an IDF soldier at that location. The trial of the soldier opened on August 1, 2010, but the reading of the indictment was immediately postponed at the request of the defense. There were questions about whether the investigation had been handled properly. As of March 2011, the trial was still in recess.[6]

Despite the large number of preliminary investigations, it was clear by early 2011 that the Israeli military and legal procedures had nearly completely exonerated the actions of the IDF in Operation Cast Lead. Israel accepted moral or legal responsibility for only a handful of the hundreds of deaths of Palestinian civilians in the operation. Israel's internal infrastructure for investigations into the law of war was elaborate, but the number of individuals actually held accountable was very small.

Ironically, while Israel was publicly excoriating the Goldstone Report, the government and the military were quietly enacting reforms that responded to some of the report's most pressing concerns.[7] Beginning in 2010, the Israel military announced a series of changes in practice intended to minimize harm in the future to a civilian population caught in the middle of a conflict. Israel conspicuously did not credit the push of the Goldstone Report for these changes. It presented them instead as part of the normal process of continuous improvement that its armed services undertook. Israel did have a long-standing record of self-scrutiny, but it strained credibility to believe that Goldstone's critique of Israeli practices was irrelevant to these changes, even if supporters of Israel were loath to admit it.

Under the new rules, the IDF would make more extensive use of legal advisers during battle itself, integrating their advice more completely into time-sensitive decision-making. Israel also announced new written guidelines, mandating that advance research on civilian infrastructure—food, water, power, religious sites, and other vital necessities—would now have to be integrated into the planning of any military campaign. Rather than giving unspecific warnings about upcoming attacks, the IDF would now make available clearer information about where civilians could find safe havens and identify evacuation routes. And even though its internal investigations had justified nearly all the destruction of private property during Cast Lead on the grounds of military necessity, the IDF issued a new standing order that clarified and limited what property could be destroyed, and on what grounds. Finally, the army placed strict limits on the use of white phosphorous, effectively eliminating its use as a battleground smokescreen. All of these issues represented changes that responded directly to issues raised in the Goldstone Report. Critics also noted that the IDF had learned that public perception matters. "The most radical change in IDF thinking since Goldstone has been in the realm of media relations," one observer noted. "Now there is a firm consensus in the army that the way military actions are perceived is at least as important as their physical impact."[8]

During 2010 and 2011, Richard Goldstone was also watching closely how the U.N. itself was following up on his report. In 2010, the HRC appointed a new group, under the leadership of former U.S. judge Mary McGowan Davis, to assess how thoroughly the Israelis and the Palestinians had fulfilled their obligations, as outlined in the Goldstone Report, to investigate Operation Cast Lead and to make appropriate changes to their practice.[9] The Israeli government, showing its consistent opposition to the "Goldstone process," refused to cooperate with the Davis team's investigations.[10]

In March 2011, the Davis Mission presented its findings to the HRC. The Davis Report credited the Israeli government with initiating a large number of investigations. When it came to independence, impartiality, promptness, and transparency, however, Davis raised a number of serious questions. Her report shed a harsh light on the small number of prosecutions, and on evidence that suggested that Israel was doling out light punishments even to those convicted of wrongdoing.[11] The transparency of which Israel was so proud, in other words, might be something of a sham. The MAG appeared to Davis to have had a practice of selectively releasing the information that it wished to, while ignoring the great majority of requests for information from interested parties.

The Davis Report was hardly a ringing endorsement of the Israeli investigative process—except in comparison to the leadership of Hamas. The Hamas leadership told Judge Davis that they did not have access to the persons involved in launching the rockets, so no investigations had been undertaken. The Davis team held Hamas responsible for failing to make "genuine efforts" to conduct inquiries.[12] No such efforts seemed likely to be made in the future.

By 2011, a clear picture had emerged. Israel continued to conduct investigations, but with a minimum of actual accountability. The Palestinians simply justified their own actions against civilians as legitimate resistance outside the normal considerations of the laws of war. The difference between the Israeli and Palestinian reactions began to gnaw at Richard Goldstone. Lawyerly by temperament, he preferred even a flawed process to no process at all.

After months of defending the Gaza report in the media, Richard Goldstone decided that he had said enough. The heightened level of rhetoric left relatively little space for nuanced discussion of the issues, and toward the end of 2009 he began to decline requests to speak about its contents publicly. Yet he was never one to retreat from civilized discourse. Indeed, over the course of 2010 and 2011, he happily accepted opportunities to maintain private dialogues that would permit more reasoned conversations. As Goldstone found new interlocutors, some of whom were diehard opponents of the report's conclusions, he kept himself open to new ideas and perspectives gleaned through the process of personal exchange.

On January 27, 2010, when Richard Goldstone gave a talk in Luce Hall at Yale University, the public controversy was still swirling. Just a few days earlier Alan Dershowitz had published a lengthy denunciation of the report, and the famed Harvard lawyer made a point of telling the press that he had severed ties with its author.[13] Goldstone told the organizers of the Yale event that he had nothing further to say about Gaza at the moment. He would speak in broader terms about his career in the area of international criminal law, under the title "Accountability for War Crimes."

The hall was packed in anticipation of the famous judge's appearance. As he was finishing his lecture to polite applause, a commotion broke out in the back of the auditorium. Two men were struggling to unfurl a banner, with large black words printed on a white background. When the men stretched the banner out completely, it was twelve feet across, and even across thirty rows of seats, the speaker could read it clearly:

1890–1906 THE DREYFUS AFFAIR
1903 THE PROTOCOLS OF THE ELDERS OF ZION
2009 THE GOLDSTONE REPORT

The intent was clear. Richard Goldstone's report, the banner suggested, stood in a nefarious historical progression. It followed the unjust persecution of the French Jewish army captain, Alfred Dreyfus, at the end of the nineteenth century, and it was a successor to the anonymous tract, first published in the early twentieth century, that blamed the Jewish people for everything from the death of Jesus to the multiple corruptions of modern life. By impugning the good name of Israel, the banner suggested, Richard Goldstone had joined the long line of those who actively participated in the persecution of the Jews.[14]

The two men holding the banner said nothing. An awkward silence settled over the hall. Richard Goldstone could see from the podium that one of the men was dressed in the garb of an ultra-Orthodox Jew, with a black hat from which curly hair spilled down his face. After an uncomfortable spell, the men rolled up their banner and departed.[15]

During the postlecture reception, Richard Goldstone was surprised to be approached by the orthodox Jewish man who had been holding the banner in the lecture hall. "Do you believe everything that you wrote in that report?" the man asked truculently.

"Well, yes," the judge replied. "We came to our conclusions based on the evidence that was available to us."

"Then it is obvious," the man continued, "that there is a great deal that you do not know. So what I want to know it this: what will you do when the report that you have written is proved false, when it is proved that every accusation that you have made about Israel is a sham and a lie?"

Goldstone looked the man in the eye. "In that case," he said evenly, "I would rejoice."

The corners of the man's mouth turned upward through his curly beard. "At that time," the man said, "I will be there to welcome you back to the Jewish people."[16]

For a time, Richard Goldstone forgot the encounter. But for his interlocutor, Rabbi Shmully Hecht, it represented one of the defining moments of his life.

A native New Yorker, a Hasidic rabbi, a controversial real estate magnate, and the leader of a private Jewish club in New Haven, Hecht felt that he had not yet found a way to make his mark in a wide way on the well-being of the Jewish people.[17] The Goldstone Report stirred him to action in a way that few other things had in recent years. He read the full text of the *Protocols of the Elders of Zion* and as much of Hitler's *Mein Kampf* as he could stomach. While he was appalled by the language of the explicit enemies of the Jews, he found a fellow Jew's apostasy even harder to take. He could not bring himself to read the actual text of the Goldstone Report, but he decided that he knew enough to develop a strong set of opinions. He believed that the report charged that the army of the state of Israel was singling out innocent babies to slaughter—this was a charge that he found beyond absurd. Such a thing went against everything in Jewish tradition and in Jewish practice, and it was unthinkable for a Jewish army. (It was also a wildly distorted perception of the Mission's conclusions.) There was no question in Hecht's mind that such a slander had to be combated in the most direct and powerful way possible.

Hecht believed that something dramatic was necessary to jolt Richard Goldstone's soul. He was convinced, from what he read, that at bottom, Judge Goldstone as a Jew could not possibly believe what he had written. He believed that he had to find a way to reach Goldstone's soul, his *neshama*, and to shock him into a new discovery of his subterranean connection to the Jewish people. When Goldstone admitted at the Yale reception after the unfurling of Hecht's banner that he would rejoice if he were proved wrong, Shmully Hecht knew that his own mission had just begun.

Months passed. In September 2010, a friend forwarded Goldstone's email address. It was shortly before Rosh Hashanah, the Jewish New Year, the time when Jews traditionally seek *tshuvah*, a turning of the soul, a renewal of the spirit as each individual confronts his or her sins and seeks God's blessing for the year to come. In the spirit of the season, the rabbi decided to change his approach. He wrote to Richard Goldstone, reminded him of how they had met the previous January, and simply wished him a sweet and happy new year.

Goldstone responded within hours. He was seldom one to hold a grudge. Maintaining lines of communication with his antagonists was more his style, and he appreciated the rabbi's gesture. He mentioned to Hecht that he would be teaching a short course at Yale later in the autumn.

When Goldstone arrived in New Haven, Hecht invited him for breakfast. The judge promptly accepted. Over the course of a few weeks, the men met for three long sessions, sitting in the rabbi's brightly lit kitchen eating bagels and cream cheese while his wife was feeding and bundling Hecht children off to school.

Before the meeting, Hecht had spoken with Alan Dershowitz, who had urged the rabbi to help the judge to "find new facts" and therefore change his conclusions. But Hecht chose the Jewish route to saving Richard Goldstone's soul, drawing his narratives from the books of Jewish commentary, the Mishnah and the Talmud. He chose tales of instruction, stories of men who had lost their way but who found a path back to God's favor and who had the wherewithal and the courage to admit their sins in public.

He told Richard the story from the Mishnah of the two ancient rabbis who battled bitterly over when was the proper date for the observance of Yom Kippur, the day of atonement. The date depended on a proper reading of the phases of the moon. Eventually, one rabbi won the argument. The other conceded through a public confession. The winning rabbi was both a teacher and a student, Hecht explained. He was a teacher because he was right. But he was a student, too, because he learned something from the example of courage that the losing rabbi showed in admitting the error of his ways.

Richard Goldstone told his own stories as well, the tales of his own life. He recalled the thrill of Israel's Independence Day when as an eight-year-old he waved a flag in the streets. He talked about his mother Kitty's activities in the Jewish community in Johannesburg. And he related the story of his own bar mitzvah, telling Hecht about how the Reform rabbi had urged the Goldstone family to celebrate at the orthodox synagogue, so as not to offend the sensibilities of the boy's paternal grandfather.[18] The rabbi talked about his own family as well, and the bond between the two men shifted from hesitant exchange toward friendship.

On the Middle East, the two men agreed to disagree. The rabbi's vision was for an undivided Israel, an unapologetic Jewish state that extended from the Mediterranean to the Jordan River, absorbing the West Bank and its myriad of Jewish holy sites. The judge also wanted to see a thriving Israel, but he wanted dignity, freedom, and self-determination for the Palestinian people. Between sessions on the Talmud, Hecht did not hesitate to press Goldstone by email on finding a way to modify the conclusions of his report. In their correspondence, Goldstone pushed back at Hecht's robust defense of Israel. In response to one set of articles that Hecht sent him, Goldstone replied, "The omissions and simplistic statements obfuscate as much as they elucidate. You know that the history is much more complicated than portrayed."

The conversations in Shmully Hecht's kitchen touched Richard Goldstone deeply. He had had many conversations over many years about law and politics and society and actions on behalf of the powerless and the oppressed. And he had faced the anger of those near and far who found his views wrongheaded or even offensive. But he rarely had the chance to sit down with a fellow human being—a rabbi no less—and talk about his own place in the world. It struck him forcefully that he was sitting at the kitchen table with someone who first confronted him in anger, but who now treated him with something approaching love. He found Hecht's politics unconvincing, but the conversations with a man who had once believed him a traitor opened the judge to new possibilities of personal transformation.

At the end of their last breakfast, shortly before Goldstone was scheduled to leave New Haven, Shmully made a request. The rabbi knew from their talks that when Richard was a teenager, he had kept for several years the practice of daily Jewish prayer. Hecht asked whether Richard would pray with him

now, whether he would don the *tefillin*, the sacred wooden boxes that obser-
vant Jews bind around their foreheads and one arm each weekday morning.
The judge hesitated. He had enjoyed the talks with the rabbi, but prayer as
such no longer had particular meaning for him. The rabbi persisted, asking it
as a personal favor. Goldstone's new friend had extended himself so generously, and he did not wish to offend him by saying no. So it came to pass in
Shmully Hecht's New Haven kitchen that Richard Goldstone, for the first
time in more than fifty years, tied the leather straps that bound one wooden
box to the center of his forehead and another around his left arm. With the
rabbi's help, since his memory of the prayers was misty, he pledged his faith
to the God whose divine hand had brought the Jews safely out of Egypt.

By the middle of 2010, the intensity of the controversy over the Goldstone
Report began to settle down. For one thing, other events in the Middle East
came to dominate the headlines. In May 2010, the Israeli navy intercepted a
Turkish ship, the *Marmara*, which was en route to Gaza on a mission to provide supplies for the Palestinian population and to call attention to the ongoing Israeli blockade. When the Israelis boarded the *Marmara*, a struggle broke
out, and nine people were killed on board. In the face of an international outcry, the Israeli government appointed an independent commission to investigate, with members from both inside and outside of Israel. The Turkel Commission, as it came to be called, represented a significant departure from the
aftermath of Operation Cast Lead, a more credible move toward independent
investigation than internal probes by the IDF.[19]

By early 2011, Richard Goldstone was seeing his Mission's report in a new
light. Among other things, he was now increasingly frustrated by the one-
dimensional role that others were forcing him to play on the public stage.
He was willing to stand behind his critiques of Israeli policy, but he deeply
resented the extent to which the Goldstone Report was being used as a ral-
lying cry by those who wished to undermine or even destroy the Israeli state.
In the wake of the report, an enterprising merchant in Gaza had done a brief
business in black-and-white *keffiyehs*, the Arab headdresses made famous by
Yasser Arafat, with Goldstone's name emblazoned in celebration across the
center.[20] Over the next year, Goldstone received a string of speaking invitations from organizations whose missions, as far as he understood them,
often crossed from sympathy for the Palestinian plight to direct attacks on the
legitimacy of Israel. When an NGO called the Russell Tribunal convened to

conduct a (nonjudicial) hearing in 2010 in Barcelona to condemn Israeli oppression of Palestinians, the Goldstone Report was a key component of the "evidence" presented.[21]

Perhaps, in the highly politicized global debate over the Israeli-Palestinian conflict, Goldstone should not have been surprised. After all, many critics had warned since the very month when he accepted the HRC's mandate that his report would be used as a weapon to delegitimize Israel. Seeing his work embraced as a tool to fight Zionism, however, hit him particularly hard.

He was spending the winter and spring of 2011 at Stanford Law School, the latest of his posts as a visiting faculty member. When he received an invitation to speak before the Leonard M. Friedman Bar Association, an organization of Jewish lawyers in Sacramento, he gladly accepted.

Delivered on January 20, 2011, Goldstone's Friedman Lecture represented a subtle shift of tone in his public stance on the report.[22] In substance, the general outline was what he had said many times before: he told again the story of how he renegotiated the mandate, of how he hoped that Israel would cooperate, and how the Mission came to the conclusion that Israel had failed in its duty to sufficient protect civilian lives.

Yet he also gave considerable credit to the later Israeli response. He noted that the investigation of the deaths of the twenty-one members of the al-Samouni family—though it was taking a very long time—appeared to be a serious probe of military wrongdoing. Goldstone told the Sacramento lawyers what the Israeli media had reported most recently—that the air strike on the home might have been the result of a fuzzy aerial photograph. The photograph, which showed several men of the house out collecting firewood, was interpreted as showing Palestinians preparing to launch a rocket. It was a great pity, Goldstone said, that the Mission did not have this information earlier. This account might not have fully exonerated the IDF, but it might have changed the Mission's finding that the strike deliberately attacked civilians.

When it came to the central conclusion of the report, the judge was not yet ready to back away. He said defiantly that the personal attacks aimed at him came not because his report "delegitimized" Israel, but because supporters of Israel did not wish to face the report's conclusion that its army may have acted, especially in its assault on civilian infrastructure, with intent to punish the people of Gaza. He noted that if delegitimization meant criticizing the policies of the Israeli government, "then there are many thousands of Israelis who are themselves involved in 'delegitimizing' Israel." He protested that lumping legitimate criticism of Israeli policy with attacks on the existence of the country "has the effect of diluting the evil call for the destruction of Israel."[23]

Goldstone ended the talk by relaying, in outline form, the story of his developing friendship with Shmully Hecht. He told of Shmully's public protest, and of the conversations that followed. The men's friendship, he told the California lawyers, was not based on their political differences, but on their common love for Israel and the Jewish people. "That I deeply value and respect this friendship I need hardly say," Goldstone concluded. "The lesson, I would suggest, is that the Jewish tradition is to debate differences rather than to dismiss them or allow them to degenerate into personal ad hominem attacks."

The shift in tone in the Friedman lecture represented a public counterpart to a different tone in the private conversations within Richard Goldstone's own family. His daughter Nicky's emotional roller-coaster had continued over the previous year, as the pressures on her within the tightknit Jewish community in Toronto remained intense. Friends and neighbors shunned her, and she felt particularly protective of her son Ben, whose school performed a "threat assessment" in the wake of his grandfather's report. Nicky's husband Adam provided an oasis of calm, but Nicky's emotions sometimes got the better of her, and on more than one occasion she had erupted at one or the other of her parents.[24]

When friends asked Richard Goldstone whether he would have taken on the Mission if he had to do it all over again, he answered yes and no. Yes, because even now he felt at a deep level that he had an obligation to use his good offices to ensure justice for *all* the world's victims. But had he foreseen what the response would do to his family . . . well, in that case he would have reluctantly left the task to someone else.

On April 1, 2011, readers of the *Washington Post* and online readers around the world woke up to an astonishing article on the op-ed page. It ran under the headline, "Reconsidering the Goldstone Report on Israel and War Crimes." The byline was "Richard Goldstone."[25]

"We know a lot more today about what happened in the Gaza war of 2008–09 than we did when I chaired the fact-finding mission," the op-ed began. "If I had known then what I know now, the Goldstone Report would have been a different document."

"The allegations of intentionality by Israel were based on the deaths of and injuries to civilians in situations where our fact-finding mission had no evidence on which to draw any other reasonable conclusion," Goldstone wrote. "While the investigations published by the Israeli military and recognized in the U.N. committee's report have established the validity of some incidents that we investigated in cases involving individual soldiers, they also indicate that civilians were not intentionally targeted as a matter of policy."

This statement effectively retracted one of the key tenets of the original Goldstone Report: Israeli "intent," as a matter of policy, to punish Palestinian civilians. There was a lawyerly quality to the retraction. The op-ed did not say clearly that Goldstone himself had decisively changed his mind. It stated only that that Israeli reports "indicate" that Palestinian civilians were not deliberate targets. Yet it represented a striking if ambiguous departure from the Mission head's previous insistence on the integrity of the report's conclusions. Richard Goldstone would no longer assert with confidence that Israeli policy explained the devastation in Gaza.

Goldstone cited as his primary example the strike on the home of the al-Samouni family, now explained by Israel as the result of a bad interpretation of an aerial photograph. He also reserved the brunt of his anger in the op-ed for Hamas, asking the HRC to condemn the "heinous acts" of the continuing rocket attacks and the recent "inexcusable and cold-blooded recent slaughter" of an Israeli family in a West Bank settlement community. He contrasted the Israeli system of investigations—which he admitted had shortcomings—with the complete absence of accountability by Hamas.

The story of Goldstone's "retraction" riveted the Jewish world and the international human rights community, as it rocketed around the internet in the succeeding days in early April 2011.

Among many in Israel, the response was angry self-righteousness. Too little too late, said the *Jerusalem Post*. The report had already done its damage by giving credence to the idea that Israel was responsible for the murder of women and children.[26] An apology isn't good enough, said commentator David Horovitz. Goldstone must now work unstintingly to undo the damage that he has caused.[27] "There can be no forgiveness for such a one-sided report," said former prime minister Ehud Olmert. "There can be no mercy for those who caused this damage to the state of Israel." Columnist Ben Caspit put it even more strongly in the Israeli paper *Maariv*: "The despicable and shameful act that he perpetrated is contrary to the most fundamental moral values, natural justice and common sense to the extent that it negates his right to absolution."[28]

Israeli leaders moved quickly to interpret Goldstone's change on the matter of intent as a definitive invalidation of *all* of the report's conclusions. Prime Minister Benjamin Netanyahu called for the Goldstone Report to be "consigned to the dustbin of history."[29] The Ministry of Foreign Affairs planned a global public relations campaign to take advantage of the new development. There were calls for Goldstone to go further—not only to retract a principal conclusion, but to seek formally the withdrawal of the report from the U.N.

While Israeli leaders were claiming validation, there was a perceptible sense of deflation in the human rights community. Jessica Montell of B'Tselem had already voiced her hesitation that the finding of Israeli intent was a step too far, but now she was concerned that Goldstone's reversal would let Israel off the hook altogether. Israel still has a lot to answer for, she wrote a few days after the judge's op-ed. "Goldstone's praise of Israel's investigations seems a bit premature."[30] Kenneth Roth of Human Rights Watch claimed that the reaction to Goldstone's op-ed was overblown, that the world should remain focused on the extensive aspects of the Mission's report that went beyond the question of purposeful harm. Aryeh Neier of the Open Society Foundation publicly questioned Goldstone's wisdom in issuing his retraction before the Israeli investigations had been fully completed.

For others, the lesson in the retraction was Richard Goldstone's moral courage—the ability to change his mind and to say so publicly. "Goldstone has given us an example of someone who is willing, despite everything, to acknowledge when mistaken and to come forward and own up," said one editorial. "This is heroism of the first order: an act of taking responsibility in that rarest of public acts—unforced admission of error. For this act, we owe him a vote of thanks, if only in showing, by personal example and at risk of his own standing, that moral courage means getting to the truth, rather than merely asserting some imaginary moral high ground."[31] A host of contenders came forward to take credit for Goldstone's change of heart: the South African Jews who met with him after the bar mitzvah, an Israeli law professor who appeared on a panel with him in California, correspondents like the retired engineer Maurice Ostroff, and, more privately, Rabbi Shmully Hecht.[32] Some strongly pro-Israel commentators took proud credit for the public pressure on the judge. "Rather than get a pass for his behavior," said Caroline Glick, "Goldstone got ostracized. . . . Obviously these attacks had an effect on him that attempts to appease him would not have."[33]

In the Arab world, the conclusion was that Richard Goldstone buckled under the intense pressure that the Jewish community had placed upon him.[34] "After 18 months of what seemed a wholly personal introspection, accompanied by an endless campaign of pressure and intimidation by Zionist and pro-Israel groups," wrote one commentator from Lebanon, "the man finally surrendered."[35] A spokesman for the Palestinian political party Fatah put it more bluntly in a leaflet distributed in Gaza City: "Goldstone has committed a crime by supporting the perpetrator against the victim."[36]

Some of Goldstone's own friends were sympathetic to his predicament, but still critical about the outcome. "My own view is that he and his family were subjected to unbearable pressure, and he cracked," said Gilbert Marcus, who had accompanied Goldstone to his meeting with the South African Zionists. "I think you have to be sympathetic to what he was subjected to. You've got to recognize his human frailty. But you have to simultaneously appreciate that judges are meant to have the fortitude to withstand pressure. You have to recognize the impact and the damage that it caused. That's my conclusion."[37]

Some of those who had been most public in supporting the courage of the Goldstone Report now felt the sting of betrayal. "We have a new verb, 'to Goldstone,'" wrote Roger Cohen in the *New York Times*. "Its meaning: To make a finding and then retract it for an uncertain motive. . . . The contortions of his about-face are considerable."[38] Richard Falk, a prominent critic of Israeli policy, called the op-ed "a personal tragedy for such a distinguished international civil servant, especially as the retraction is not persuasive on its merits, and, as might have been predicted, deeply disappointed his supporters while failing to satisfy his critics."[39] Cherif Bassiouni, whose investigations had laid a partial foundation for Goldstone's work at The Hague, now chided his old friend and told him in a private letter that he would have advised against the retraction. "Now you must right the wrong that has been done," Bassiouni wrote to Goldstone, since others have spun the result "in ways that you had not intended."[40]

Several aspects of Goldstone's op-ed were striking departures from the judge's usual careful style. For one thing, he did not coordinate at all with the three other members of the fact-finding Mission. The report, after all, also bore the names of Christine Chinkin, Hina Jilani, and Desmond Travers, but the Mission head had neither consulted with them nor given them the courtesy of an advance word of his intentions. He knew that it was likely that they would not support his change of heart.[41] So he went ahead on his own, a marked change for a man who had preached and practiced collaboration throughout his career as a judge, prosecutor, and investigator.

The other members of the Mission, scattered around the world, were blindsided. The op-ed came as "a bolt from the blue," remembered Christine Chinkin, who was in the United States at the time. She tracked down Travers and Jilani, who shared her "sense of shock." Well aware of the pressures that Goldstone was under, they also felt obliged to stand up for the integrity of their original work. Chinkin's own email address "collapsed" under the weight of so many inquirers asking for an explanation.[42]

Ten days after Goldstone's retraction, Christine Chinkin, Hila Jilani, and Desmond Travers published an article in the *Guardian* that reaffirmed their conclusions and distanced themselves from the judge's new position. "Nothing of substance has appeared that would in any way change the context, findings or conclusions of that report with respect to any of the parties to the Gaza conflict," the other three Mission members wrote. "We firmly stand by [the report's] conclusions."[43]

The op-ed was also puzzling because, when examined closely, it was clear that its reasoning was not up to Goldstone's usual high standards. The case that he presented for changing his mind was thin. There had been three pillars of the Goldstone Report's claim that Israel intentionally punished the people of Gaza: the lack of plausible explanations for the scale and extent of the harm, the public statements by Israeli political and military leaders, and the testimony of former Israeli soldiers who described, in the Mission's view, a pattern of callous disregard for civilian well-being. With regard to the facts on the ground, the Israeli government had still presented no clear and persuasive explanation for the scale of civilian suffering in Gaza. The statements of the Israeli leaders and soldiers were still part of the public record—nothing had changed with regard to those pillars of the argument since 2009. So, too, the testimonies of the "Breaking the Silence" soldiers.

Goldstone's op-ed cited with approval the recent U.N. report of Judge Mary McGowan Davis, claiming that this recent study showed that Israel was serious about its internal investigations. In fact, the Davis Report took a much tougher tone on the pace and the outcomes of the Israeli investigations than the op-ed suggested. Davis argued that Israel had not, in fact, conducted a credible internal investigation about the question of whether Israeli leaders instituted a policy of collective punishment. She also highlighted the telling gap between the impressive number of Israeli investigations and the unim-pressive number of individuals who had actually been held accountable as a result of those outcomes. Goldstone would later describe his references to the Davis Report as simply a timely "peg" for the op-ed; the record suggests that it was a stronger "peg" as timing for the op-ed than it was as a signifi-cant cache of new information.

The truth was that there was really little new evidence to overturn the Goldstone Mission's original conclusions. It was also true that the evidence in the original report on the issue of intent was thin from the start. Goldstone and his fellow Mission members had inferred that Israel had a systematic pol-icy to punish the Palestinian people from indirect evidence. Goldstone's change of heart in April 2011 reflected the weakness of the original evidence, more than a dramatic change in the state of knowledge.

Read closely, it was clear that Goldstone's op-ed did not categorically reject the idea that Israel intended to harm Palestinian civilians. It merely said that new Israeli reports "indicate" that there was no such policy—an "indication" that one would in fact expect from the Israeli government. The judge, in effect, had overturned his own original judgment on appeal. The evidence in the original investigation did not support the "conviction"—that Israel had a pol-icy to harm civilians. The op-ed left open the possibility that evidence not available to the Mission might still have painted Israeli intent in an unfavor-able light. He effectively changed the verdict to "not guilty," a concession that the case could not be proved, rather than Israel was altogether innocent.

Despite Benjamin Netanyahu's contention, Goldstone did not attempt to withdraw the report as a whole. Even if Israel had no policy to attack civil-ians, it was still a war crime if its military failed to take adequate precautions to distinguish between civilian and military targets. It was still a war crime if Israel's tactics caused harm to civilians that was disproportionate to the mil-itary ends. The Goldstone Report had provided evidence and drawn many conclusions about war crimes that did not depend on the existence of an Israeli policy. Nothing in the Mission head's April 2011 op-ed retracted these many aspects of the original report.

In the weeks and months following the op-ed, Goldstone mostly declined to elaborate further on its message, leaving observers to speculate widely on its meaning and its author's motives. He seemed content to allow observers to reach startlingly different conclusions. He declined to take any action to withdraw the report from the U.N., a move that would in any case be meaningless because the document was now "owned" by the body that commissioned it. He seemed content to allow the report's impact to dissipate in a cloud of murkiness.

That cloud of murkiness took a toll on Richard Goldstone's reputation and stature. His critics took the retraction as vindication of their own merciless attacks on his integrity. Those who had defended the report saw a man who had refused to stick to his guns. A giant of international criminal justice had abandoned the path of principle for what seemed to many the path of expedience. Even in the eyes of his closest friends, Richard Goldstone seemed diminished. He had paid a steep price for his willingness to step into the fray.

There is another way to look at it. His dramatic action had an enormous benefit that was overlooked in the swirl of competing theories. By stepping back from the more far-reaching conclusions of the Mission, he revived the opportunity to consider the laws of war in all the complexity and nuance that they demanded. If the original Goldstone Report no longer generated as much heat around the question of intent, then it brought to the fore the challenging questions about how best to protect civilian lives in the complex circumstances of asymmetric warfare. Seen in this light, Goldstone's *Washington Post* op-ed was a heroic gesture—a distinguished figure exposing himself to further opprobrium in the service of creating space for more penetrating ongoing consideration of the principles that mattered most.

For example, what if one of the root causes of civilian suffering in Gaza was not policy, but permissiveness? Israeli soldiers at all levels had a great deal of authority to make real-time decisions. Indeed, such independence and initiative at all levels was one of the defining characteristics of the IDF, saluted in such contemporary accounts as *Start-Up Nation* for its innovative and entrepreneurial spirit.[44] In situations where individual units and even individual soldiers had considerable discretion to decide what was necessary from a military point of view and what was necessary to protect one's fellow soldiers, then "intent" became something quite different. It opened the possibility that harm to civilians—rather than being something perpetrated by design—was at least in some quarters considered an acceptable by-product of military action. Neither wholly intentional nor wholly unintentional, the devastation in Gaza could lie in a moral middle ground that resisted codification and made accountability a challenge.

Goldstone's enigmatic op-ed puzzled so many people because in fact it raised uncomfortable questions for everyone about the whole process of accountability for war crimes.[45] Supporters wanted to see Israel entirely exonerated, but Goldstone could not go that far. Proponents of a stronger system of global justice preferred to see bright lines of accountability, but the aftermath of the Goldstone Report exposed the challenges of applying legal guidelines to complex moral situations. Toward the end of his career, the man who had played a leading role in the application of the laws of war reminded the world that humanitarian law was still a work in progress and would always struggle to keep up with the changing complexities of human conflict.[46]

EPILOGUE

Legacies

FOLLOWING THE FURY over the Gaza report, the Goldstones shuttled between American university campuses, as Richard continued his stint as a sage and teacher in the international justice community. He accepted an intriguing assignment in 2013 to investigate the mysterious plane crash that killed U.N. secretary-general Dag Hammarskjöld in 1961.[1] He retired from regular teaching posts in 2017, although he remained active as a lecturer and a board member on organizations connected with global justice issues.[2] After many years of short visits, he and Noleen began to spend more time in South Africa, eventually moving back to their seaside apartment in Cape Town. While the pace of Goldstone's professional activities began to wind down, the legacy of his achievements continued to reverberate in the far-flung locales where he had done his most significant work.

A quarter century after the commission on public violence that Goldstone chaired, South Africa remained the world's preeminent example of a successful transition from repression to democracy. Participants in its (relatively) peaceful revolution exported their knowledge and experience to other countries seeking ways to recover from a repressive and violent past. The state of South African democracy was not, however, altogether healthy. The ANC, the party of Mandela, had devolved into corruption under the leadership of President Jacob Zuma, who was finally pushed out as president in early 2018. Persistent poverty and accelerating economic inequality marred the South African experiment. Following Zuma's departure, the ANC turned to Cyril Ramaphosa, whom Goldstone had first met in the 1980s, to try to restore good governance and attack the nation's deep-seated problems.

The contributions of the Goldstone Commission—and of the judiciary in general—to the South African transition remained underrecognized. The roles of Mandela, Tambo, Tutu, Mbeki, and other Black leaders justifiably commanded the narrative. Yet the achievements of these men depended in fundamental ways on the premise that law was an essential tool for establishing public good. Goldstone's work as a judge and his leadership of the commission on public violence remained preeminent examples of how law could be used to undermine an undemocratic regime.

In The Hague, the international criminal tribunals for the former Yugoslavia and Rwanda wound down their work after two decades. Following Goldstone's departure in 1996, a series of successors in the OTP built on the foundation that he had established to bring, eventually, nearly all of the major figures in both conflicts to the bar of justice. The ICTR completed its final trial in 2015, after issuing 93 indictments, and sentencing 62 defendants. The ICTY closed its doors in 2017, having indicted 161 and sentenced 90.[3]

Not everything had run smoothly, especially when it came to the prosecution of the "big fish." The ICTY eventually indicted Slobodan Milosević in 1999, but the Serbian president managed to turn his four-year trial into a series of opportunities for self-serving speeches about the injustices being perpetrated against the Serbian people by Western countries and by the tribunal itself. Milosević was still presenting his protracted defense when, after four years of trial, he died in prison in The Hague.[4]

The Milosević debacle was not the only failing of the tribunals. The complexities of international law and the cumbersome U.N. bureaucracy made for frequent inefficiencies; the tribunals cost the U.N. member states more than $2.5 billion each by the time that all was said and done. The tension between accountability and fairness created inconsistent rulings, and the rulings of the Appeals Chamber sometimes baffled the global legal community. Even after the fall of Milosević and the establishment of a stable government under Paul Kagame in Rwanda, it continued to be difficult to locate suspects and bring them to justice.[5]

It was embarrassing that for many years, the other two "big fish," Radovan Karadžić and Ratko Mladić, remained at large. Goldstone's successors at the OTP tried a variety of methods to pressure and shame governments into finding a way to bring the two architects of the Bosnian genocide into custody, but nothing seemed to work. Then, in 2008, the Serbian government abruptly announced that it had located and arrested Karadžić. The psychiatrist turned political leader had let his hair and his beard grow out. He had been living under a pseudonym on the outskirts of Belgrade, making his way as a practitioner of alternative medicine. Mladić was finally arrested in 2011, also in Serbia.

The trials of Karadžić and Mladić were protracted affairs, each absorbing more than four years of motions and proceedings. Yet in the end, both men were found guilty in separate trials of war crimes, crimes against humanity, and genocide. By 2018, twenty-three years after Richard Goldstone signed the first indictments against the leading perpetrators of ethnic cleansing, both were in prison, likely destined to spend the rest of their lives behind bars.[6]

Peace, deterrence, impunity, efficiency, closure—the tribunals were supposed to deliver them all. In the gap between the promise and the reality, dark doubts and critiques thrived. But the hopes were impossibly high. Outsized ideals obscured in some quarters the remarkable ways that the courts did, in fact, change the course of human history and consciousness.

The tribunals provided life—and teeth—to international treaties that outlawed genocide, offered protections for civilians in times of war, and asserted that certain atrocities were so monstrous that they should be considered crimes against humanity itself. Duly constituted courts of law pronounced that rape was not simply a violent act of sex, but that it could be considered an illicit tool of warfare.[7] They held commanders responsible for outrages that their underlings perpetrated, even when the commanders themselves did not issue the direct orders. They ruled that coded speech, when expressly intended to provoke violence, could be considered incitement to genocide.[8] They made it clear that an array of violent actions targeted at people as members of groups constituted a fundamental violation not only of conscience but of law in the modern world.

The Yugoslavia and Rwanda tribunals led to new international courts. Some were designed to address specific situations: the aftermath of horrific violence in Sierra Leone; the bloody attempt to suppress an independence movement in East Timor by Indonesia, the assassination of Prime Minister Rafic Hariri in Lebanon; the genocide perpetrated by the Khmer Rouge in Cambodia.[9] The founders of these courts borrowed some features and legal principles from Yugoslavia and Rwanda, and adapted them to local legal and political circumstances. The ICC was created at an international conference in Rome in 1998, and it came into existence in 2002. By 2018, 123 countries were members of the ICC, but it was still a work in progress, not yet a truly "international" institution.[10] Global politics competed with legal and moral ideals, and some of the world's largest nations—China, India, Russia, the United States—refused to sign on. Nevertheless, its presence and its principles permeated every contemporary discussion about the protection of civilians in times and places of armed conflict. The laws of war, the prohibition against genocide, and the protection of civilians were no longer abstract, distant, and purely voluntary.

Meanwhile, the proceedings at The Hague and Arusha created an extraordinary historical record. The history of the Holocaust in Europe had emerged fitfully, unsystematically, in ways that even seventy years later allowed many to deny the scale and intent of the slaughter of the Jews and millions of others. No such denial was plausible for the events of the 1990s in the Balkans and the Great Lakes. The stories of thousands, begun in the Rule 61 hearings launched under Richard Goldstone's leadership in The Hague, and continued through hundreds of thousands of hours of testimony in the trials, provided a searing, detailed account of the crimes at every level. The stories of Ibro Osmanović, witness FWS-87, and thousands like them became available forever as an undeniable portion of the truth, a compelling lesson for future generations.

The legacy of Goldstone's Gaza report was less tangible. Israel made some changes to its protocols (without giving credit to the report), but subsequent conflicts spurred the same debates over proportionality and accountability.

In 2014, Israel launched Operation Protective Edge, a response to not only more rocket fire but also the presence of underground tunnels that Hamas had built in order to smuggle fighters into Israeli territory. Protective Edge, like Cast Lead both an air and ground operation, proceeded at an even higher pitch than its predecessor. The conflict cost more than 2,000 Gazans their lives, and more than 10,000 were wounded. Thirteen Israeli civilians were killed by rocket fire, and sixty-six soldiers died in the fighting. The disproportionate numbers gave rise to the same criticisms of Israel that had dominated the world news in 2009, although Israeli public opinion, particularly outraged by the revelations about the tunnels, strongly supported the conflict as a defensive measure against terrorism.

One again the U.N. swung into action. Navi Pillay, still the high commissioner for human rights, criticized violations by both Hamas and Israel. The HRC voted to appoint another commission of inquiry, this one to be led by William Schabas, a Canadian expert on human rights and humanitarian law. As with Goldstone, supporters of Israel launched a series of preemptive attacks on Schabas, charging that he had a record of anti-Israel bias. This time the critics won. Schabas resigned as the chair of the commission of inquiry in February 2015. He was replaced by Mary McGowan Davis, the U.S. judge who had undertaken the follow-up investigation that played a part in Goldstone's retraction. Once again Israel refused to cooperate with the U.N. process, forcing Davis and her colleagues to rely on NGO reports and social media for much of their information about what happened inside Gaza. Davis's Mission issued its report in June 2015, once again saying that there was strong evidence that both Hamas and Israel had committed war crimes, but devoting the bulk of the report to Israeli violations.[11]

Without the dramatic gesture of a global Jewish hero criticizing Israel, the Davis Report in 2015 made fewer waves than the Goldstone Report of 2009. The HRC duly issued a resolution that exclusively condemned Israel and ignored the report's conclusions about Hamas. (The United States was the only country to oppose the resolution.)[12] The process was coming to feel like a ritual in which all of the actors were playing their assigned parts.

Richard Goldstone declined to comment during the press during Protective Edge, and he by and large avoided the topic of the Israeli-Palestinian conflict in both his public and his private conversations. The wounds were still deep, and he could not see a productive way to contribute, given the intensity of reaction both to his original report and to his retraction of some of its conclusions. The Goldstone Report lived on as an object lesson.

Richard Goldstone was devoted not to the grand gesture, but to the persistent application of core values. He helped advance, as much as any other single individual, three principles that were widely saluted in rhetoric, but often ignored in practice.

The first was accountability. From Sebokeng to Srebrenica to Gaza, Goldstone trained his efforts on finding those responsible for human suffering, and bringing them to justice. This was not born from a taste for punishment. Instead, Goldstone grasped the human hunger for justice not as retribution, but as a collective expression of human aspirations for improving the world. He always gave priority to the stories and needs of victims, witnesses, and survivors—the men, women, and children whose lives counted for so little in the minds of the perpetrators. He believed firmly that the record of their narratives was essential to binding the wounds of broken societies and establishing a firm foundation for reconciliation and recovery. Prison sentences for the men and women in the dock were important, but not as important as the process of the trials themselves: the stories of victims, the respect for the rule of law, the triumph of reason, tempered and fortified by compassion.

The second principle that Goldstone advanced was equality before the law. It was easy to articulate, but equally easy to shunt aside. In South Africa, he exposed the crimes of the apartheid government, but his commission did not spare the ANC and other parties of resistance. Serbs, Croatians, and Muslims alike stood trial in The Hague for crimes committed during the brutal war in the Balkans. More courageously, he took on, as a Jew, the heavy responsibility of judging Israel's conduct of warfare, precisely because he believed that principles of justice needed to be applied close to home, as well as on distant continents. The principle of equality exposed Goldstone to a constant stream of criticism, if not invective, because many partisans despised balance and wanted to see justice applied only to others. He eventually waffled on his final conclusions about the Gaza conflict, but by his own lights he was simply extending his commitment to following where the evidence led him.

Third, Goldstone stood for a commitment to the vitality and centrality of international institutions, of particular importance in an era when nationalism and xenophobia began to seize large swaths of the global community. He believed deeply in the U.N., even when his experience as a prosecutor and investigator revealed deep-seated problems of inefficiency, small-minded politics, and even corruption within the organization. He saw no alternative. He saw large human institutions as inherently fallible, and he believed fervently that his job was to provide a course correction, not to try to overturn the ship. Goldstone was not a career international public servant; he could easily have turned his back on the frustrations and imperfections of international institutions like the U.N. Instead, he provided a model of global public service built on principles of integrity and a mastery of geopolitics.

Richard Goldstone, was, of course, more than a collection of principles. His life of courage and controlled passion offers insights into the intricacies of human character.

A South African raised in the context of racism and oppression, Goldstone's choices in his personal life and on the bench demonstrated the complexities of living with integrity in an unjust society.

A professional who savored the pleasures of the good life, he undertook his work in the grand belief that the material, personal, and family blessings that he enjoyed should be shared by all.

A man who began his career in a world where patriarchy ruled, he gradually acquired a bedrock commitment to righting the wrongs done to women in wartime and in peace.

A Jew for whom the ideal of Israel as a shining moral example burned brightly, he paid a heavy price for his efforts to hold that nation to the highest standards.

A lightning rod for outrage in an era of polarized rhetoric, he stood for rights-based values and reasoned inquiry.

A judge who understood the imperfections of the law, he charted a course for the future of justice.

ACKNOWLEDGMENTS

My greatest debt in writing this book is to Richard Goldstone himself, who generously cooperated with every stage of the research.

I have known Richard since 1998, when he first spoke at Brandeis University, at a time when I was just launching a new center dedicated to global issues. He joined the advisory board of the International Center for Ethics, Justice and Public Life, and chaired the board from 2009 to 2016. Richard also played a vital role in the establishment and leadership of one of the center's flagship programs, the Brandeis Institute for International Judges. We became friends as well as colleagues.

I approached Richard about writing this volume in late 2011, while the controversy over the Gaza report was still very much alive. Given his prominence in three different locales—South Africa, The Hague, and the Middle East—I felt that his life and work offered a unique narrative for understanding the story of human rights and international justice in our time.

Richard agreed to sit for on-the-record interviews, and he also provided me with access to his personal papers. (I did not, however, have access to his email correspondence, where much of his real business was conducted since the 1990s.) He introduced me to friends and colleagues who might shed light on his work.

Goldstone's excellent memoir, *For Humanity*, gives an autobiographical account of his career through his tenure in The Hague. We agreed from the beginning that the story as told in *this* book would be mine. He understood that it was my job as a historian to offer the facts as I found them, and to come to independent conclusions.

For five years, we met for interviews as opportunities presented themselves in Boston, New Haven, New York City, Washington, D.C., Stanford, Budapest, Johannesburg, and Cape Town. Through this period, I cross-checked information and perspectives with Richard, but I did not share my work in progress. In November 2017, I sent the substantially complete manuscript to him and his wife Noleen. They corrected errors of fact, and they offered occasional suggestions for improvements in editing.

Richard conspicuously did not quarrel with any of my "big picture" interpretations about his life and work. This is not because he agrees with everything that I have written. Indeed, I am quite sure that he does not. His restraint testifies to his strength of character, and his willingness to live up to the original terms of our agreement. I doubt that there are many people who could match his equanimity.

More than forty family members, friends, colleagues, and antagonists of Richard Goldstone sat down with me to share their memories and perspectives. (They are listed in the bibliographical note.) I am grateful for their candor and insights, without which this volume would be significantly poorer. I am particularly grateful to Richard's wife Noleen and to the Goldstones' daughters, Glenda Goldstone Brener and Nicole Goldstone, who were willing to share intimate details about particularly challenging moments in their lives. Richard's brother David Goldstone spent hours scanning hard-to-find newspaper clippings from his personal collection to supplement my own research.

At Brandeis University, my professional home for nearly twenty-six years, I was blessed with a supportive administration, outstanding faculty and staff colleagues, and smart and energetic students. President Jehuda Reinharz established the International Center for Ethics, Justice and Public Life, and then bravely entrusted me with its leadership. Provosts Marty Krauss, Irv Epstein, and Lisa Lynch consistently supported the center, including the balance between research, teaching, and program development that I struck. My longtime center colleagues—Cynthia Cohen, Marci McPhee, Barbara Strauss, Leigh Swigart, and David Weinstein—created as warm and vibrant a community as anyone could hope to work in. David Briand, who did excellent work on the Ad Hoc Tribunals Oral History project, also contributed valuable research and editing to the chapters on the tribunals in this volume. I was fortunate to receive valuable research assistance from a number of Brandeis University students and recent alumni, including Nahum Gilliatt, Alex Glomset, Dina Kapengut, Shelby Magid, and Miriam Sievers.

In South Africa, Marc Schulman, then a law student at the University of the Witwatersrand, assembled an indispensable record of Richard Goldstone's cases as a judge. I also benefited from the help of the librarians in the Historical Papers Research Archives at the William Cullen Library at Wits. Anthony Katz of the *South African Jewish Report* helped me locate important materials and pointed me in promising directions.

I wrote the first drafts of the first chapters of the book during a fellowship at the Blue Mountain Center in the Adirondack Mountains in the summer of 2013. I am grateful to the center for providing an ideal atmosphere for taking risks and moving ideas forward, and to my fellow residents who provided encouragement and insightful commentary at a critical stage of the project.

This book has benefited from the comments of informed and careful readers. My thanks go to Linda Carter, Adam Dodek, Sylvia Fuks Fried, Sue Horton, and Leigh Swigart, all of whom saved me from embarrassing errors and contributed positive suggestions for improvement. Naturally, I alone am responsible for any errors that remain after their input.

My family has inspired and supported me for a lifetime. My father David, who died while I was working on this book, defined integrity not so much through words but through the loving and ethical way in which he lived. My mother Susan has passed along to me her high standards as a writer. My sons have now gotten to the age where I am learning more from them than they are from me. I have benefited from Ben's skills as a reporter, Eli's deep knowledge of Africa, Theo's perspective on Israeli society, and Sam's critical insights into what makes a book successful. I cannot possibly keep pace with the enormous creative energies of my wife, Maggie, but her love is for me (impossibly) both anchor and sail in a turbulent world.

NOTES

PROLOGUE

1. "Justice Richard Goldstone Receives MacArthur Award for International Justice," News Release, MacArthur Foundation, May 25, 2009, https://www.macfound.org/press/press-releases/justice-richard-goldstone-receives-macarthur-award-for-international-justice/. The video of the event is available at https://www.macfound.org/videos/174/.
2. *Joint Statement: Hudson Institute; International Association of Jewish Lawyers and Jurists,* video, HRC, September 30, 2009, http://www.un.org/webcast/unhrc/archive.asp?go=090930.

CHAPTER 1   DIVISIONS

1. This account of Goldstone's early recollections is based on an interview with Richard Goldstone by Daniel Terris, April 11, 2012.
2. "Obituary: Albert Jacobson, Reef Pioneer," n.d., Richard Goldstone's private papers.
3. Richard Goldstone, interview by Daniel Terris, April 12, 2012.
4. A court, for example, had ruled that Coloured people in the Cape Province still had the right to vote, even though non-Whites in the rest of the country were disenfranchised.
5. This section relies on Gideon Shimoni, *Community and Conscience: The Jews in Apartheid South Africa* (Hanover, N.H.: Brandeis University Press, 2003).
6. Ibid.
7. All Whites in South Africa were considered to be "Europeans," regardless of their country of origin.
8. By the time that Richard Goldstone was born, Yiddish was spoken in fewer than a quarter of South African Jewish households.
9. Richard's younger brother David was not born until Richard was twenty.
10. *King Edward VII Magazine,* December 1956, p. 27.
11. Geoffrey Mansell, interview by Daniel Terris, January 4, 2013.
12. T.R.H. Davenport and Christopher C. Saunders, *South Africa: A Modern History,* 5th ed. (Hampshire, England: Macmillan Press, 2000).
13. Benas Levy, interview by Daniel Terris, June 16, 2015.
14. Richard Goldstone, interview by Daniel Terris, October 19, 2013.
15. Bruce K. Murray, *Wits, the "Open" Years: A History of the University of the Witwatersrand, Johannesburg, 1939–1959* (Johannesburg: Witwatersrand University Press, 1997), 166.
16. "History of Wits," University of the Witwatersrand, http://www.wits.ac.za/aboutwits/introducingwits/3162/short_history_of_the_university.html.

17. Murray, *Wits, the "Open" Years*, 167–168.

18. There were smaller numbers in the other faculties: there would be four, for example, who would enter in Richard Goldstone's class when he entered law school in 1960, according to Goldstone's recollection.

19. Murray, *Wits, the "Open" Years*, 47.

20. Richard Goldstone, *For Humanity: Reflections of a War Crimes Investigator* (New Haven, Conn.: Yale University Press, 2000), 2.

21. Murray, *Wits, the "Open" Years*, 315.

22. Ibid.

23. Richard Goldstone interview, October 19, 2013.

24. Goldstone, *For Humanity*, 3.

25. Richard Goldstone interview, April 12, 2012.

26. Richard Goldstone interview, October 19, 2013.

27. The transcript of this recording has been preserved in the University of the Witwatersrand archives. This account is based on that transcript, in addition to interviews with Richard Goldstone.

28. Murray, *Wits, the "Open" Years*, 318.

29. *Cape Argus*, February 18, 1959, from notes in the University of the Witwatersrand archives.

30. Murray, *Wits, the "Open" Years*, 318.

31. *Sunday Times*, February 22, 1959, in the University of the Witwatersrand archives.

32. Goldstone, *For Humanity*, 4.

33. Ibid.

34. Richard Goldstone interview, October 19, 2013.

CHAPTER 2   THE STRIVER

1. In the South African system, students first earned an undergraduate BA in law over three years. Goldstone completed this degree at the end of 1959. He then entered a two-year program to earn a second undergraduate degree for professional training in law (LLB), which he earned at the end of 1961.

2. This was Richard Goldstone's own estimate. Richard Goldstone, interview by Daniel Terris, April 12, 2012.

3. This account of the roots of South African law draws on John Dugard, *Human Rights and the South African Legal Order* (Princeton, N.J.: Princeton University Press, 1978); Albie Sachs, *Justice in South Africa* (Berkeley: University of California Press, 1973); Stephen Ellmann, *In a Time of Trouble: Law and Liberty in South Africa's State of Emergency* (New York: Oxford University Press, 1992); and David Dyzenhaus, *Judging the Judges, Judging Ourselves: Truth, Reconciliation and the Apartheid Legal Order* (Oxford: Hart Publishers, 2003).

4. Ellmann, *In a Time of Trouble*, 2.

5. Noleen Goldstone, interview by Daniel Terris, April 11, 2012.

6. Benas Levy, interview by Daniel Terris, January 5, 2013.

7. Dennis Davis and Michelle Le Roux, *Precedent and Possibility: The (Ab)Use of Law in South Africa* (Cape Town: Double Storey, 2009), 42.

8. Richard Goldstone, *For Humanity: Reflections of a War Crimes Investigator* (New Haven, Conn.: Yale University Press, 2000), 5.

9. Geoffrey Mansell, interview by Daniel Terris, January 4, 2013.

10. Ibid.

11. Richard Goldstone, interview by Daniel Terris, April 12, 2012.

12. Noleen Goldstone, interview by Daniel Terris, June 15, 2015.

13. Gideon Shimoni, *Community and Conscience: The Jews in Apartheid South Africa* (Hanover, N.H.: Brandeis University Press, 2003), 152.

14. See *Zionist Record*, December 18, 1992, 3.

15. Richard Goldstone interview, April 12, 2012.

16. "History of ORT," ORT, http://www.ort.org/about-us/history/.

17. Goldstone was president of World ORT from 1997 to 2004.

18. See, generally, Marjorie N. Feld, *Nations Divided: American Jews and the Struggle over Apartheid* (New York: Palgrave Macmillan, 2014).

19. Richard Goldstone interview, April 12, 2012.

20. See Samuel Moyn, *The Last Utopia: Human Rights in History* (Cambridge, Mass.: Harvard University Press, 2010).

21. Dugard, *Human Rights and the South African Legal Order*; Sachs, *Justice in South Africa*.

22. Quoted in Michael Corbett, "Guaranteeing Fundamental Freedoms in a New South Africa," Hoernle Lecture, South African Institute of Race Relations, May 7, 1990, 5.

23. Richard Goldstone interview, April 12, 2012.

24. Goldstone, *For Humanity*, 5.

25. These figures are from 1978. See Dugard, *Human Rights and the South African Legal Order*, 10.

26. Ibid., 35.

27. Sachs, *Justice in South Africa*, 35–36.

28. Ibid., 133–134.

29. Raymond Wacks, "Judges and Injustice," *South African Law Journal* 101(1984), 266–285.

30. John Dugard, "Should Judges Resign? A Reply to Professor Wacks," *South African Law Journal* 101(1984), 286–294.

31. Goldstone, *For Humanity*, 5.

CHAPTER 3   CRACKS IN THE WALL

1. Judgment, *S v. Boshoff and Others*, Transvaal Provincial Division, 1981 (1) SA 393 (T), October 14, 1980.

2. Richard Goldstone, personal communication to Daniel Terris, December 18, 2015.

3. Judgment, *S v. Sekwati*, Transvaal Provincial Division Court, 1982 (1) SA 626 (T), November 6, 1981.

4. See David Dyzenhaus, *Judging the Judges, Judging Ourselves: Truth, Reconciliation and the Apartheid Legal Order* (Oxford: Hart Publishers, 2003).

5. Judgment, *S v. Govender*, Transvaal Provincial Division Court, 1986 (3) SA 969 (T), November 30, 1982.

6. Kate O'Regan, interview by Daniel Terris, January 8, 2013; Navi Pillay, interview by Daniel Terris, October 30, 2014; and Justice Moloto, interview by Daniel Terris, May 6, 2014.

7. Justice Moloto interview, May 6, 2014.

8. Kate O'Regan interview, January 8, 2013.

9. Nicole Goldstone, interview by Daniel Terris, November 12, 2012.

10. Peta Krost, "On a Crusade for a Gentler Mindset," undated newspaper clipping in Richard Goldstone's papers.

11. Richard Goldstone, interview by Daniel Terris, October 19, 2013; ibid.

12. Judgment, *S v. Khumalo*, Witwatersrand Local Division Court, 1984 (4) SA 642 (W), May 9, 1984; Cathy Stagg, "Enthusiastic Response for Judge Goldstone," *Star*, December 19, 1989.

13. Nicole Goldstone interview, November 12, 2012.

14. Richard Goldstone, *For Humanity: Reflections of a War Crimes Investigator* (New Haven, Conn.: Yale University Press, 2000), 9.

15. Transcript of interview with Zwelakhe Sisulu for the video *A Tribute to South African Judge Richard Goldstone*, produced by Pippa Scott. The video can be found at https://www.youtube.com/watch?v=cDqQThmoRCw.

16. Transcript of interview with Zwelakhe Sisulu.

17. Goldstone, *For Humanity*, 10–11.

18. Transcript of interview with Richard Goldstone for *Tribute to South African Judge Richard Goldstone*.

19. Transcript of interview with Mathatha Tsedu for *Tribute to South African Judge Richard Goldstone*. The gift that Goldstone brought to Tsedu was a stack of *National Geographic* magazines.

20. Goldstone, *For Humanity*, 9.

21. Richard Goldstone, interview by Daniel Terris, April 11, 2012.

22. Ibid.

23. Judgment, *S v. Ndaba and Others*, Transvaal Provincial Division, 1987 (1) SA 237 (T), September 30, 1985.

24. He was also worried that if he overturned the punishment it would result in a longer prison term for the men (ibid.).

25. Richard Goldstone interview, April 11, 2012.

26. Judgment, *S v. Gwebu*, Witwatersrand Local Division, 1988 (4) SA 155 (W), May 18, 1987.

27. Richard Goldstone interview, April 11, 2012.

28. David Margolick, "Breaking One of South Africa's Barriers," *New York Times*, September 16, 1989; Vernon Grigg, interview by Daniel Terris, March 8, 2013.

29. Richard Goldstone interview, April 11, 2012.

30. Ibid.

31. Ibid.

32. *Dlomo* case, cited in Ayal Rosenberg, *Richard Goldstone: Apartheid Judge* (self-pub., Amazon Digital Services, 2012), loc. 1283 of 8609, Kindle.

33. Albie Sachs, interview by Daniel Terris, September 11, 2014.

34. Gilbert Marcus, interview by Daniel Terris, June 16, 2015.

35. "Remarks by the Honourable Justice Richard J. Goldstone at a Panel Discussion during the Meeting in Cape Town of the World Jurist Association" (1997). Pamphlet in Richard Goldstone's personal papers.

36. See chapter 18.

37. Goldstone was not alone in this point of view. Other prominent South African opponents of apartheid, such as Helen Suzman, also opposed international sanctions.

38. Richard Goldstone, "Address to Graduating Class of King Edward VII School" (1988). Typescript in Richard Goldstone's personal papers.

39. Ibid.

CHAPTER 4   DEMONSTRATIONS

1. "The Judge Who Has Striven for Peace Is Not Finished Yet," *Star*, December 29, 1992.

2. Christopher Wren, "De Klerk and Mandela Discuss Future," *New York Times*, December 14, 1989.

3. "F. W. De Klerk's Speech at the Opening of Parliament 2 February 1990," Nelson Mandela Foundation, https://www.nelsonmandela.org/omalley/index.php/site/q/03lvo2039 /04lvo2103/05lvo2104/06lvo2105.htm.

4. "South Africa's New Era; Transcript of Mandela's Speech at Cape Town City Hall: 'Africa It Is Ours!,'" *New York Times*, February 12, 1990.

5. Richard Goldstone, interview by Daniel Terris, January 3, 2013.

6. Richard Goldstone, *For Humanity: Reflections of a War Crimes Investigator* (New Haven, Conn.: Yale University Press, 2000), 2.

7. *Truth and Reconciliation Commission of South Africa Report*, 1999, vol. 2, 563. Available at http://www.justice.gov.za/trc/report/finalreport/Volume%202.pdf.

8. "No One to Blame for Sithole's Death," *Star*, March 6, 1990.

9. The UDF was the umbrella political anti-apartheid movement that had operated inside South Africa on behalf of the banned ANC.

10. JJ Du Toit, interview by Daniel Terris, January 14, 2013.

11. Richard Goldstone, *Report of the Commission of Enquiry into the Incidents at Sebokeng, Boipatong, Lekoa, Sharpeville, and Evaton on 26 March 1990*, June 27, 1990, 65. Typescript available in the Historical Papers Research Archive, University of the Witwatersrand.

12. Ibid., 66.

13. Ibid., 62.

14. This principle has been applied in international conflicts, not for the most part in policing situations, though the principle of "superior responsibility" can be applied to civilian leaders.

15. It should be noted that the counsel for the victims, George Bizos, did not argue for vigorous prosecution of the commanders.

16. Goldstone, *Report of the Commission of Enquiry*, 70.

17. President de Klerk did not release the report for three months after Goldstone submitted it, apparently in part because he did not want to disrupt negotiations that led to an agreement called the "Pretoria Minute" in August 1990.

18. George Bizos, interview by Daniel Terris, January 4, 2013.

19. Chris Moerdyk, "'Sebokeng' Judge Is Not Known for Pussyfooting," *Star*, September 8, 1990.

20. *Truth and Reconciliation Commission of South Africa Report*, vol. 3, 670.

21. Ben Temkin, *Buthelezi: A Biography* (Portland, Oreg.: Frank Cass, 2003).

22. Monthly reports by the Independent Board of Inquiry into Informal Repression through this period document this violence in detail. An extensive set of these reports can be found in the Historical Papers Research Archive in the William Cullen Library at the University of the Witwatersrand (http://www.historicalpapers.wits.ac.za).

23. See "The National Peace Accord and Its Structures," Nelson Mandela Centre of Memory, https://www.nelsonmandela.org/omalley/index.php/site/q/03lv02424/04lv03275/05lv03294/06lv03321.htm.

24. George Bizos interview, January 4, 2013.

25. Richard Goldstone, interview by Daniel Terris, January 3, 2013.

26. Goldstone, *For Humanity*, 26.

27. Mike Robertson, "Justice of the Peace," *Sunday Times*, October 27, 1991.

28. Richard Goldstone interview, January 3, 2013.

29. The account of the work of the Commission that follows here and in the next chapter are based on the records of the Commission and contemporary media sources. The only book that has focused at length on the Commission's work is Anthea Jeffery, *People's War: New Light on the Struggle for South Africa* (Johannesburg: Jonathan Ball, 2009).

30. No relation to Clayton Sizwe Sithole.

31. Albie Sachs, interview by Daniel Terris, September 11, 2014.

32. Richard Goldstone interview, January 3, 2013.

33. Richard Goldstone, interview by Padraig O'Malley, January 28, 1992, http://www.nelsonmandela.org/omalley/index.php/site/q/03lv00017/04lv00344/05lv00607/06lv00654.htm.

34. Goldstone Commission, *Second Interim Report of the Goldstone Commission*, April 29, 1992, in *Goldstone Commission, 1991–1994: A Compilation of Reports, Press Releases & Submissions* (Johannesburg: Human Rights Institute of South Africa, 2006). This was published as a CD-ROM. Selected documents of the Goldstone Commission are also available at https://searchworks.stanford.edu/view/2740653.

35. Goldstone, *For Humanity*, 30.

36. This account draws on James G. R. Simpson, *The Boipatong Massacre and South Africa's Democratic Transition* (Leiden: African Studies Centre, 2011); and Bill Keller, "39 in South Africa Die in a Massacre," *New York Times,* June 19, 1992.

37. Keller, "39 in South Africa Die in a Massacre."

38. Simpson, *Boipatong Massacre,* 32.

39. David Beresford, "Mandela Calls a Halt to Talks," *Guardian,* June 22, 1992.

40. Goldstone, *For Humanity,* 31.

41. "Turning a Deaf Ear to Goldstone," *Star,* July 7, 1992.

42. "Appeal to Mandela; Stick with the Negotiations," *Ottawa Citizen,* June 24, 1992.

43. Richard Goldstone, "Statement at the Preliminary Hearing into the Boipatong Massacre," News Release, Goldstone Commission, July 6, 1992. Typescript in Richard Goldstone personal papers.

44. Peter Waddington, *Report of the Inquiry into the Police Response to, and Investigation of, Events in Boipatong on 17 June 1992,* Goldstone Commission, July 20, 1992, in *Goldstone Commission, 1991–1994.*

45. Richard Goldstone interview, January 28, 1992.

46. JJ Du Toit interview, January 14, 2013.

47. Princeton N. Lyman, interview by Daniel Terris, April 21, 2014.

48. Richard Goldstone interview, January 28, 1992.

CHAPTER 5   THE THIRD FORCE

1. David B. Ottoway, "South African Judge Makes His Mark with Evenhanded Probe of Violence," *Washington Post,* July 12, 1992.

2. Goldstone Commission, *Report on the Regulation of Gatherings,* January 15, 1993, in *Goldstone Commission, 1991–1994: A Compilation of Reports, Press Releases & Submissions* (Johannesburg: Human Rights Institute of South Africa, 2006).

3. Philip Heymann interview by Daniel Terris, October 3, 2014.

4. JJ Du Toit, interview by Daniel Terris, January 14, 2013.

5. Philip Heymann interview, October 3, 2014.

6. Richard Goldstone, interview by Daniel Terris, January 3, 2013.

7. Richard Goldstone, *For Humanity: Reflections of a War Crimes Investigator* (New Haven, Conn.: Yale University Press, 2000), 39.

8. "Goldstone Backs UN Secretary-General's Recommendations," *BBC Summary of World Broadcast,* August 10, 1992; "Judge Seeks an Amnesty," *Courier-Mail,* August 10, 1992.

9. "ANC Wants Political Crimes to Be Disclosed before General Amnesty Introduced," *BBC Summary of World Broadcast,* August 11, 1992.

10. Bill Keller, "Pretoria Offers an Amnesty Plan, but Mandela's Group Refuses It," *New York Times,* August 14, 1992.

11. Goldstone Commission, *Report on the Investigation Units of the Goldstone Commission: 1 October 1992–30 September 1993,* November 26, 1993.

12. Patti Waldmeir, *Anatomy of a Miracle: The End of Apartheid and the Birth of the New South Africa* (New York: W. W. Norton, 1997).

13. JJ Du Toit interview, January 14, 2013.

14. Goldstone Commission, *Allegations Published in the Vrye Weekblad Dated 30 October 1992 Concerning a Third Force*, May 27, 1993, in *Goldstone Commission, 1991–1994*.

15. In 1989, for example, allegations regarding two widely feared units, the blandly named Civil Cooperation Bureau and a South African Defence Force unit called C10 had been splashed across the headlines. Two insiders, Dirk Coetzee and Butana Almond Nofomela, told dramatic tales of assassination squads and dirty tricks to the local and the international press.

16. National Peace Accord, 1991, in *Goldstone Commission, 1991–1994*.

17. Richard Goldstone interview, January 3, 2013.

18. News Release, Goldstone Commission, November 16, 1992, in *Goldstone Commission, 1991–1994*.

19. "National Party Comments on Statement by Goldstone Commission," *BBC Summary of World Broadcasts*, November 18, 1992.

20. David Beresford, "Top S African Army Officers Caught in Web of Suspicion," *Guardian*, November 18, 1992.

21. F. W. De Klerk, *The Last Trek—a New Beginning: The Autobiography* (London: Macmillan, 1998), 260.

22. Bill Keller, "Mandela, Shifting Strategy, Offers Whites an Assured Share of Power," *New York Times*, November 20, 1992.

23. "Shocks from the Steyn Report," *Mail & Guardian*, January 31, 1997. Available at http://mg.co.za/article/1997-01-31-shocks-from-the-steyn-report.

24. De Klerk, *Last Trek*, 264.

25. Alan Cowell, "De Klerk Concedes Military Had Role in Township Strife," *New York Times*, December 20, 1992.

26. Bill Keller, "Cape Town Journal; in a Wary Land, the Judge Is Trusted (to a Point)," *New York Times*, March 8, 1993.

27. *Sowetan*, April 29, 1993.

28. *Jewish Voice*, February 1, 1993.

29. Richard Goldstone, "Address to Durban Press Club" (1992). Typescript in Richard Goldstone's personal papers.

30. "The Judge Who Has Striven for Peace Is Not Finished Yet," *Star*, December 29, 1992.

31. Richard Goldstone, interview by Padraig O'Malley, December 6, 1993, http://www.nelsonmandela.org/omalley/index.php/site/q/03lv00017/04lv00344/05lv00607/06lv00654.htm.

32. De Klerk, *Last Trek*, 258.

33. Ibid., 264.

34. Richard Goldstone interview, January 3, 2013.

35. Ibid.

36. Ibid.

37. Mandela to Nicky Goldstone, August 4, 1993, in Richard Goldstone's personal papers.

38. This account draws on Goldstone Commission, *Interim Report: Criminal Political Violence by Elements within the South African Police, the Kwazulu Police and the Inkatha Freedom Party*, March 18, 1994, in *Goldstone Commission, 1991–1994*.

39. Eugene de Kock and Jeremy Gordin, *A Long Night's Damage: Working for the Apartheid State* (Saxonwold, South Africa: Contra Press, 1998).

40. Goldstone, *For Humanity*, 52.

41. JJ Du Toit interview, January 14, 2013.

42. The Goldstone Commission report states that the meeting was with de Klerk and Coetsee. Goldstone says in *For Humanity* that he met with de Klerk alone.

43. Goldstone Commission, *Interim Report*.

44. JJ Du Toit interview, January 14, 2013.

45. Goldstone Commission, *Interim Report*.

46. Errol and Ruth Friedmann, interview by Daniel Terris, January 9, 2013.

47. Goldstone, *For Humanity*, 54–55.

48. Ibid., 57.

49. The Human Rights Institute of South Africa was still a functioning NGO in South Africa as of early 2018 (http://www.hurisa.org.za).

50. See Stephen Ellmann, *In a Time of Trouble: Law and Liberty in South Africa's State of Emergency* (New York: Oxford University Press, 1992).

CHAPTER 6   IN THE FOOTSTEPS OF ROBERT JACKSON

1. This account is based on Rule 61 Hearing, *The Prosecutor of the Tribunal against Dragan Nikolić Also Known as "Jenki" Nikolić*, ICTY, October 9, 1995. The archives of the ICTY are available via the website of the U.N. Mechanism for International Criminal Tribunals at http://www.unmict.org.

2. Indictment, *The Prosecutor of the Tribunal against Dragan Nikolić Also Known as "Jenki" Nikolić*, ICTY, IT-94-2-I, November 4, 1994.

3. Richard Goldstone, interview by Daniel Terris, November 5, 2014. In 1992 he had said to a Jewish group that they should take note of the suffering of Muslims in Croatia. *Zionist Record*, December 18, 1992.

4. Ibid.; George Bizos, interview by Daniel Terris, January 4, 2013.

5. Richard Goldstone, *For Humanity: Reflections of a War Crimes Investigator* (New Haven, Conn.: Yale University Press, 2000), 21.

6. Antonio Cassese, personal communication to Richard Goldstone, July 1, 1994.

7. Richard Goldstone, interview by Daniel Terris, April 11, 2012.

8. Richard Goldstone, personal communication to Antonio Cassese, July 5, 1994.

9. Cassese to Goldstone, July 1, 1994.

10. Richard Goldstone interview, April 11, 2012.

11. Richard Goldstone, interview by David P. Briand and Leigh Swigart, March 9, 2015, International Center for Ethics, Justice and Public Life, Robert D. Farber University Archives and Special Collections Department, Brandeis University. This collection of oral history interviews can be accessed at http://www.brandeis.edu/ethics/internationaljustice /oral-history/index.html.

12. Richard Goldstone interview, November 5, 2014.

13. See, generally, Leslie Benson, *Yugoslavia: A Concise History* (New York: Palgrave Macmillan, 2003); and Steven L. Burg and Paul Shoup, *The War in Bosnia-Herzegovina: Ethnic Conflict and International Intervention* (Armonk, N.Y.: M. E. Sharpe, 1999).

14. *Final Report of the Commission of Experts Established Pursuant to Security Council Resolution 780 (1992)*, U.N., S/1994/674, May 27, 1994, http://www.icty.org/x/file/About /OTP/un_commission_of_experts_report1994_en.pdf.

15. "The Conflicts," ICTY, http://www.icty.org/en/about/what-former-yugoslavia /conflicts.

16. "'Hello, 911? This Is Bosnia,'" *New York Times*, May 28, 1992.

17. *Bosnia and Herzegovina Death Camps for Muslims*, television segment aired on Penny Marshall, *News at Ten*, August 6, 1992 (London: ITN Archive reference t06089201.htm), videotape.

18. Michael P. Scharf, *Balkan Justice: The Story behind the First International War Crimes Trial since Nuremberg* (Durham, N.C.: Carolina Academic Press, 1997).

19. *The Path to the Hague: Selected Documents on the Origins of the ICTY* (New York: U.N., 1996), 43–45.

20. *Resolution 780 (1992)*, U.N. Security Council, S/RES/780 (1992), October 6, 1992.

21. David Scheffer, *All the Missing Souls: A Personal History of the War Crimes Tribunals* (Princeton, N.J.: Princeton University Press, 2012), 22.

22. *Resolution 827 (1993)*, U.N. Security Council, S/RES/827 (1993), May 25, 1993.

23. Larry D. Johnson, interview by David P. Briand and Leigh Swigart, February 18, 2015, Ad Hoc Tribunals Oral History Project, International Center for Ethics, Justice and Public Life, Robert D. Farber University Archives and Special Collections Department, Brandeis University, http://www.brandeis.edu/ethics/internationaljustice/oral -history/interviews/johnson.html, 11.

24. *Charter of the United Nations and Statute of the International Court of Justice* (New York: U.N., 1945).

25. Even earlier, the Americans had considered Luis Moreno Ocampo of Argentina, but he lacked the support of his own government. Ocampo would later become the first chief prosecutor for the International Criminal Court (ICC). See David Scheffer, "Three Memories from the Year of Origin, 1993," *Journal of International Criminal Justice* 2, no. 2 (2004), 353.

26. Scheffer, *All the Missing Souls*, 31.

27. Scharf, *Balkan Justice*.

28. Gary Jonathan Bass, *Stay the Hand of Vengeance: The Politics of War Crimes Tribunals* (Princeton, N.J.: Princeton University Press, 2000).

29. Roger Cohen, "Serbs Put a Serb on Trial for War Crimes," *New York Times*, June 12, 1994.

30. Goldstone, *For Humanity*, 21.

31. Pierre Hazan, *Justice in a Time of War: The True Story behind the International Criminal Tribunal for the Former Yugoslavia* (College Station: Texas A&M University Press, 2004).

32. John H. F. Shattuck, *Freedom on Fire: Human Rights Wars and America's Response* (Cambridge, Mass.: Harvard University Press, 2003), 143–144.

33. Goldstone, *For Humanity*, 23–24.

34. *Resolution 936 (1994)*, U.N. Security Council, S/RES/936 (1994), July 8, 1994.

35. David Beresford, "Goldstone to Take War Crimes Job," *Guardian*, July 9, 1994.

36. Anthony Lewis, personal communication to Richard Goldstone, July 12, 1994.

37. Hazan, *Justice in a Time of War*. Christian Chartier, personal communication to Daniel Terris, December 18, 2014.

38. Madeleine Bunting, "The Evil That Men Do," *Guardian*, August 19, 1994.

39. Goldstone, *For Humanity*, 74.

40. Robert H. Jackson, "Opening Statement before the International Military Tribunal, November 21, 1945," Robert H. Jackson Center, https://www.roberthjackson.org/speech-and-writing/opening-statement-before-the-international-military-tribunal/.

41. Steve Coll, "In the Shadow of the Holocaust," *Washington Post*, September 25, 1994.

CHAPTER 7   A PATCHWORK COURT

1. Catherine Cissé, interview by Daniel Terris, May 8, 2014.

2. Minna Schrag, interview by Daniel Terris, May 1, 2014.

3. Richard Goldstone, *For Humanity: Reflections of a War Crimes Investigator* (New Haven, Conn.: Yale University Press, 2000), 81.

4. Antonio Cassese, personal communication to Richard Goldstone, July 14, 1995.

5. Graham Blewitt, interview by Daniel Terris, June 30, 2014.

6. Ibid.

7. ICTY, *Second Annual Report of the International Tribunal for the Prosecution of Persons Responsible for Serious Violations of International Humanitarian Law Committed in the Territory of the Former Yugoslavia since 1991*, U.N., A/50/365 S/1995/728, August 23, 1995.

8. Gary Jonathan Bass, *Stay the Hand of Vengeance: The Politics of War Crimes Tribunals* (Princeton, N.J.: Princeton University Press, 2000), 221.

9. Robert Marquand, "US Must Support War Crimes Prosecution," *Christian Science Monitor*, August 30, 1994.

10. "An Exercise in Hypocrisy? Will the UN's War-Crimes Tribunal in Bosnia Ever Hear a Case?," *60 Minutes*, CBS News, October 2, 1994.

11. ICTY, *Second Annual Report*. The OTP also received support from private foundations like the Open Society Foundations. See Richard Goldstone, "In Aryeh's Footsteps: The Strengthening of International Justice," in *The Rise of International Justice: A Collection of Essays and Reminiscences Dedicated to Aryeh Neier* (n.p.: Open Society Foundations, 2013), 91–96.

12. Marquand, "US Must Support War Crimes Prosecution."

13. Richard Goldstone, interview by Daniel Terris, April 22, 2014; Goldstone, *For Humanity*, 86.

14. Goldstone, *For Humanity*, 82.

15. Richard Goldstone interview, April 22, 2014.

16. Bass, *Stay the Hand of Vengeance*, 220.

17. "Living History Interview with Judge Richard Goldstone (Chief Prosecutor for the Yugoslav and Rwandan War Crimes Tribunals)," *Transnational Law & Contemporary Problems* 5, no. 2 (1995), 373–385.

18. Christian Chartier, personal communication to Daniel Terris, December 18, 2014.

19. Clare Dyer, "Judge of Our Inactions," *Guardian*, October 1, 1994.

20. Chartier to Terris, December 18, 2014.

21. Richard Goldstone interview, April 22, 2014.

22. The title was formally approved by the Protocol Committee of the U.N.

23. Goldstone, *For Humanity*, 88–89.

24. Richard Goldstone interview, April 22, 2014.

25. Goldstone, *For Humanity*, 96.

26. Richard Goldstone interview, April 22, 2014.

27. Goldstone, *For Humanity*, 95.

28. Terree Bowers interview, June 30, 2014; Graham Blewitt interview, June 30, 2014; Goldstone, *For Humanity*, 96.

29. "Co-Operation between Bosnia and the International Tribunal Formally Acknowledged," News Release, ICTY, December 3, 1994, http://www.icty.org/sid/10305.

30. Minna Schrag interview, May 1, 2014; Terree Bowers interview, June 30, 2014.

31. Graham Blewitt interview, June 30, 2014.

32. John Hagan, *Justice in the Balkans: Prosecuting War Crimes in the Hague Tribunal* (Chicago: University of Chicago Press, 2003).

33. Minna Schrag interview, May 1, 2014.

34. Ibid.; Terree Bowers interview, June 30, 2014.

35. Richard Goldstone interview, April 22, 2014.

36. "An Exercise in Hypocrisy?"

CHAPTER 8   BIG FISH, LITTLE FISH

1. M. Cherif Bassiouni, introduction to Pierre Hazan, *Justice in a Time of War: The True Story Behind the International Criminal Tribunal for the Former Yugoslavia* (College Station: Texas A&M University Press, 2004); Graham Blewitt, interview by Daniel Terris, June 30, 2014.

2. John Hagan, *Justice in the Balkans: Prosecuting War Crimes in the Hague Tribunal* (Chicago: University of Chicago Press, 2003), 68.

3. Ibid., 69, 78; Graham Blewitt interview, June 30, 2014.

4. Hagan, *Justice in the Balkans*, 69.

5. *Christian Science Monitor*, August 19, 1994.

6. Richard Goldstone, *For Humanity: Reflections of a War Crimes Investigator* (New Haven, Conn.: Yale University Press, 2000), 87.

7. Robert H. Jackson, "Opening Statement before the International Military Tribunal, November 21, 1945," Robert H. Jackson Center, https://www.roberthjackson.org/speech-and-writing/opening-statement-before-the-international-military-tribunal/.

8. For example, the International Court of Justice and the European Court of Human Rights.

9. Richard Goldstone, "War Crimes: A Question of Will," *World Today* 53, no. 4 (April 1997), 106–108.

10. Aryeh Neier, interview by Daniel Terris, November 6, 2014.

11. Goldstone, *For Humanity*, 105; Hagan, *Justice in the Balkans*, 68.

12. Rule 61 Hearing, *The Prosecutor of the Tribunal against Dragan Nikolić Also Known as "Jenki" Nikolić*, ICTY, October 9, 1995.

13. Roger Cohen, "Ex-Guard for Serbs Tells of Grisly 'Cleansing' Camp," *New York Times*, August 1, 1994.

14. Indictment, *The Prosecutor of the Tribunal against Dragan Nikolić Also Known as "Jenki" Nikolić*, ICTY, IT-94-2-I, November 4, 1994. The ICTY Statute required that a single judge confirm an indictment before it could be issued.

15. Theodor Meron et al., "Where Do We Go from Here? New and Emerging Issues in the Prosecution of War Crimes and Acts of Terrorism: A Panel Discussion," *Social Research* 69, no. 4 (2002), 1174–1206.

16. Ed Vulliamy, "In Times of Trial," *Guardian*, October 31, 1995.

17. Goldstone, *For Humanity*, 85; Richard Goldstone, "Prosecuting Rape as a War Crime," *Case Western Reserve Journal of International Law* (2002), 278.

18. Patricia Viseur Sellers and Kaoru Okuizumi, "Prosecuting International Crimes: An Inside View," *Transnational Law and Contemporary Problems* 45 (Spring 1997), 46–80.

19. *Resolution 827 (1993)*, U.N. Security Council, S/RES/827 (1993), May 25, 1993; Goldstone, "Prosecuting Rape as a War Crime," 278.

20. ICTY Rule 96.

21. Goldstone, "Prosecuting Rape as a War Crime," 278.

22. Richard Goldstone interview, March 19, 2014.

23. Ibid.

24. Patricia Viseur Sellers, interview by Susana SáCouto, June 1, 2016, International Center for Ethics, Justice and Public Life, Robert D. Farber University Archives and Special Collections Department, Brandeis University, 20–21. This collection of oral history interviews can be accessed at http://www.brandeis.edu/ethics/internationaljustice/oral-history/index.html.

25. Sellers saw the support that Goldstone and Graham Blewitt provided for her work as crucial to its success (ibid., 23).

26. ICTY, *Second Annual Report of the International Tribunal for the Prosecution of Persons Responsible for Serious Violations of International Humanitarian Law Committed in the*

Territory of the Former Yugoslavia since 1991, U.N. A/50/365 S/1995/728, August 23, 1995, para. 122.

27. "Prosecute Bosnia's War Criminals," *New York Times*, January 4, 1995.

CHAPTER 9   THE PAPER TIGER

1. Claude Jorda of France was elected in 1994.

2. Michael P. Scharf, *Balkan Justice: The Story behind the First International War Crimes Trial since Nuremberg* (Durham, N.C.: Carolina Academic Press, 1997), 64–65; Daniel Terris and Leigh Swigart, "Who Are International Judges?," in *The Oxford Handbook of International Adjudication*, ed. Cesare P. R. Romano, Karen J. Alter, and Yuval Shany (Oxford: Oxford University Press, 2013), 619–638.

3. Richard Goldstone, interview by Daniel Terris, March 19, 2014; Gabrielle Kirk McDonald, interview by Daniel Terris, July 14, 2014.

4. Richard Goldstone and Noleen Goldstone, interview by Daniel Terris, May 10, 2014.

5. Graham Blewitt, interview by Daniel Terris, June 30, 2014.

6. Christian Chartier, personal communication to Daniel Terris, December 18, 2014.

7. Ibid.

8. Gary Jonathan Bass, *Stay the Hand of Vengeance: The Politics of War Crimes Tribunals* (Princeton, N.J.: Princeton University Press, 2000), 219.

9. Richard Goldstone interview, March 19, 2014; Graham Blewitt interview, June 30, 2014.

10. Pierre Hazan, *Justice in a Time of War: The True Story behind the International Criminal Tribunal for the Former Yugoslavia* (College Station: Texas A&M University Press, 2004).

11. Antonio Cassese, personal communication to Richard Goldstone, January 30, 1995.

12. Memo from Richard Goldstone to ICTY Judges, May 1, 1995. Typescript in Richard Goldstone's personal papers.

13. Gabrielle Kirk McDonald interview, July 14, 2014. Cassese and Abi-Saab made a similar case to Aryeh Neier, the head of the Open Society Foundations, a key private supporter of the ICTY. Aryeh Neier, interview by Daniel Terris, November 6, 2014.

14. ICTY, *Second Annual Report of the International Tribunal for the Prosecution of Persons Responsible for Serious Violations of International Humanitarian Law Committed in the Territory of the Former Yugoslavia since 1991*, U.N. A/50/365 S/1995/728, August 23, 1995.

15. Ian Traynor, "CIA Blames Serbs for Worst Terror," *Guardian*, March 10, 1995.

16. Cassese to Goldstone, January 30, 1995. Other letters from winter and spring 1995 discussed these topics.

17. Richard Goldstone, *For Humanity: Reflections of a War Crimes Investigator* (New Haven, Conn.: Yale University Press, 2000), 101.

18. Richard Goldstone memo to ICTY Judges, May 1, 1995.

19. Cassese to Goldstone, January 30, 1995.

20. Memo from Richard Goldstone to ICTY Judges, March 22, 1995.

21. It is not wholly clear which of the versions of this detailed dossier, if any, Goldstone circulated to the judges as a group.

22. Richard Goldstone interview, March 19, 2014.

23. Ibid.

24. Roger Cohen, "Tribunal to Cite Bosnia Serb Chief as War Criminal," *New York Times*, April 24, 1995.

25. Roger Cohen, "In the Dock: Balkan Nationalism," *New York Times*, April 30, 1995.

26. Elizabeth Odio Benito, personal communication to Richard Goldstone, May 2, 1995.

27. Richard Goldstone interview, March 19, 2014.

28. ICTY, *Second Annual Report*.

29. Minna Schrag, interview by Daniel Terris, May 1, 2014; Terree Bowers, interview by Daniel Terris, June 30, 2014.

30. Terree Bowers interview, June 30, 2014.

31. William Drozdiak, "Noted Jurist Says Bias Contains 'Seeds of Genocide'; South African Who Probed Police Abuses at Home Turns to War Crimes in Balkans, Rwanda," *Washington Post*, July 2, 1995.

32. This account is based on Rule 61 Hearing, *Prosecutor v. Radovan Karadžić and Ratko Mladić*, ICTY, IT-95-18-R61, July 5, 1996.

33. Drozdiak, "Noted Jurist Says Bias Contains 'Seeds of Genocide.'"

34. Minna Schrag interview, May 1, 2014.

35. Mirko Klarin, interview by Daniel Terris, May 7, 2014.

36. Bass, *Stay the Hand of Vengeance*, 229.

37. JJ Du Toit, interview by Daniel Terris, January 14, 2013; Richard Goldstone interview, March 19, 2014.

38. Richard Goldstone interview, March 19, 2014; Graham Blewitt interview, June 30, 2014; Bass, *Stay the Hand of Vengeance*, 229.

39. ICTY, *Second Annual Report*.

40. Anthony Lewis, "Abroad at Home: Crimes against Humanity," *New York Times*, July 28, 1995.

41. A. M. Rosenthal, "On My Mind; Arresting the Negotiators," *New York Times*, July 28, 1995.

42. Goldstone, *For Humanity*, 103.

CHAPTER 10   THE BARGAINING CHIP

1. John H. F. Shattuck, *Freedom on Fire: Human Rights Wars and America's Response* (Cambridge, Mass.: Harvard University Press, 2003), 157–160.

2. Gary Jonathan Bass, *Stay the Hand of Vengeance: The Politics of War Crimes Tribunals* (Princeton, N.J.: Princeton University Press, 2000), 231.

3. Richard C. Holbrooke, *To End a War* (New York: Random House, 1998), 107.

4. Wilbur G. Landrey, "Justice Promised for Bosnia Victims," *St. Petersburg Times*, October 22, 1995.

5. Ed Vulliamy, "In Times of Trial," *Guardian*, October 31, 1995.

6. Michael P. Scharf, *Balkan Justice: The Story behind the First International War Crimes Trial since Nuremberg* (Durham, N.C.: Carolina Academic Press, 1997), 87; Stephen Engelberg, "Panel Seeks U.S. Pledge on Bosnia War Criminals," *New York Times*, November 3, 1995.

7. Engelberg, "Panel Seeks U.S. Pledge on Bosnia War Criminals."

8. "Three 'JNA' Officers from a Belgrade-Based Brigade Charged with the Mass Killing of Non-Serb Men Forcibly Removed from the Vukovar Hospital," News Release, ICTY, November 9, 1995, http://www.icty.org/sid/7223.

9. "The Vice-President of Herceg-Bosna and Five Other Prominent Bosnian Croats Indicted for the 'Ethnic Cleansing' of the Lasva Valley Area," News Release, ICTY, November 13, 1995, http://www.icty.org/sid/7222.

10. Gabrielle Kirk McDonald, interview by Daniel Terris, July 14, 2014. Goldstone does not recollect the conversation, but does not deny that it took place. (Richard Goldstone interview by Daniel Terris, March 19, 2014.) The Lašva Valley indictments expanded those under indictment to Serbs and Croats. In the spring of 1996, Goldstone and the OTP issued indictments for war crimes committed by Bosnian Muslims in the Čelebići case.

11. Glyn Morgan, interview by David P. Briand and Leigh Swigart, May 25, 2015, Ad Hoc Tribunals Oral History Project, International Center for Ethics, Justice and Public Life, Robert D. Farber University Archives and Special Collections Department, Brandeis University. This collection of oral history interviews can be accessed at http://www.brandeis.edu/ethics/internationaljustice/oral-history/index.html.

12. Goldstone was right to worry. On October 20, U.S. satellite imagery revealed heavy excavation work of a large trench near Srebrenica. By October 30, the site had been smoothed over and the heavy equipment was gone. David Scheffer, *All the Missing Souls: A Personal History of the War Crimes Tribunals* (Princeton, N.J.: Princeton University Press, 2012), 41.

13. Michael Dobbs, "War Crimes Prosecutor Says U.S. Information Insufficient," *Washington Post*, November 7, 1995.

14. Scheffer, *All the Missing Souls*, 40. Scheffer also notes that on November 1, 1995, two days after Goldstone's letter was written and before it was published, the State Department delivered a large batch of new data to the ICTY.

15. Elaine Sciolino, "U.S. Says It Is Withholding Data from War Crimes Panel," *New York Times*, November 8, 1995.

16. "U.S. Promises Data to War Crimes Panel," *New York Times*, November 9, 1995.

17. Elaine Sciolino, "Clinton Makes Case to Congress for Putting U.S. Troops in Bosnia," *New York Times*, November 15, 1995.

18. Scheffer, *All the Missing Souls*, 40.

19. Indictment, *Prosecutor v. Radovan Karadžić and Ratko Mladić*, ICTY, IT-95-18-I, November 14, 1996.

20. Richard Goldstone interview, March 19, 2014.

21. Bass, *Stay the Hand of Vengeance*, 244.

22. Holbrooke, *To End a War*, 231–312.

23. Scharf, *Balkan Justice*, 88; Elaine Sciolino, "Bosnian Talks Snag on Fate of Two Serbs," *New York Times*, November 17, 1995.

24. Shattuck, *Freedom on Fire*, 206–213.

25. Elaine Sciolino, Roger Cohen, and Stephen Engelberg, "Balkan Accord: The Play-by-Play," *New York Times*, November 23, 1995.

26. Shattuck, *Freedom on Fire*, 212.

27. Scharf, *Balkan Justice*, 88.

28. *The General Framework Agreement for Peace in Bosnia and Herzegovina*, December 14, 1995, http://www.osce.org/bih/126173?download=true.

29. "The Tribunal Welcomes the Parties' Commitment to Justice," News Release, ICTY, November 24, 1995, http://www.icty.org/sid/7220.

30. Scheffer, *All the Missing Souls*, 132.

31. Aryeh Neier, *War Crimes: Brutality, Genocide, Terror, and the Struggle for Justice* (New York: Times Books, 1998).

32. Scheffer, *All the Missing Souls*, 130.

33. Theodor Meron, "Answering for War Crimes; Lessons from the Balkans," *Foreign Affairs* 76, no. 1 (1997), 2–8.

34. Jane Perlez, "NATO Backs Off Helping Bosnia War Crimes Panel," *New York Times*, January 20, 1996.

35. Ibid.

36. Eve-Ann Prentice, "NATO Joins Forces with War Crimes Teams to Seek Out Mass Graves," *The Times*, January 23, 1996; John Pomfret, "NATO, Prosecutor Debate Bosnia Aims," *Washington Post*, January 23, 1996.

37. Richard Goldstone, *For Humanity: Reflections of a War Crimes Investigator* (New Haven, Conn.: Yale University Press, 2000), 116.

38. Jane Perlez, "War Crimes Tribunal on Bosnia Is Hampered by Basic Problems," *New York Times*, January 28, 1996.

39. Richard Goldstone interview, March 19, 2014.

40. She is named in Indictment, *The Prosecutor against Drazen Erdemovic*, ICTY, IT-96-22, May 22, 1996.

41. See chapter 9.

42. Hagan, *Justice in the Balkans*, 76.

43. "Press Statement by Justice R.J. Goldstone," News Release, ICTY, March 7, 1996, http://www.icty.org/sid/7404.

44. Jon Swain, "Ghosts of Bosnia Wait for Justice," *Sunday Times*, May 26, 1996.

45. "Erdemovic and Kremenovic Transferred to the Hague," News Release, ICTY, March 30, 1996, http://www.icty.org/en/sid/7387.

46. Bass, *Stay the Hand of Vengeance*, 220.

47. "The Judges Request That the International Tribunal Be Exempted of Budgetary Remains," News Release, ICTY, October 9, 1995, http://www.icty.org/sid/7224.

48. Goldstone, *For Humanity*, 104.

49. Richard Goldstone interview, March 19, 2014.

50. "Nelson Mandela, U.N. Kingmaker?," *US News & World Report*, February 5, 1996. Goldstone always maintained a sense of humor about these speculations. Some sardonic critics began to refer to him publicly as "Richard-Richard," an allusion to his ostensible

bid to succeed Boutros Boutros-Ghali in the post. On at least one occasion, Goldstone called a newspaper office and announced himself as "Richard-Richard" to a startled reporter. David Beresford, "Goldstone to Take War Crimes Job," *Guardian*, July 9, 1994.

51. Goldstone, *For Humanity*, 117.

52. Graham Blewitt interview, June 30, 2014; Richard Goldstone interview, March 19, 2014.

53. Richard Goldstone interview, March 19, 2014.

54. *Resolution 1047*, U.N. Security Council, S/RES/1047(1996), February 23, 1996.

CHAPTER 11   IN THE DOCK

1. Louise McElvogue, "Court TV Prepares for Next Big Case," *Los Angeles Times*, November 13, 1995.

2. Richard Goldstone, interview by Daniel Terris, March 19, 2014.

3. Jonathan Freedland, "War Crimes Trial of Serb 'Torturer' Will Keep US Viewers Hooked," *Guardian*, September 28, 1995.

4. Michael P. Scharf, *Balkan Justice: The Story behind the First International War Crimes Trial since Nuremberg* (Durham, N.C.: Carolina Academic Press, 1997), 83.

5. Ed Vulliamy, "In Times of Trial," *Guardian*, October 31, 1995.

6. The prosecutor's request for a Rule 61 hearing was originally made in May 1995. See ICTY, *Second Annual Report of the International Tribunal for the Prosecution of Persons Responsible for Serious Violations of International Humanitarian Law Committed in the Territory of the Former Yugoslavia since 1991*, U.N. A/50/365 S/1995/728, August 23, 1995, para. 16.

7. On issues of translation at the ICTY, see Ellen Elias-Bursać, *Translating Evidence and Interpreting Testimony at a War Crimes Tribunal* (London: Palgrave Macmillan, 2015), and Ellen Elias-Bursać, interview by David P. Briand and Leigh Swigart, February 9, 2016, Ad Hoc Tribunals Oral History Project, International Center for Ethics, Justice and Public Life, Robert D. Farber University Archives and Special Collections Department, Brandeis University.

8. Review of Indictment Pursuant to Rule 61 of the Rules of Procedure and Evidence, *The Prosecutor of the Tribunal against Dragan Nikolić Also Known as "Jenki" Nikolić*, ICTY, IT-94-2-R61, October 20, 1995.

9. *Rules of Procedure and Evidence (Original Version)*, ICTY, February 11, 1994, http://www.icty.org/x/file/Legal%20Library/Rules_procedure_evidence/IT032_original_en.pdf.

10. See Gabrielle Kirk McDonald, interview by David P. Briand and Leigh Swigart, July 15, 2015, Ad Hoc Tribunals Oral History Project, International Center for Ethics, Justice and Public Life, Robert D. Farber University Archives and Special Collections Department, Brandeis University.

11. Goldstone's opening statement in Rule 61 Trial Transcript, *The Prosecutor of the Tribunal against Dragan Nikolić Also Known as "Jenki" Nikolić*, ICTY, IT-94-2-R61, October 9, 1995; Ian Traynor, "Serb War Crime Hearing Makes Legal History," *Guardian* October 10, 1995.

12. Richard Goldstone interview, March 19, 2014.

13. Review of Indictment, *Prosecutor v. Nikolić.*

14. Ibid.

15. Gabrielle Kirk McDonald, interview by Daniel Terris, July 14, 2014.

16. Trial Transcript, *The Prosecutor of the Tribunal against Kunarac et al. "Foča,"* ICTY, IT-96-23/1, April 4, 2000; Trial Judgment, *The Prosecutor of the Tribunal against Kunarac et al. "Foča,"* ICTY, IT-96-23/1, February 22, 2001.

17. Parallel cases were also developing under Goldstone's leadership in the Rwanda tribunal. See chapter 12.

18. ICTY, *Third Annual Report of the International Tribunal for the Prosecution of Persons Responsible for Serious Violations of International Humanitarian Law Committed in the Territory of the Former Yugoslavia since 1991,* U.N., A/51/292 S/1996/665, August 16, 1996, 10.

19. John Hagan, *Justice in the Balkans: Prosecuting War Crimes in the Hague Tribunal* (Chicago: University of Chicago Press, 2003), 81.

20. Richard Goldstone interview, March 19, 2014.

21. Freedland, "War Crimes Trial of Serb 'Torturer' Will Keep US Viewers Hooked."

22. For a detailed account of the assembly of the Tadić defense team, see Alphons Orie, interview by David P. Briand and Linda Carter, May 21, 2015, Ad Hoc Tribunals Oral History Project, International Center for Ethics, Justice and Public Life, Robert D. Farber University Archives and Special Collections Department, Brandeis University.

23. Richard Goldstone interview, March 19, 2014. Richard Goldstone, *For Humanity: Reflections of a War Crimes Investigator* (New Haven, Conn.: Yale University Press, 2000), 119.

24. Trial Transcript, *Prosecutor v. Duško Tadic a/k/a "Dule,"* ICTY, IT-94-1-T, May 7, 1996.

25. Hagan, *Justice in the Balkans,* 80.

26. Scharf, *Balkan Justice,* 120.

27. Gabrielle Kirk McDonald interview, July 15, 2015.

28. Scharf, *Balkan Justice,* 121.

29. There was evidence, however, that the televised coverage was reaching at least some viewers in the Balkans. See Julian Borger, "Bosnia Sees Justice Being Done," *Guardian,* June 12, 1996.

30. Richard Goldstone interview, March 19, 2014.

31. Hagan, *Justice in the Balkans,* 82.

32. Geoffrey Robertson, *Crimes against Humanity: The Struggle for Global Justice* (New York: New Press, 2000), 89; Gary Jonathan Bass, *Stay the Hand of Vengeance: The Politics of War Crimes Tribunals* (Princeton, N.J.: Princeton University Press, 2000), 207.

33. William Drozdiak, "Noted Jurist Says Bias Contains 'Seeds of Genocide'; South African Who Probed Police Abuses at Home Turns to War Crimes in Balkans, Rwanda," *Washington Post,* July 2, 1995.

34. The *Čelebići* case was the first prosecution of Bosnian Muslims for war crimes committed against Serbs. See Trial Judgment, *Prosecutor v. Mucić and Others ("Čelebići"),* ICTY, IT-96-21, November 16, 1998.

CHAPTER 12   RWANDA

1. This account draws on Judgment, *Prosecutor v. Théoneste Bagosora and Others*, ICTR, ICTR-98-41-T, December 18, 2008, pp. 176–183.

2. Jerry Gray, "Rwanda Plans to Try Thousands for Massacres, New Leader Says," *New York Times*, August 3, 1994.

3. Paul Lewis, "Rwanda Agrees to a U.N. War-Crimes Tribunal," *New York Times*, August 9, 1994; John H. F. Shattuck, *Freedom on Fire: Human Rights Wars and America's Response* (Cambridge, Mass.: Harvard University Press, 2003), 64–68.

4. David Scheffer, *All the Missing Souls: A Personal History of the War Crimes Tribunals* (Princeton, N.J.: Princeton University Press, 2012), 76–77.

5. Raymond Bonner, "U.N. Commission Recommends Rwanda 'Genocide' Tribunal," *New York Times*, September 29, 1994.

6. Scheffer, *All the Missing Souls*, 79.

7. Chris McGreal, "Rwanda and UN Clash on War Trials," *Guardian*, November 5, 1994.

8. *Resolution 955*, U.N. Security Council, S/RES/955, November 8, 1994, https://documents-dds-ny.un.org/doc/UNDOC/GEN/N95/140/97/PDF/N9514097ċ.pdf?OpenElement.

9. Catherine Cissé, interview by Daniel Terris, May 8, 2014.

10. Jon Henley, "War Crimes Judge Says Rwanda a Simpler Task than Yugoslavia," *Guardian*, November 19, 1994.

11. Richard Goldstone, *For Humanity: Reflections of a War Crimes Investigator* (New Haven, Conn.: Yale University Press, 2000), 111.

12. Richard Goldstone, interview by Daniel Terris, March 19, 2014.

13. He made fourteen trips over the course of his tenure. Goldstone, *For Humanity*, 113.

14. *Resolution 955*, Article 15.

15. Richard Goldstone interview, March 19, 2014.

16. Goldstone, *For Humanity*, 114.

17. Richard Goldstone interview, March 19, 2014.

18. ICTR, *Report of the International Criminal Tribunal for the Prosecution of Persons Responsible for Genocide and Other Serious Violations of International Humanitarian Law Committed in the Territory of Rwanda and Rwandan Citizens Responsible for Genocide and Other Such Violations Committed in the Territory of Neighbouring States between 1 January and 31 December 1994*, U.N., S/1996/778, September 24, 1996, para. 12 (hereafter *Annual Report 1996*).

19. Paul Lewis, "U.N. Report Comes Down Hard on Rwandan Genocide Tribunal," *New York Times*, February 13, 1997.

20. Richard Goldstone interview, March 19, 2014.

21. Graham Blewitt, interview by Daniel Terris, June 30, 2014.

22. In February 1997, four months after Richard Goldstone had left his post as chief prosecutor, the internal investigations office of the U.N. delivered a scathing report on the management of the ICTR. The report listed a litany of failures: poor employment practices, budget irregularities, and a series of personality clashes that hindered the effective-

ness of both the prosecutor's office in Kigali and the main administrative office of the tribunal in Arusha. The principal blame in the report landed on the deputy prosecutor and the registrar—both of them appointed by Boutros Boutros-Ghali. The new secretary-general, Kofi Annan, fired both men within weeks of the report. While Richard Goldstone did not bear direct responsibility, these lapses occurred on his watch. It was difficult for him to view the achievements in Arusha with the same pride that he had about the survival and the achievements of the Yugoslavia court in The Hague. See Lewis, "U.N. Report Comes Down Hard on Rwandan Genocide Tribunal."

23. "Statement of Dr. Andronico O. Adede, Registrar of the ICTR, Announcing the Tribunal's First Indictment," News Release, ICTR, December 12, 1995, http://unictr.unmict .org/en/news/statement-dr-andronico-o-adede-registrar-ictr-announcing-tribunals -first-indictment.

24. Ibid.

25. "400 Suspects Listed in '94 Rwanda Killings," *New York Times*, April 6, 1995.

26. "Statement of Dr. Andronico O. Adede, Registrar of the ICTR, Announcing the Tribunal's First Indictment."

27. Scheffer, *All the Missing Souls*, 109.

28. Ibid., 110.

29. *Resolution 978*, U.N. Security Council, S/RES/978 February 27, 1995, https:// documents-dds-ny.un.org/doc/UNDOC/GEN/N95/054/92/PDF/N9505492.pdf ?OpenElement.

30. ICTR, *Annual Report 1996*, para. 51–56.

31. Donatella Lorch, "Kenya Refuses to Hand Over Suspects in Rwanda Slayings," *New York Times*, October 6, 1996.

32. Barbara Crossette, "Rwanda Atrocity Inquiries Focus on Former Officer," *New York Times*, March 28, 1996.

33. Goldstone, *For Humanity*, 112.

34. Richard Goldstone interview, March 19, 2014.

35. Madeline Morris, "The Trials of Concurrent Jurisdiction: The Case of Rwanda," *Duke Journal of Comparative & International Law* 7 (1997), 349–374.

36. These costly, fruitless plane flights later become, unfairly, one of the items for which the ICTR was taken to task by a U.N. investigation into the mismanagement of funds at the tribunal.

37. James C. McKinley, "Rwanda War Crimes Tribunal Indicts 2 Men in Jail in Zambia," *New York Times*, February 20, 1996.

38. Trial Judgment, *The Prosecutor versus Jean-Paul Akayesu*, ICTR, ICTR-96-4-T, February 2, 1998.

39. Diane Marie Amann, "International Decisions: Prosecutor v. Akayesu, Case ICTR-96-4-T, International Criminal Tribunal for Rwanda, September 2, 1998," *American Journal of International Law* 93(1999), 195–199.

40. Trial Judgment, *The Prosecutor versus Jean-Paul Akayesu*.

41. John Hagan, *Justice in the Balkans: Prosecuting War Crimes in the Hague Tribunal* (Chicago: University of Chicago Press, 2003), 93.

42. ICTY, *Third Annual Report of the International Tribunal for the Prosecution of Persons Responsible for Serious Violations of International Humanitarian Law Committed in the Territory of the Former Yugoslavia since 1991*, U.N., A/51/292 S/1996/665, August 16, 1996.

43. Theodor Meron et al., "Where Do We Go from Here? New and Emerging Issues in the Prosecution of War Crimes and Acts of Terrorism: A Panel Discussion," *Social Research* 69, no. 4 (2002), 1177–1206.

44. Richard Goldstone, "Assessing the Work of the United Nations War Crimes Tribunals," *Stanford Journal of International Law* 33, no. 1 (1997), 8.

CHAPTER 13   GLOBETROTTER

1. Mandela's speech can be found at http://www.sahistory.org.za/archive/speech-president -nelson-mandela-inauguration-constitutional-court-johannesburg-14-february-1.

2. The court ruled that the death penalty was unconstitutional. Judgment, *The State versus T. Makwanyane and M. Mchunu*, Constitutional Court of South Africa, CCT/3/94, June 6, 1995.

3. The history and links to the text can be found at https://www.concourt.org.za/index .php/constitution/the-text.

4. Judgment, *National Coalition for Gay and Lesbian Equality and Another v Minister of Justice and Others*, Constitutional Court of South Africa, CCT 11/98, October 9, 1998; and Judgment, *National Coalition for Gay and Lesbian Equality and Others v Minister of Home Affairs and Others*, Constitutional Court of South Africa, CCT 10/99, December 2, 1999.

5. Judgment, *August and Another v Electoral Commission and Others*, Constitutional Court of South Africa, CCT 8/99, April 1, 1999.

6. Judgment, *Minister of Health and Others v Treatment Action Campaign and Others (No 1)*, Constitutional Court of South Africa, CCT 9/2002, July 5, 2002.

7. Kate O'Regan, interview by Daniel Terris, January 8, 2013.

8. Albie Sachs, interview by Daniel Terris, September 11, 2014.

9. Richard Goldstone, interview by Daniel Terris, January 13, 2013.

10. See chapter 18.

11. Judgment, *President of the Republic of South Africa and Another v Hugo*, Constitutional Court of South Africa, CCT 11/96, April 18, 1997.

12. "Goldstone Clears Truth Commissioner," News Release, South African Press Association, December 2, 1997, http://www.justice.gov.za/trc/media%5C1997%5C9712 /s971202n.htm.

13. See http://www.brandeis.edu/ethics/internationaljustice/biij/index.html.

14. See, generally, for this section, Independent International Commission on Kosovo, *The Kosovo Report: Conflict, International Response, Lessons Learned* (Oxford: Oxford University Press, 2000).

15. Goldstone's involvement was at the request of Swedish prime minister Goran Persson, and he was encouraged to accept the position by both Nelson Mandela and court president Arthur Chaskalson.

16. Independent International Commission on Kosovo, *Kosovo Report*, 8.

17. See Daniel Terris and Galia Golan, "Introduction," in *The Responsibility to Protect at 10: The Challenge of Protecting the World's Most Vulnerable Populations*, ed. Daniel Terris and Galia Golan (Brandeis University, 2015), https://www.brandeis.edu/ethics/pdfs/internationaljustice/r2p/march%202015%20papers/r2p-intro.pdf.

18. Chris Barron, "US Invasion of Iraq Puts International Law at Risk," *Sunday Times*, March 30, 2003. Goldstone also spoke out against what he considered excesses of the U.S. war on terrorism, and also on the U.S. position on torture. See Richard Goldstone, "International Law and Justice and America's War on Terrorism," *Social Research* 69, no. 4 (2002), 1045–1054; and Richard Goldstone, "Combating Terrorism: Zero Tolerance for Torture," *Case Western Reserve Journal of International Law* 37 (2006), 343–348.

19. Kate O'Regan interview, January 8, 2013.

20. Richard Goldstone interview, January 13, 2013.

21. A copy of the tribute remarks by Deputy Chief Justice Pius Langa is in Richard Goldstone's personal papers.

22. Goldstone, "Combating Terrorism: Zero Tolerance for Torture."

23. Theodor Meron et al., "Where Do We Go from Here? New and Emerging Issues in the Prosecution of War Crimes and Acts of Terrorism: A Panel Discussion," *Social Research* 69, no. 4 (2002), 1177–1206; Richard Goldstone, "Advances in International Human Rights Law," *International Law Forum du droit international* 6 (2004), 136–140.

24. For this section, see, generally, Jeffrey A. Meyer and Mark G. Califano, *Good Intentions Corrupted: The Oil-for-Food Program and the Threat to the U.N.* (New York: Public Affairs, 2006).

25. Richard Goldstone, interview by Daniel Terris, April 22, 2014.

26. The dispute involving the two staff members who interviewed Kofi Annan became public when the pair resigned, taking with them confidential documents and hurrying to Washington, D.C., to make their case to Congress. Goldstone was convinced that the investigators had prejudged Annan, and his view carried the day in the commission's report.

27. Richard Goldstone interview, April 22, 2014.

28. Goldstone's responsibilities on the OFP Commission, which involved administration of the project's sensitive archives, continued until 2013.

CHAPTER 14   CAST LEAD

1. *Public Hearings in Geneva*, U.N. Fact Finding Mission on the Gaza Conflict, July 6, 2009, Morning Session, http://www.ohchr.org/EN/HRBodies/HRC/SpecialSessions/Session9/Pages/FactFindingMission.aspx.

2. Sheryl Gay Stolberg and Ethan Bronner, "Rocket Hits City in Israel as Bush Hails Anniversary," *New York Times*, May 15, 2008; Yaakov Katz, "Ashkelon Early Warning System Was Disconnected Weeks Ago," *Jerusalem Post*, May 15, 2008; Yaakov Katz, Herb Keinon, and Yaakov Lappin, "As Bush Meets PM, Rocket Strikes Ashkelon Mall," *Jerusalem Post*, May 15, 2008.

3. This account is based on *Human Rights in Palestine and Other Occupied Arab Territories: Report on the United Nations Fact-Finding Mission on the Gaza Conflict*, HRC, A/HRC/12/48, September 25, 2009, paras. 653–703. A link to this report is available at https://www.ohchr.org/EN/HRBodies/HRC/SpecialSessions/Session9/Pages/FactFindingMission.aspx. See also Taghreed El-Khodary, "Gazans Express Grief and Rage over Deaths Outside U.N. School," *New York Times*, January 9, 2009.

4. Taghreed El-Khodary and Isabel Kershner, "Israeli Shells Kill 40 at Gaza U.N. School," *New York Times*, January 7, 2009.

5. Ibid.

6. *The Operation in Gaza: Factual and Legal Aspects*, Israeli Ministry of Foreign Affairs, July 2009, http://www.mfa.gov.il/MFA_Graphics/MFA%20Gallery/Documents/Gaza Operation%20w%20Links.pdf, p. 5.

7. *Human Rights in Palestine*, paras. 181–183.

8. The name of Operation Cast Lead ("Oferet Yetzukah") echoes a poem by Chaim Bialik: "My teacher gave me a dreidel / Cast in lead / Do you know why he did so? / To celebrate Chanukah!"

9. El-Khodary and Kershner, "Israeli Shells Kill 40 at Gaza U.N. School."

10. *Report of the Human Rights Council on Its Ninth Special Session*, U.N., A/HRC/S-9/2, February 27, 2009, http://www.ohchr.org/EN/HRBodies/HRC/SpecialSessions/Session9/Pages/9thSpecialSession.aspx.

11. Robb London, "Life, Liberty, and the Pursuit of Dignity," *Harvard Law Today*, October 22, 2008.

12. Much of this account of Goldstone's decision to chair the Fact-Finding Mission is from an interview I conducted with Richard Goldstone on April 12, 2012.

13. "Gaza: World's Leading Investigators Call for War Crimes Inquiry," United Nations Information System on the Question of Palestine, https://unispal.un.org/DPA/DPR/unispal.nsf/0/F4CB07EBCC6183828525757F004FD965. The letter was released to the public on March 16, 2009, after Goldstone received the request described below from Navi Pillay, but before he had been named as chair of the Mission.

14. Ibid., para. 364.

15. See chapter 12.

16. Richard Goldstone, personal communication to Navi Pillay, March 9, 2009.

17. Geoffrey Mansell interview, January 4, 2013; Claudia Braude, "Goldstone's Gambit: The Man Behind U.N. Report," *Forward*, September 16, 2009.

18. The account of this one-on-one conversation is based on my interviews with Richard Goldstone, supplemented by my interview with Navi Pillay on October 30, 2014. I was unable to reach Martin Uhomoibhi to hear the account from his perspective.

19. "Near Verbatim Transcript of Press Conference by the President of the Human Rights Council, Martin Ihoeghian Uhomoibhi (Nigeria) and Justice Richard J. Goldstone on the Announcement of the Human Rights Council Fact-Finding Mission on the Conflict in the Gaza Strip," News Release, U.N., April 3, 2009. A link to this transcript is available at https://www.ohchr.org/EN/HRBodies/HRC/SpecialSessions/Session9/Pages/FactFindingMission.aspx.

20. *Rain of Fire: Israel's Unlawful Use of White Phosphorus in Gaza*, Human Rights Watch, March 25, 2009, https://www.hrw.org/report/2009/03/25/rain-fire/israels-unlawful-use -white-phosphorus-gaza. Human Rights Watch also published a report in August 2009 on the impact of rocket fire from Gaza on Israeli civilians. See *Rockets from Gaza: Harm to Civilians from Palestinian Armed Groups' Rocket Attacks*, Human Rights Watch, August 2009, https://www.hrw.org/report/2009/08/06/rockets-gaza/harm-civilians -palestinian-armed-groups-rocket-attacks.

21. *Evidence of the Use of the Civilian Population as Human Shields*, Meir Amit Intelligence and Terrorism Information Center at the Israeli Intelligence Heritage and Commemoration Center, February 4, 2009, http://www.terrorism-info.org.il/en/18321.

22. *Summary by the Secretary-General of the Report of the United Nations Headquarters Board of Inquiry into Certain Incidents in the Gaza Strip between 27 December 2008 and 19 January 2009*, U.N., A/63/855-S/2009/250, May 15, 2009.

23. Alan Baker, "Goldstone Mission Just Another Unfair UN Fact-Finding Farce, I'm Afraid," *Jerusalem Post*, April 13, 2009.

24. Avi Bell, "Let's Seek a True Legal Investigation of the Gaza War," *Jerusalem Post*, April 17, 2009.

25. "The Speech Banned as 'Inadmissible' by the U.N. Human Rights Council," UN Watch, https://www.unwatch.org/speech/.

26. "UN Watch Calls on Goldstone Gaza Inquiry to Denounce Biased Mandate," News Release, UN Watch, May 5, 2009, https://www.unwatch.org/un-watch-calls-goldstone -gaza-inquiry-denounce-biased-mandate/.

27. Baker, "Goldstone Mission."

28. Paul Gordon Lauren, "To Preserve and Build on Its Achievements and to Redress Its Shortcomings: The Journey from the Commission on Human Rights to the Human Rights Council," *Human Rights Quarterly* 29, no. 2 (2007), 307–345.

29. Felice D. Gaer and Christen Broecker, eds., *The United Nations High Commissioner for Human Rights: Conscience for the World* (Leiden: Brill, 2014), 225. Overall, in its first ten years (2006–2016), the HRC devoted 33 percent of its country-specific special sessions and 29 percent of its country-specific resolutions to Israel. See *Country-Specific Scrutiny by the UN Human Rights Council: Changes Documented During US Membership, 2009–2015*, Jacob Blaustein Institute for the Advancement of Human Rights, February 2, 2016, http://www.jbi-humanrights.org/jacob-blaustein-institute/2016/02/country-specific -scrutiny-by-the-un-human-rights-council-changes-documented-during-us-membership -200.html.

30. *Report of the Human Rights Council on Its Ninth Special Session*, U.N. HRC, February 27, 2009.

31. The United States, under President George W. Bush, had chosen not to stand for election to the group, and was therefore not a member in January 2009.

32. Netanyahu took office on March 31, 2009.

33. *Human Rights in Palestine*, para. 434.

34. Ibid., para. 436.

35. Ibid., paras. 446–448.

36. Richard Goldstone interview, April 22, 2014.

37. Daniel Reisner, interview by Daniel Terris, December 21, 2014.

CHAPTER 15   GAZA

1. For biographical information on all of the Mission members, see "United Nations Fact Finding Mission on the Gaza Conflict," http://www.ohchr.org/EN/HRBodies/HRC/SpecialSessions/Session9/Pages/FactFindingMission.aspx.

2. Hilary Charlesworth, Christine Chinkin, and Shelley Wright, "Feminist Approaches to International Law," *American Journal of International Law* 85, no. 4 (1991), 613–645.

3. Christine Chinkin, "The Legality of NATO's Action in the Former Republic of Yugoslavia (FRY) under International Law," *International and Comparative Law Quarterly* 49, no. 4 (2000), 910–925.

4. *Report of the High-Level Fact-Finding Mission to Beit Hanoun Established under Council Resolution S-3/1*, HRC, A/HRC/9/26, September 1, 2008.

5. "Asma Jahangir and Hina Jilani," Robert F. Kennedy Center for Justice and Human Rights, http://rfkcenter.org/asma-jahangir-e-hina-jilani.

6. Desmond Travers, interview by Hanan Chehata, 2010, *Middle East Monitor*, February 2, 2010, https://hananchehata.wordpress.com/2010/02/02/gaza-is-the-only-gulag-in-the-western-hemisphere-maintained-by-democracies-closed-off-from-food-water-air-says-colonel-desmond-travers-co-author-of-the-goldstone-report-in-an-exclusive-memo/. Travers was a last-minute substitute for appointment to the mission; an Irish general had withdrawn for health reasons.

7. Desmond Travers, interview by Daniel Terris, October 20, 2014.

8. *House of Cards: NGOs and the Goldstone Report*, NGO Monitor, October 1, 2009, https://www.ngo-monitor.org/reports/_house_of_cards_ngos_and_the_goldstone_report.

9. This section draws on Nathan Shachar, *The Gaza Strip: Its History and Politics: From the Pharaohs to the Israeli Invasion of 2009* (Brighton: Sussex Academic Press, 2010), and Jean-Pierre Filiu, *Gaza: A History* (Oxford: Oxford University Press, 2014).

10. Shachar, *Gaza Strip*, 23.

11. Ibid., 48–49.

12. Ibid., 79.

13. *CIA World Factbook*, 2009, https://www.cia.gov/library/publications/download/download-2009.

14. "Justice Richard Goldstone and Former Israeli Ambassador Dore Gold Discuss the U.N. Gaza Report," News Release, Brandeis University, November 6, 2009.

15. Richard Goldstone, interview by Daniel Terris, November 6, 2014.

16. "UN Investigator 'Shocked' by Scale of Destruction in Gaza," *Haaretz*, June 4, 2009; E. B. Solomont, "As UN Team Enters Gaza, Barak Insists Israel Won't Cooperate," *Jerusalem Post*, June 2, 2009.

17. Richard Goldstone interview, November 6, 2014.

18. "Justice Richard Goldstone and Former Israeli Ambassador Dore Gold Discuss the U.N. Gaza Report."

19. *Chronological Review of Events Relating to the Question of Palestine*, U.N. Division for Palestinian Rights, June, 2009, https://unispal.un.org/DPA/DPR/unispal.nsf/0/0BAC 855C16904DAA852575F3004BFE25.

20. "Goldstone: Israeli Refusal Will Not Stop Gaza Probe," *Ma'an News*, June 4, 2009.

21. Richard Goldstone interview, November 6, 2014.

22. See, among many others, Dan Kosky, "Goldstone's Sins of Omission," *Guardian*, September 16, 2009.

23. Christine Chinkin, interview by Daniel Terris, October 29, 2014.

24. *Human Rights in Palestine and Other Occupied Arab Territories: Report on the United Nations Fact-Finding Mission on the Gaza Conflict*, HRC, A/HRC/12/48, September 25, 2009, http://www.ohchr.org/EN/HRBodies/HRC/SpecialSessions/Session9/Pages /FactFindingMission.aspx., paras. 822–843.

25. *Conclusion of Investigations into Central Claims and Issues in Operation Cast Lead-Part 2*, Israeli Ministry of Foreign Affairs, April 22, 2009, http://mfa.gov.il/MFA/ForeignPolicy /Terrorism/Pages/Conclusion_of_%20Investigations_into_Central_Claims_and _Issues_in_Operation_Cast_Lead-Part2_22-Apr-200.aspx.

26. Richard Goldstone interview, November 6, 2014.

27. *Public Hearings in Gaza*, U.N. Fact-Finding Mission on the Gaza Conflict, June 28, 2009, Morning Session, http://www.ohchr.org/EN/HRBodies/HRC/SpecialSessions /Session9/Pages/FactFindingMission.aspx.

28. Ibid.

29. Michael Lerner, "Interview with Richard Goldstone," *Tikkun*, October 1, 2009.

30. *Human Rights in Palestine*, paras. 706–735.

31. Taghreed El-Khodary and Isabel Kershner, "For Arab Clan, Days of Agony in a Cross-Fire," *New York Times*, January 10, 2009.

32. Rory McCarthy, "Amid Dust and Death, a Family's Story Speaks for the Terror of War," *Guardian*, January 19, 2009.

33. El-Khodary and Kershner, "For Arab Clan, Days of Agony in a Cross-Fire."

34. Michael Bleby, "Goldstone Walks a Fine Line in an Ancient War Zone," *Business Day*, August 4, 2009.

35. *Public Hearings in Gaza*, June 28–29, 2009.

36. *Public Hearings in Geneva*, U.N. Fact-Finding Mission on the Gaza Conflict, July 6–7, 2009, http://www.ohchr.org/EN/HRBodies/HRC/SpecialSessions/Session9/Pages /FactFindingMission.aspx.

37. "Justice Richard Goldstone and Former Israeli Ambassador Dore Gold Discuss the U.N. Gaza Report."

38. Hillel Neuer and Melissa Cramer, "A Case Study in UN Hypocrisy," *National Post* (Canada), July 17, 2009.

39. Richard Goldstone interview, November 6, 2014; Desmond Travers interview, October 20, 2014.

40. Richard Goldstone interview, November 6, 2014.

41. Christine Chinkin interview, October 29, 2014; Desmond Travers interview, October 20, 2014.

42. Bleby, "Goldstone Walks a Fine Line in an Ancient War Zone."

CHAPTER 16   THE GOLDSTONE REPORT

1. The September 15 version was a preliminary release. The version cited in this volume is the official version released on September 25. *Human Rights in Palestine and Other Occupied Arab Territories: Report on the United Nations Fact-Finding Mission on the Gaza Conflict*, HRC, A/HRC/12/48, September 25, 2009, https://www.ohchr.org/EN/HRBodies/HRC/SpecialSessions/Session9/Pages/FactFindingMission.aspx.

2. Ibid., para. 159.

3. Ibid., para. 150.

4. Ibid., para. 185. Israel has generally preferred to use the word "fence" or the phrase "security barrier."

5. Ibid., paras. 596–652.

6. Ibid., paras. 653–703.

7. Ibid., paras. 903–1031.

8. Ibid., paras. 704–885.

9. For the discussion of intent, see ibid., paras. 1177–1216 and 1880–1895.

10. Ibid., paras. 1192–1199.

11. Ibid., paras. 1204–1205.

12. Ibid., paras. 802–808.

13. Breaking the Silence, *Soldiers' Testimonies from Operation Cast Lead, Gaza, 2009*, June 2009, http://www.breakingthesilence.org.il/testimonies/publications.

14. By putting the word in quotation marks in the text, the authors were apparently conceding that they had found no official expression or endorsement of these practices.

15. *Human Rights in Palestine*, para. 812.

16. According to the statute of the ICC, "The Court shall have jurisdiction in respect of war crimes in particular when committed as part of a plan or policy or as part of a large-scale commission of such crimes." "Rome Statute of the International Criminal Court," (1998), Article 8, Section 1.

17. *Human Rights in Palestine*, paras. 439–498.

18. "In this respect, the operations were in furtherance of an overall policy aimed at punishing the Gaza population for its resilience and for its apparent support for Hamas, and possibly with the intent of forcing a change in such support. The Mission considers this position to be firmly based in fact, bearing in mind what it saw and heard on the ground, what it read in the accounts of soldiers who served in the campaign, and what it heard and read from current and former military officers and political leaders whom the Mission considers to be representative of the thinking that informed the policy and strategy of the military operations" (ibid., para. 1884).

19. Richard Goldstone, "Statement by Richard Goldstone on Behalf of the Members of the United Nations Fact Finding Mission on the Gaza Conflict," News Release, HRC, September 29, 2009.

20. As distinct from war crimes, which could involve incidents on a smaller scale and without the standard of "systematic" attack against a population.

21. *Human Rights in Palestine*, paras. 1300–1335.

22. Ibid., paras. 1682–1691.

23. Goldstone, "Statement by Richard Goldstone on Behalf of the Members of the United Nations Fact Finding Mission on the Gaza Conflict."

CHAPTER 17   OUTRAGE

1. Neil MacFarquhar, "Inquiry Finds Gaza War Crimes from Both Sides," *New York Times*, September 16, 2009.

2. Haviv Rettig Gur, "UN Probe Alleges Israeli Crimes against Humanity in Gaza," *Jerusalem Post*, September 16, 2009.

3. Donald Macintyre, "Israelis Hit Back at UN Report Alleging War Crimes in Gaza," *Independent*, September 17, 2009.

4. David Harris, "The Goldstone Report: Three Strikes and You're Out!," *Huffington Post*, https://www.huffingtonpost.com/david-harris/the-goldstone-report-thre_b_291480 .html.

5. Max Boot, "The Goldstone Report," *Commentary*, September 16, 2009.

6. Ehud Barak, "At the UN, Terrorism Pays," *Wall Street Journal*, September 25, 2009.

7. See Galit Raguan, "Adjudicating Armed Conflict in Domestic Courts: The Experience of Israel's Supreme Court," in *Yearbook of International Humanitarian Law Volume 13, 2010*, ed. M. N. Schmitt, L. Arimatsu, and T. McCormack (The Hague: Asser Institute, 2011), 61–95; and David Kretzmer, *The Occupation of Justice: The Supreme Court of Israel and the Occupied Territories* (Albany: State University of New York Press, 2002).

8. Isabel Kershner and Neil MacFarquhar, "Israel Rejects Findings of U.N. Inquiry on Gaza War," *New York Times*, September 17, 2009.

9. *Guidelines for Israel's Investigation into Operation Cast Lead*, B'Tselem, February, 2009, https://www.btselem.org/download/200902_operation_cast_lead_position_paper _eng.pdf.

10. Haviv Rettig Gur, "B'tselem: Goldstone Report Wrong in Its Fundamental Accusations against Israel," *Jerusalem Post*, September 30, 2009.

11. *Israel Today* columnist Dan Margalit, quoted in the *Sydney Morning Herald*, September 17, 2009, and quoted in the *Australian*, October 20, 2009.

12. Charles Abelsohn, quoted in Gur, "UN Probe Alleges Israeli Crimes against Humanity in Gaza."

13. Kim Hawkey, "Jews Say Goldstone Is a 'Modern Cain,'" *Sunday Times*, October 4, 2009.

14. "Dershowitz: Goldstone Is a Traitor to the Jewish People," *Haaretz*, January 31, 2010.

15. Kershner and MacFarquhar, "Israel Rejects Findings of U.N. Inquiry on Gaza War"; Brendan Boyle, "Goldstone Denies He Betrayed Jewish State," *Sunday Times*, November 15, 2009.

16. Yossi Alpher, "The Goldstone Disconnect," *Forward*, October 2, 2009.

17. Ethan Bronner, "Israel Poised to Challenge a U.N. Report on Gaza," *New York Times*, January 23, 2010.

18. Larry Derfner, "A Wake-Up Call from Judge Goldstone," *Jerusalem Post*, September 16, 2009.

19. Amira Hass, "The One Thing Worse Than Denying the Gaza Report," *Haaretz*, September 16, 2009.

20. Roger Cohen, "An Ordinary Israel," *New York Times*, October 16, 2009.

21. Jimmy Carter, "Goldstone and Gaza," *New York Times*, November 6, 2009.

22. Kershner and MacFarquhar, "Israel Rejects Findings of U.N. Inquiry on Gaza War."

23. MacFarquhar, "Inquiry Finds Gaza War Crimes from Both Sides."

24. "Islamic Jihad Chief Views Goldstone Report, Abbas Position, Palestinian Division," *BBC Monitoring Middle East*, October 9, 2009.

25. Ramzy Baroud, "Justice at Last?," *Khaleej Times*, September 24, 2009.

26. Mary Robinson, "Accounting for Gaza," *Daily News Egypt*, October 6, 2009.

27. Richard Goldstone, "Justice in Gaza," *New York Times*, September 17, 2009.

28. Richard Goldstone, "Who's Being Unfair?," *Jerusalem Post*, September 21, 2009.

29. Richard Goldstone, interview by Bill Moyers, October 23, 2009, *Bill Moyers Journal*, http://www.pbs.org/moyers/journal/10232009/transcript1.html?print, part 1, p. 3; Sharon Otterman, "Gaza Report Author Asks U.S. to Clarify Concerns," *New York Times*, October 23, 2009.

30. Gal Beckerman, "Goldstone: 'If This Was a Court of Law, There Would Have Been Nothing Proven,'" *Forward*, October 7, 2009.

31. Tovah Lazaroff, "UN Report a 21st Century Blood Libel, Scholar Says in Geneva," *Jerusalem Post*, September 30, 2009.

32. Richard Goldstone, interview by Bill Moyers, October 23, 2009, Part 1, 6.

33. Michael Lerner, "Interview with Richard Goldstone," *Tikkun*, October 1, 2009.

34. Errol and Ruth Friedmann, interview by Daniel Terris, January 9, 2013; Benas Levy, interview by Daniel Terris, January 5, 2013.

35. Nicole Goldstone, interview by Daniel Terris, November 12, 2012; Benas Levy interview, January 5, 2013.

36. Nicole Goldstone, personal communication to Richard and Noleen Goldstone, October 4, 2009, in Richard Goldstone's papers.

37. Richard Goldstone, personal communication to Nicole Goldstone, October 4, 2009, in Richard Goldstone's papers.

38. Nicole Goldstone interview, November 12, 2012.

39. Richard Goldstone, "Statement by Richard Goldstone on Behalf of the Members of the United Nations Fact Finding Mission on the Gaza Conflict," News Release, HRC, September 29, 2009.

40. *Report of the Human Rights Council on Its Twelfth Session*, HRC, A/HRC/12/50, February 25, 2010.

41. She claimed only "two pages" for Israeli victims. But the whole section on Palestinian rocket fire into Israel actually comprised 20 of the 429 pages in the final version of the report. Mirela Siderer, "Statement by Mirela Siderer," News Release, HRC, September 29, 2009.

42. "Gaza Probe 'Fatal Blow' to Peace," *BBC News*, October 1, 2009.

43. Neil MacFarquhar, "Palestinians Halt Push on War Report," *New York Times*, October 2, 2009.

44. *Report of the Human Rights Council on Its Twelfth Session*.

45. MacFarquhar, "Palestinians Halt Push on War Report."

46. Isabel Kershner and Neil MacFarquhar, "Furor Sends Palestinians into Shift on U.N. Report," *New York Times*, October 8, 2009.

47. Tovah Lazaroff and Haviv Rettig Gur, "Israel: Resolution Endorsing One-Sided Gaza Report Harms Regional Peace Efforts," *Jerusalem Post*, October 18, 2009.

48. *Report of the Human Rights Council on Its Twelfth Session*.

49. David Landau, "The Gaza Report's Wasted Opportunity," *New York Times*, September 20, 2009.

50. Moshe Halbertal, "The Goldstone Illusion," *New Republic*, November 6, 2009.

51. Moshe Halbertal, interview by Daniel Terris, November 3, 2014.

52. Ibid.

53. See also Michael Walzer, "Responsibility and Proportionality in State and Nonstate Wars," *Parameters* (2009), 40–52 (written before the Goldstone Report).

54. Moshe Halbertal, personal communication to Daniel Terris, January 7, 2018.

CHAPTER 18   BAR MITZVAH

1. The Jewish population in South Africa had also declined precipitously in recent decades. By 2016, the Jewish population of the country was only 70,000, just over half of what it had been fifty years earlier. See Geoff Sifrin, "In Troubled Post-Mandela South Africa, a Fight or Flight Dilemma for the 70,000 Jews," *Times of Israel*, July 27, 2016.

2. Avrom Krengel, interview by Daniel Terris, January 15, 2013.

3. Avrom Krengel, "Goldstone Report," *South African Jewish Report*, September 25–October 2, 2009; Zev Krengel, "Israel Found Guilty from the Outset," *South African Jewish Report*, September 25–October 2, 2009.

4. Avrom Krengel interview, January 15, 2013. See chapter 16 for a clear refutation of Krengel's claim that the report had "no evidence to back it up."

5. Warren Goldstein, "It Looks Like Law, but It's Just Politics," *Jerusalem Post*, October 15, 2009; Warren Goldstein, "Report Replete with Procedural and Substantive Injustices," *South African Jewish Report*, October 30–November 6, 2009.

6. Gideon Shimoni, *Community and Conscience: The Jews in Apartheid South Africa* (Hanover, N.H.: Brandeis University Press, 2003).

7. Richard Goldstone, "Nelson Mandela, Iconic Leader for Jews of South Africa—and World," *Forward*, December 5, 2013.

8. *Report of the High-Level Fact-Finding Mission to Beit Hanoun Established under Council Resolution S-3/1*, HRC, A/HRC/9/26, September 1, 2008.

9. "Damning UN Report on Gaza Strike," *BBC*, http://news.bbc.co.uk/2/hi/middle _east/7623583.stm.

10. Amir Mizroch, "The Unforgiven," *Jerusalem Post*, October 2, 2009.

11. The South African Human Rights Commission did declare these statements "hate speech," the first time that anti-Israel statements had received that designation in South Africa. See Kevin Bloom, *Hating Goldstone: The Jewish Community against the Judge* (Johannesburg: Parktown Publishers, 2012), 22. In 2017 a court compelled Masuku to apologize. See Jeanette Chabalala, "Bongani Masuku Guilty of Hate Speech, Must Apologise to SA Jewish Board of Deputies," *News24*, June 29, 2017.

12. Mizroch, "The Unforgiven."

13. Chris Gevers, *Applying Universal Jurisdiction in SA Law*, Open Society Initiative for Southern Africa, April 25, 2012, http://www.osisa.org/law/blog/applying-universal -jurisdiction-sa-law.

14. *Human Rights in Palestine and Other Occupied Arab Territories: Report on the United Nations Fact-Finding Mission on the Gaza Conflict*, HRC, A/HRC/12/48, September 25, 2009, https://www.ohchr.org/EN/HRBodies/HRC/SpecialSessions/Session9/Pages /FactFindingMission.aspx, para. 185.

15. Ibid., footnote to para. 1855.

16. Benas Levy, interview by Daniel Terris, January 5, 2013; Geoffrey Mansell, interview by Daniel Terris, January 4, 2013.

17. Quoted in Arthur Chaskalson and George Bizos, "Chaskalson, Bizos Defend Goldstone," *IOL*, http://www.iol.co.za/news/politics/chaskalson-bizos-defend-goldstone-471161.

18. R. W. Johnson, "Who Is Richard Goldstone?," *Radio Free Europe*, October 20, 2009.

19. Bloom, *Hating Goldstone*, 8.

20. Ayal Rosenberg, "Goldstone: A Critique of Self-Apotheosis," October 9, 2009, http://www.scribd.com/doc/21359334/Goldstone-V2; Ayal Rosenberg, *Richard Goldstone: Apartheid Judge* (self-pub., Amazon Digital Services, 2012).

21. Tehiya Barak, "Judge Goldstone's Dark Past," *Yediot Aharanot*, May 10, 2010.

22. Ibid.

23. Nathan Guttman, "Israelis Condemn Goldstone's Role in South Africa during Apartheid; but His Supporters Say That He Worked to Dismantle the System," *Forward*, May 21, 2010.

24. See chapters 3–5.

25. Chaskalson and Bizos, "Chaskalson, Bizos Defend Goldstone."

26. See https://www.congress.gov/bill/111th-congress/house-resolution/867.

27. Glenda Goldstone Brener, interview by Daniel Terris, June 15, 2015.

28. Julian Brener, interview by Daniel Terris, June 15, 2015; Richard Goldstone, interview by Daniel Terris, January 13, 2013.

29. Avrom Krengel interview, January 15, 2013; Bloom, *Hating Goldstone*, 23.

30. Julian Brener interview, June 15, 2015.

31. Moira Schneider, "Goldstone 'Barred' from Grandson's Bar Mitzvah," *South African Jewish Report*, April 16–23, 2010.

32. Barry Bearak, "South African Judge May Be Kept from Grandson's Bar Mitzvah," *New York Times*, April 16, 2010.

33. Schneider, "Goldstone 'Barred' from Grandson's Bar Mitzvah."

34. "Judge Goldstone Deserves Our Support and Our Thanks," *Cape Times*, April 26, 2010.

35. Daniel Terris, "Attacking Richard Goldstone," *Los Angeles Times*, April 21, 2010.

36. Albie Sachs, "Address by Justice Albie Sachs to the Cape Town Press Club (April 21, 2010)," *Writing the Wrongs*, May 1, 2010, http://writingtw.blogspot.com/2010_04_25 _archive.html; "Sachs Breaks Silence on Goldstone Fracas," *Mail&Guardian*, April 22, 2010.

37. Avrom Krengel interview, January 15, 2013.

38. Siggi Suchard, personal communication to Richard Goldstone, April 16, 2010.

39. Warren Goldstein, "This Isn't about Goldstone, It's about Judaism," *Jerusalem Post*, April 22, 2010.

40. Richard Goldstone interview, January 13, 2013.

41. Quoted in Chris McGreal, "Goldstone Family Drawn into Row over Gaza Report," *Guardian*, April 30, 2010.

42. Bloom, *Hating Goldstone*, 23; Richard Goldstone interview, January 13, 2013.

43. Gill Marcus, interview by Daniel Terris, January 11, 2013.

44. The Torah portion can be found at http://ajrca.edu/parshat-emor-2/.

45. Julian Brener interview, June 15, 2015.

46. Gilbert Marcus, interview by Daniel Terris, June 16, 2015.

47. Bloom, *Hating Goldstone*, 24.

48. Richard Goldstone, "My Mandate on Gaza Was Even-Handed, My Loyalty Is to Justice," *Guardian*, May 5, 2010.

49. Richard Goldstone interview, January 13, 2013.

50. Gilbert Marcus interview, June 16, 2015.

51. Richard Goldstone interview, January 13, 2013.

52. Letty Cottin Pogrebin, "The Unholy Assault on Richard Goldstone," in *The Goldstone Report: The Legacy of the Landmark Investigation of the Gaza Conflict*, ed. Adam Horowitz, Lizzy Ratner, and Philip Weiss (New York: Nation Books, 2011), 413.

CHAPTER 19   RETRACTION

1. The work of investigations was principally performed by the Military Police Criminal Investigation Division, which looked into thousands of cases per year; in 2009 only 7 percent of those cases involved Palestinian complainants. *Gaza Operation Investigations: An Update*, Israeli Ministry of Foreign Affairs, January 2010, http://mfa.gov.il/MFA _Graphics/MFA%20Gallery/Documents/GazaOperationInvestigationsUpdate.pdf, paras. 14–25.

2. Ibid.; *Gaza Operation Investigations: Second Update*, Israeli Ministry of Foreign Affairs, July 2010, http://mfa.gov.il/MFA_Graphics/MFA%20Gallery/Documents/GazaUpdate July2010.pdf.

3. *Gaza Operation Investigations: An Update*, para. 124; *Gaza Operation Investigations: Second Update*, para. 23.

4. *Gaza Operation Investigations: An Update*, paras. 142–182; *Gaza Operation Investigations: Second Update*, paras. 141–145.

5. The account of the Israeli cases as of March 2011 is in *Report of the Committee of Independent Experts in International Humanitarian and Human Rights Law Established Pursuant to Council Resolution 13/9 (Davis Report)*, HRC, A/HRC/16/24, March 18, 2011, paras. 24–35. See also Jessica Montell, "Beyond Goldstone: A Truer Discussion about Israel, Hamas, and the Gaza Conflict," *Haaretz*, April 5, 2011.

6. In August 2012, the military prosecution agreed to a plea bargain with the solider, known publicly only as "Soldier S." He was to serve forty-five days in prison for "unlawful use of a weapon." "When War Criminals Walk Free," *Haaretz*, August 14, 2012.

7. The following paragraphs draw on Leslie Susser, "Pushed by Goldstone, Israeli Army Embraces New 'Smart' Warfare," *Jewish Telegraph Agency*, April 11, 2011, and Yonah Jeremy Bob, "Analysis: The Goldstone Report's Positive Effects," *Jerusalem Post*, October 25, 2012. See also *Gaza Operation Investigations: Second Update*, paras. 146–157.

8. Susser, "Pushed by Goldstone, Israeli Army Embraces New 'Smart' Warfare."

9. *Davis Report*.

10. Ibid., para. 13.

11. The report noted that in the case of a Palestinian boy used as booby trap, the Israeli soldiers involved received just three-month suspended sentences. Ibid., paras. 30–32.

12. Ibid., para. 63.

13. Alan Dershowitz, "The Case against the Goldstone Report: A Study in Evidentiary Bias," DASH Repository, https://dash.harvard.edu/bitstream/handle/1/3593975/DershowitzGoldstone.pdf?sequence=2.

14. "Video: Rabbi Shmully Hecht Challenges Professor Goldstone at Yale," *Matsav.com*, January 31, 2010, http://matzav.com/video-rabbi-shmully-hecht-challenges-professor-goldstone-at-yale.

15. This account and the description of the friendship between Goldstone and Rabbi Shmully Hecht are based on interviews with both of them. Richard Goldstone, interview by Daniel Terris, January 13, 2013; Shmully Hecht, interview by Daniel Terris, November 3, 2014; Shmully Hecht, interview by Daniel Terris, November 19, 2014.

16. Richard Goldstone, "Reflections Two Years after the Gaza War" (Sacramento, California: Leonard M. Friedman Bar Association Annual Dinner, 2011); typescript in Richard Goldstone papers. Shmully Hecht interview, November 3, 2014.

17. Rishabh Bhandari and Hannah Schwarz, "For Rent," *Yale Daily News*, April 18, 2014.

18. See chapter 1.

19. *Second Report—the Turkel Commission*, Public Commission to Examine the Maritime Incident of 31 May 2010, February 2013, http://www.humanrightsvoices.org/assets/attachments/documents/turkel.report.2.pdf.

20. "Gift Shop Markets 'Goldstone' Headscarves," *Right Vision News*, October 6, 2009.

21. *Report*, Russell Tribunal on Palestine, January 2012, http://www2.ohchr.org/english/bodies/cerd/docs/ngos/RussellTribunalOnPalestine_Israel80.pdf.

22. Goldstone, "Reflections Two Years after the Gaza War."

23. Ibid., 19–20.

24. Nicole Goldstone, interview by Daniel Terris, November 12, 2012.

25. Richard Goldstone, "Reconsidering the Goldstone Report on Israel and War Crimes," *Washington Post*, April 1, 2011.

26. "Goldstone's Example," *Jerusalem Post*, April 4, 2011.

27. David Horovitz, "Goldstone, the Belated Penitent," *Jerusalem Post*, April 3, 2011.

28. Quoted in Ethan Bronner, "Israel Grapples with Retraction on U.N. Report," *New York Times*, April 3, 2011.

29. Joshua Mitnick, "In Israel, Goldstone's Gaza War Retraction Triggers 'Earthquake' of Vindication," *Christian Science Monitor*, April 3, 2011.

30. Montell, "Beyond Goldstone."

31. "Goldstone Displays Rare Moral Courage," *Sydney Morning Herald*, April 5, 2011.

32. Avi Bell, "Richard Goldstone's Legacy," *Jerusalem Post*, April 3, 2011; Tovah Lazaroff and Gil Shefler, "Goldstone Critics Ponder Their Roles in About-Face," *Jerusalem Post*, April 6, 2011.

33. Caroline B. Glick, "Richard Goldstone and Palestinian Statehood," *Jerusalem Post*, April 5, 2011.

34. Khaled Abu Toameh and Tovah Lazaroff, "Palestinians Unimpressed with Goldstone's About-Face," *Jerusalem Post*, April 4, 2011.

35. *Daily Star*, April 5, 2011.

36. "News in Brief," *Jerusalem Post*, April 6, 2011.

37. Gilbert Marcus, interview by Daniel Terris, June 16, 2015.

38. Roger Cohen, "The Goldstone Chronicles," *New York Times*, April 7, 2011.

39. Richard Falk, "The Goldstone Report without Goldstone," *Journal of Palestine Studies* 41, no. 1 (2011), 96–111.

40. M. Cherif Bassiouni, personal communication to Richard Goldstone, April 8, 2011.

41. Richard Goldstone interview, January 13, 2013.

42. Christine Chinkin, interview by Daniel Terris, October 29, 2014.

43. Hina Jilani, Christine Chinkin, and Desmond Travers, "Goldstone Report: Statement Issued by Members of UN Mission on Gaza War," *Guardian*, April 14, 2011.

44. Dan Senor and Saul Singer, *Start-Up Nation* (New York: Twelve, 2009).

45. Ethan Bronner and Jennifer Medina, "Past Holds a Clue to Goldstone's Shift on the Gaza War," *New York Times*, April 19, 2011.

46. In May 2012, more than one year after Goldstone's op-ed, the MAG announced an end to the investigation of the incident in which twenty-one members of the al-Samouni family died. In his final report, the MAG announced that no further criminal or disciplinary action would be taken. The only repercussion from the incident was that a single officer had been given a "command sanction," which would prevent him from taking charge of a certain level of operations during active combat. The MAG said that the

evidence did not support the al-Samouni family members' own testimony that they were ordered into the residence by the Israeli military, but he offered no reason why he had dismissed the Palestinians' account. The Israeli report concluded that there was no criminal intent to kill the family members, and it also concluded that the soldiers involved had shown neither recklessness nor negligence. It was a wartime situation, and accidents happened. The Israeli investigation cited most prominently by Richard Goldstone in his speeches and in his *Washington Post* article had come to naught. Jessica Montell, "No Closure in Killing of 21 Gaza Family Members," *Jerusalem Post*, July 5, 2012.

EPILOGUE

1. Hammarskjöld Commission, *Report of the Commission of Inquiry*, 2013, http://www.hammarskjoldcommission.org/index.html.
2. His board commitments included, among others: the international advisory committee of the Coalition for the International Criminal Court (chair); the international advisory committee of the International Center for Transitional Justice (chair); the advisory board of the International Center for Ethics, Justice and Public Life, Brandeis University (chair); the international committee of the American Academy of Arts and Sciences; and the board of Physicians for Human Rights.
3. For statistical overviews, see http://unictr.unmict.org/en/tribunal (for the ICTR) and http://www.icty.org/en/content/infographic-icty-facts-figures (for the ICTY).
4. See *The Prosecutor of the Tribunal Against Slobodan Milošević*, ICTY, IT-02-54. The records are available at http://www.icty.org/en/cases/party/738/4.
5. A final dramatic and embarrassing indicator of the ICTY's shortcomings occurred in one of the tribunal's last acts. On November 29, 2017, the Appeals Chamber delivered a verdict in the case of Slobodan Praljak, a Croatian general who had been sentenced to twenty years for war crimes and crimes against humanity. After the court read its judgment—which overturned some aspects of Praljak's conviction but did not reduce his twenty-year sentence—the accused delivered a statement in which he rejected the court's authority and professed his innocence. As he spoke, he dramatically removed a small vial of liquid from his coat and swallowed. Hours later he was dead, leaving baffled observers to wonder how he had managed to obtain poison in the ICTY prison. Marlise Simons, "Croatian War Criminal Dies after Swallowing Poison in Court," *New York Times*, November 29, 2017. See also the account of an independent review of the incident, which generally cleared the ICTY of malfeasance, at http://www.icty.org/en/press/statement-on-the-independent-review-regarding-the-passing-of-slobodan-praljak.
6. Both appealed their convictions, which as of 2018 were in process through the U.N. Mechanism for International Criminal Tribunals. See http://www.unmict.org/en/cases/mict-13-55 and http://www.unmict.org/en/cases/mict-13-56.
7. Richard Goldstone, "Prosecuting Rape as a War Crime," *Case Western Reserve Journal of International Law* 34 (2002), 277–285.

8. See Nahimana et al., ICTR, ICTR-99-52. The records are available at http://unictr .unmict.org/en/cases/ictr-99-52.

9. See William Schabas, "International Criminal Courts," in *The Oxford Handbook of International Adjudication*, ed. Cesare P. R. Romano, Karen J. Alter, and Yuval Shany (Oxford: Oxford University Press, 2014), 205–224.

10. Up-to-date information about membership in the ICC can be found at https://asp .icc-cpi.int/en_menus/asp/states%20parties/pages/the%20states%20parties%20to%20 the%20rome%20statute.aspx.

11. See the text of the report and related documents at http://www.ohchr.org/EN/HR Bodies/HRC/CoIGazaConflict/Pages/ReportCoIGaza.aspx.

12. Barak Ravid, "UN Human Rights Council Adopts Resolution Condemning Israel over Gaza War Report," *Haaretz*, July 3, 2015.

BIBLIOGRAPHIC ESSAY

The starting point for Richard Goldstone's life and work is his memoir, *For Humanity: Reflections of a War Crimes Investigator* (New Haven, Conn.: Yale University Press, 2000). This volume covers, in Goldstone's typically pithy and witty style, his career through his tenure as the chief prosecutor in The Hague.

For understanding the complex situation of Jews in apartheid South Africa, the indispensable volume is Gideon Shimoni, *Community and Conscience: The Jews in Apartheid South Africa* (Hanover, N.H.: Brandeis University Press, 2003). An informative book that covers the interaction between the global Jewish community and the anti-apartheid movement is Marjorie N. Feld, *Nations Divided: American Jews and the Struggle over Apartheid* (New York: Palgrave Macmillan, 2014).

On South African law during the apartheid era, I relied on several books by two prominent figures who were friends of Richard Goldstone, Albie Sachs and John Dugard, including Sachs's *Justice in South Africa* (Berkeley: University of California Press, 1973), and Dugard's *Human Rights and the South African Legal Order* (Princeton, N.J.: Princeton University Press, 1978). Two later scholarly volumes are also helpful: Stephen Ellmann, *In a Time of Trouble: Law and Liberty in South Africa's State of Emergency* (New York: Oxford University Press, 1992), and David Dyzenhaus, *Judging the Judges, Judging Ourselves: Truth, Reconciliation and the Apartheid Legal Order* (Oxford: Hart Publishers, 2003).

The Historical Papers Research Archive at the William Cullen Library at the University of the Witwatersrand is a treasure trove of primary sources for South African history, including the era in which Goldstone was active. Many important papers are available online at http://www.historicalpapers.wits.ac.za.

The work of Goldstone's Commission of Inquiry regarding the Prevention of Public Violence and Intimidation in South Africa is not well documented in the secondary literature. The best compilation of the Commission's work is *Goldstone Commission, 1991–1994: A Compilation of Reports, Press Releases & Submissions* (Johannesburg: Human Rights Institute of South Africa, 2006), published as a CD-ROM. Many of the original Commission reports and other documents are available online through the Stanford University library at https://searchworks.stanford.edu/view/2740653.

A number of books recount the early years of the International Criminal Tribunal for the former Yugoslavia, including Michael P. Scharf, *Balkan Justice: The Story behind the First International War Crimes Trial since Nuremberg* (Durham, N.C.: Carolina Academic Press, 1997), John Hagan, *Justice in the Balkans: Prosecuting War Crimes in the Hague Tribunal* (Chicago: University of Chicago Press, 2003), and Pierre Hazan, *Justice in a Time of War: The True Story behind the International Criminal Tribunal for the Former Yugoslavia* (College Station: Texas A&M University Press, 2004). Two excellent accounts by journalists mix narrative about the broader conflicts in the Balkans and Rwanda with accounts of the justice process: Elizabeth Neuffer, *The Key to My Neighbor's House: Seeking Justice in Bosnia and Rwanda* (New York: Picador, 2001), and Philip Gourevitch, *We Wish to Inform You That Tomorrow We Will Be Killed with Our Families: Stories from Rwanda* (New York: Farrar, Straus and Giroux, 1998).

The archives of the Yugoslavia and Rwanda tribunals are available via the website of the U.N. Mechanism for International Criminal Tribunals at http://www.unmict.org. With both courts now closed, this mechanism handles any remaining appeals and also serves as the official repository of the tribunals' legacy. A newer primary resource, focused on the full range of individuals who staffed the tribunals, is the Ad Hoc Tribunals Oral History Project of the International Center for Ethics, Justice and Public Life at Brandeis University (http://www.brandeis.edu/ethics/internationaljustice/oral-history/index.html).

Case law of the Constitutional Court of South Africa can be found at http://www.constitutionalcourt.org.za/. The Kosovo Commission report was published as a book: Independent International Commission on Kosovo, *The Kosovo Report: Conflict, International Response, Lessons Learned* (Oxford: Oxford University Press, 2000). An informative and swift-moving narrative summary by insiders of the Oil for Food Program inquiry is Jeffrey A. Meyer and Mark G. Califano, *Good Intentions Corrupted: The Oil-for-Food Program and the Threat to the U.N.* (New York: Public Affairs, 2006).

The Goldstone report on the Gaza conflict and related documents are available at: http://www.ohchr.org/EN/HRBodies/HRC/SpecialSessions/Session9/Pages/FactFindingMission.aspx. The report inspired two collections of essays. One is generally supportive of the report's perspective: Adam Horowitz, Lizzy Ratner, and Philip Weiss, eds., *The Goldstone Report: The Legacy of the Landmark Investigation of the Gaza Conflict* (New York: Nation

Books, 2011). The other is generally critical of the findings: Gerald M. Steinberg and Anne Herzberg, eds., *The Goldstone Report "Reconsidered": A Critical Analysis* (Jerusalem: NGO Monitor, 2012).

Finally, this book relies significantly on interviews conducted mostly in person, but occasionally by telephone. Those interviewed include George Bizos, Graham Blewitt, Terree Bowers, Glenda Goldstone Brener, Julian Brener, Christian Chartier, Christine Chinkin, Catherine Cissé, JJ du Toit, Errol Friedmann, Ruth Friedmann, Nicole Goldstone, Noleen Goldstone, Richard Goldstone, Vernon Grigg, Moshe Halbertal, Shmully Hecht, Thelton Henderson, Philip Heymann, Mirko Klarin, Avrom Krengel, Benas Levy, Alon Liel, Princeton Lyman, Geoffrey Mansell, Gilbert Marcus, Francesca Marotta, Isaac Meletse, Theodor Meron, Justice Moloto, Aryeh Neier, Kate O'Regan, Diane Orentlicher, Navi Pillay, Antony Polonsky, Daniel Reisner, Albie Sachs, David Scheffer, Minna Schrag, and Desmond Travers.

INDEX

ABOUT THE AUTHOR

DANIEL TERRIS is dean of Al-Quds Bard College for Arts & Sciences at Al-Quds University in East Jerusalem and visiting professor of humanities at Bard College. He was previously the founding director of the International Center for Ethics, Justice and Public Life at Brandeis University. He is the author of *Ethics at Work: Creating Virtue in an American Corporation* and coauthor of *The International Judge: An Introduction to the Men and Women Who Decide the World's Cases.*